Shugo Chara!

5

PEACH-PIT

Translated by
Satsuki Yamashita

Adapted by
Nunzio DeFilippis and Christina Weir

Lettered by
North Market Street Graphics

BALLANTINE BOOKS · NEW YORK

Shugo Chara! volume 5 is a work of fiction. Names, characters, places, and incidents are the products of the author's imagination or are used fictitiously. Any resemblance to actual events, locales, or persons, living or dead, is entirely coincidental.

A Del Rey Manga/Kodansha Trade Paperback Original

Published in the United States by Del Rey, an imprint of The Random House Publishing Group, a division of Random House, Inc., New York.

Publication rights arranged through Kodansha Ltd.

First published in Japan in 2007 by Kodansha Ltd., Tokyo

ISBN 978-0-345-50804-1

Original cover design by Akiko Omo

Printed in the United States of America

www.delreymanga.com

9 8 7 6 5 4 3 2

Translator: Satsuki Yamashita
Adapters: Nunzio DeFilippis and Christina Weir
Lettering: North Market Street Graphics

Contents

Honorifics Explained v

Shugo Chara! volume 5 1

About the Creators 168

Translation Notes 169

Honorifics Explained

Throughout the Del Rey Manga books, you will find Japanese honorifics left intact in the translations. For those not familiar with how the Japanese use honorifics and, more important, how they differ from American honorifics, we present this brief overview.

Politeness has always been a critical facet of Japanese culture. Ever since the feudal era, when Japan was a highly stratified society, use of honorifics—which can be defined as polite speech that indicates relationship or status—has played an essential role in the Japanese language. When addressing someone in Japanese, an honorific usually takes the form of a suffix attached to one's name (example: "Asuna-san"), is used as a title at the end of one's name, or appears in place of the name itself (example: "Negi-sensei," or simply "Sensei").

Honorifics can be expressions of respect or endearment. In the context of manga and anime, honorifics give insight into the nature of the relationship between characters. Many English translations leave out these important honorifics and therefore distort the feel of the original Japanese. Because Japanese honorifics contain nuances that English honorifics lack, it is our policy at Del Rey not to translate them. Here, instead, is a guide to some of the honorifics you may encounter in Del Rey Manga.

-san: This is the most common honorific and is equivalent to Mr., Miss, Ms., or Mrs. It is the all-purpose honorific and can be used in any situation where politeness is required.

-sama: This is one level higher than "-san" and is used to confer great respect.

-dono: This comes from the word "tono," which means "lord." It is an even higher level than "-sama" and confers utmost respect.

-kun: This suffix is used at the end of boys' names to express familiarity or endearment. It is also sometimes used by men among friends, or when addressing someone younger or of a lower station.

-chan: This is used to express endearment, mostly toward girls. It is also used for little boys, pets, and even among lovers. It gives a sense of childish cuteness.

Bozu: This is an informal way to refer to a boy, similar to the English terms "kid" and "squirt."

Sempai/
Senpai: This title suggests that the addressee is one's senior in a group or organization. It is most often used in a school setting, where underclassmen refer to their upperclassmen as "sempai." It can also be used in the workplace, such as when a newer employee addresses an employee who has seniority in the company.

Kohai: This is the opposite of "sempai" and is used toward underclassmen in school or newcomers in the workplace. It connotes that the addressee is of a lower station.

Sensei: Literally meaning "one who has come before," this title is used for teachers, doctors, or masters of any profession or art.

-[blank]:   This is usually forgotten in these lists, but it is perhaps the most significant difference between Japanese and English. The lack of honorific means that the speaker has permission to address the person in a very intimate way. Usually, only family, spouses, or very close friends have this kind of permission. Known as *yobisute,* it can be gratifying when someone who has earned the intimacy starts to call one by one's name without an honorific. But when that intimacy hasn't been earned, it can be very insulting.

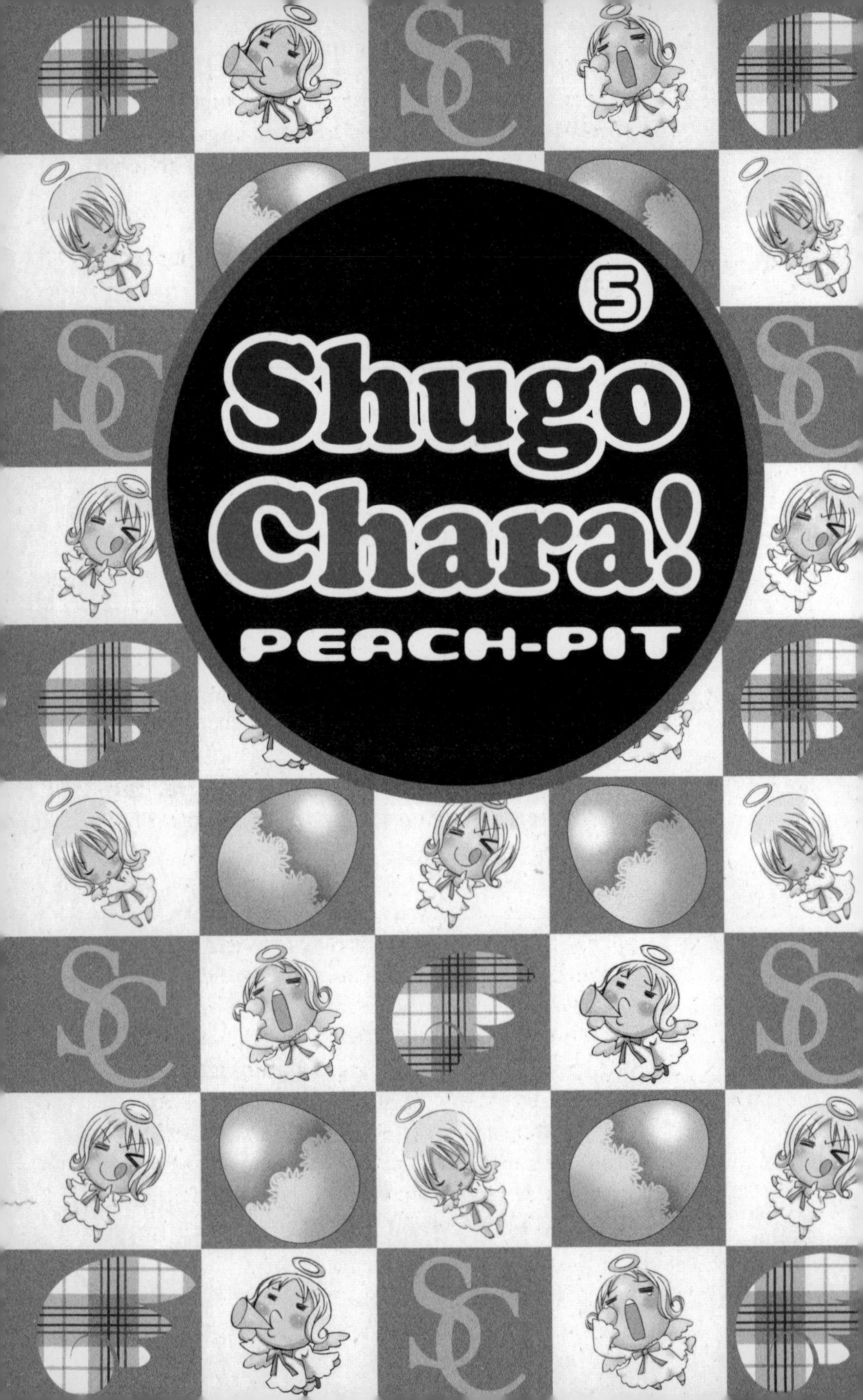
5
Shugo Chara!
PEACH-PIT

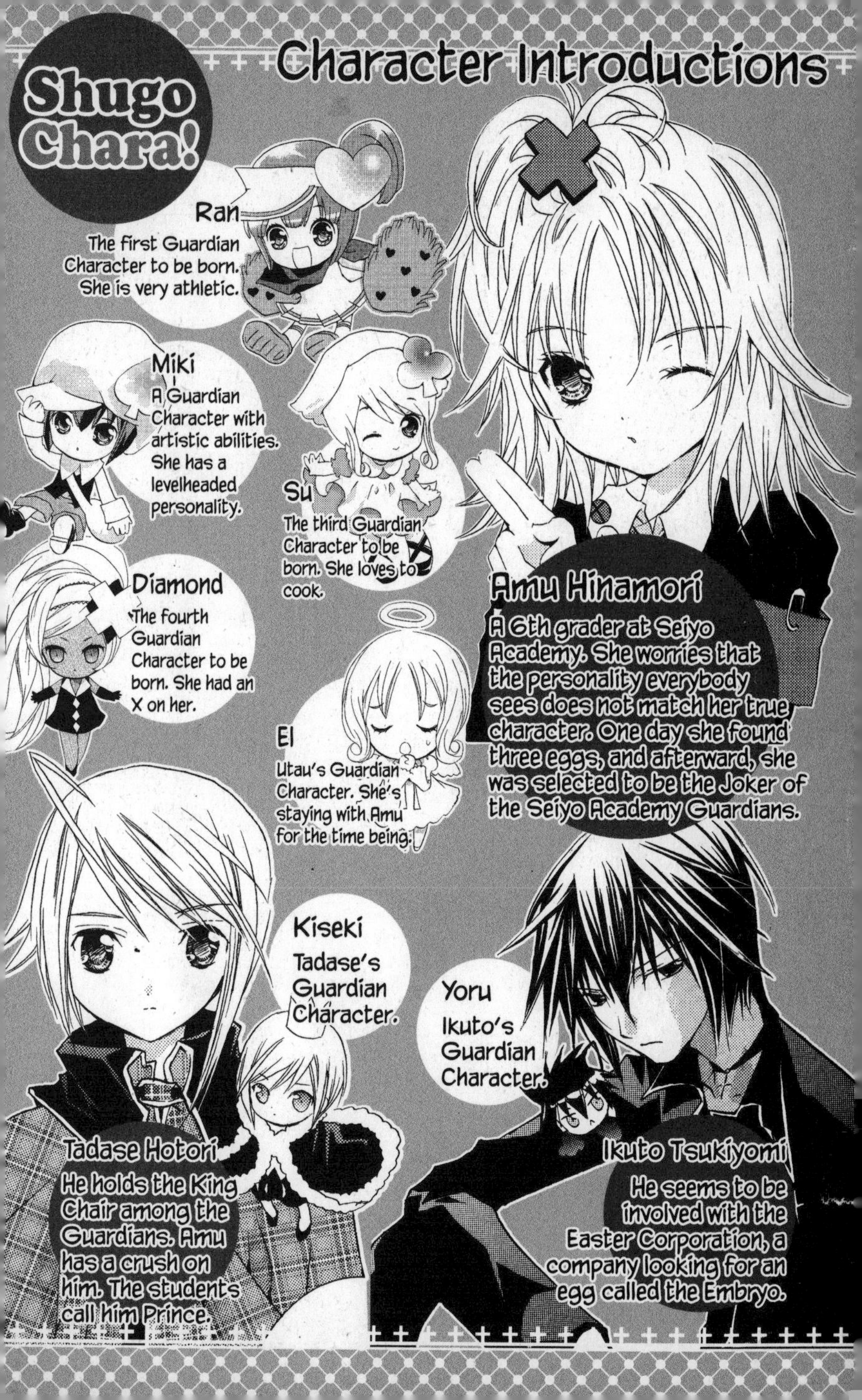
Shugo Chara!
Character Introductions
Amu Hinamori
A 6th grader at Seiyo Academy. She worries that the personality everybody sees does not match her true character. One day she found three eggs, and afterward, she was selected to be the Joker of the Seiyo Academy Guardians.
Ran
The first Guardian Character to be born. She is very athletic.
Miki
A Guardian Character with artistic abilities. She has a levelheaded personality.
Su
The third Guardian Character to be born. She loves to cook.
Diamond
The fourth Guardian Character to be born. She had an X on her.
El
Utau's Guardian Character. She's staying with Amu for the time being.
Yoru
Ikuto's Guardian Character.
Ikuto Tsukiyomi
He seems to be involved with the Easter Corporation, a company looking for an egg called the Embryo.
Kiseki
Tadase's Guardian Character.
Tadase Hotori
He holds the King Chair among the Guardians. Amu has a crush on him. The students call him Prince.

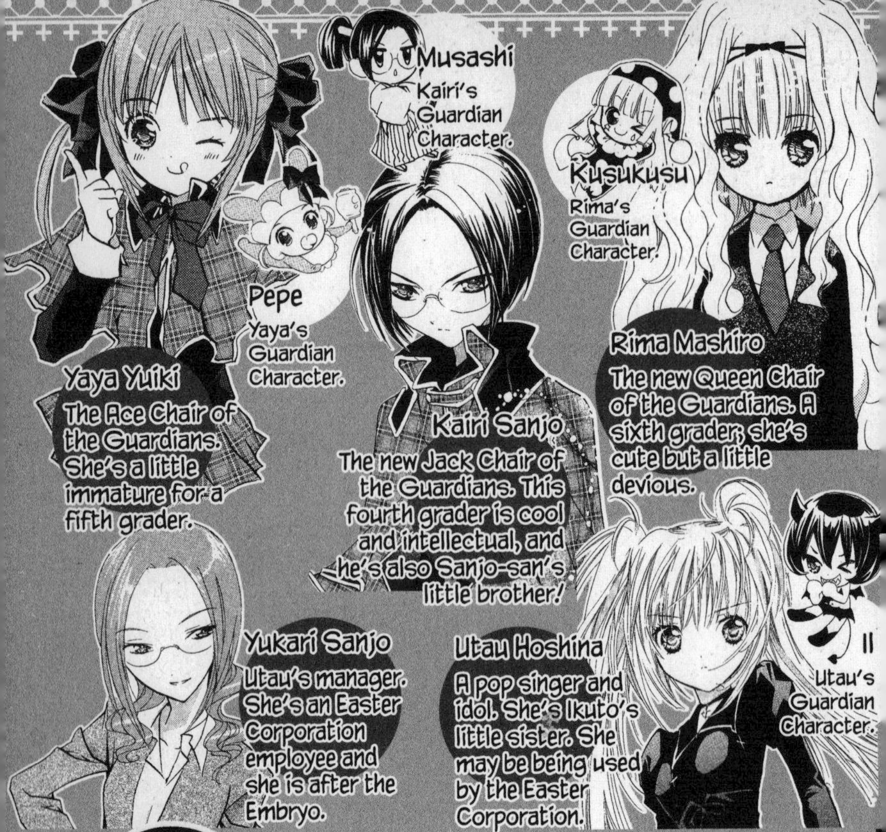
Kusukusu
Rima's Guardian Character.
Rima Mashiro
The new Queen Chair of the Guardians. A sixth grader; she's cute but a little devious.
Musashi
Kairi's Guardian Character.
Kairi Sanjo
The new Jack Chair of the Guardians. This fourth grader is cool and intellectual, and he's also Sanjo-san's little brother!
Pepe
Yaya's Guardian Character.
Yaya Yuiki
The Ace Chair of the Guardians. She's a little immature for a fifth grader.
Il
Utau's Guardian Character.
Utau Hoshina
A pop singer and idol. She's Ikuto's little sister. She may be being used by the Easter Corporation.
Yukari Sanjo
Utau's manager. She's an Easter Corporation employee and she is after the Embryo.

The Story So Far

●Everyone thinks Amu is the coolest. But that's not who she really is: Deep inside, she's shy and a little cynical. One day, she wished she could be more true to herself, and the next day she found three eggs in her bed!

●Ran, Miki, and Su hatched from the eggs. As Amu's "Guardian Characters," they claim to be Amu's "true selves." When Amu undergoes a "Character Change" with them, she can become good at sports, art, or cooking! Soon after they hatched, Amu found herself recruited to become one of the Guardians of Seiyo Academy. Ever since, she's become good friends with the other students who have Guardian Characters, including the boy she has a crush on, Tadase-kun. But in the spring, Kukai graduated and Nadeshiko went abroad to study.

●Rima and Kairi replaced them, but they're both a little weird. And to make things worse, Amu's fourth Guardian Egg has a mysterious X on it!!

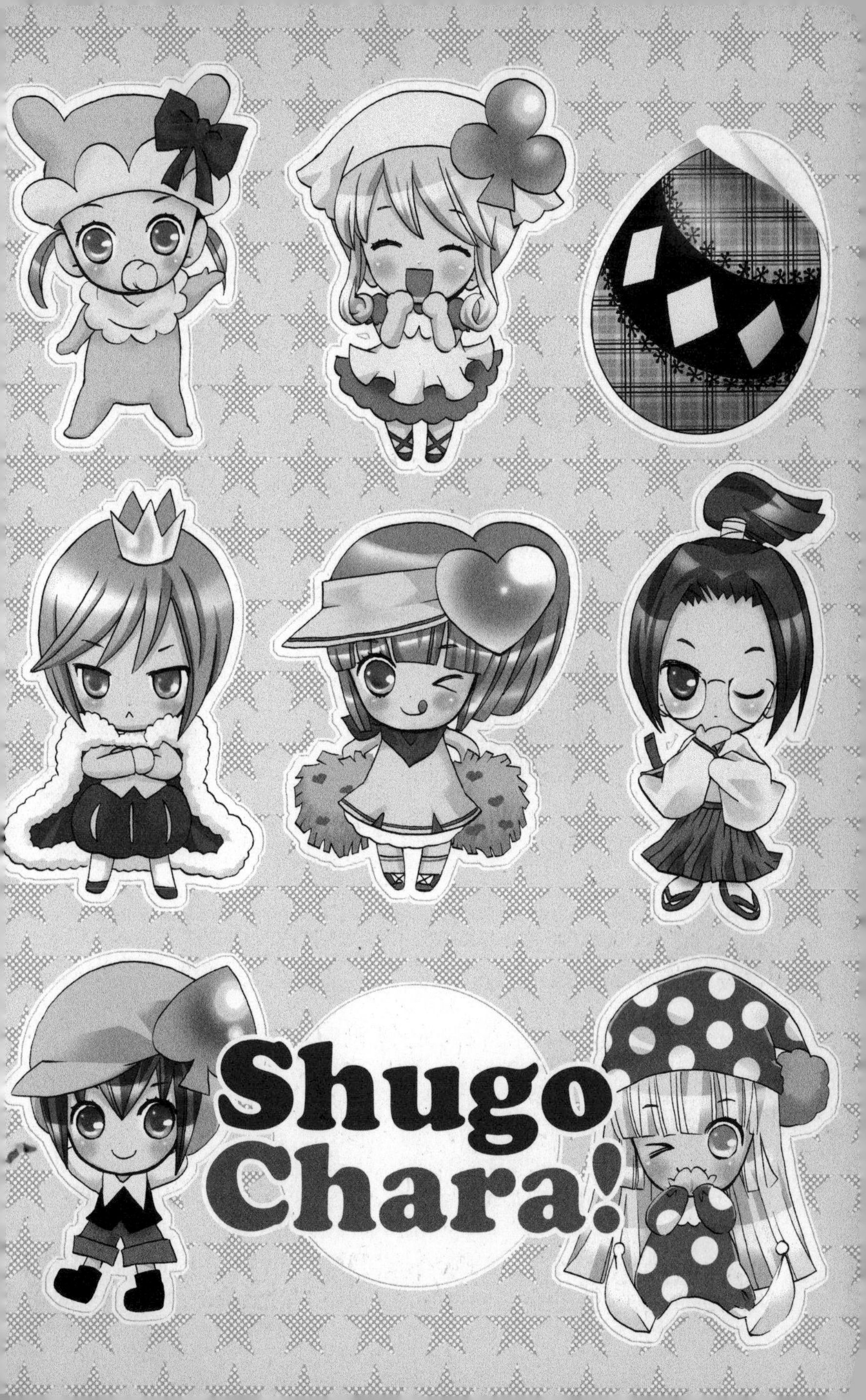
Shugo
Chara!

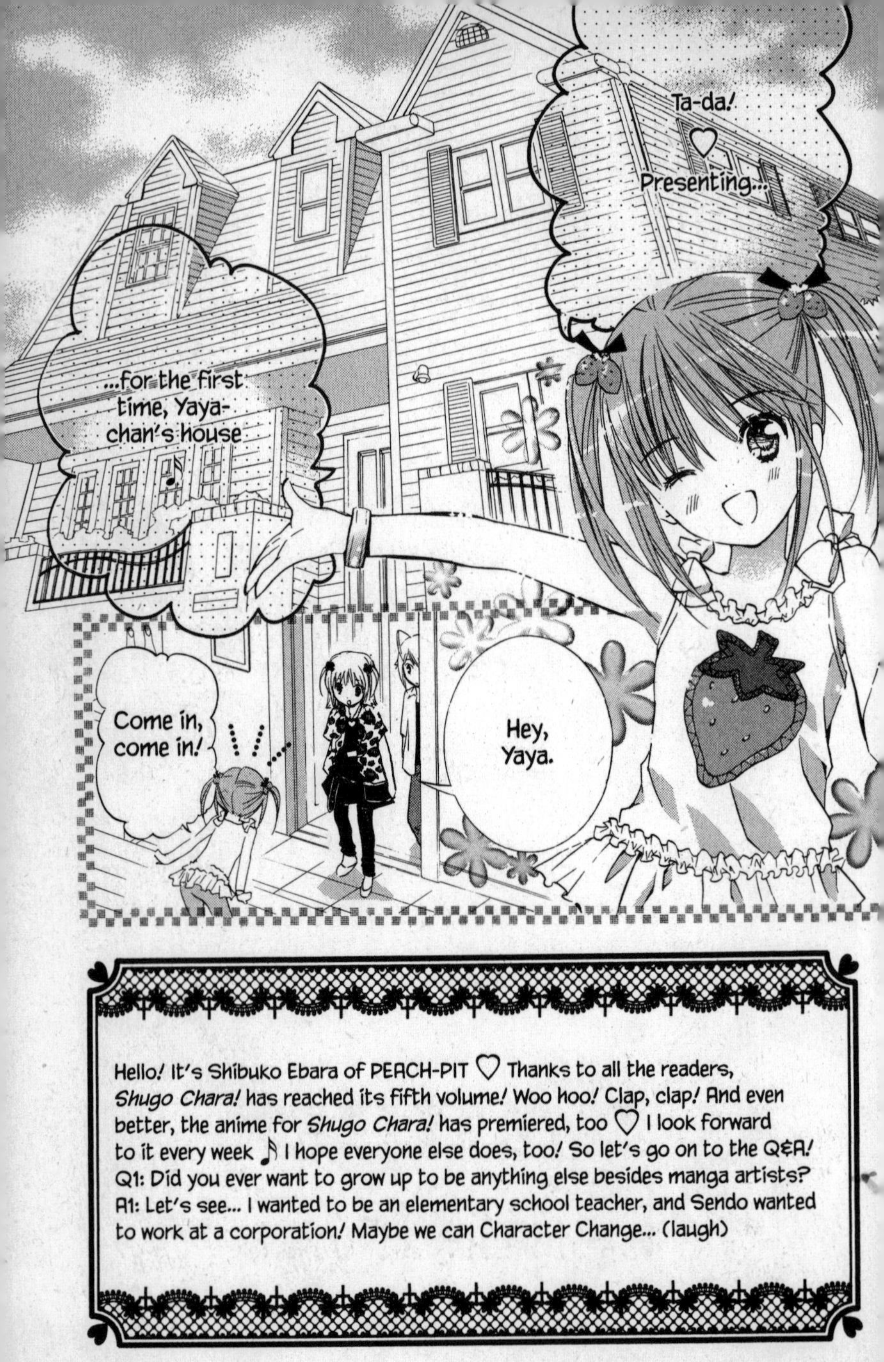
Ta-da! ♡ Presenting...
...for the first time, Yaya-chan's house
Hey, Yaya.
Come in, come in!

Hello! It's Shibuko Ebara of PEACH-PIT ♡ Thanks to all the readers, *Shugo Chara!* has reached its fifth volume! Woo hoo! Clap, clap! And even better, the anime for *Shugo Chara!* has premiered, too ♡ I look forward to it every week ♪ I hope everyone else does, too! So let's go on to the Q&A!

Q1: Did you ever want to grow up to be anything else besides manga artists?

A1: Let's see... I wanted to be an elementary school teacher, and Sendo wanted to work at a corporation! Maybe we can Character Change... (laugh)

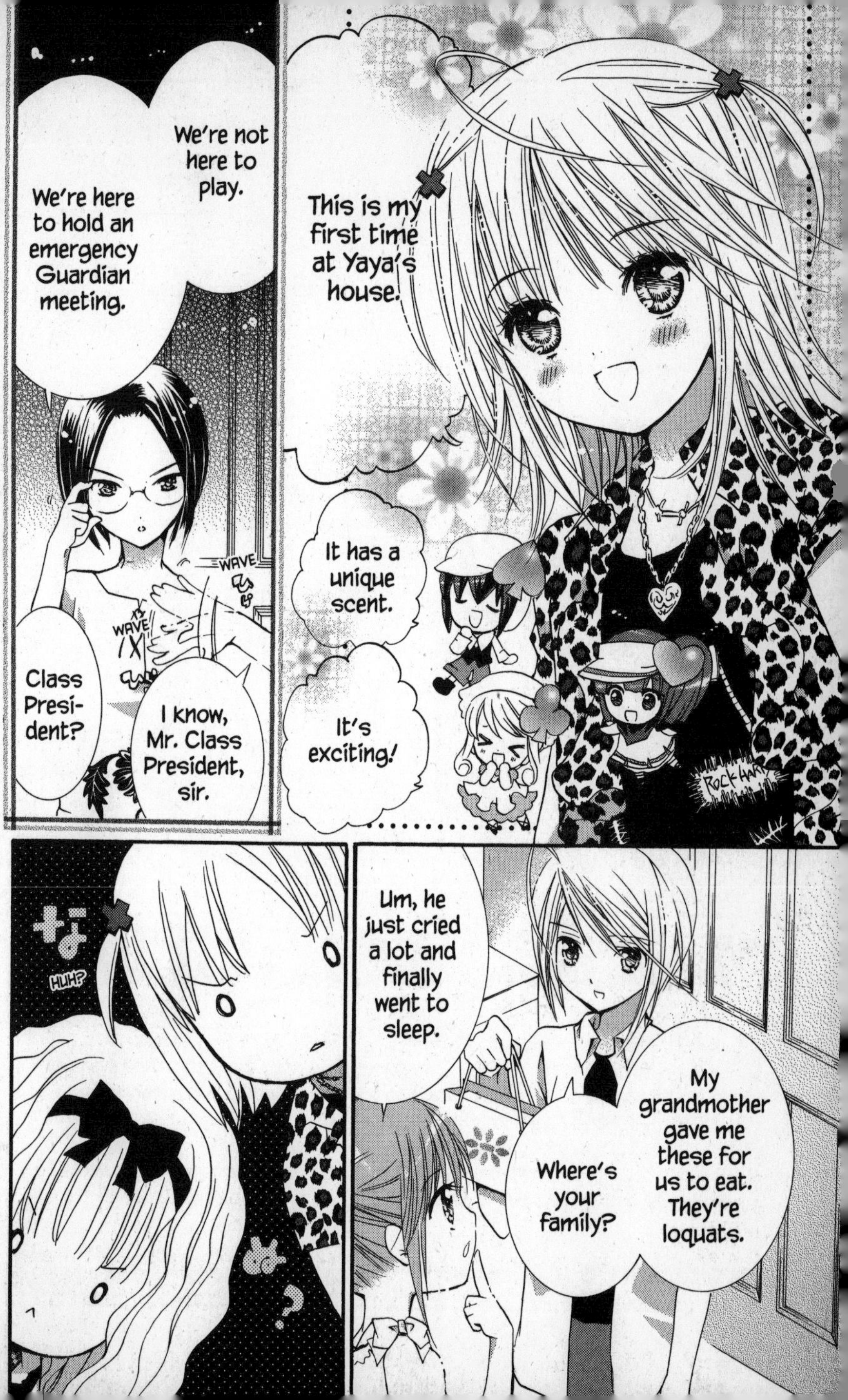
This is my first time at Yaya's house!
It has a unique scent.
It's exciting!
We're not here to play.
We're here to hold an emergency Guardian meeting.
WAVE
WAVE
Class President?
I know, Mr. Class President, sir.
My grandmother gave me these for us to eat. They're loquats.
Where's your family?
Um, he just cried a lot and finally went to sleep.
HUH?

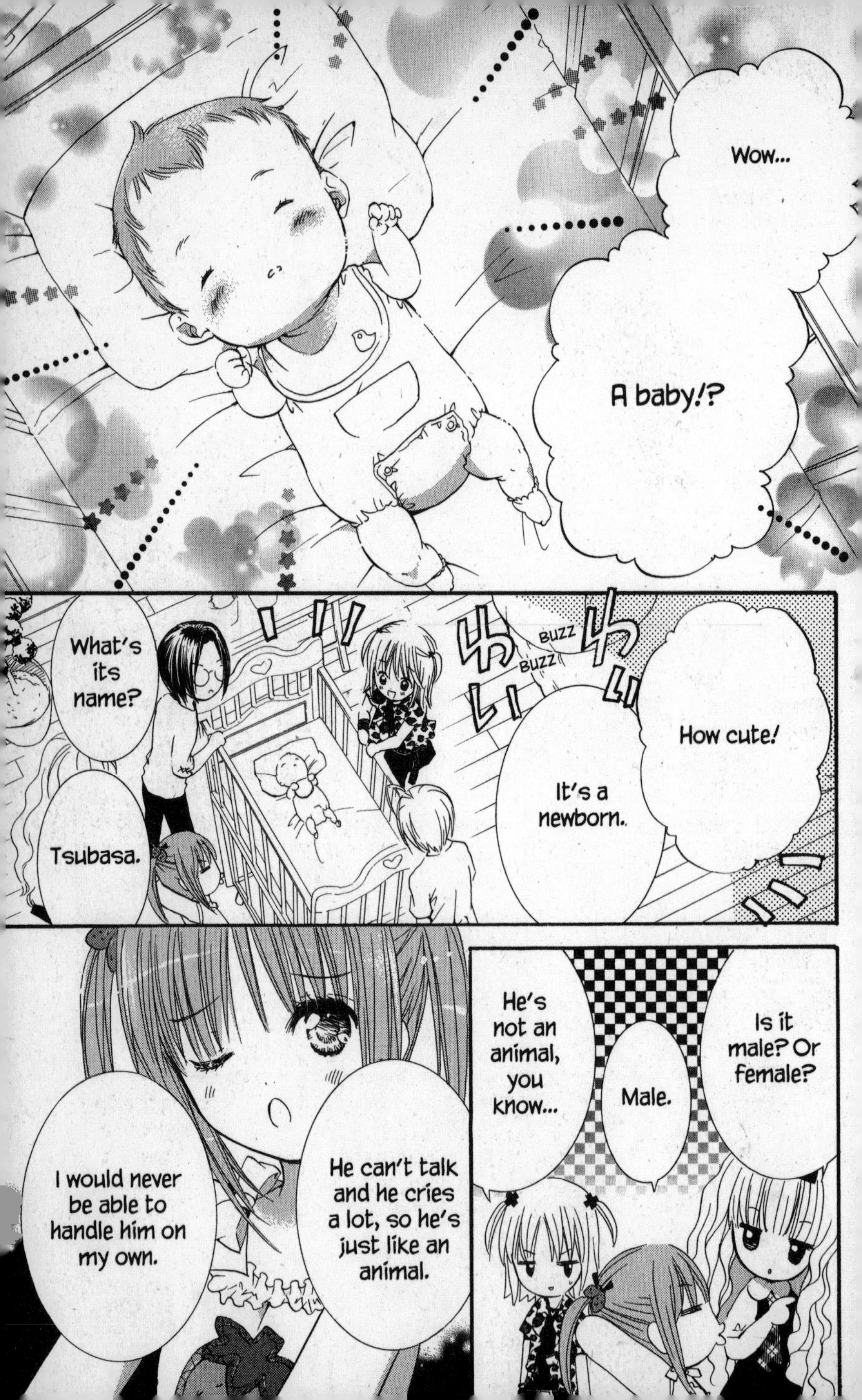

Wow...
A baby!?
How cute!
BUZZ
BUZZ
It's a newborn.
What's its name?
Tsubasa.
Is it male? Or female?
Male.
He's not an animal, you know...
He can't talk and he cries a lot, so he's just like an animal.
I would never be able to handle him on my own.

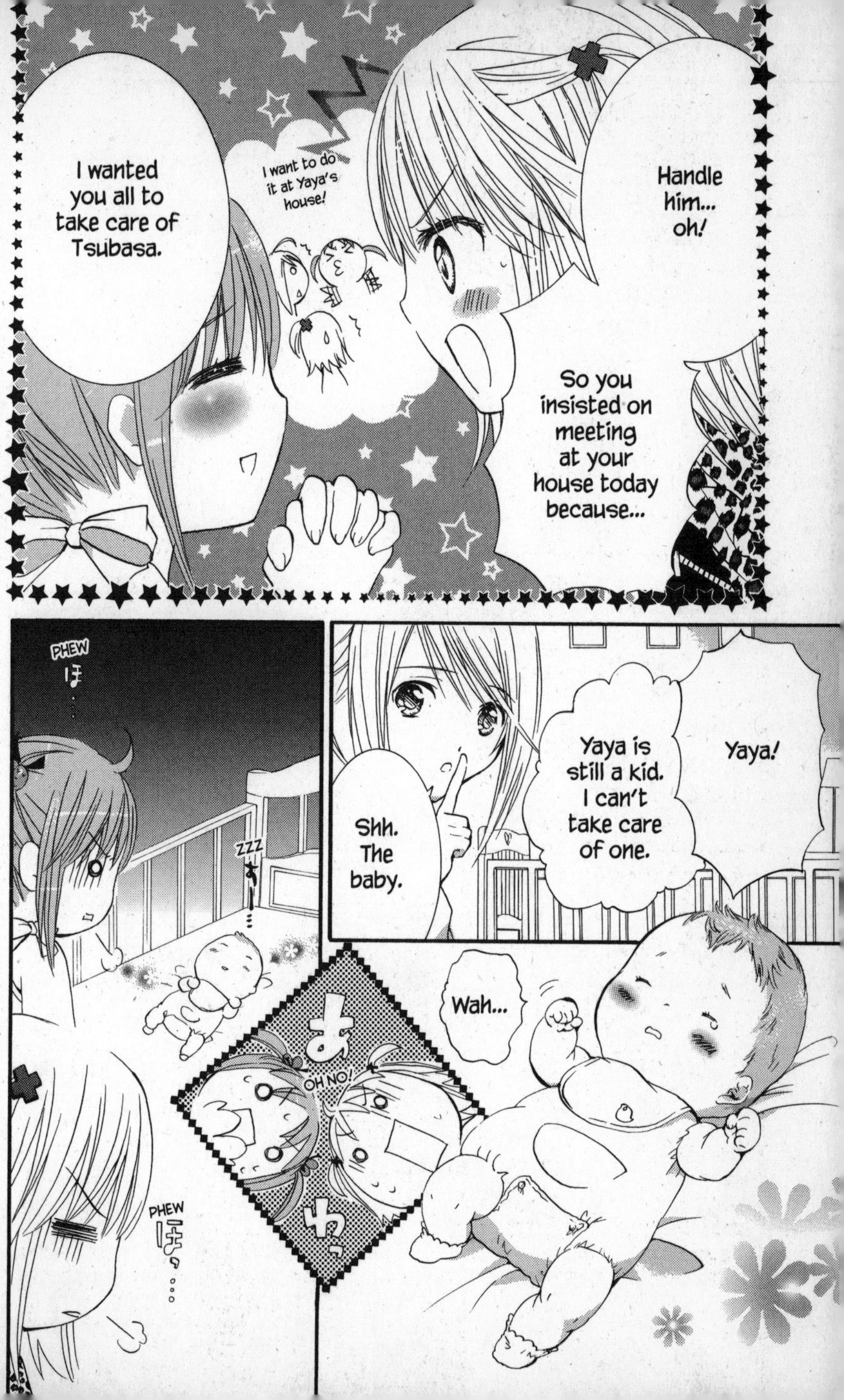
Handle him... oh!
So you insisted on meeting at your house today because...
I want to do it at Yaya's house!
I wanted you all to take care of Tsubasa.
Yaya!
Yaya is still a kid. I can't take care of one.
Shh. The baby.
Wah...
OH NO!
あわ
PHEW
ほ...
ZZZ
すー...
PHEW
ほっ...

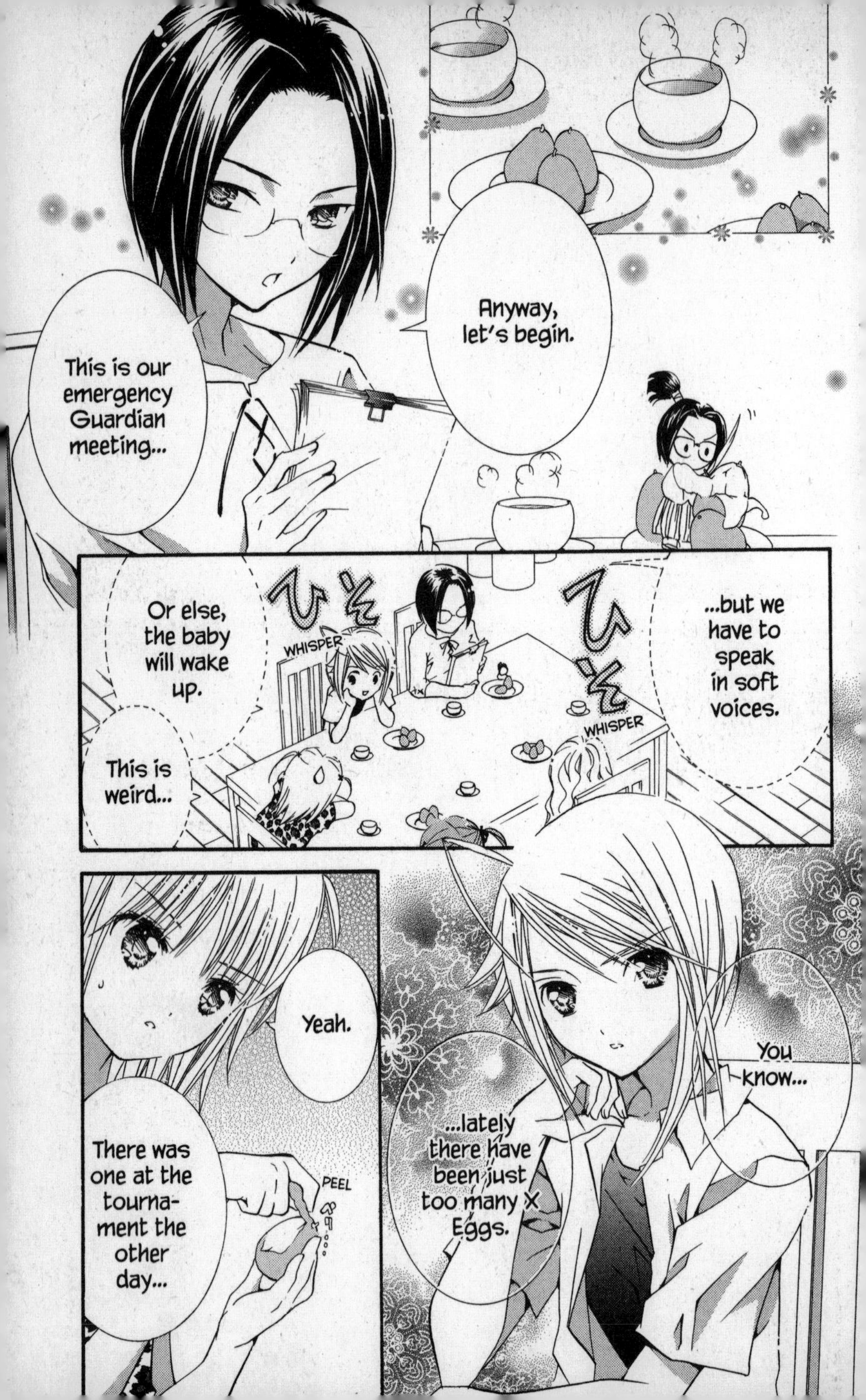

Anyway, let's begin.
This is our emergency Guardian meeting...
...but we have to speak in soft voices.
WHISPER
WHISPER
Or else, the baby will wake up.
This is weird...
You know...
...lately there have been just too many X Eggs.
Yeah.
There was one at the tournament the other day...
PEEL

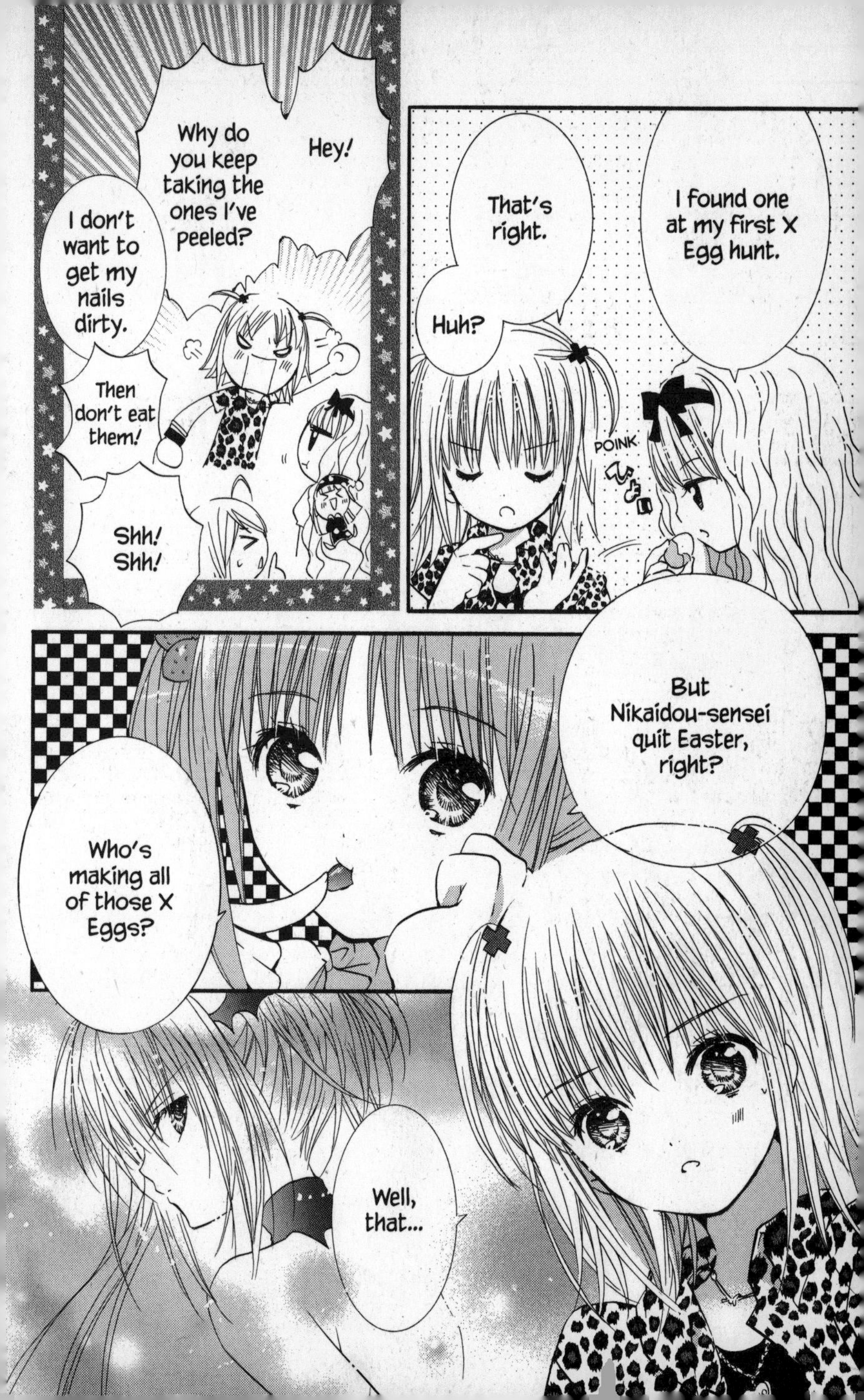
I found one at my first X Egg hunt.
That's right.
Huh?
POINK
Hey!
Why do you keep taking the ones I've peeled?
I don't want to get my nails dirty.
Then don't eat them!
Shh! Shh!
But Nikaidou-sensei quit Easter, right?
Who's making all of those X Eggs?
Well, that...

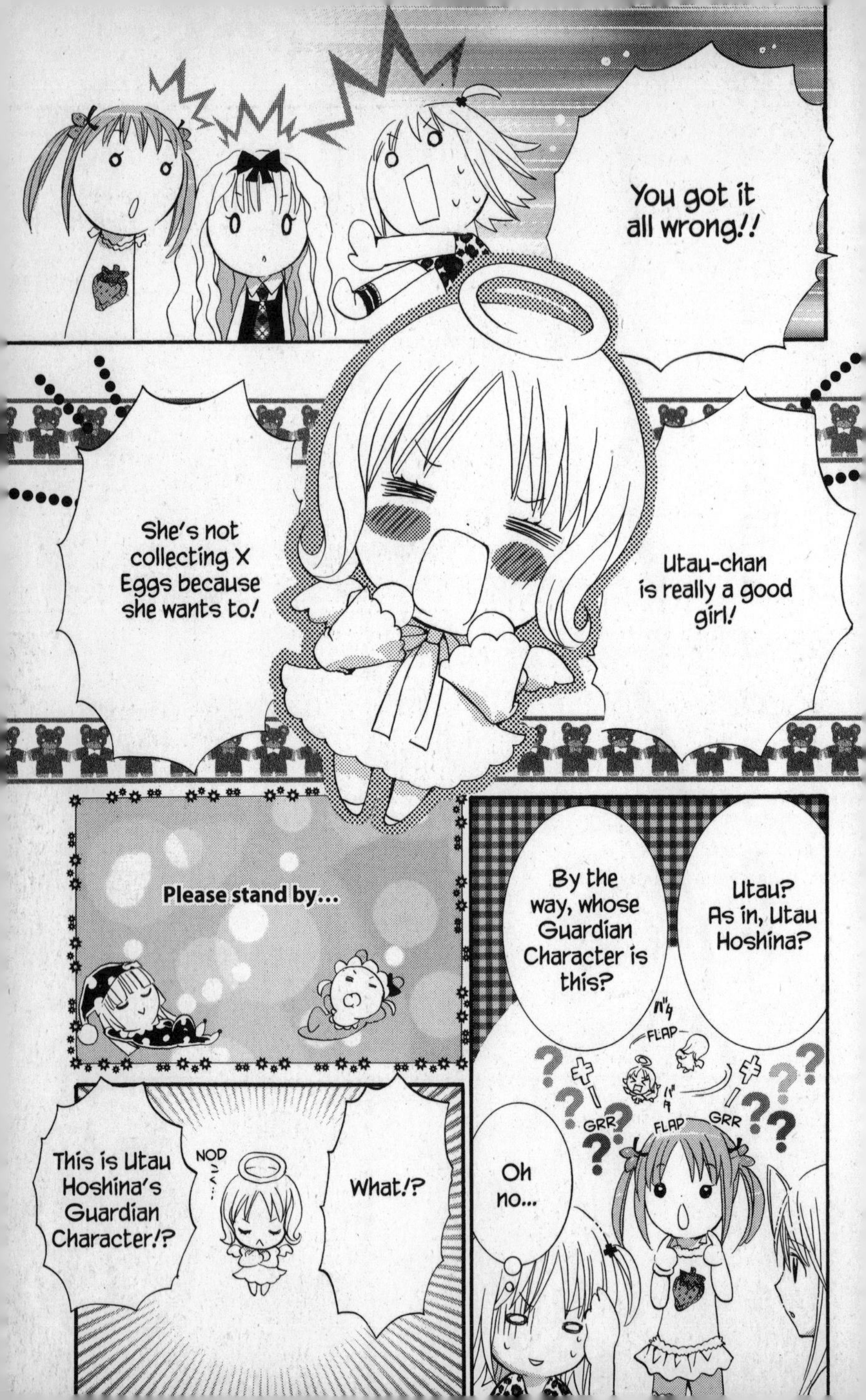

You got it all wrong!!
Utau-chan is really a good girl!
She's not collecting X Eggs because she wants to!
Utau? As in, Utau Hoshina?
By the way, whose Guardian Character is this?
FLAP
GRR
FLAP
GRR
Oh no...
Please stand by...
What!?
NOD
This is Utau Hoshina's Guardian Character!?

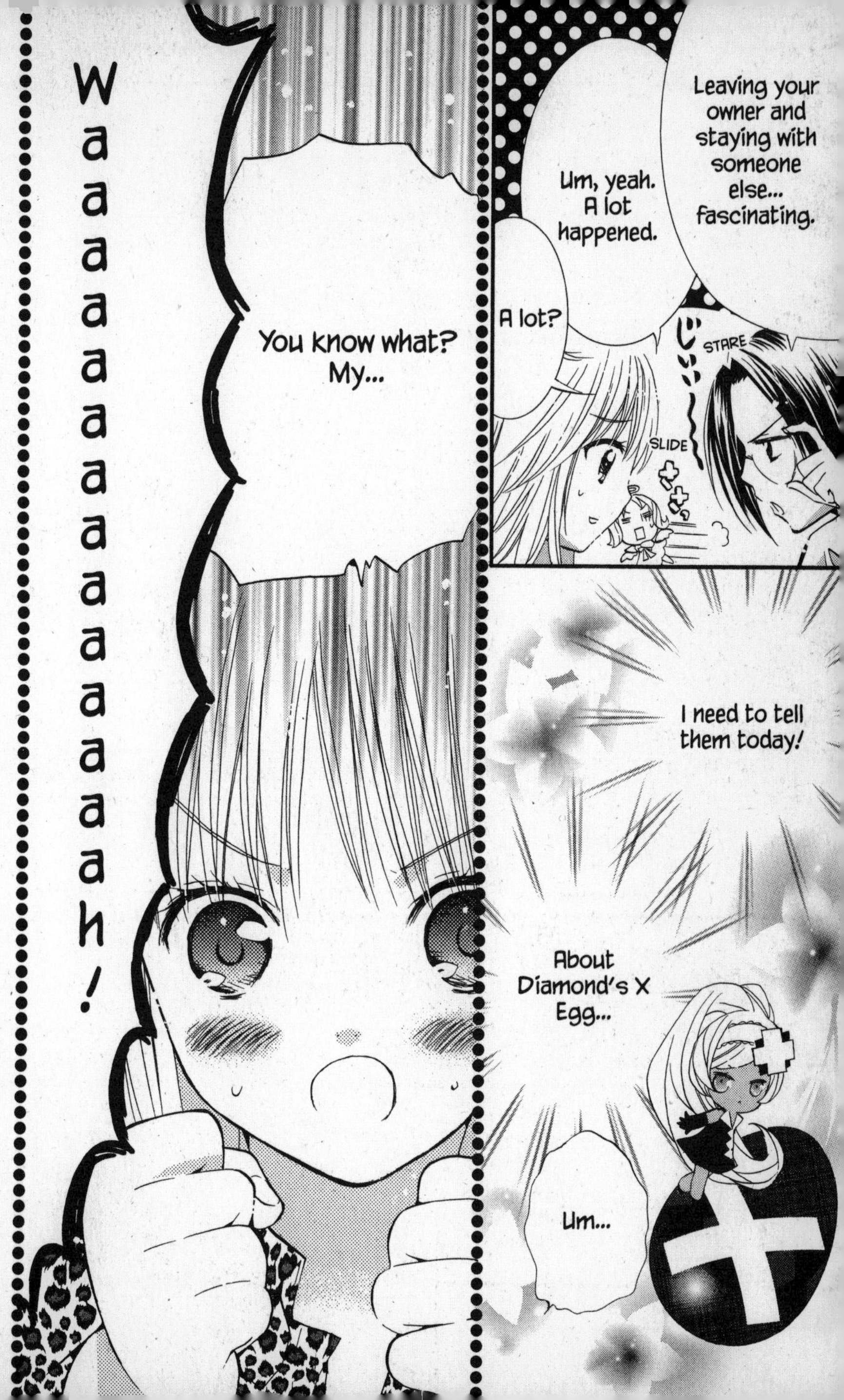
Leaving your owner and staying with someone else... fascinating.
Um, yeah. A lot happened.
A lot?
STARE
SLIDE
I need to tell them today!
About Diamond's X Egg...
Um...
You know what? My...
Waaaaaaaaaaaaaah!

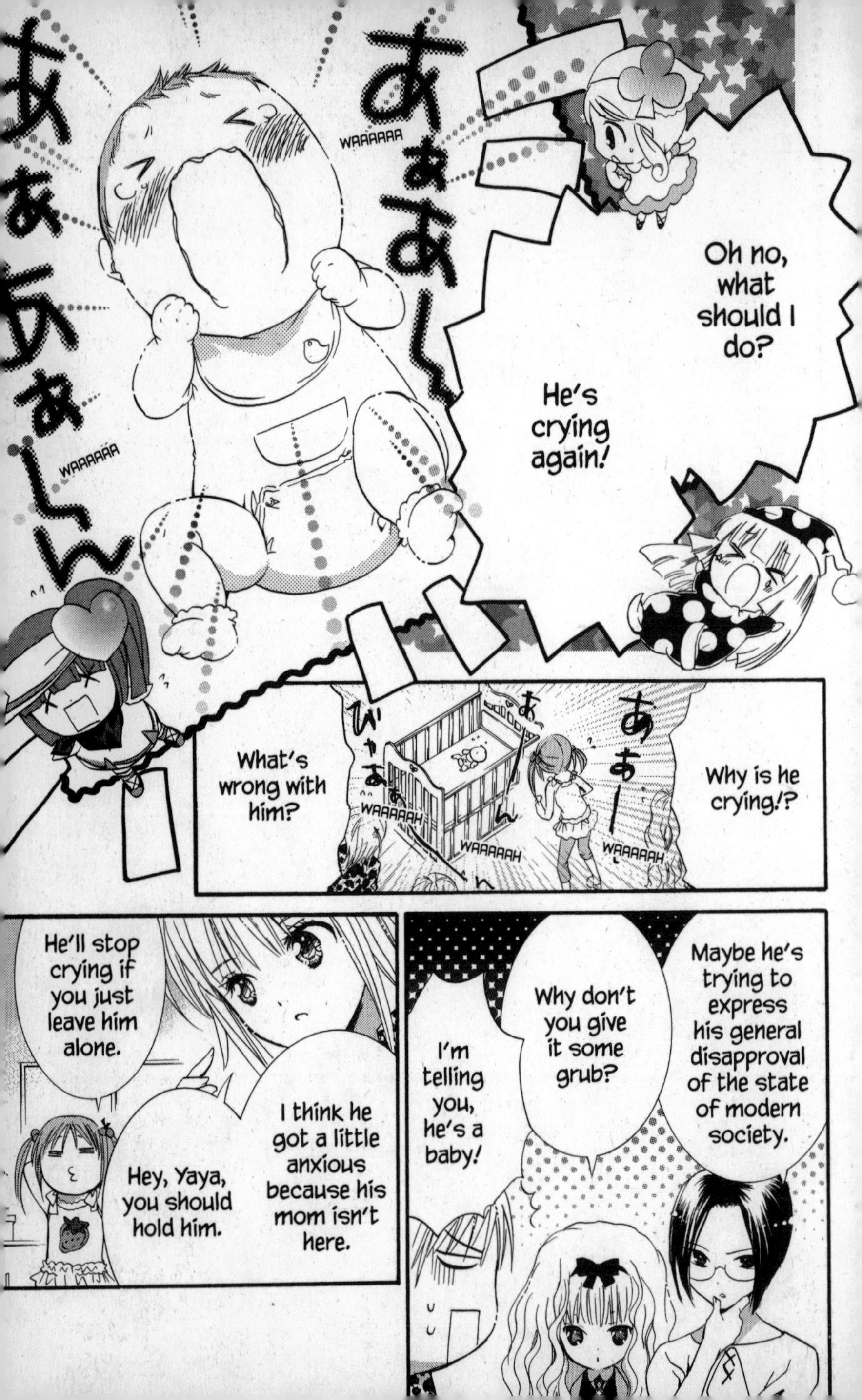
WAAAAAA
WAAAAAA
Oh no, what should I do?
He's crying again!
Why is he crying!?
What's wrong with him?
WAAAAAH
WAAAAAH
WAAAAAH
Maybe he's trying to express his general disapproval of the state of modern society.
Why don't you give it some grub?
I'm telling you, he's a baby!
He'll stop crying if you just leave him alone.
I think he got a little anxious because his mom isn't here.
Hey, Yaya, you should hold him.

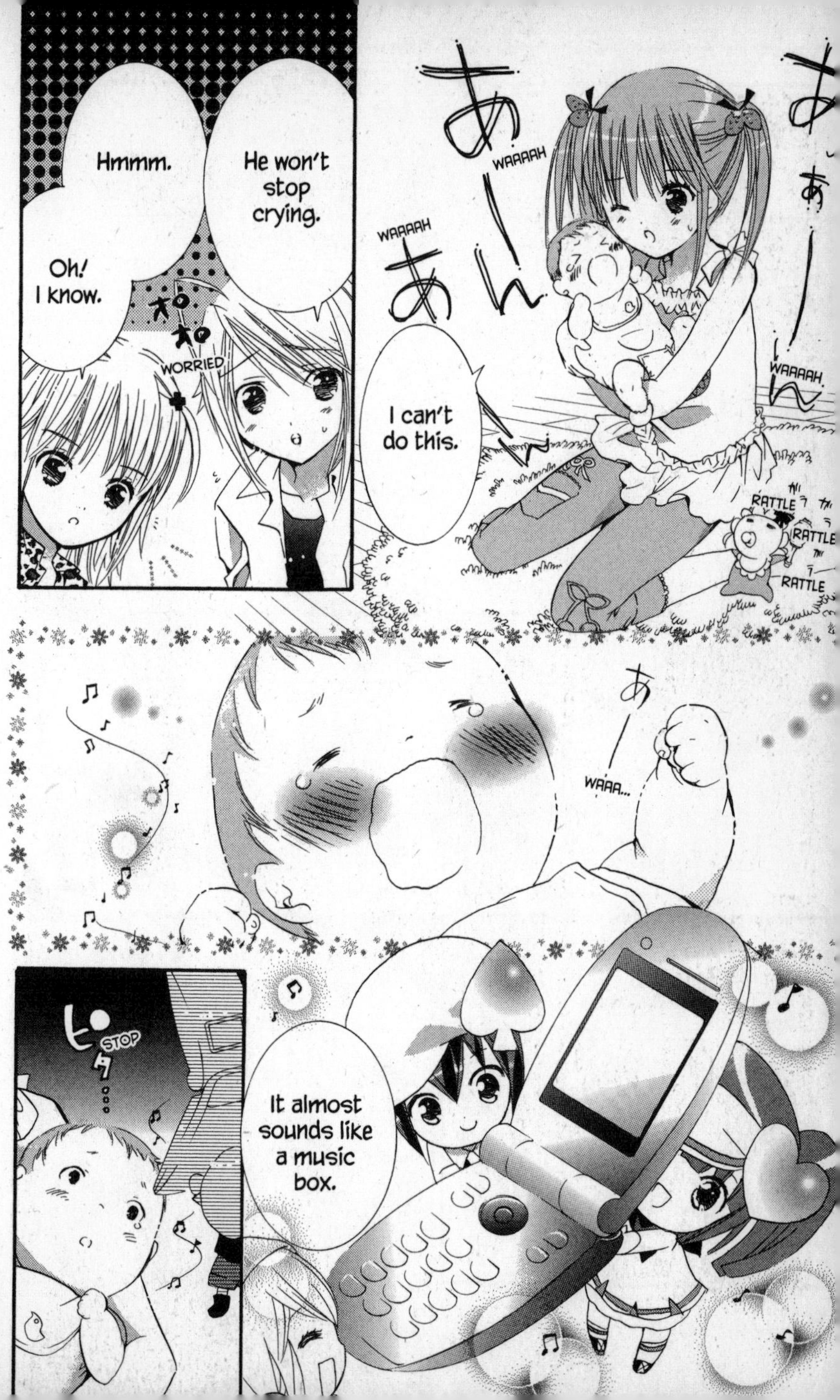
あーん
WAAAAH
あーん
WAAAAH
あ
WAAAAH
I can't do this.
RATTLE
RATTLE
RATTLE
He won't stop crying.
Hmmm.
Oh! I know.
WORRIED
あー
WAAA...
It almost sounds like a music box.
ピタ
STOP

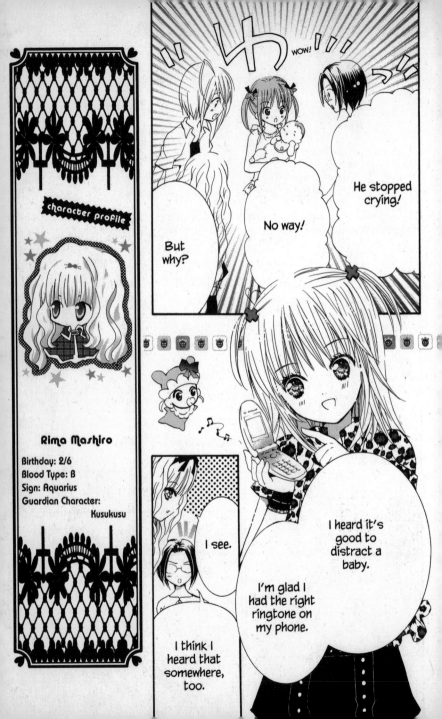

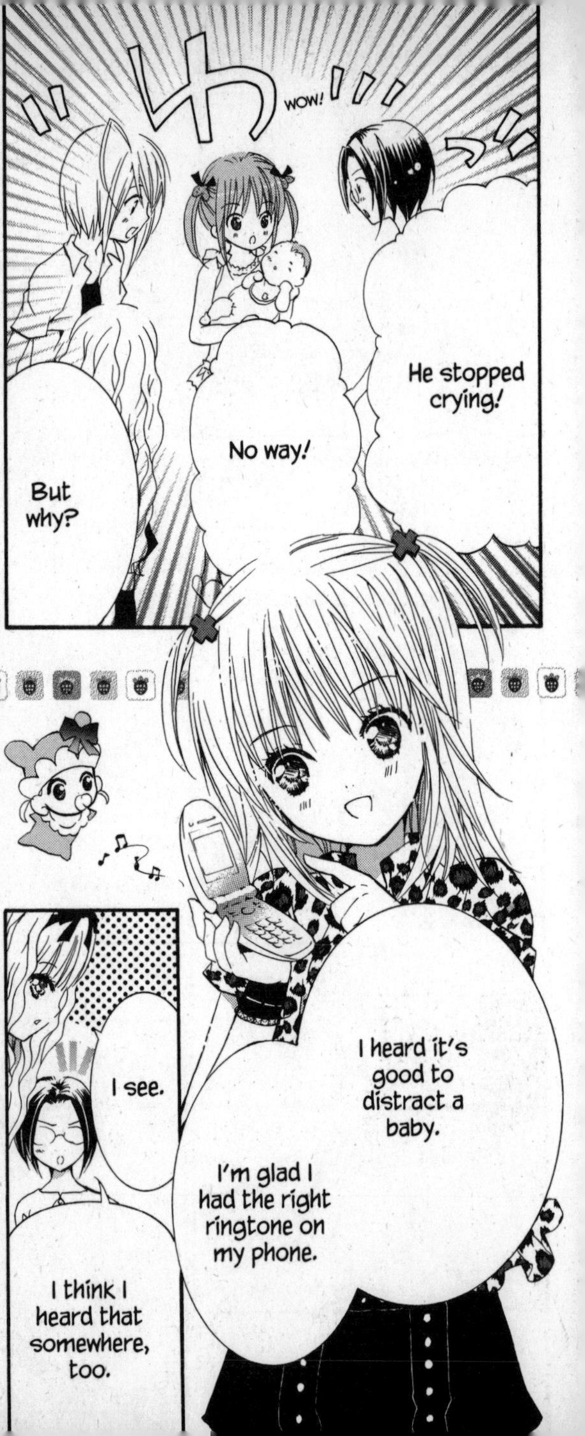
WOW!
He stopped crying!
No way!
But why?
I heard it's good to distract a baby.
I'm glad I had the right ringtone on my phone.
I see.
I think I heard that somewhere, too.

character profile

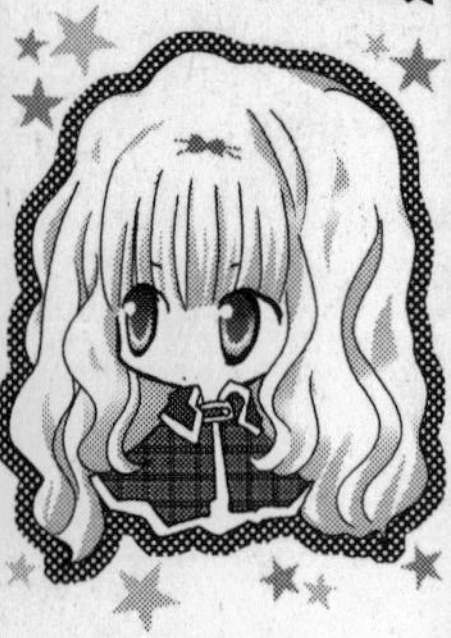

Rima Mashiro

Birthday: 2/6
Blood Type: B
Sign: Aquarius
Guardian Character:
Kusukusu

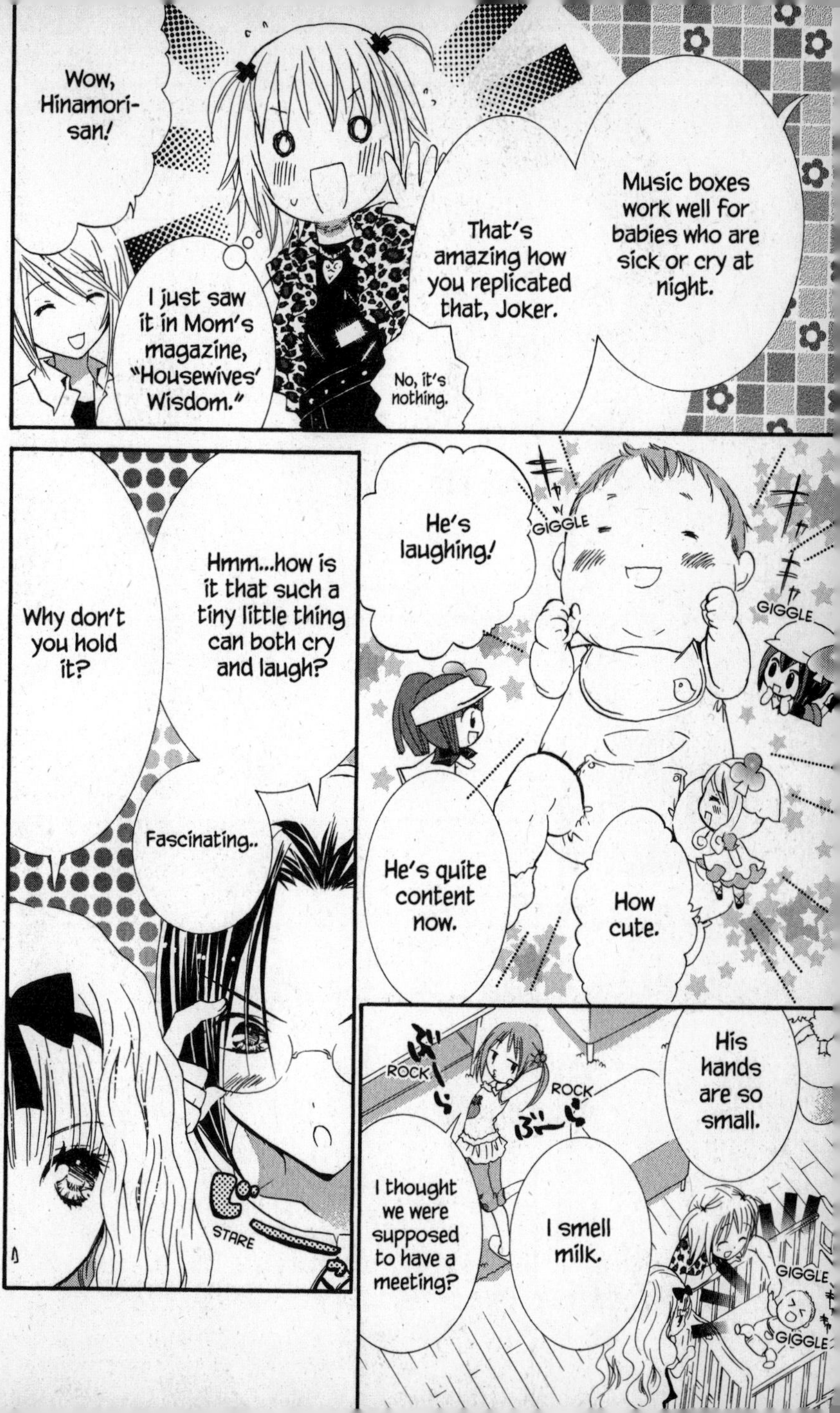
Music boxes work well for babies who are sick or cry at night.
That's amazing how you replicated that, Joker.
No, it's nothing.
Wow, Hinamori-san!
I just saw it in Mom's magazine, "Housewives' Wisdom."
GIGGLE
He's laughing!
GIGGLE
How cute.
He's quite content now.
His hands are so small.
ROCK
ROCK
I smell milk.
I thought we were supposed to have a meeting?
GIGGLE
GIGGLE
Hmm...how is it that such a tiny little thing can both cry and laugh?
Why don't you hold it?
Fascinating..
STARE

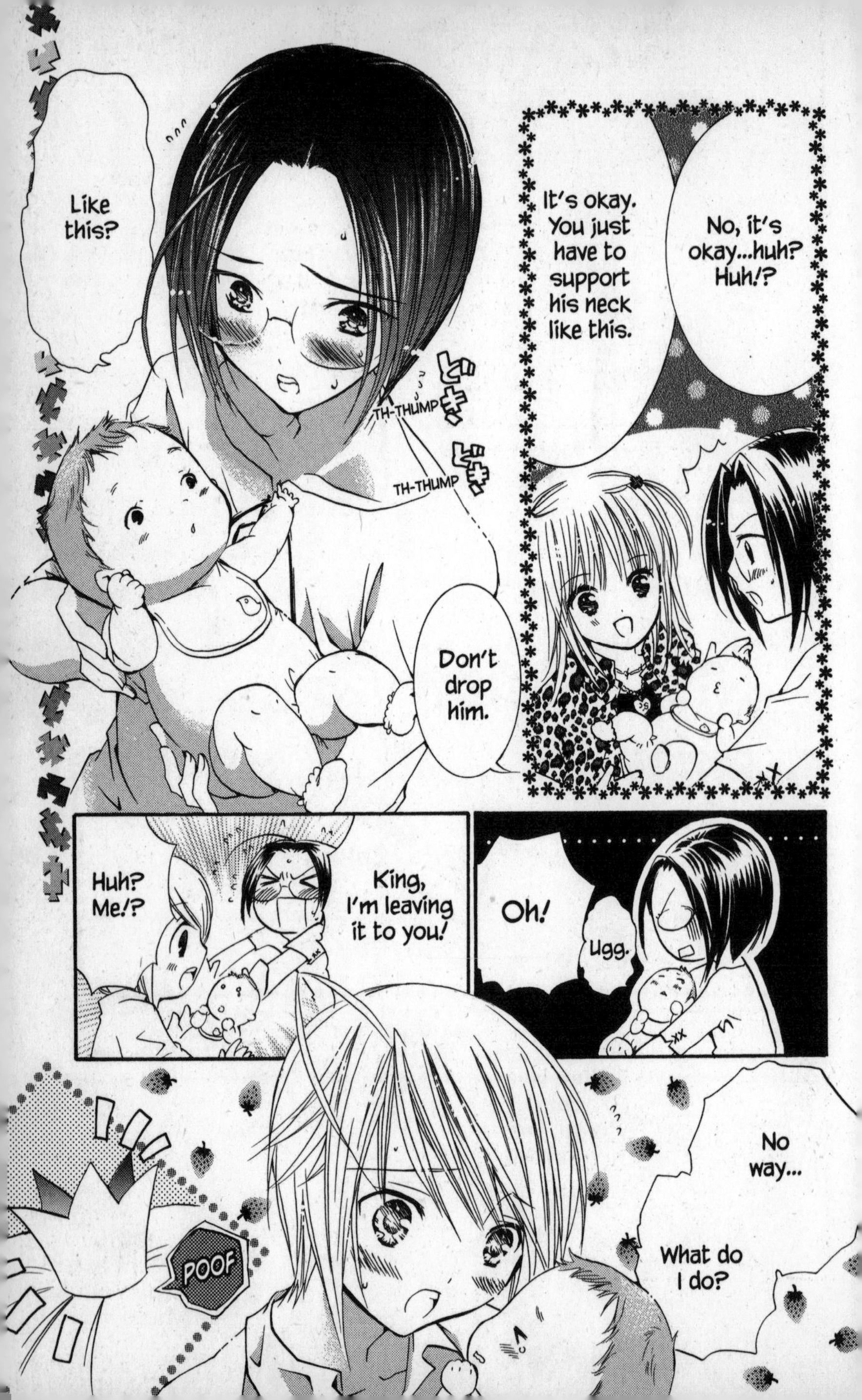

No, it's okay...huh? Huh!?
It's okay. You just have to support his neck like this.
Like this?
TH-THUMP
TH-THUMP
Don't drop him.
Oh!
Ugg.
King, I'm leaving it to you!
Huh? Me!?
No way...
What do I do?
POOF

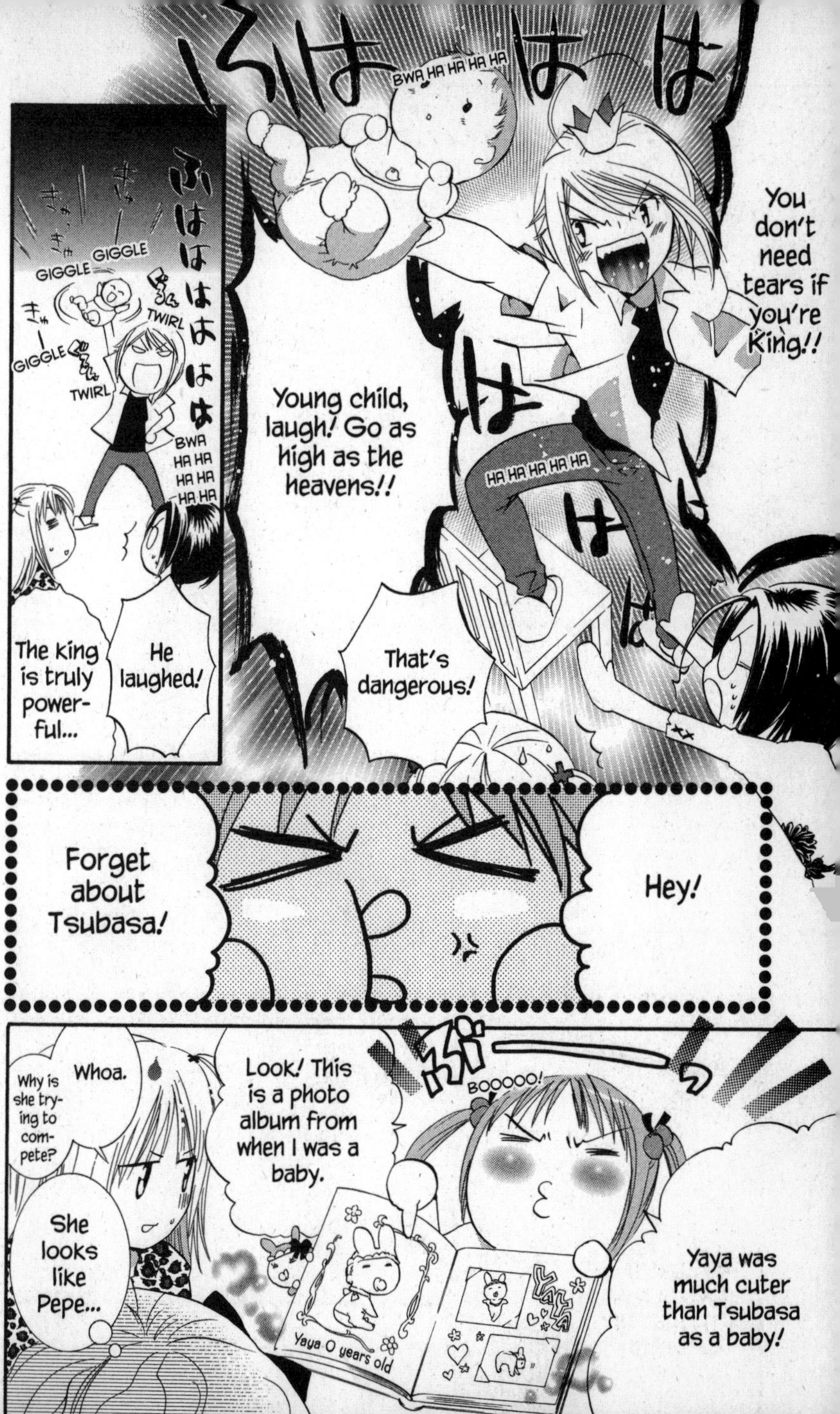
BWA HA HA HA HA
You don't need tears if you're King!!
Young child, laugh! Go as high as the heavens!!
HA HA HA HA HA
That's dangerous!
GIGGLE GIGGLE
TWIRL
GIGGLE
TWIRL
BWA HA HA HA HA HA HA
He laughed!
The king is truly power-ful...
Hey!
Forget about Tsubasa!
BOOOOO!
Yaya was much cuter than Tsubasa as a baby!
Look! This is a photo album from when I was a baby.
Yaya 0 years old
YAYA
Whoa.
Why is she try-ing to com-pete?
She looks like Pepe...

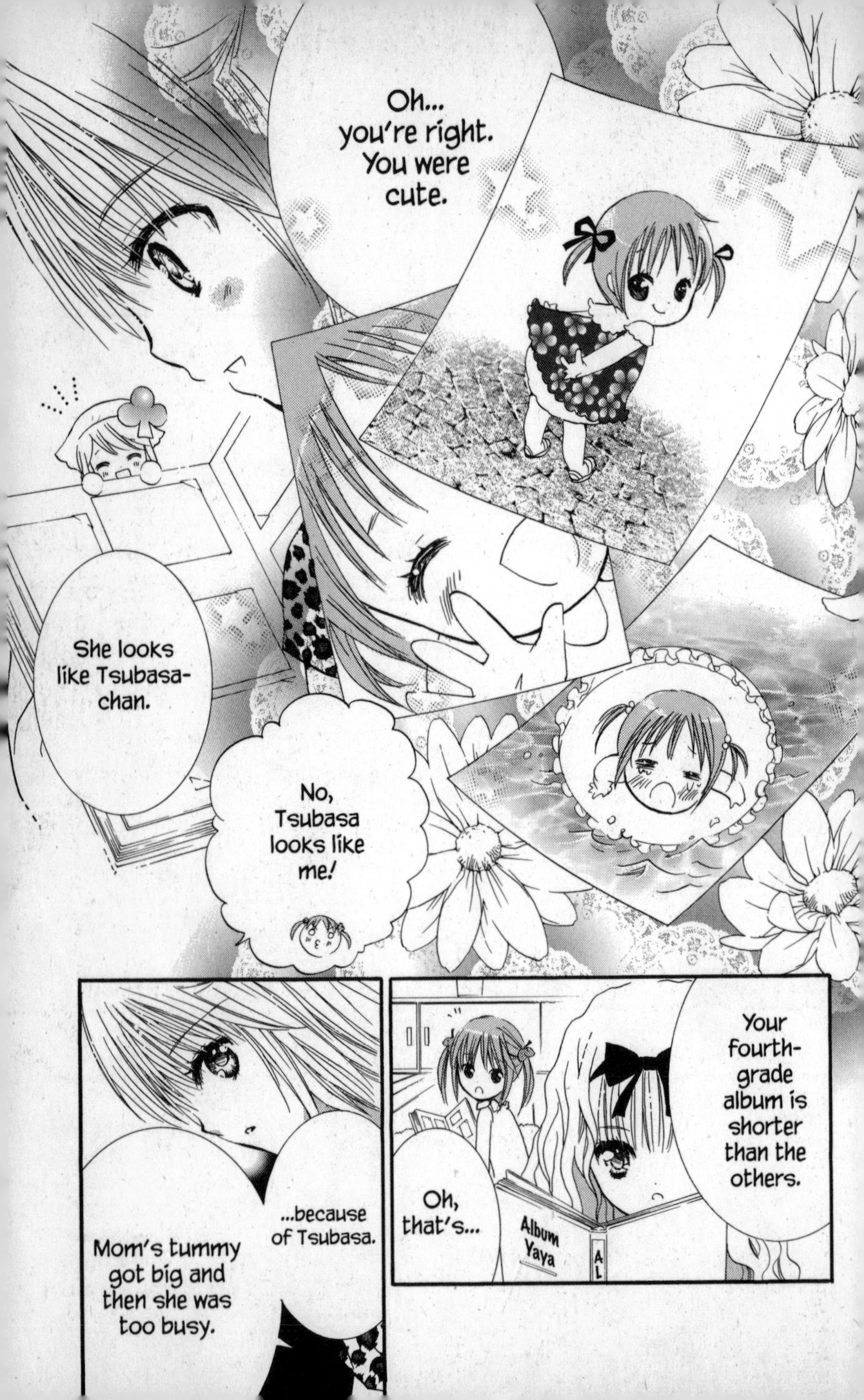
Oh... you're right. You were cute.
She looks like Tsubasa-chan.
No, Tsubasa looks like me!
Your fourth-grade album is shorter than the others.
Oh, that's...
Album Yaya
...because of Tsubasa.
Mom's tummy got big and then she was too busy.

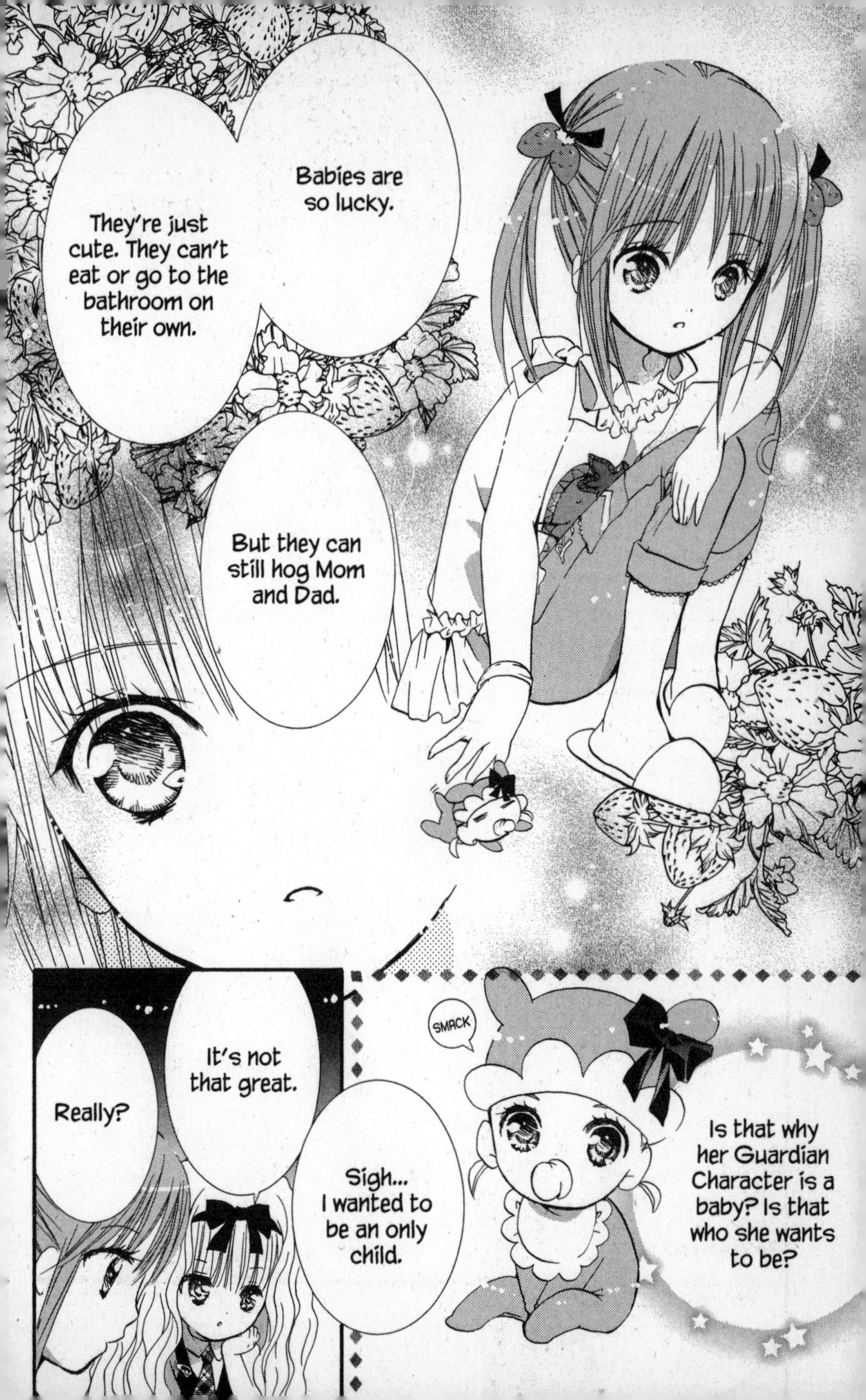
Babies are so lucky.
They're just cute. They can't eat or go to the bathroom on their own.
But they can still hog Mom and Dad.
SMACK
Is that why her Guardian Character is a baby? Is that who she wants to be?
It's not that great.
Really?
Sigh... I wanted to be an only child.

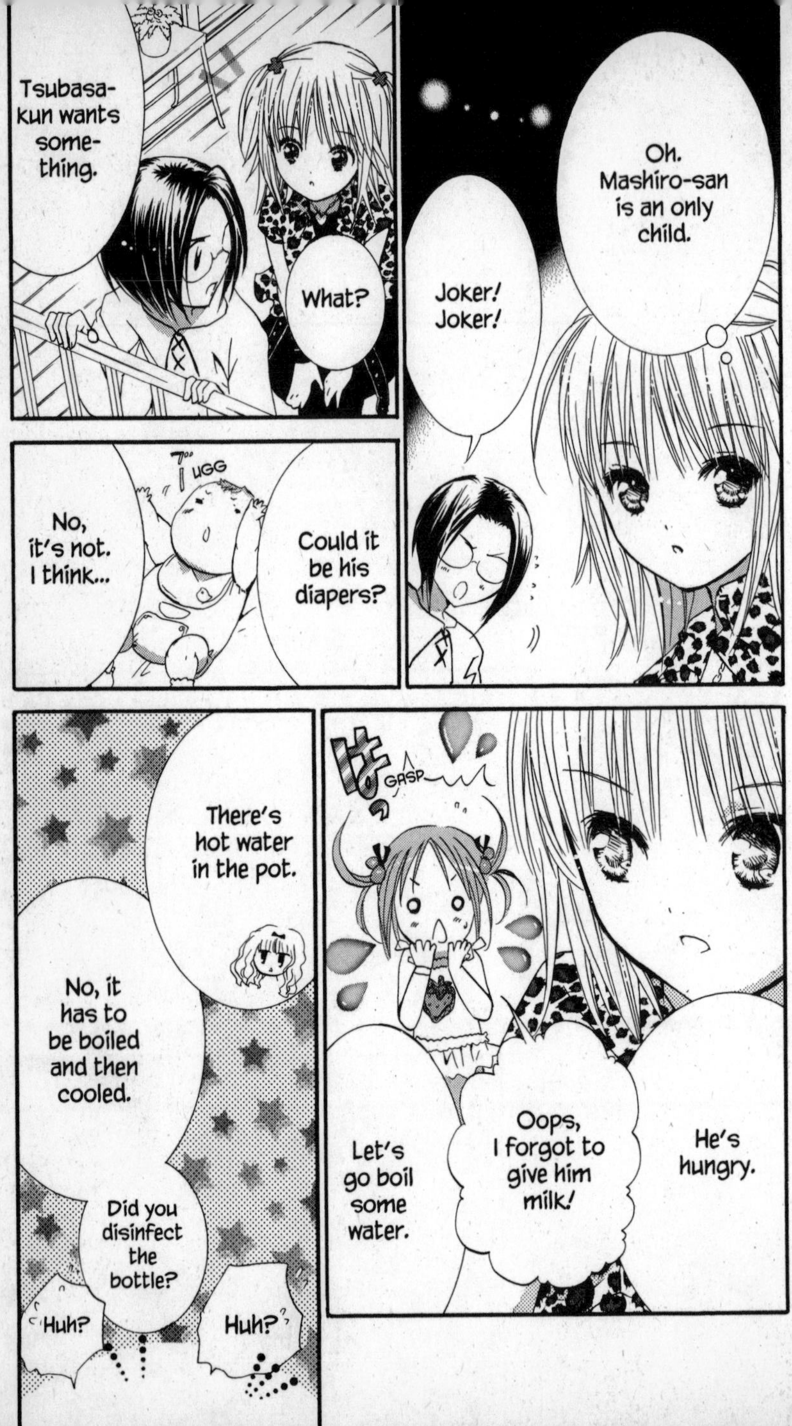
Oh. Mashiro-san is an only child.
Joker! Joker!
Tsubasa-kun wants something.
What?
Could it be his diapers?
UGG
No, it's not. I think...
He's hungry.
GASP
Oops, I forgot to give him milk!
Let's go boil some water.
There's hot water in the pot.
No, it has to be boiled and then cooled.
Did you disinfect the bottle?
Huh?
Huh?

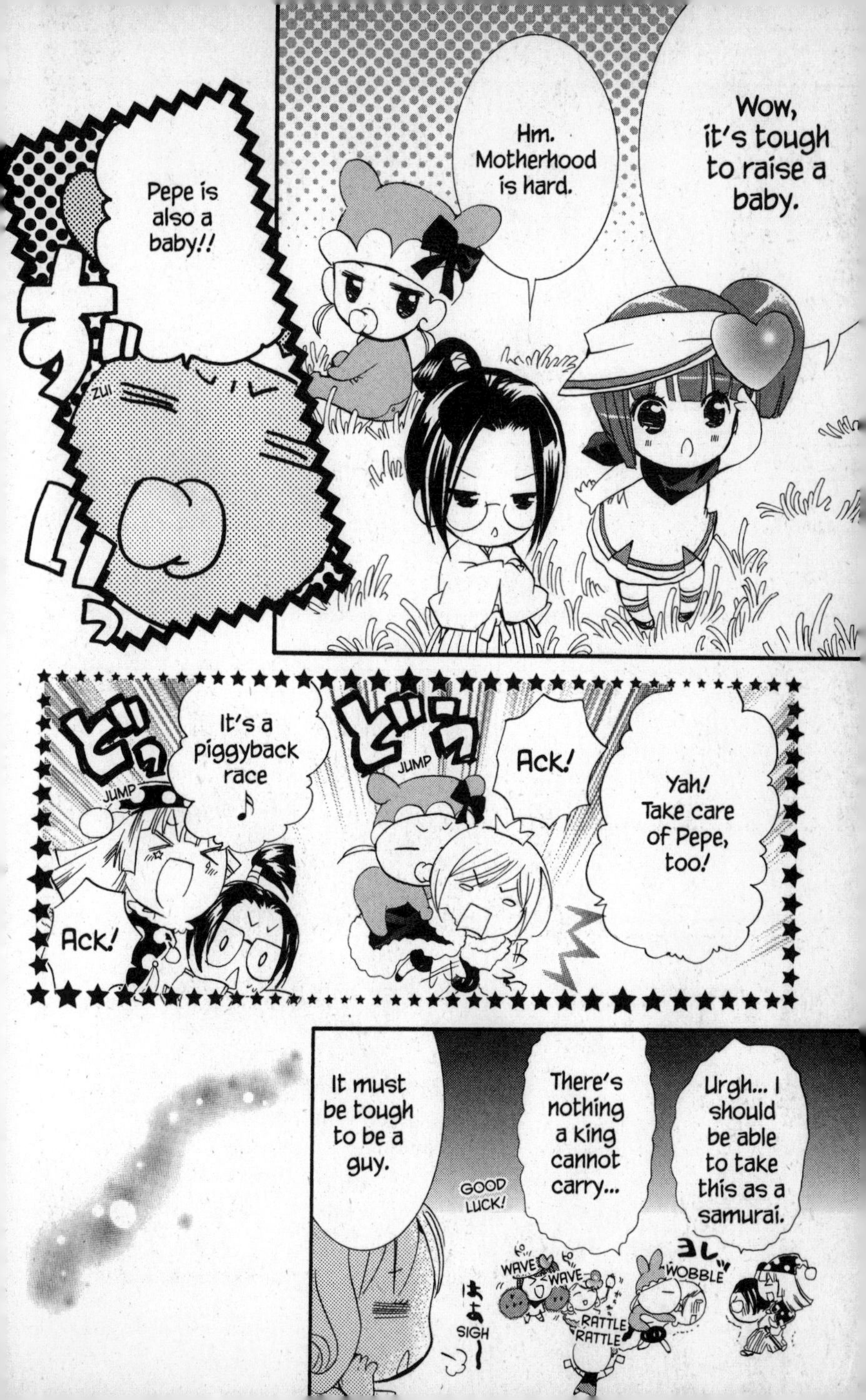
Wow, it's tough to raise a baby.
Hm. Motherhood is hard.
Pepe is also a baby!!
ZUI
Yah! Take care of Pepe, too!
Ack!
JUMP
It's a piggyback race ♪
JUMP
Ack!
Urgh... I should be able to take this as a samurai.
There's nothing a king cannot carry...
It must be tough to be a guy.
GOOD LUCK!
WOBBLE
WAVE
WAVE
RATTLE RATTLE
SIGH

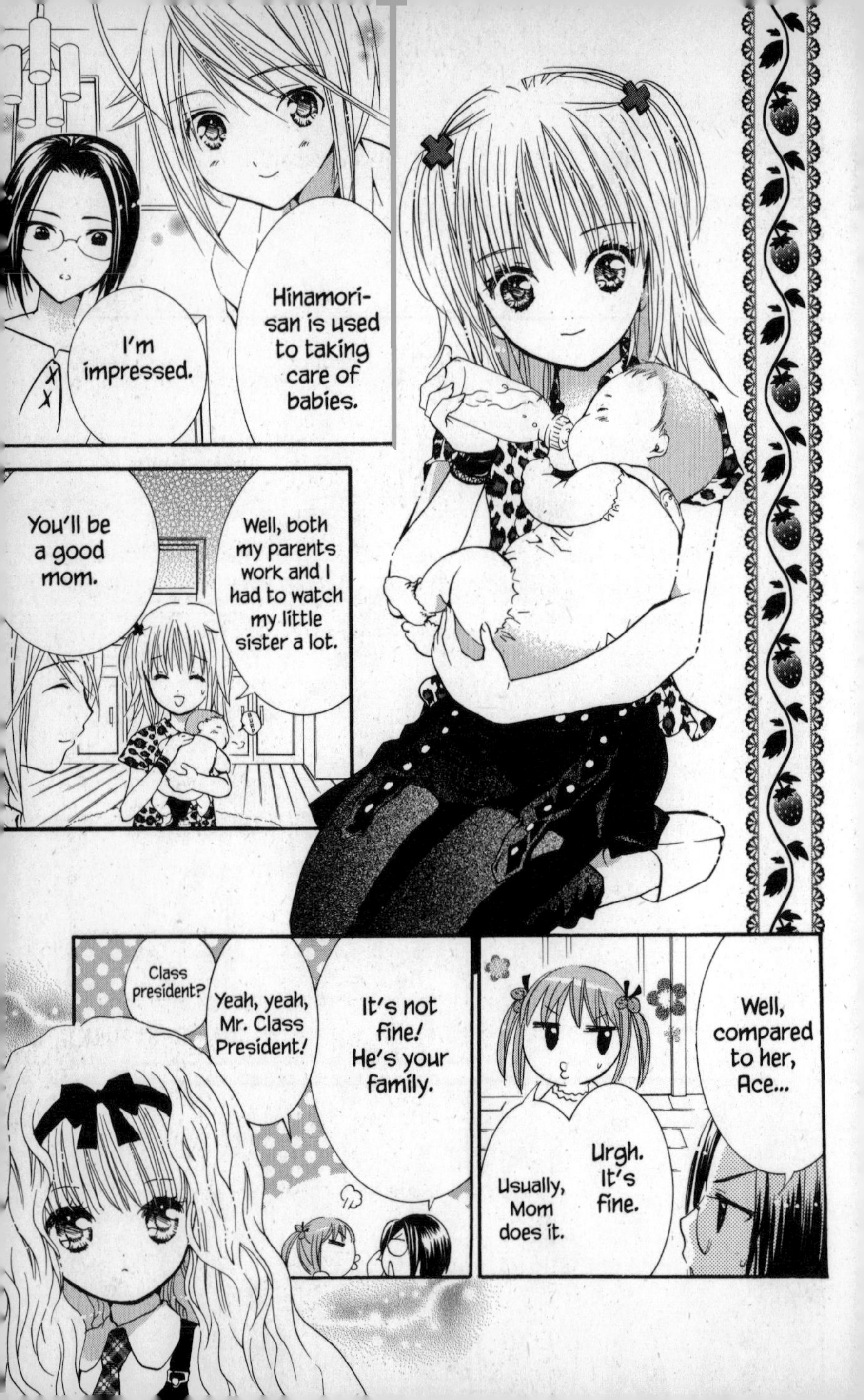
Hinamori-san is used to taking care of babies.
I'm impressed.
Well, both my parents work and I had to watch my little sister a lot.
You'll be a good mom.
BURP
Well, compared to her, Ace...
Urgh. It's fine.
Usually, Mom does it.
It's not fine! He's your family.
Yeah, yeah, Mr. Class President!
Class president?

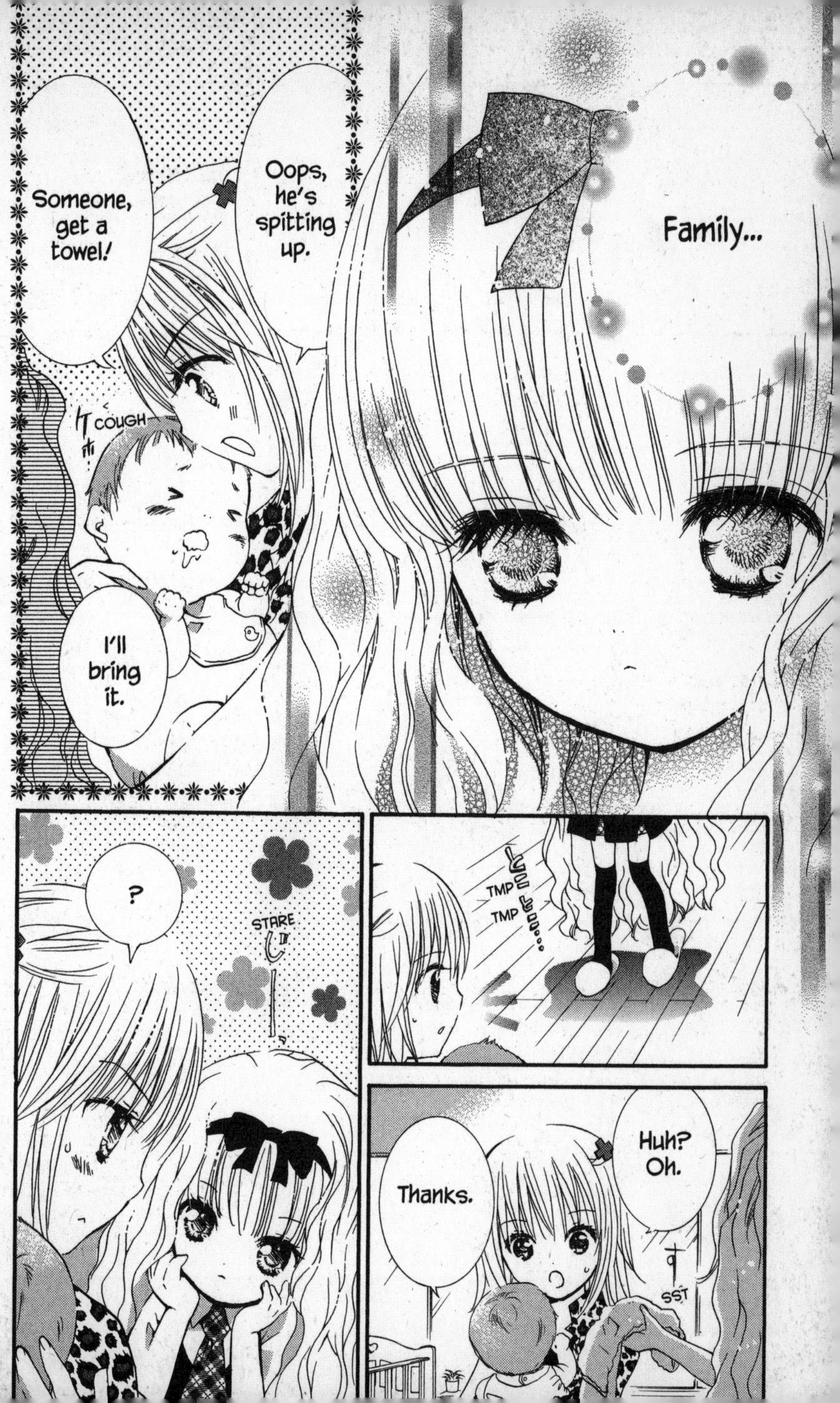
Family...
Oops, he's spitting up.
Someone, get a towel!
COUGH
I'll bring it.
TMP
TMP
Huh? Oh.
Thanks.
SST
?
STARE

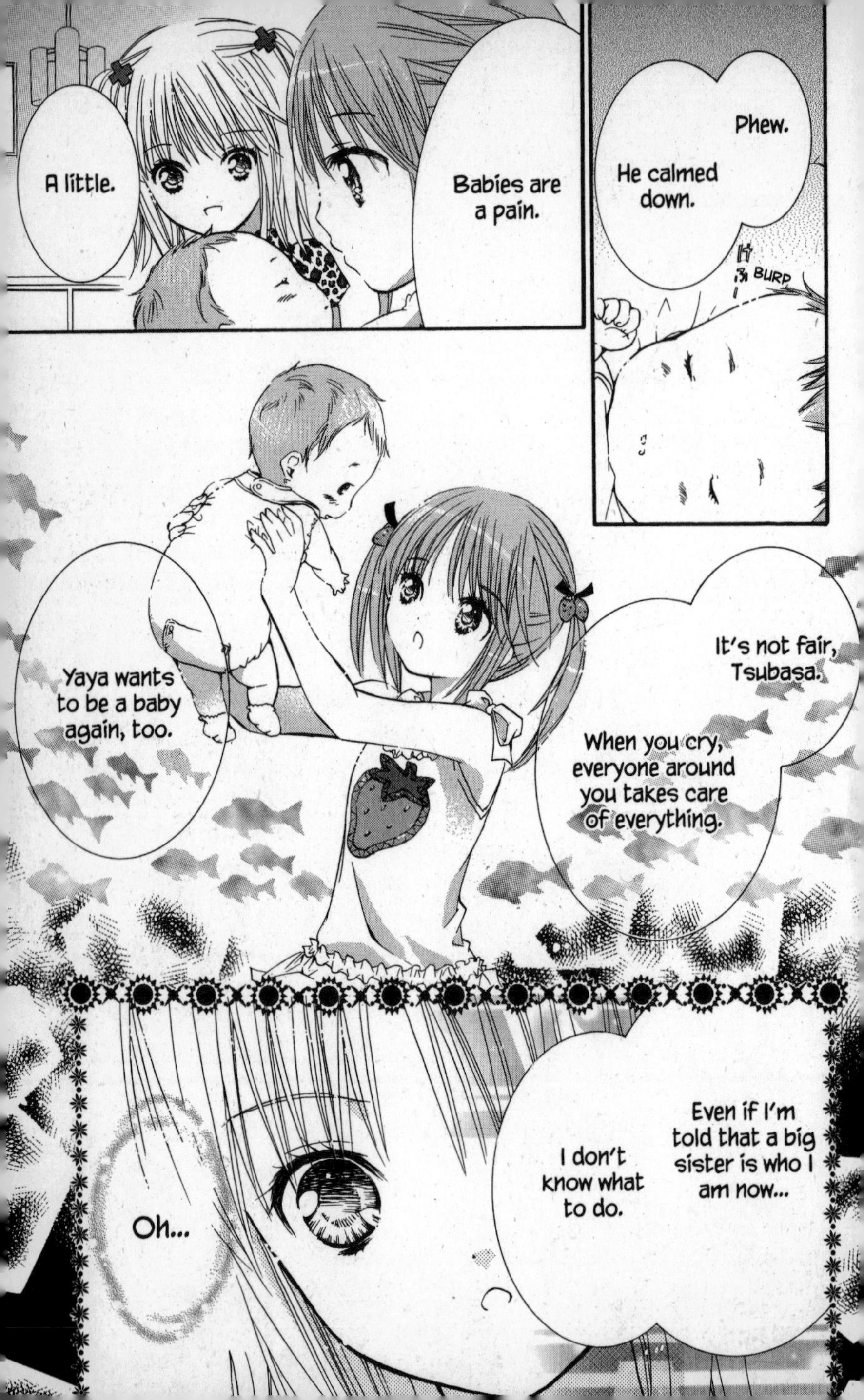
Phew.
He calmed down.
BURP
Babies are a pain.
A little.
It's not fair, Tsubasa.
When you cry, everyone around you takes care of everything.
Yaya wants to be a baby again, too.
Even if I'm told that a big sister is who I am now...
I don't know what to do.
Oh...

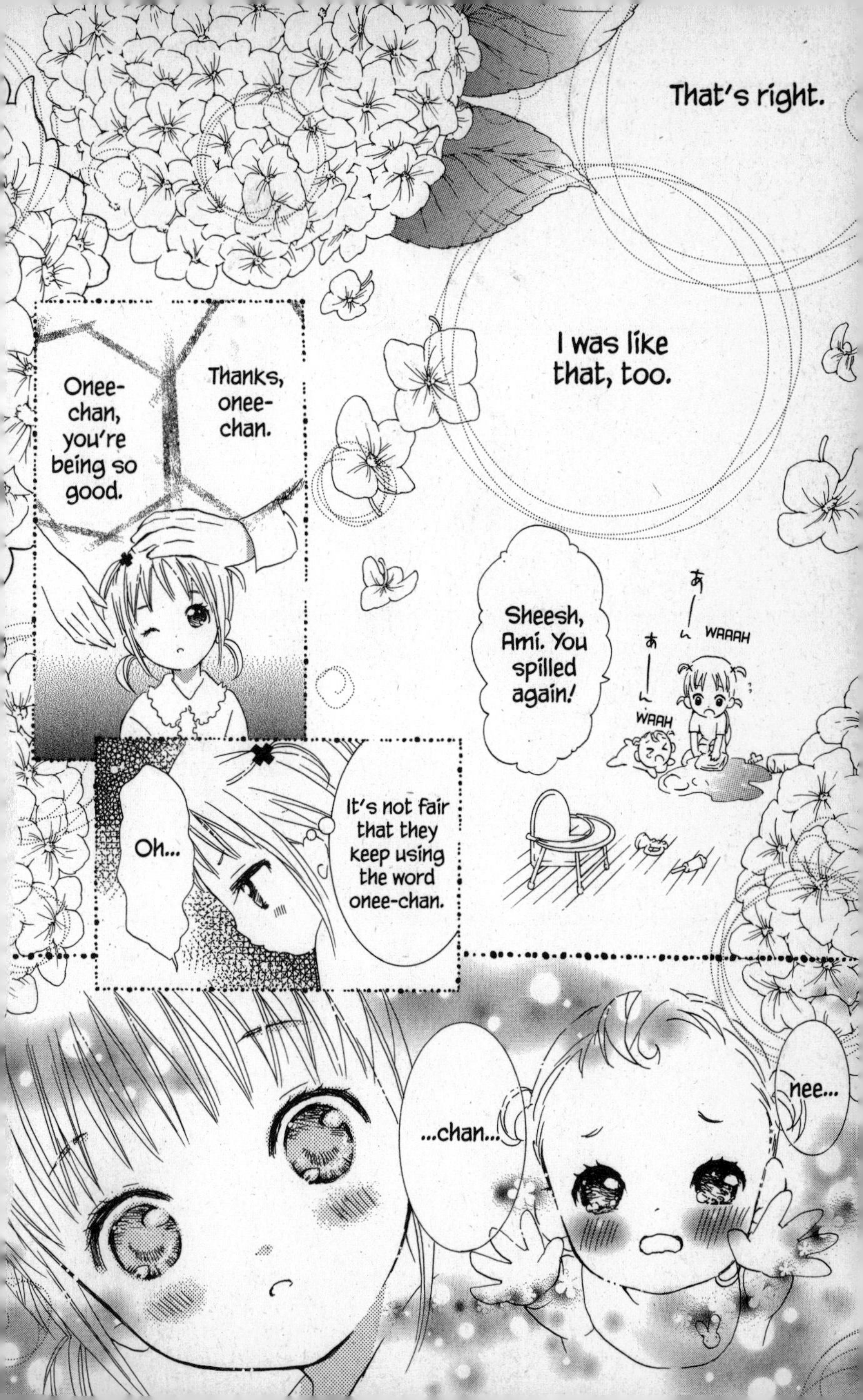

That's right.
I was like that, too.
Sheesh, Ami. You spilled again!
あーん WAAAH
あーん WAAH
Thanks, onee-chan.
Onee-chan, you're being so good.
It's not fair that they keep using the word onee-chan.
Oh...
nee...
...chan...

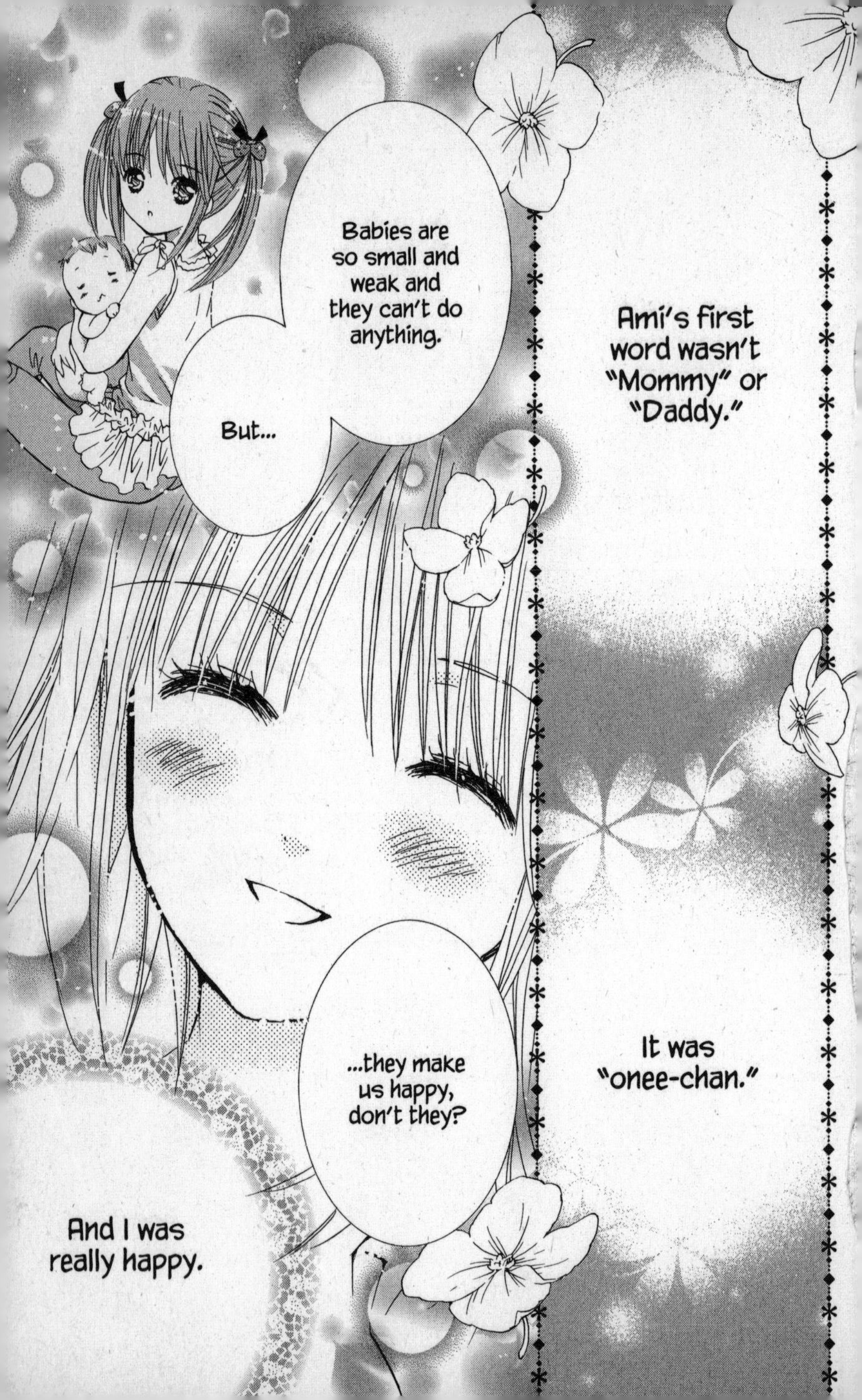
Ami's first word wasn't "Mommy" or "Daddy."
It was "onee-chan."
Babies are so small and weak and they can't do anything.
But...
...they make us happy, don't they?
And I was really happy.

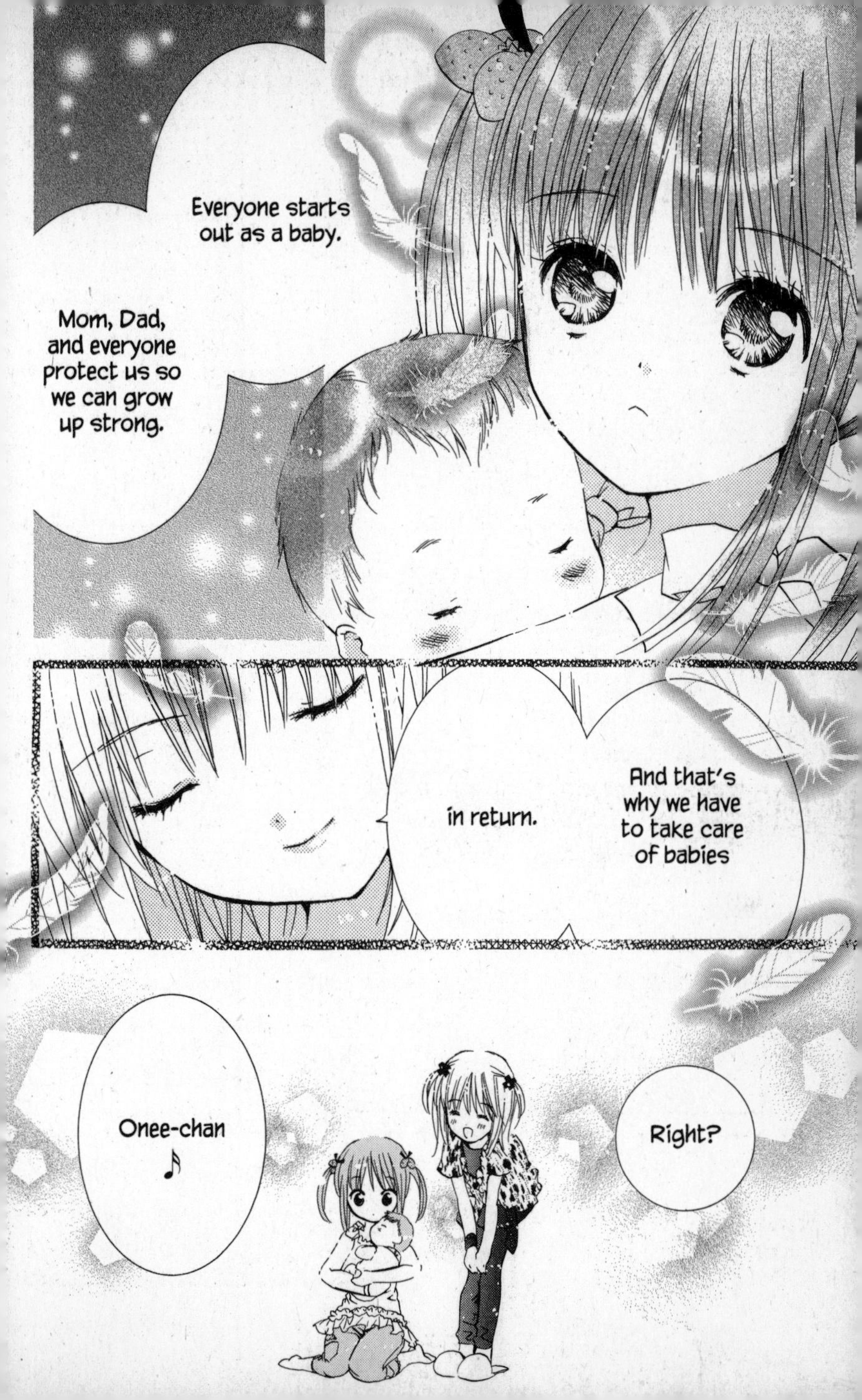
Everyone starts out as a baby.
Mom, Dad, and everyone protect us so we can grow up strong.
And that's why we have to take care of babies
in return.
Right?
Onee-chan ♪

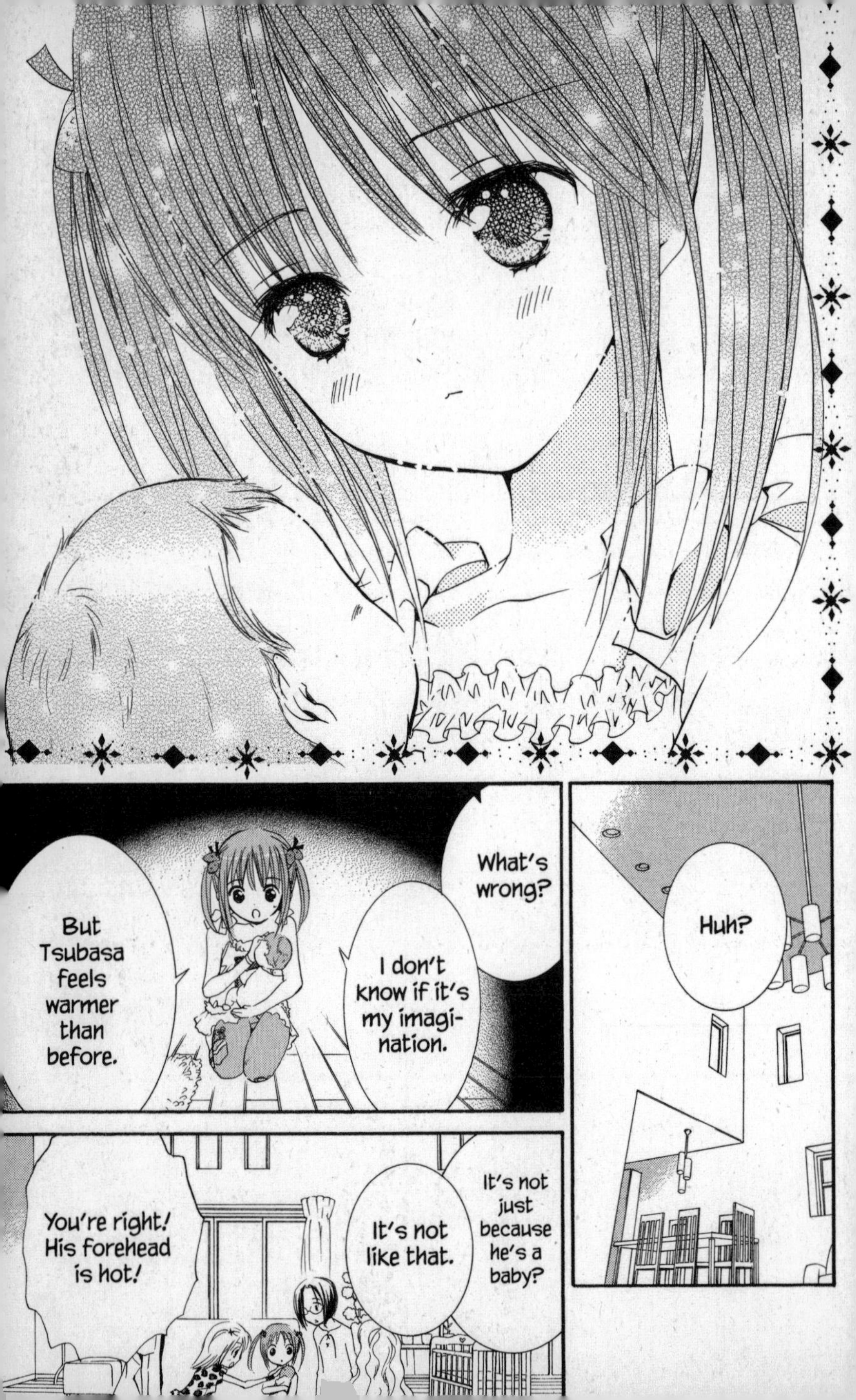
Huh?
What's wrong?
I don't know if it's my imagination.
But Tsubasa feels warmer than before.
It's not just because he's a baby?
It's not like that.
You're right! His forehead is hot!

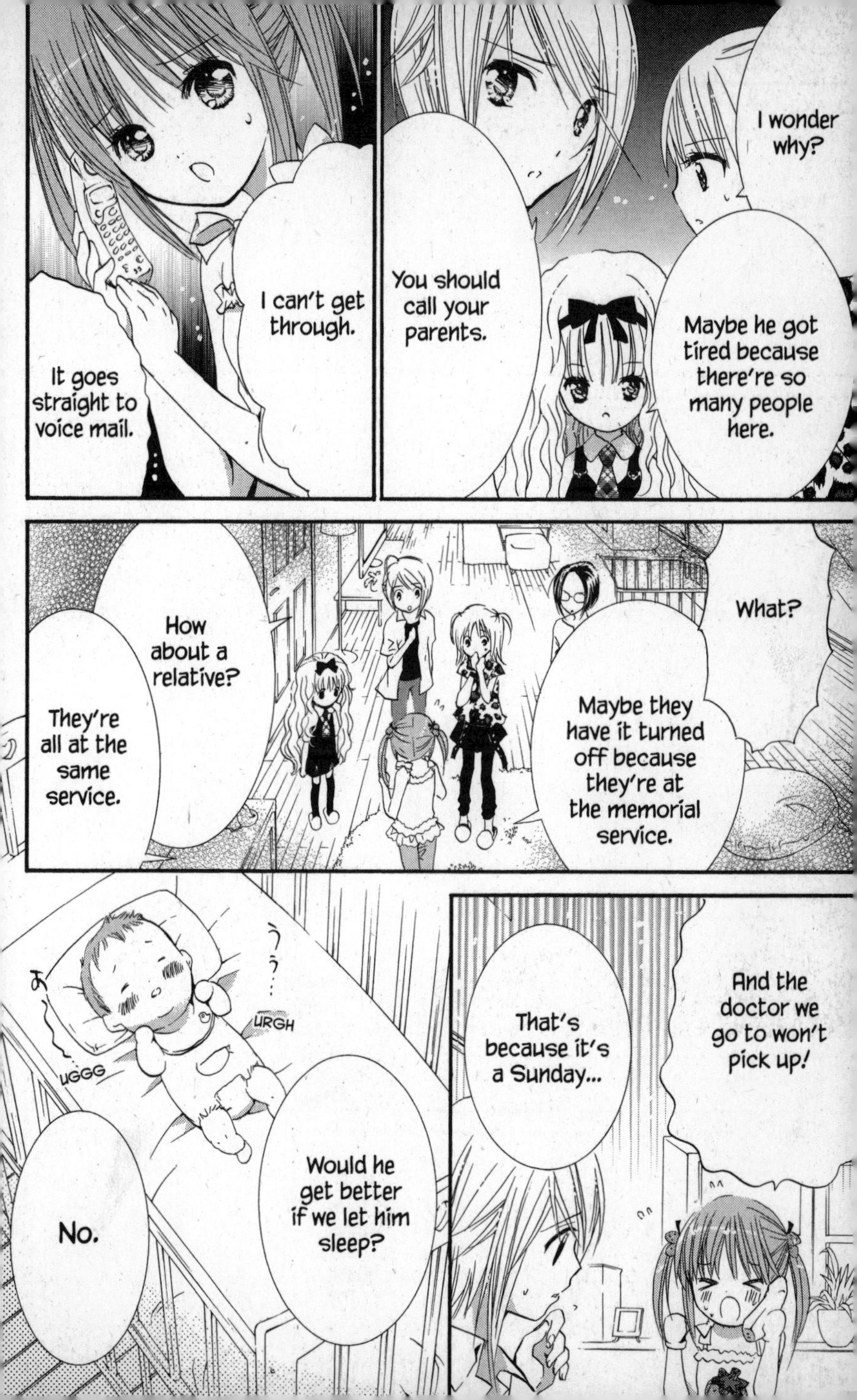
I wonder why?
Maybe he got tired because there're so many people here.
You should call your parents.
I can't get through.
It goes straight to voice mail.
What?
Maybe they have it turned off because they're at the memorial service.
How about a relative?
They're all at the same service.
And the doctor we go to won't pick up!
That's because it's a Sunday...
URGH
UGGG
Would he get better if we let him sleep?
No.

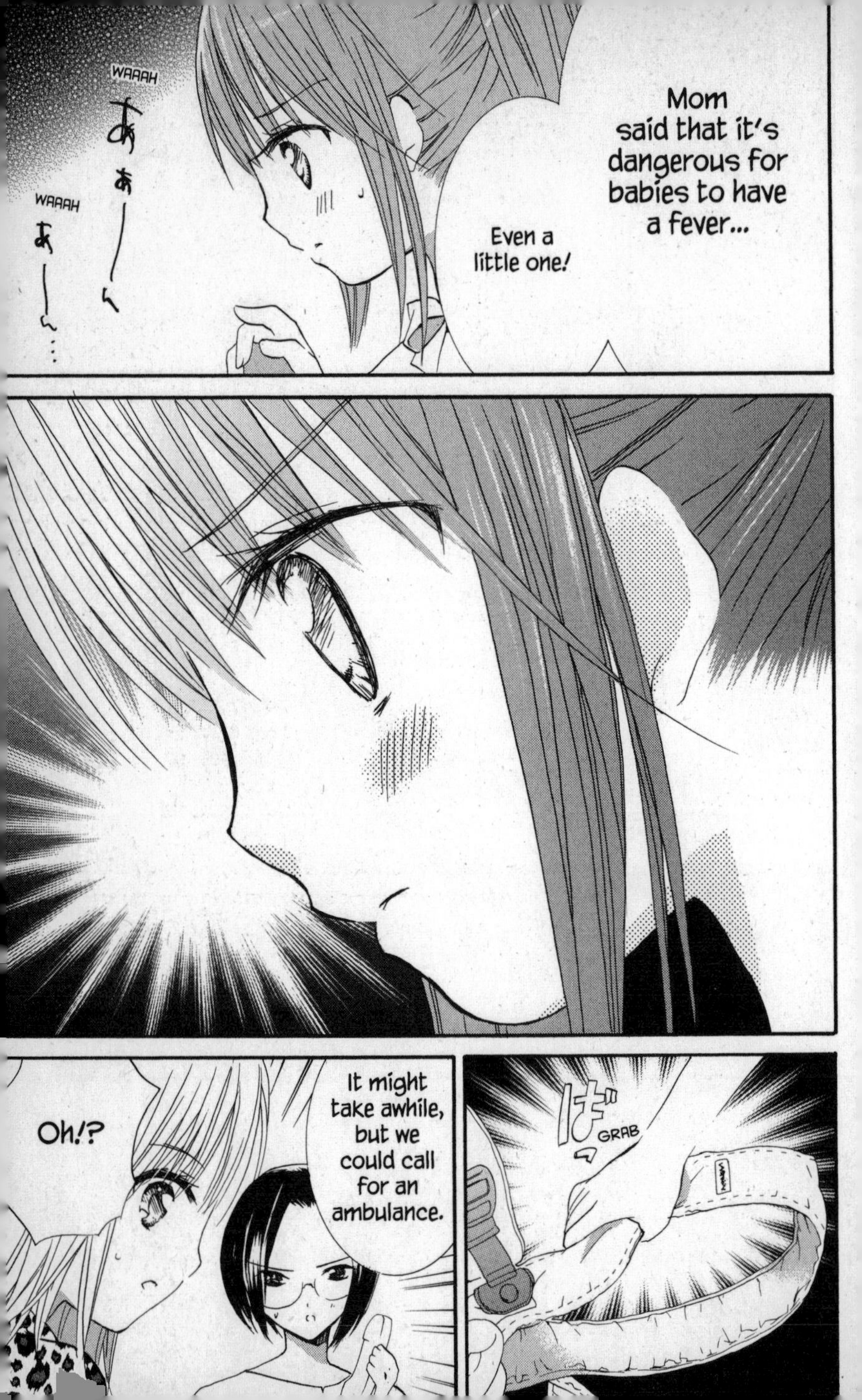
Mom said that it's dangerous for babies to have a fever...
Even a little one!
WAAAH
ああーん
WAAAH
あーん…
ばっ
GRAB
It might take awhile, but we could call for an ambulance.
Oh!?

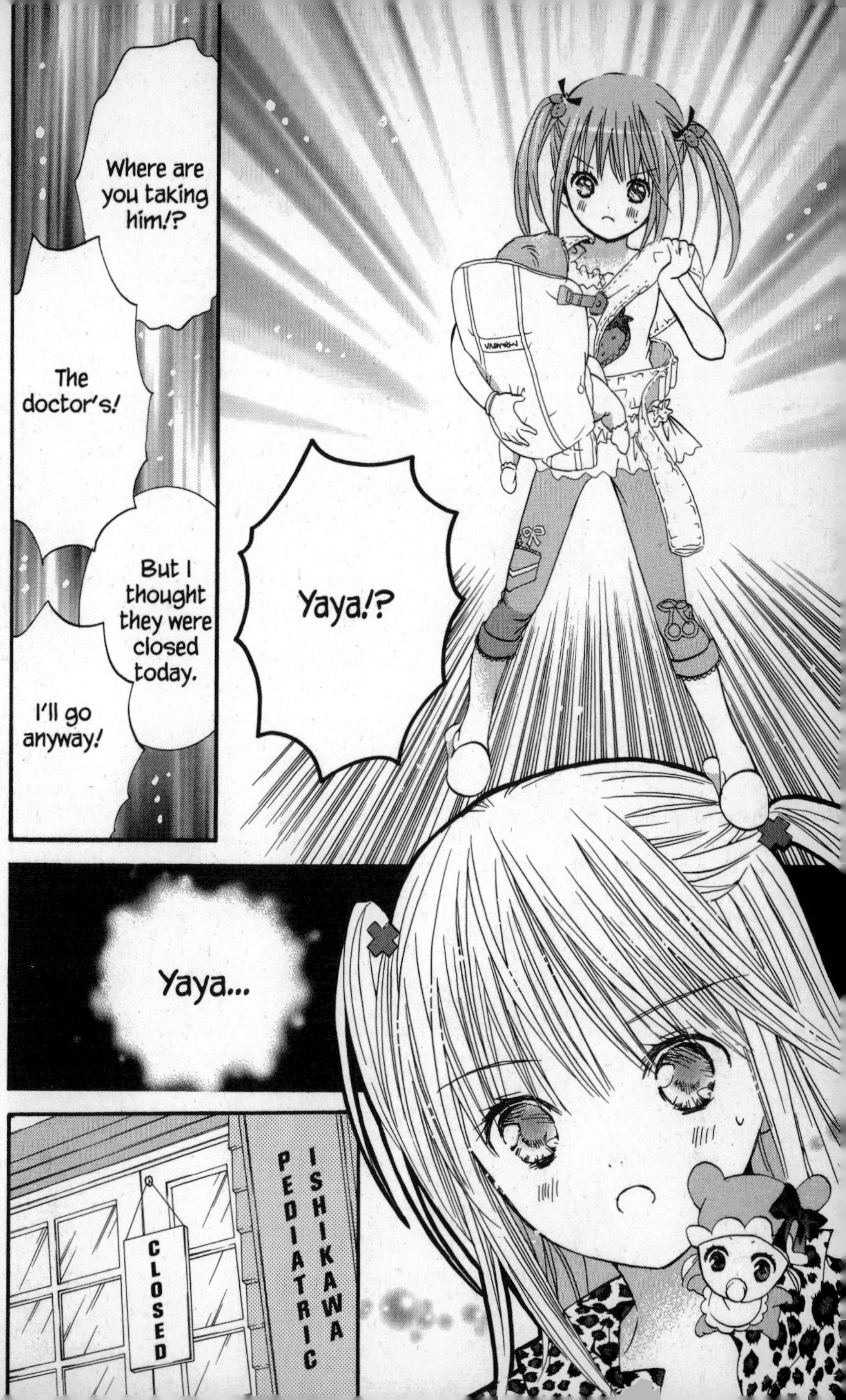
Yaya!?
Where are you taking him!?
The doctor's!
But I thought they were closed today.
I'll go anyway!
Yaya...
ISHIKAWA PEDIATRIC
CLOSED

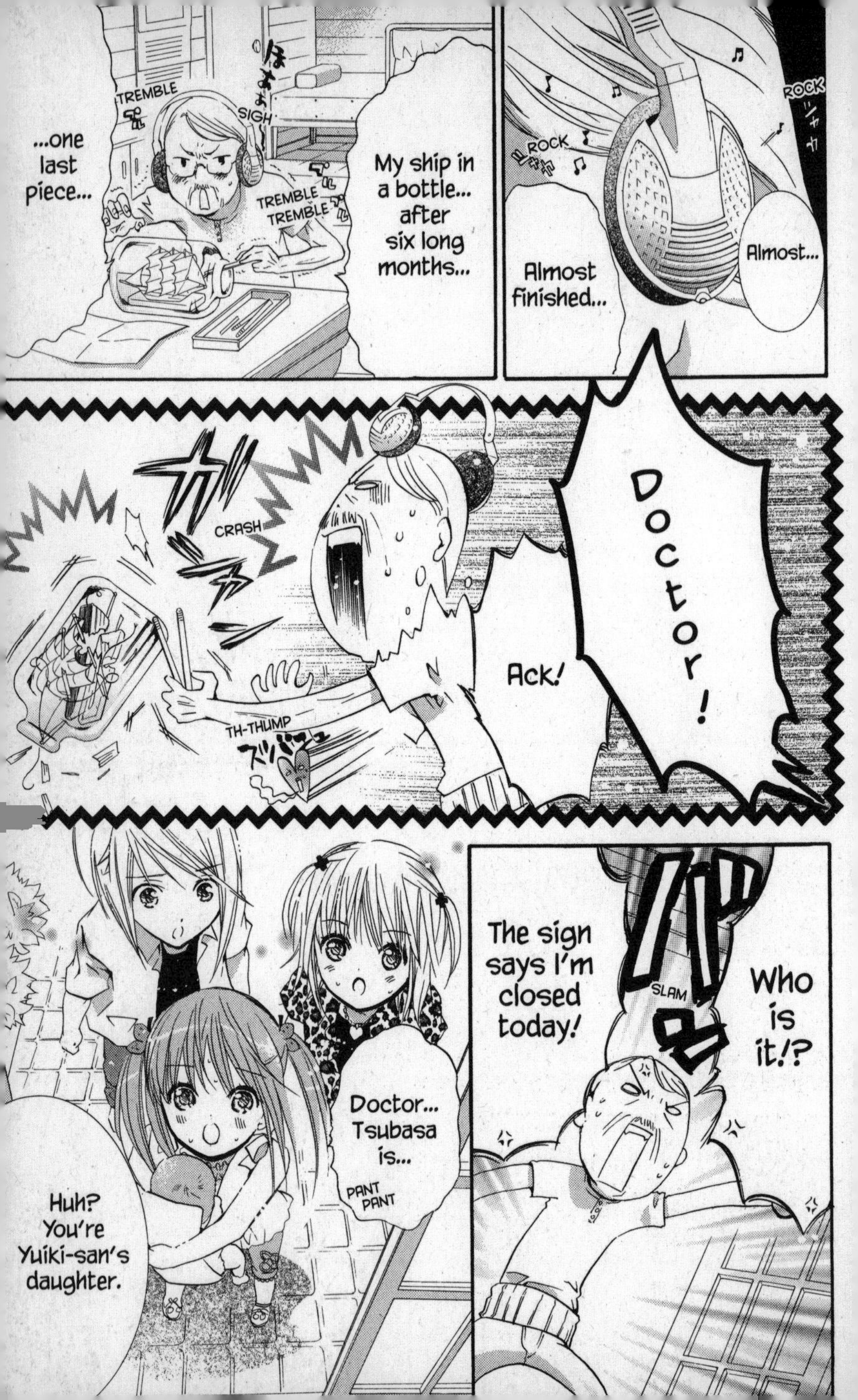
ROCK
Almost...
ROCK
Almost finished...
My ship in a bottle... after six long months...
SIGH
TREMBLE
TREMBLE TREMBLE
...one last piece...
Doctor!
Ack!
CRASH
TH-THUMP
Who is it!?
SLAM
The sign says I'm closed today!
Doctor... Tsubasa is...
PANT PANT
Huh? You're Yuiki-san's daughter.

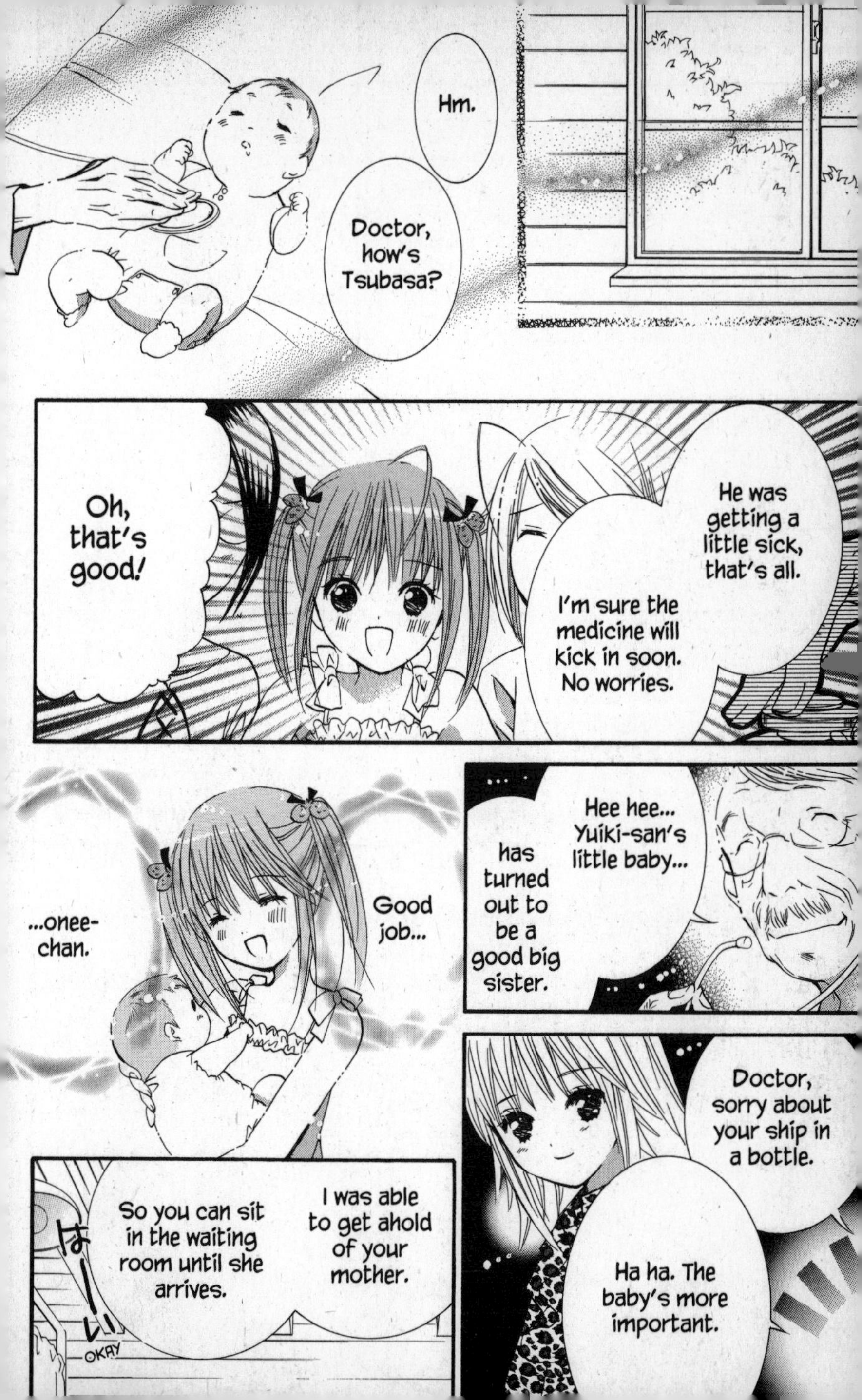
Hm.
Doctor, how's Tsubasa?
He was getting a little sick, that's all.
I'm sure the medicine will kick in soon. No worries.
Oh, that's good!
Hee hee... Yuiki-san's little baby...
has turned out to be a good big sister.
Good job...
...onee-chan.
Doctor, sorry about your ship in a bottle.
Ha ha. The baby's more important.
I was able to get ahold of your mother.
So you can sit in the waiting room until she arrives.
はーい
OKAY

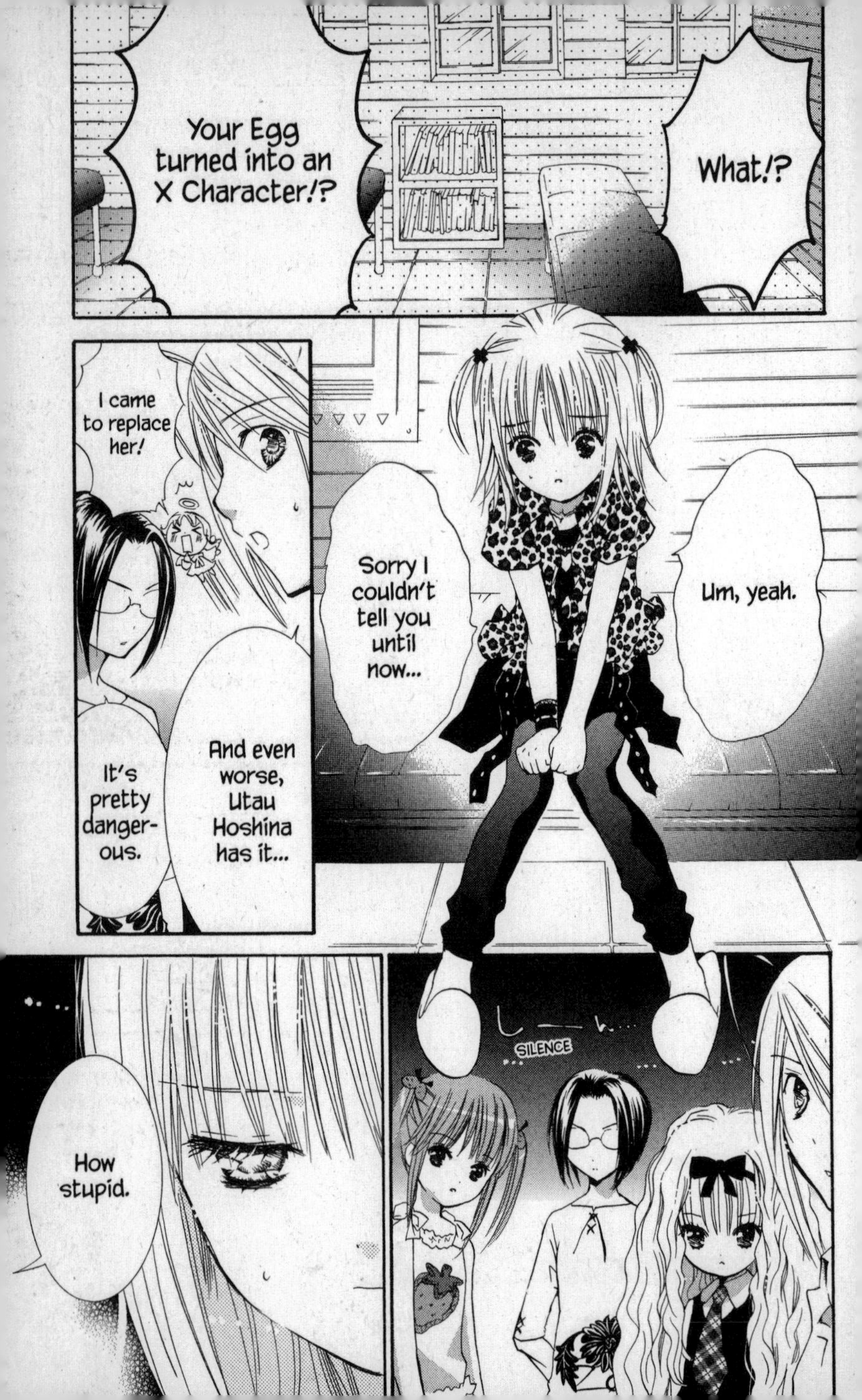
What!?
Your Egg turned into an X Character!?
Um, yeah.
Sorry I couldn't tell you until now...
I came to replace her!
And even worse, Utau Hoshina has it...
It's pretty danger-ous.
しーん…
SILENCE
…
How stupid.

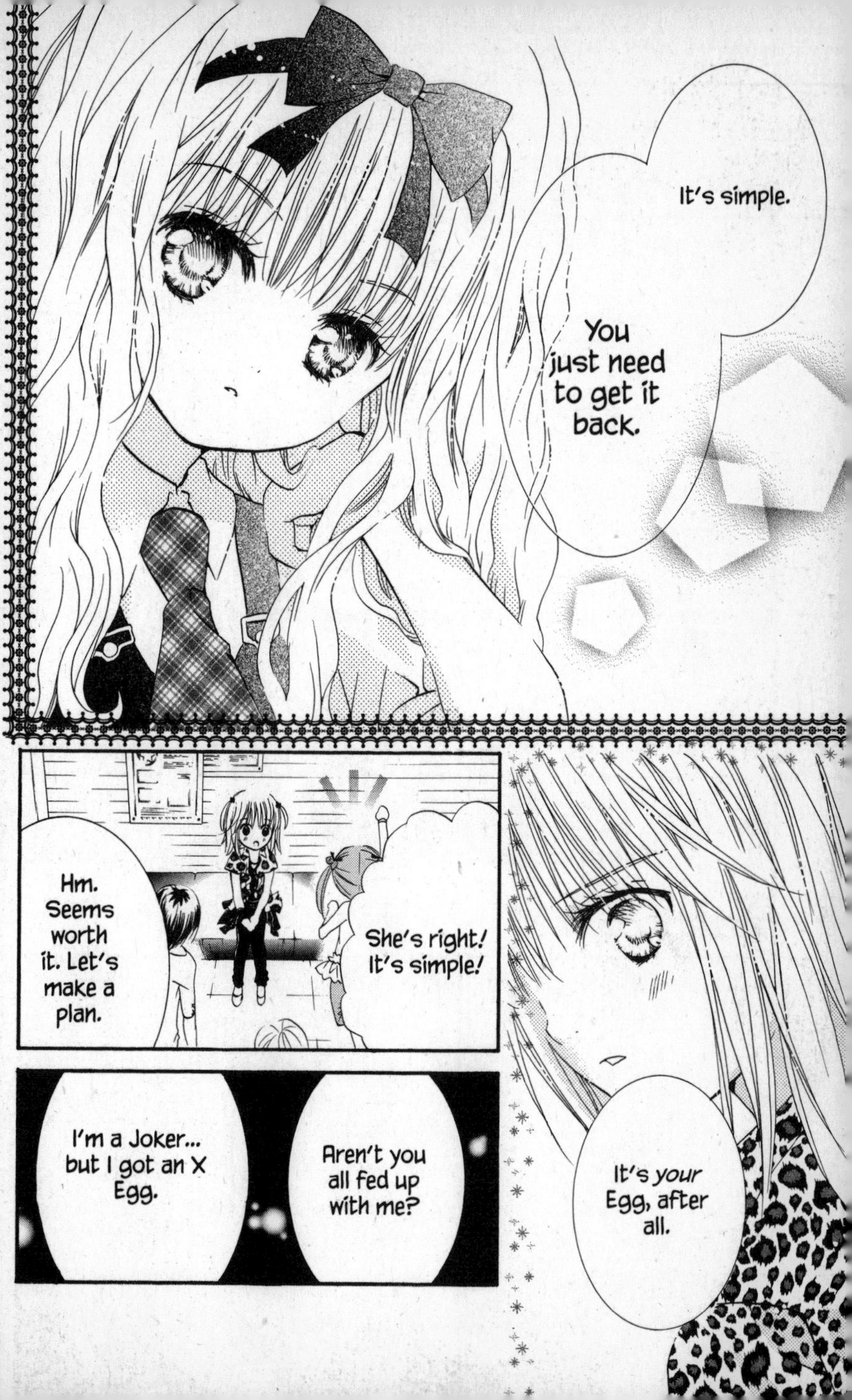
It's simple.
You just need to get it back.
It's *your* Egg, after all.
She's right! It's simple!
Hm. Seems worth it. Let's make a plan.
Aren't you all fed up with me?
I'm a Joker... but I got an X Egg.

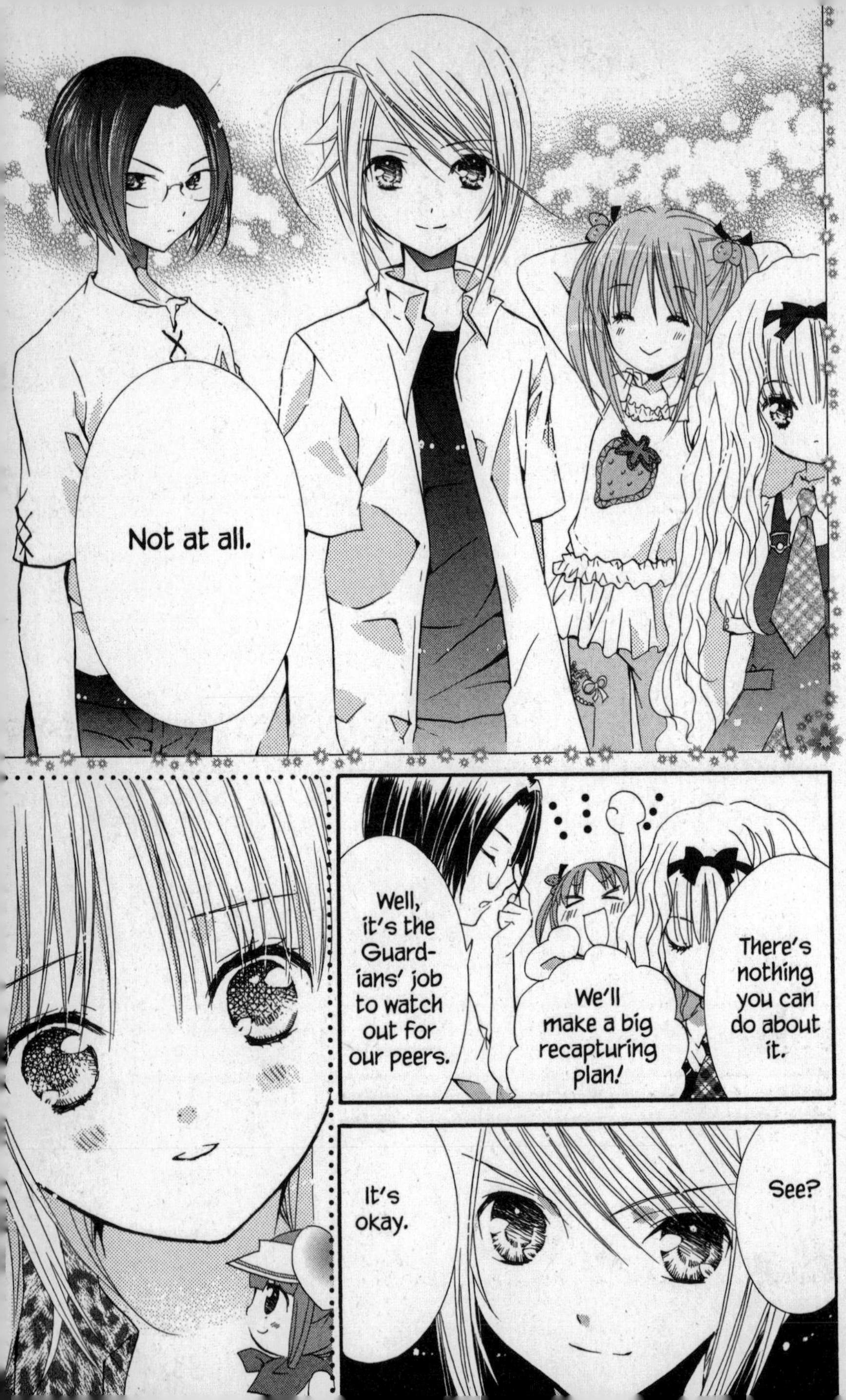
Not at all.
There's nothing you can do about it.
We'll make a big recapturing plan!
Well, it's the Guardians' job to watch out for our peers.
See?
It's okay.

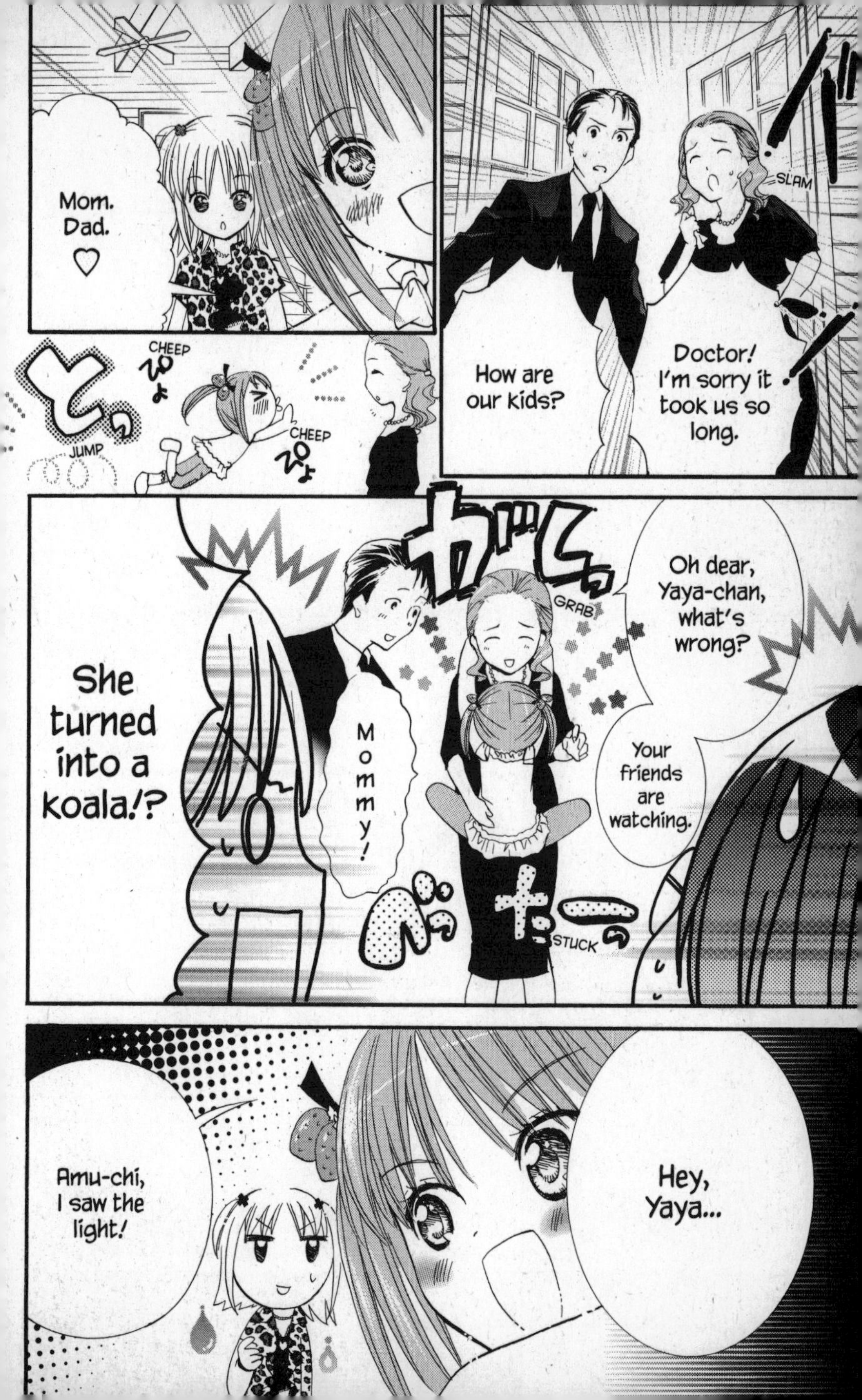
SLAM
Doctor! I'm sorry it took us so long.
How are our kids?
Mom. Dad. ♡
CHEEP
JUMP
CHEEP
GRAB
Oh dear, Yaya-chan, what's wrong?
Your friends are watching.
Mommy!
STUCK
She turned into a koala!?
Hey, Yaya...
Amu-chi, I saw the light!

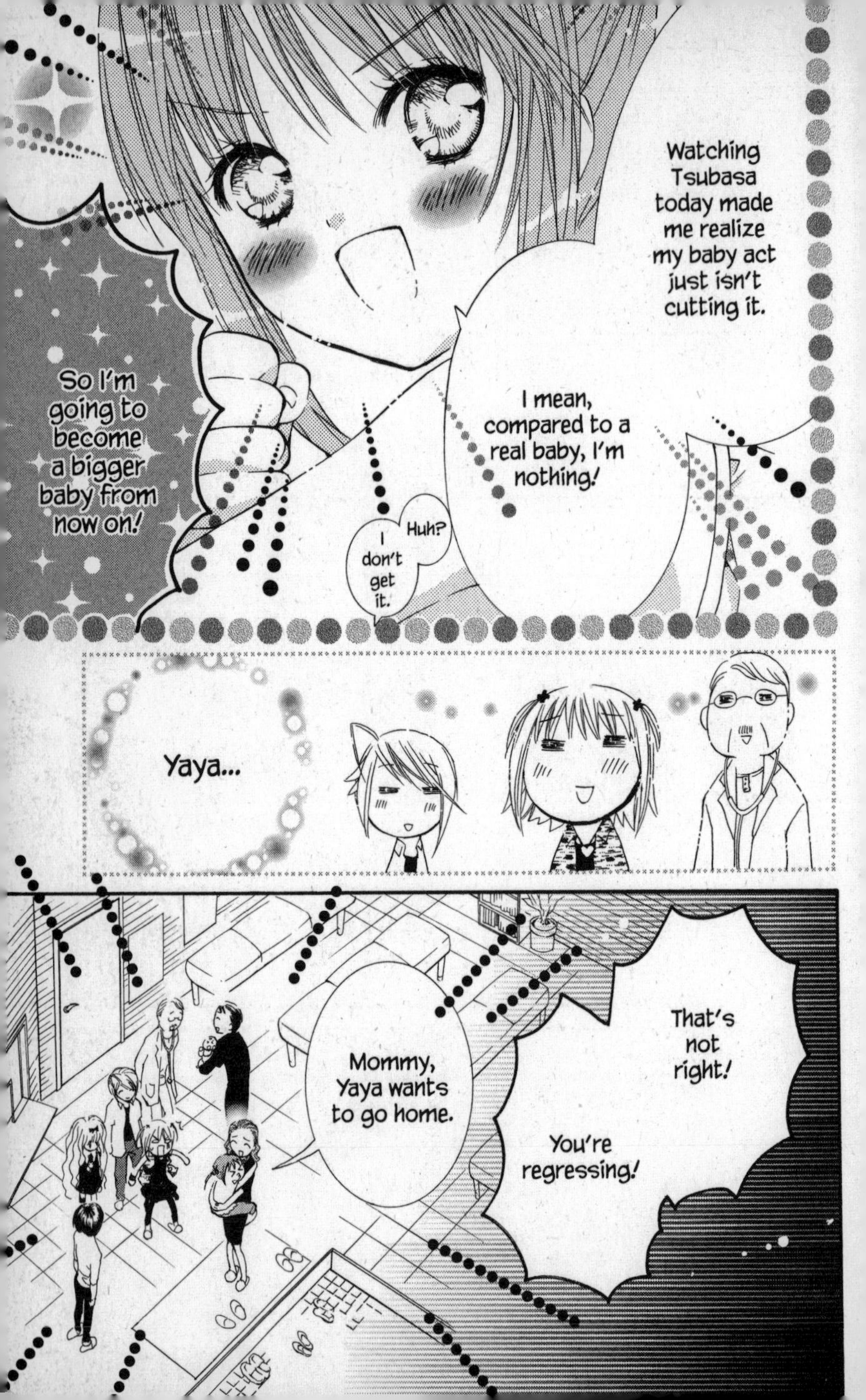
Watching Tsubasa today made me realize my baby act just isn't cutting it.
I mean, compared to a real baby, I'm nothing!
Huh? I don't get it.
So I'm going to become a bigger baby from now on!
Yaya...
That's not right!
You're regressing!
Mommy, Yaya wants to go home.

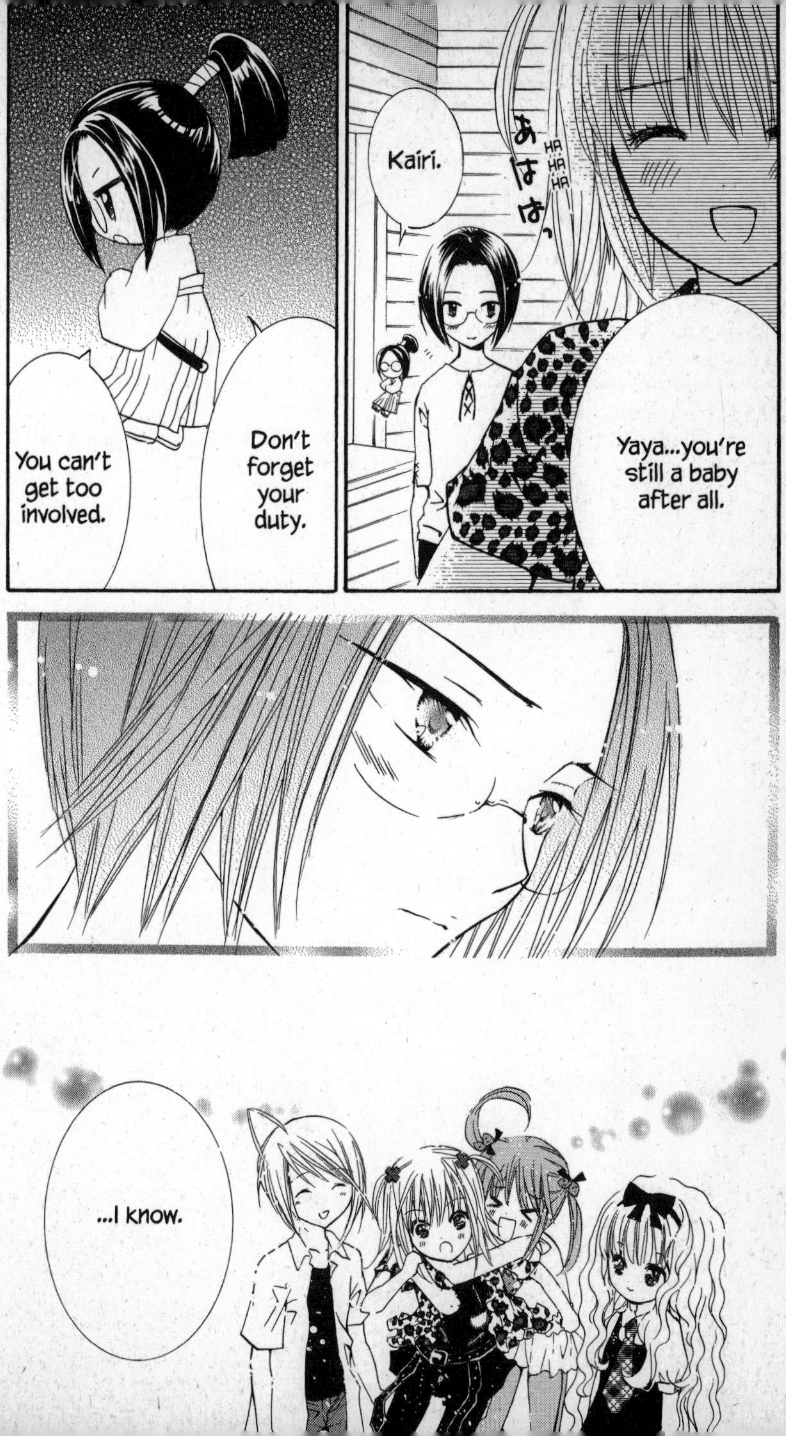
あはは
HA HA HA
Kairi.
Yaya...you're still a baby after all.
Don't forget your duty.
You can't get too involved.
...I know.

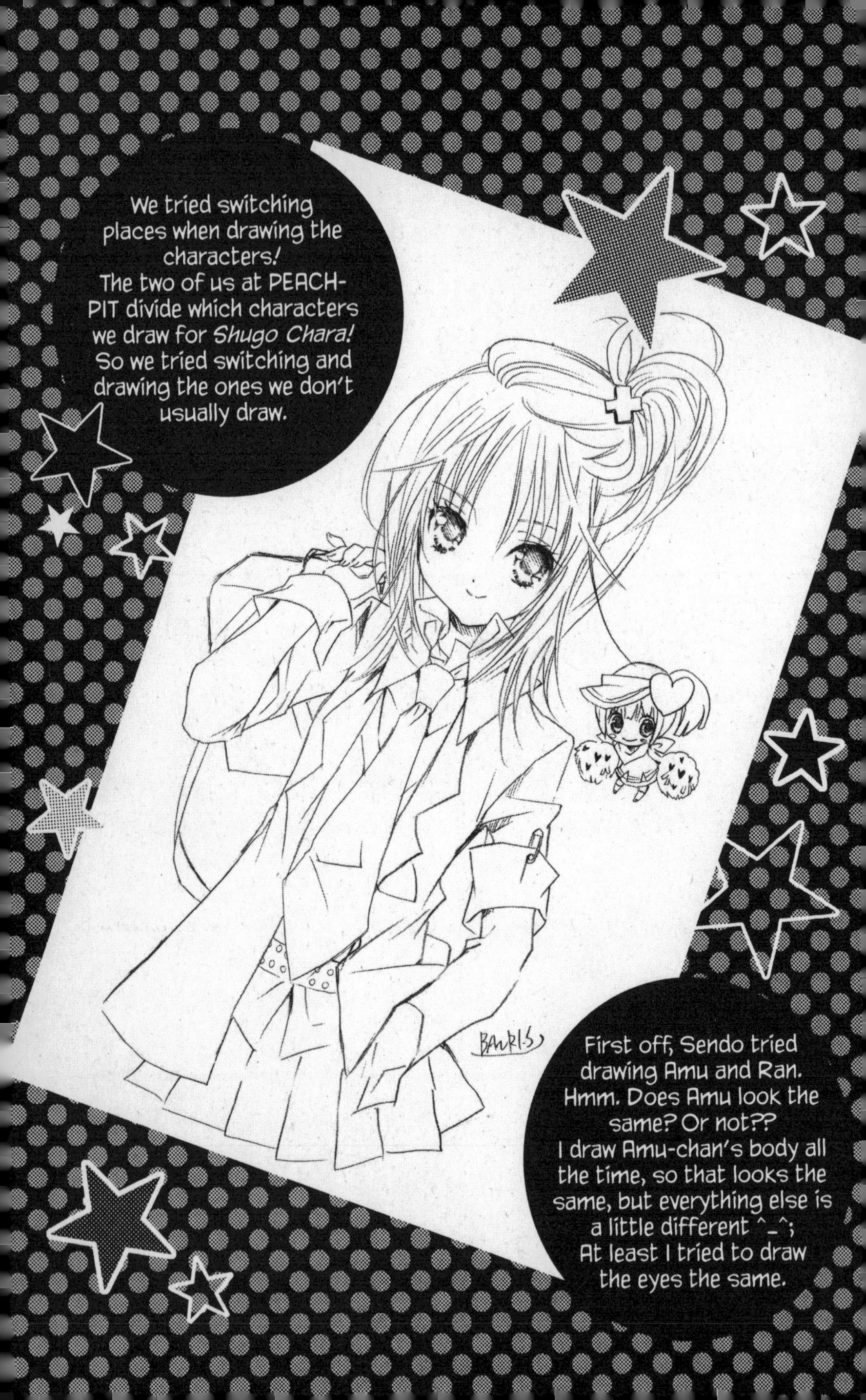
We tried switching places when drawing the characters! The two of us at PEACH-PIT divide which characters we draw for *Shugo Chara!* So we tried switching and drawing the ones we don't usually draw.
BAWRI-5
First off, Sendo tried drawing Amu and Ran. Hmm. Does Amu look the same? Or not?? I draw Amu-chan's body all the time, so that looks the same, but everything else is a little different ^_^; At least I tried to draw the eyes the same.

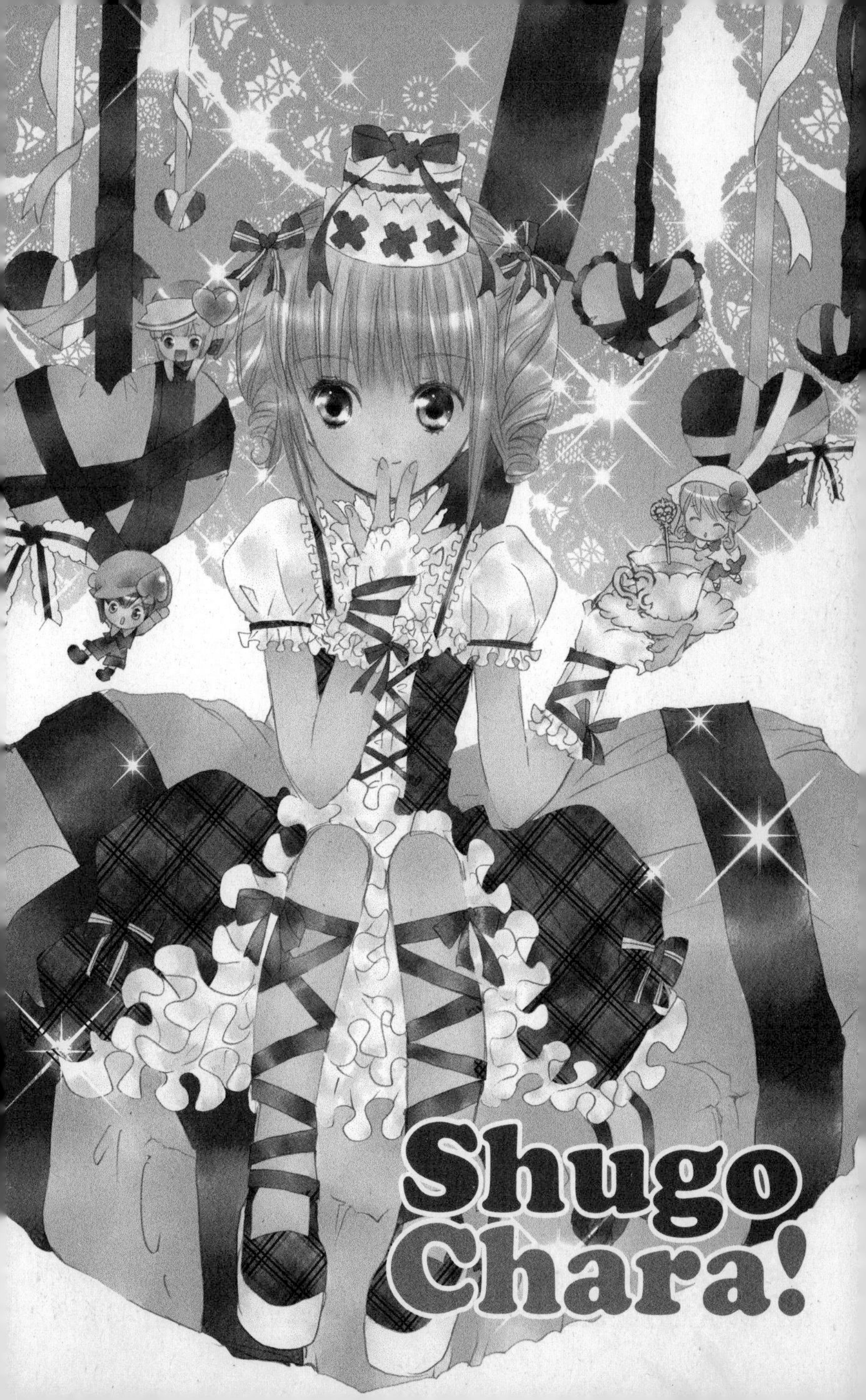
Shugo
Chara!

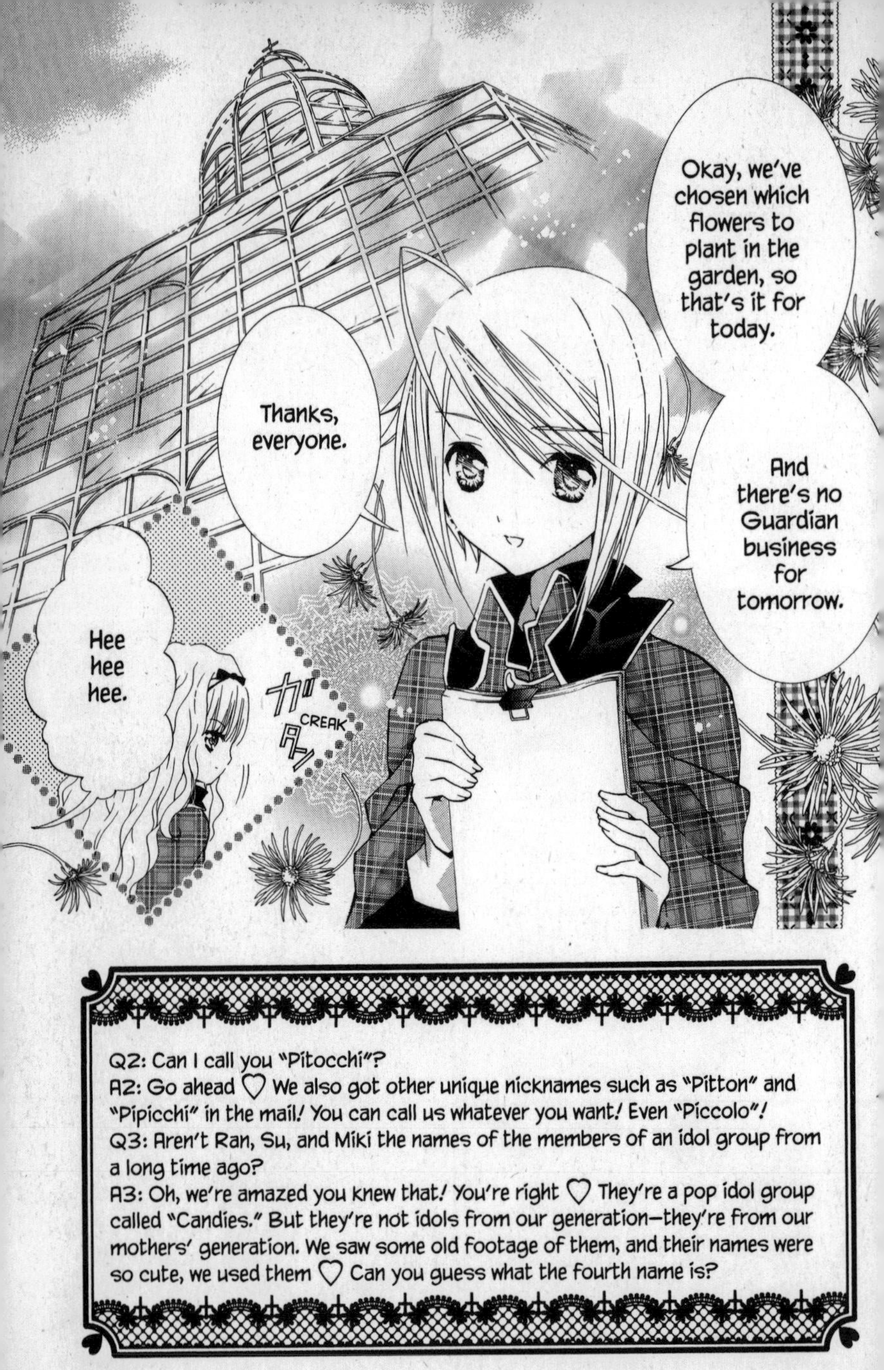
Okay, we've chosen which flowers to plant in the garden, so that's it for today.
And there's no Guardian business for tomorrow.
Thanks, everyone.
Hee hee hee.
CREAK

Q2: Can I call you "Pitocchi"?
A2: Go ahead ♡ We also got other unique nicknames such as "Pitton" and "Pipicchi" in the mail! You can call us whatever you want! Even "Piccolo"!
Q3: Aren't Ran, Su, and Miki the names of the members of an idol group from a long time ago?
A3: Oh, we're amazed you knew that! You're right ♡ They're a pop idol group called "Candies." But they're not idols from our generation—they're from our mothers' generation. We saw some old footage of them, and their names were so cute, we used them ♡ Can you guess what the fourth name is?

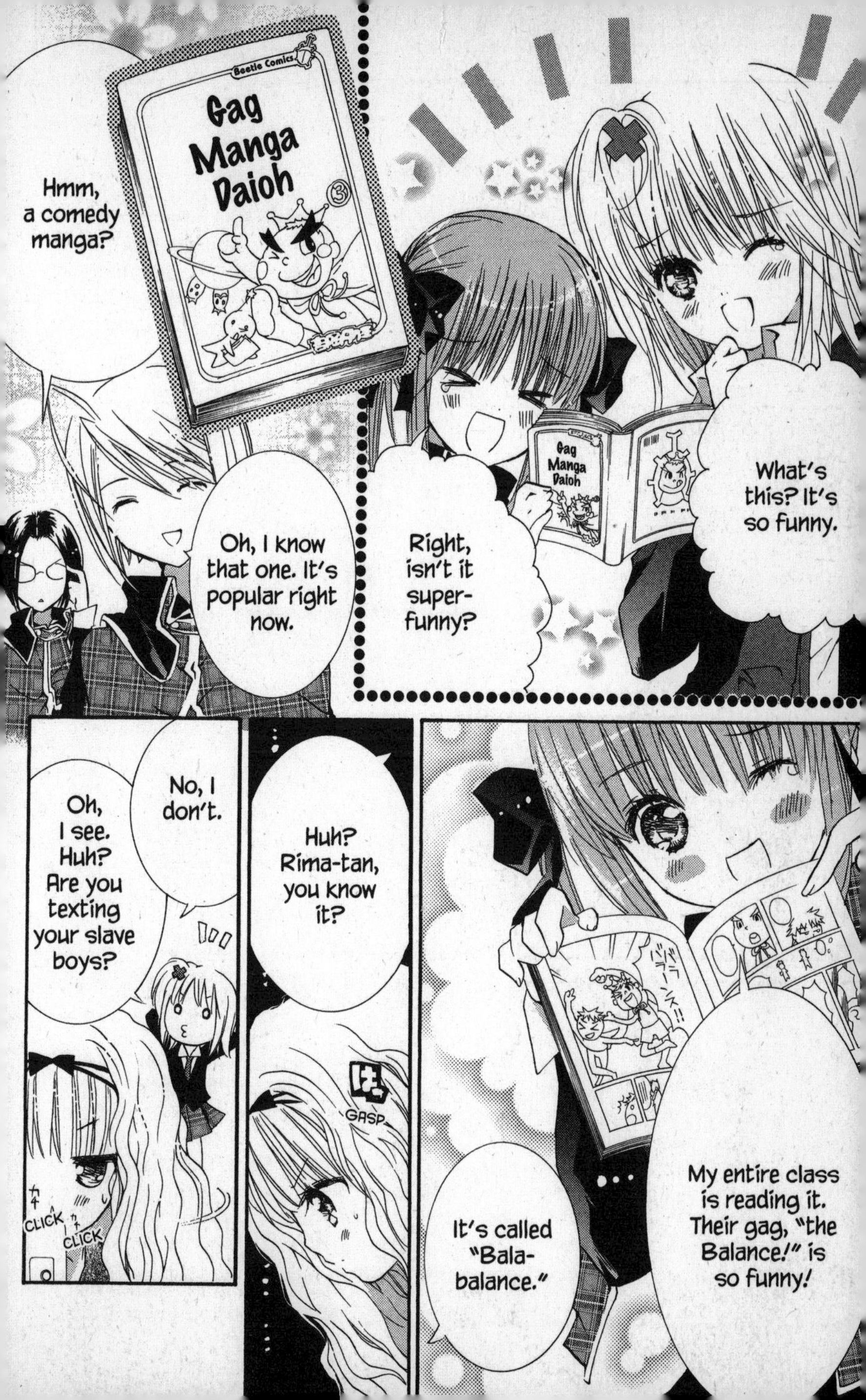
What's this? It's so funny.
Gag Manga Daioh
Right, isn't it super-funny?
Beetle Comics
Gag Manga Daioh
Hmm, a comedy manga?
Oh, I know that one. It's popular right now.
My entire class is reading it. Their gag, "the Balance!" is so funny!
It's called "Bala-balance."
Huh? Rima-tan, you know it?
GASP
No, I don't.
Oh, I see. Huh? Are you texting your slave boys?
CLICK
CLICK

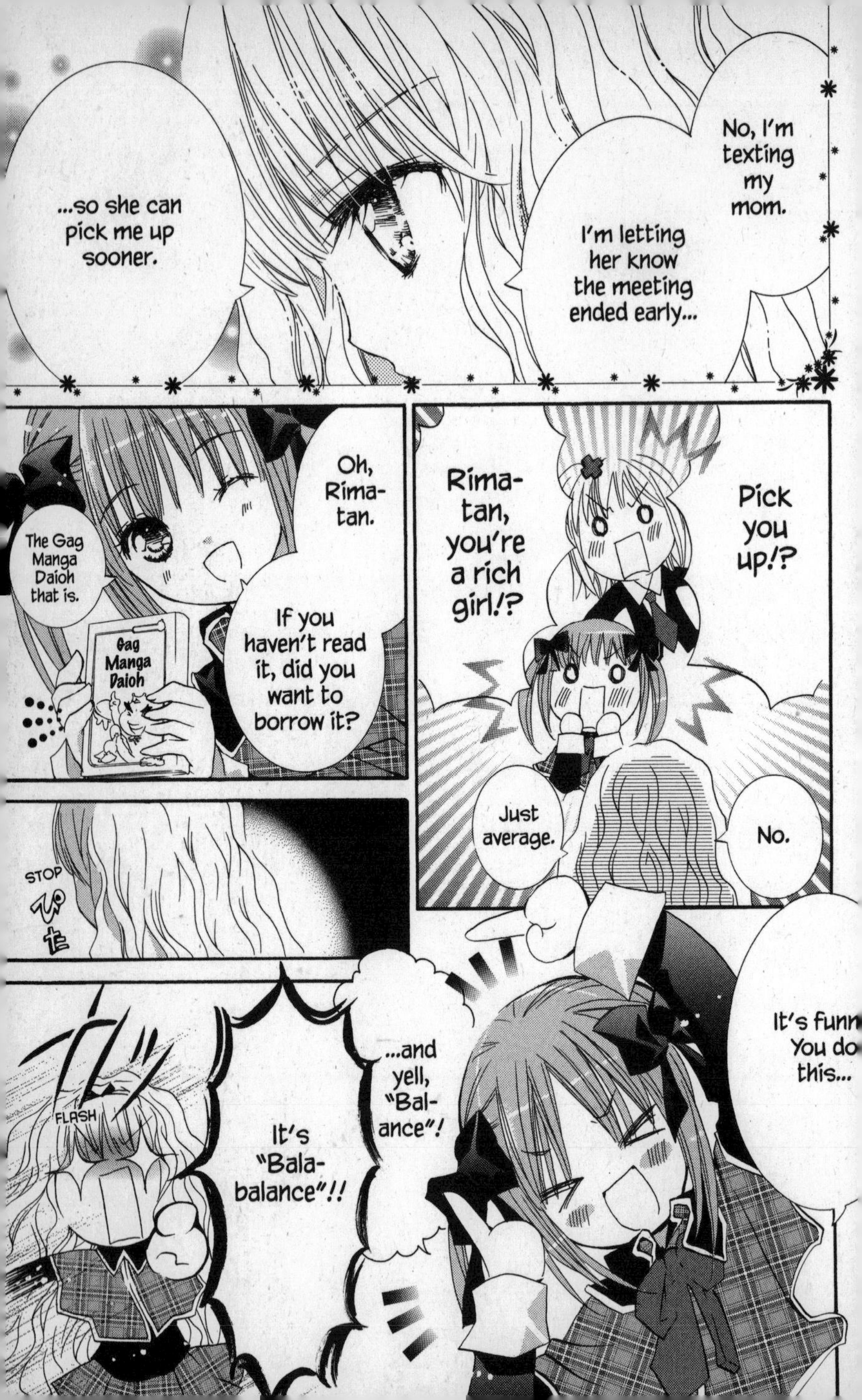
No, I'm texting my mom.
I'm letting her know the meeting ended early...
...so she can pick me up sooner.
Pick you up!?
Rima-tan, you're a rich girl!?
No.
Just average.
Oh, Rima-tan.
If you haven't read it, did you want to borrow it?
The Gag Manga Daioh that is.
Gag Manga Daioh
STOP
It's funn
You do this...
...and yell, "Bal-ance"!
It's "Bala-balance"!!
FLASH

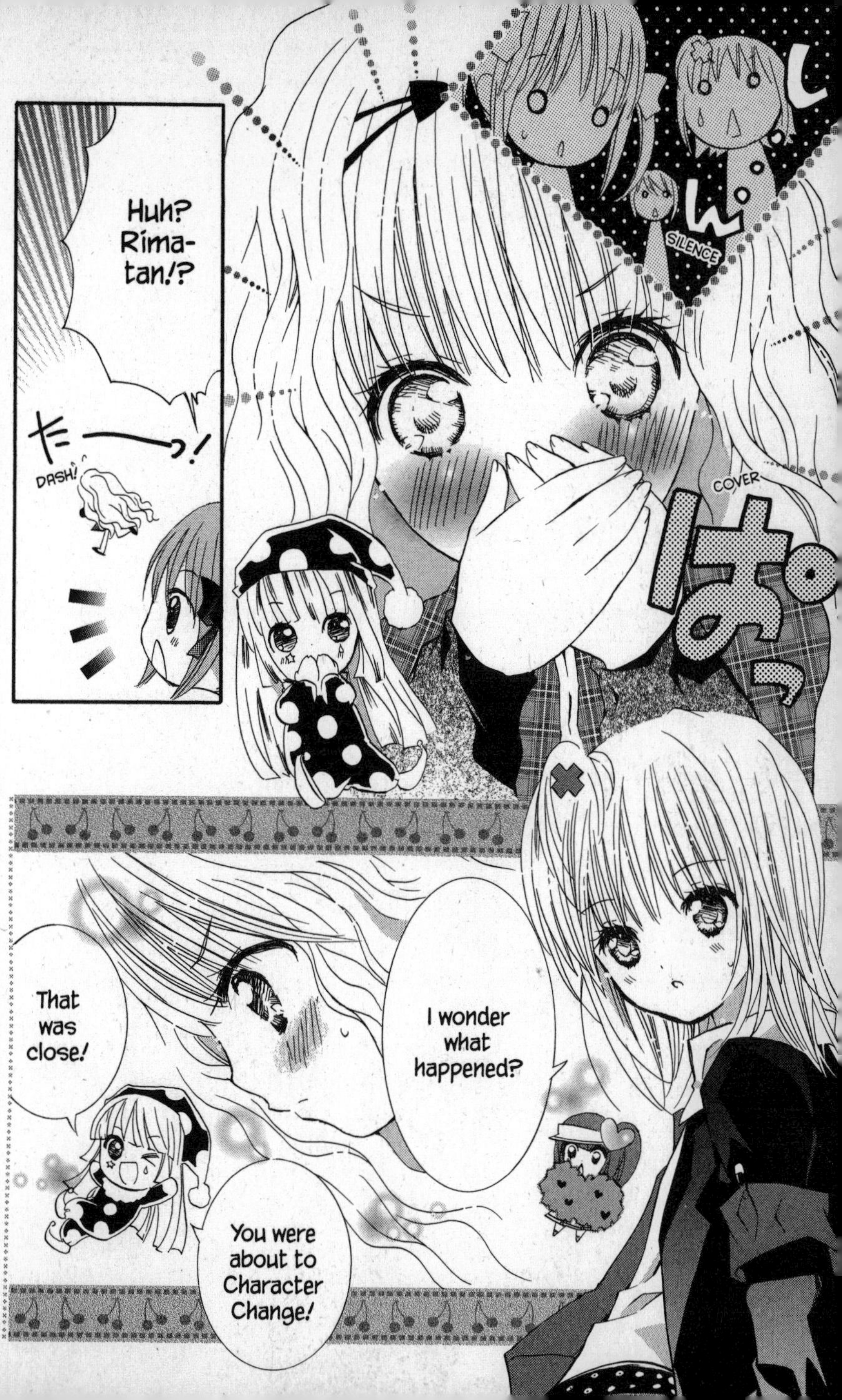
しーん
SILENCE
ぽっ
COVER
Huh? Rima-tan!?
だーっ!
DASH!
I wonder what happened?
That was close!
You were about to Character Change!

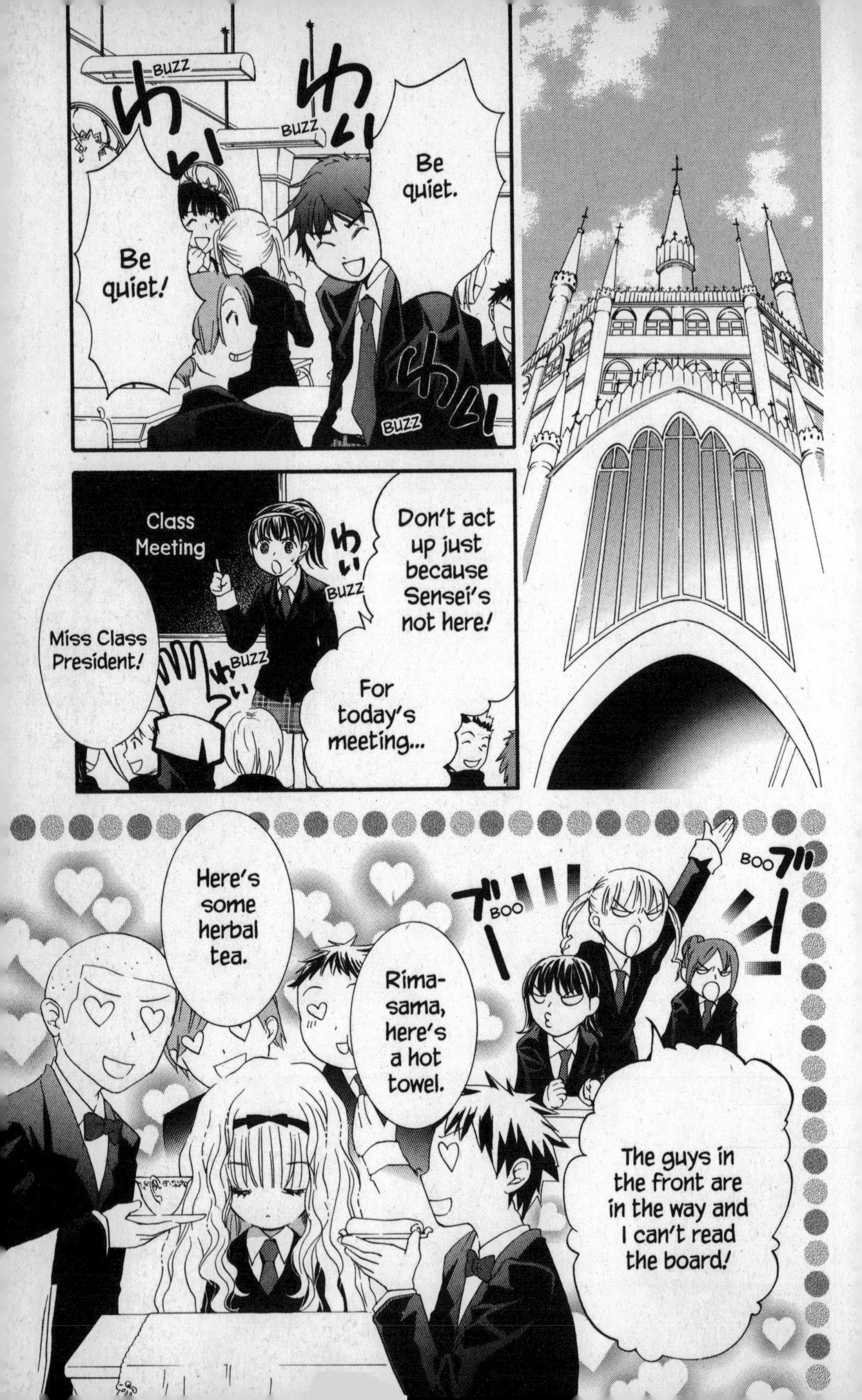
BUZZ
BUZZ
Be quiet.
Be quiet!
BUZZ
Don't act up just because Sensei's not here!
BUZZ
Class Meeting
For today's meeting...
BUZZ
Miss Class President!
BOO
BOO
The guys in the front are in the way and I can't read the board!
Rima-sama, here's a hot towel.
Here's some herbal tea.

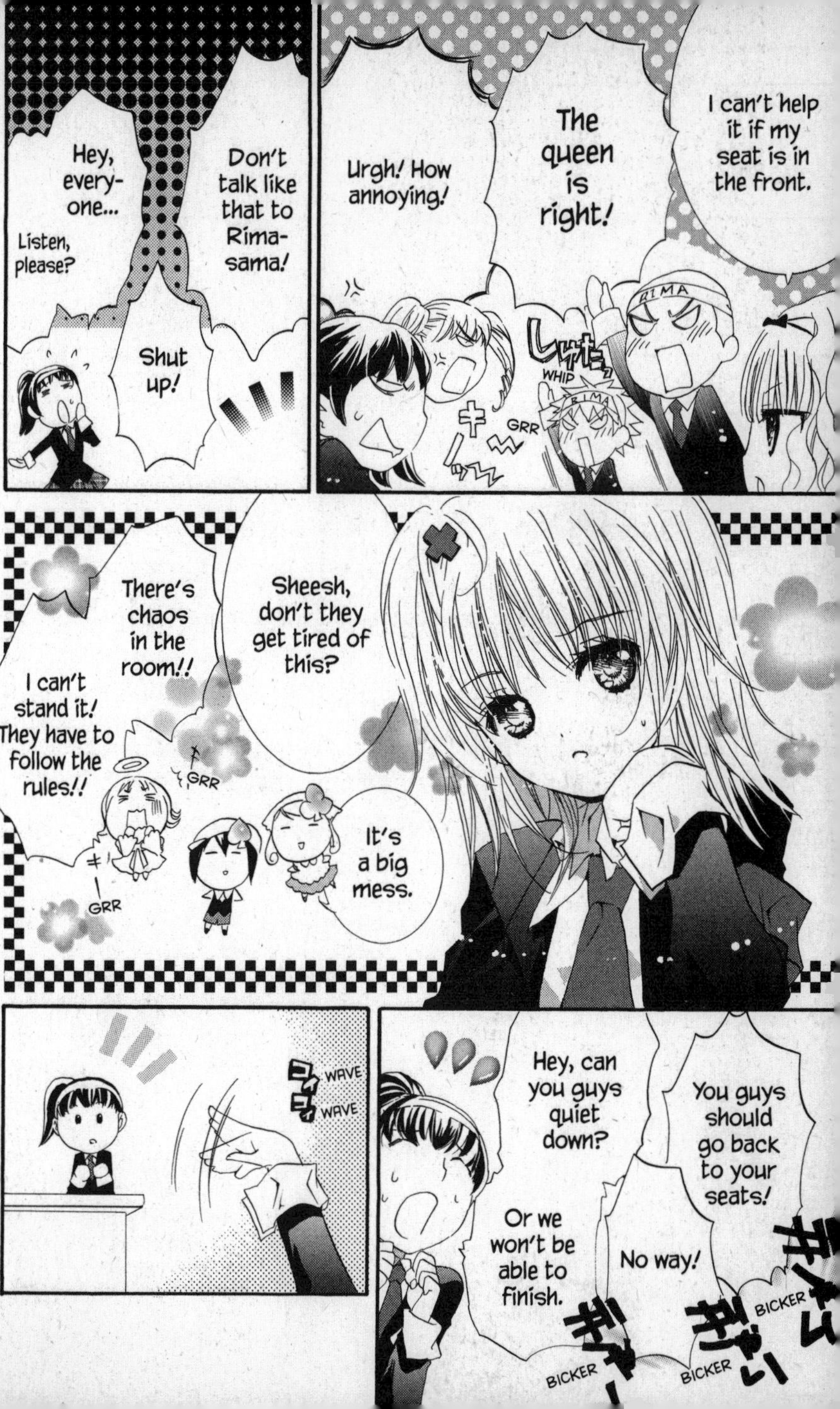
I can't help it if my seat is in the front.
The queen is right!
Urgh! How annoying!
WHIP
GRR
Don't talk like that to Rima-sama!
Hey, everyone...
Listen, please?
Shut up!
Sheesh, don't they get tired of this?
There's chaos in the room!!
I can't stand it! They have to follow the rules!!
GRR
GRR
It's a big mess.
You guys should go back to your seats!
Hey, can you guys quiet down?
No way!
Or we won't be able to finish.
BICKER
BICKER
BICKER
WAVE
WAVE

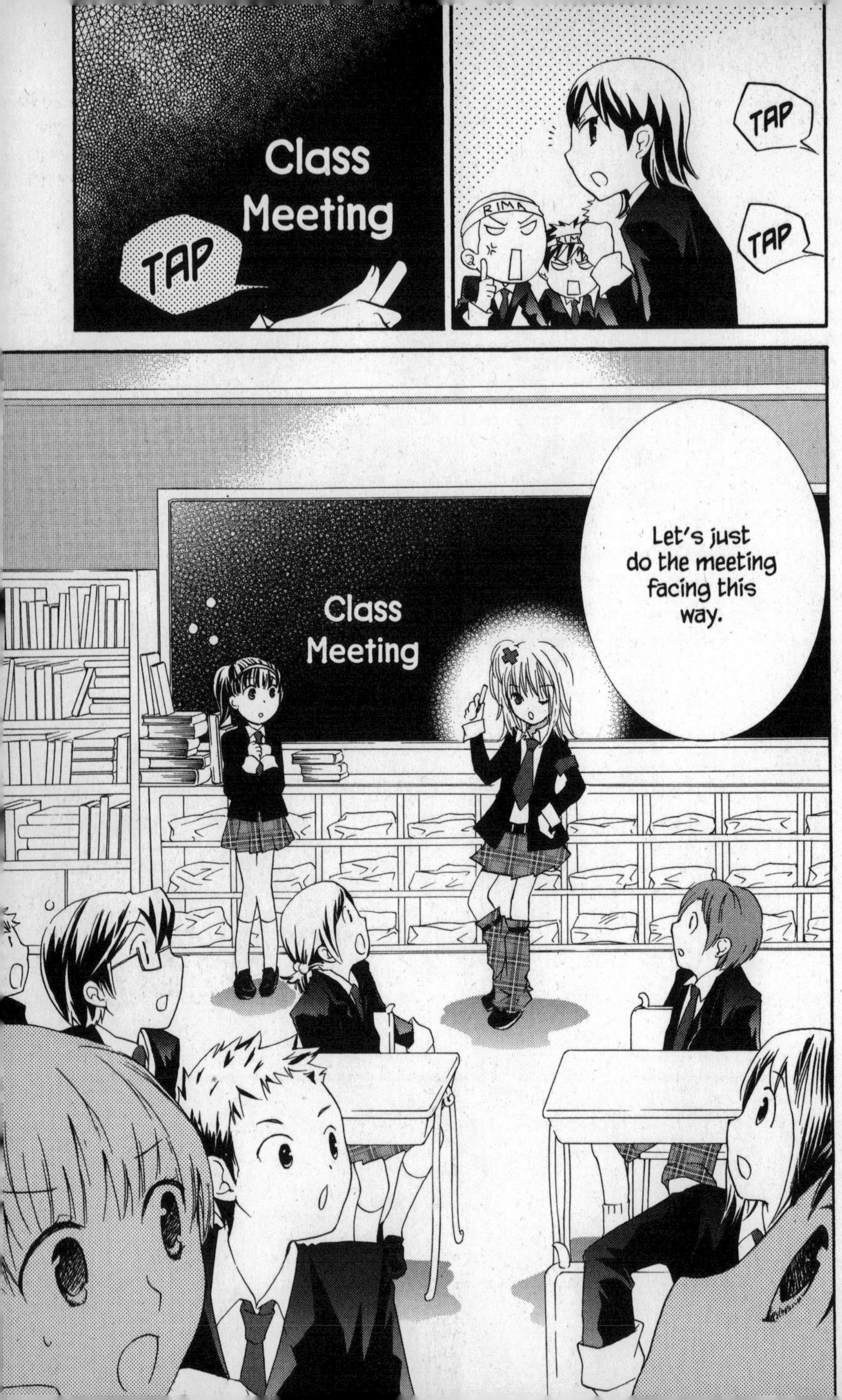
TAP
RIMA
TAP
Class Meeting
TAP
Class Meeting
Let's just do the meeting facing this way.

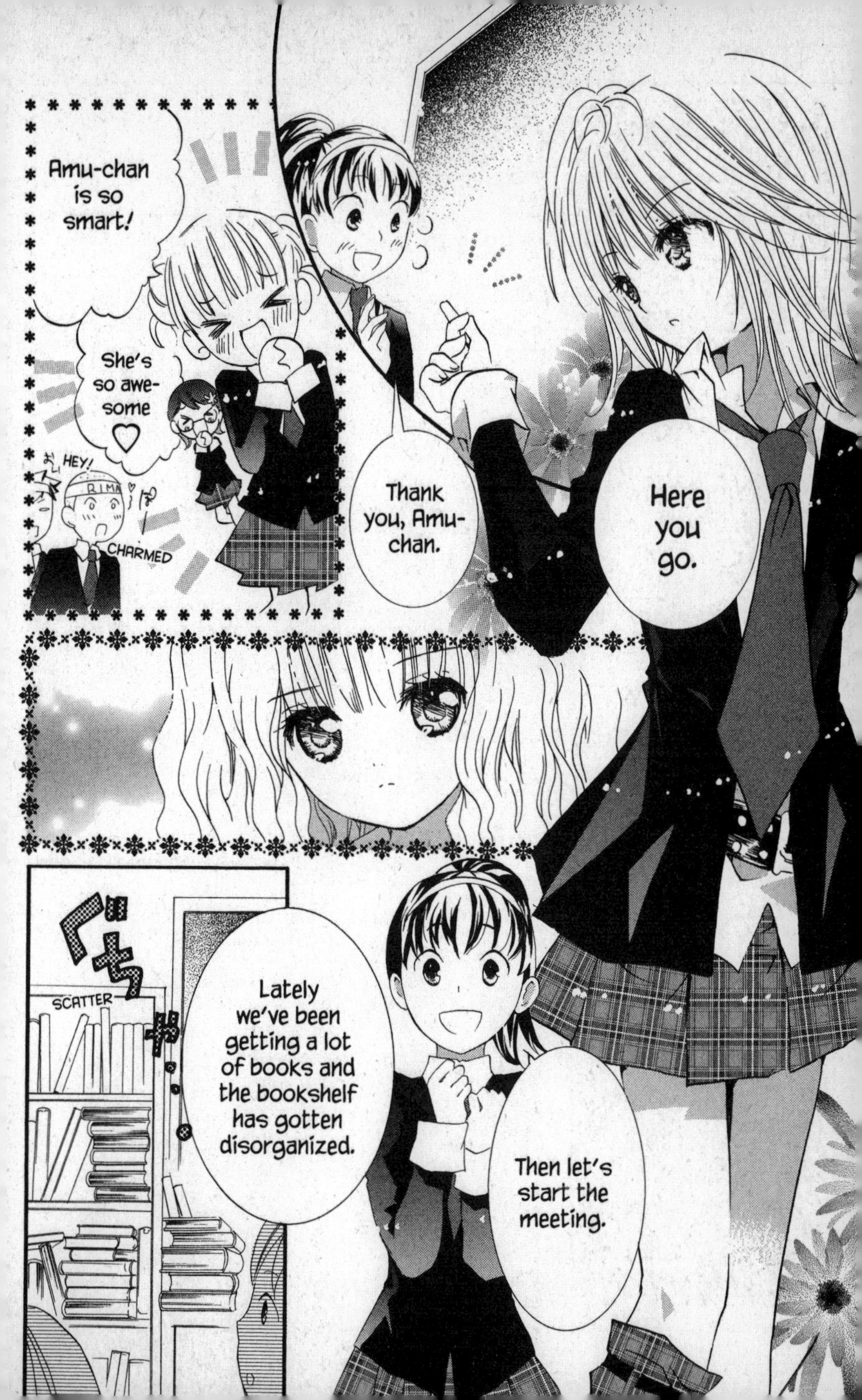
Here you go.
Thank you, Amu-chan.
Amu-chan is so smart!
She's so awe-some ♡
HEY!
RIMA
CHARMED
SCATTER
Lately we've been getting a lot of books and the bookshelf has gotten disorganized.
Then let's start the meeting.

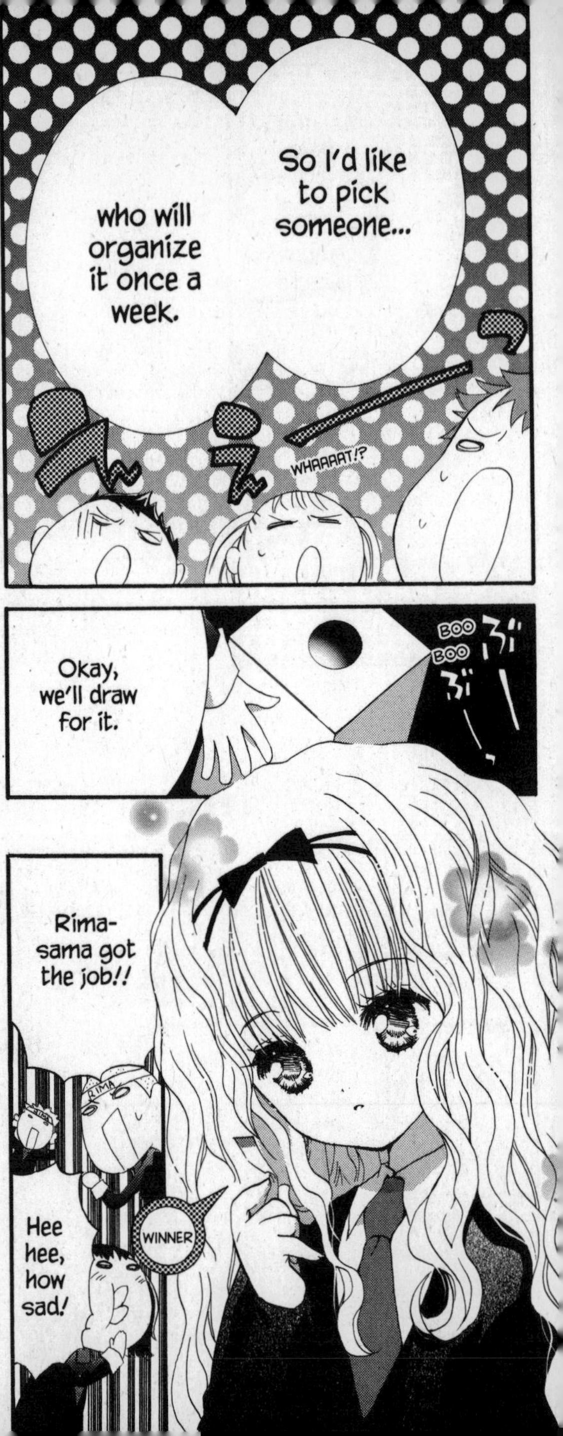
So I'd like to pick someone...
who will organize it once a week.
WHAAAAT!?
BOO BOO ぶ ぶ
Okay, we'll draw for it.
Rima-sama got the job!!
RIMA
WINNER
Hee hee, how sad!

character profile

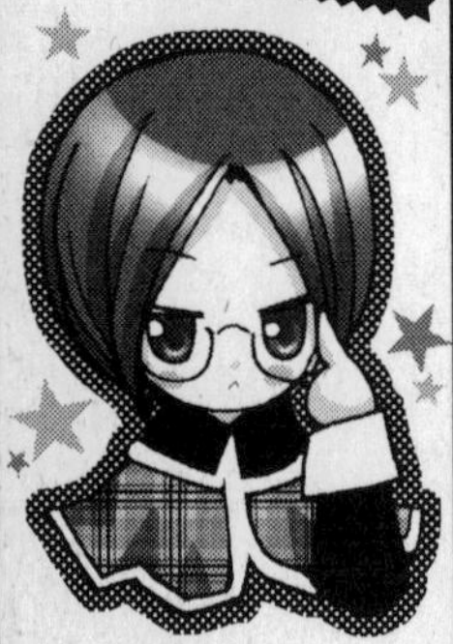

Kairi Sanjo

Birthday: 6/12
Blood Type: A
Sign: Gemini
Guardian Character: Musashi

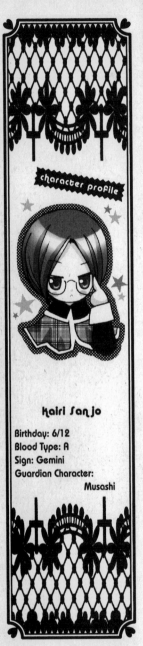

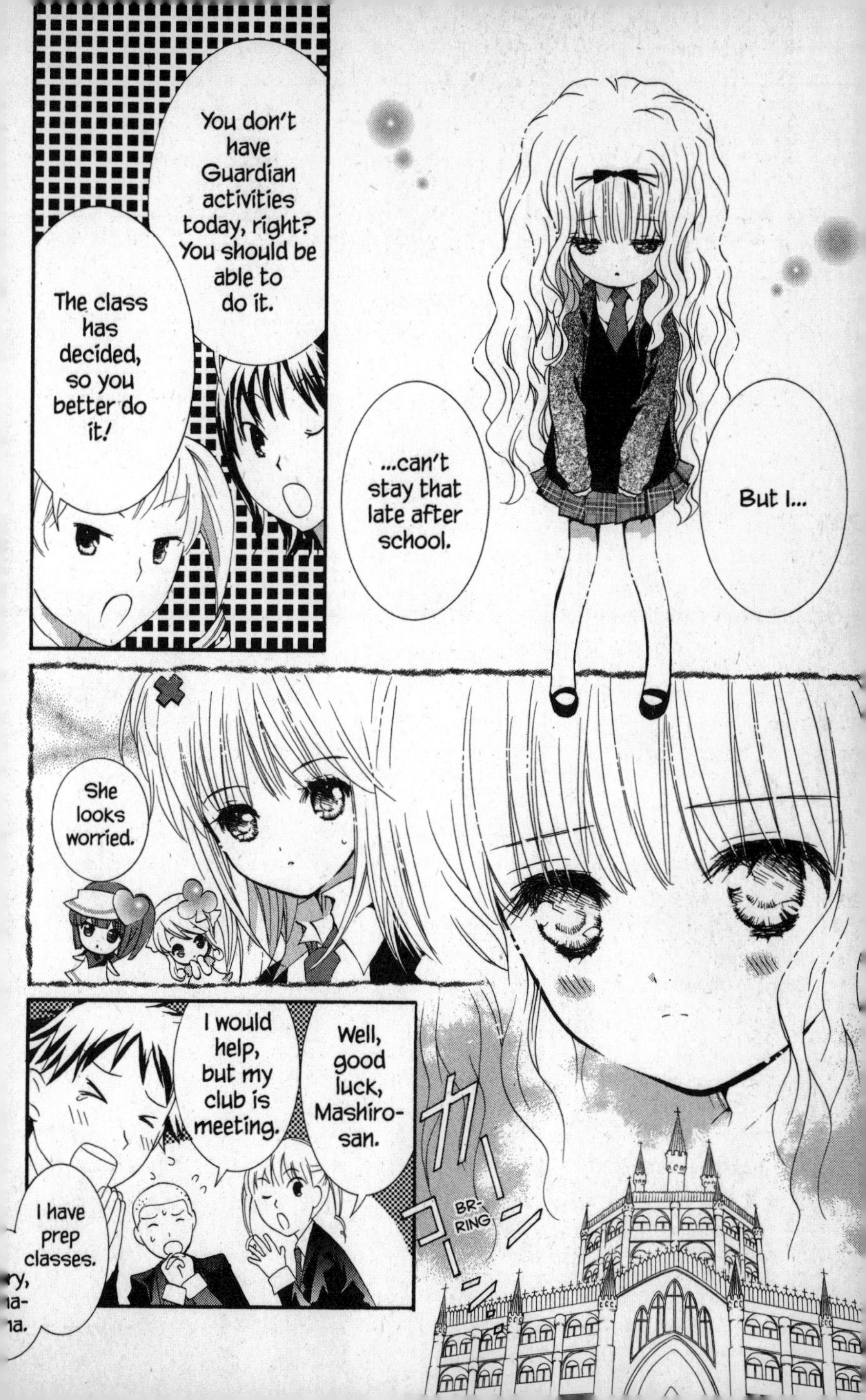
But I...
...can't stay that late after school.
You don't have Guardian activities today, right? You should be able to do it.
The class has decided, so you better do it!
BR-RING
She looks worried.
Well, good luck, Mashiro-san.
I would help, but my club is meeting.
I have prep classes.

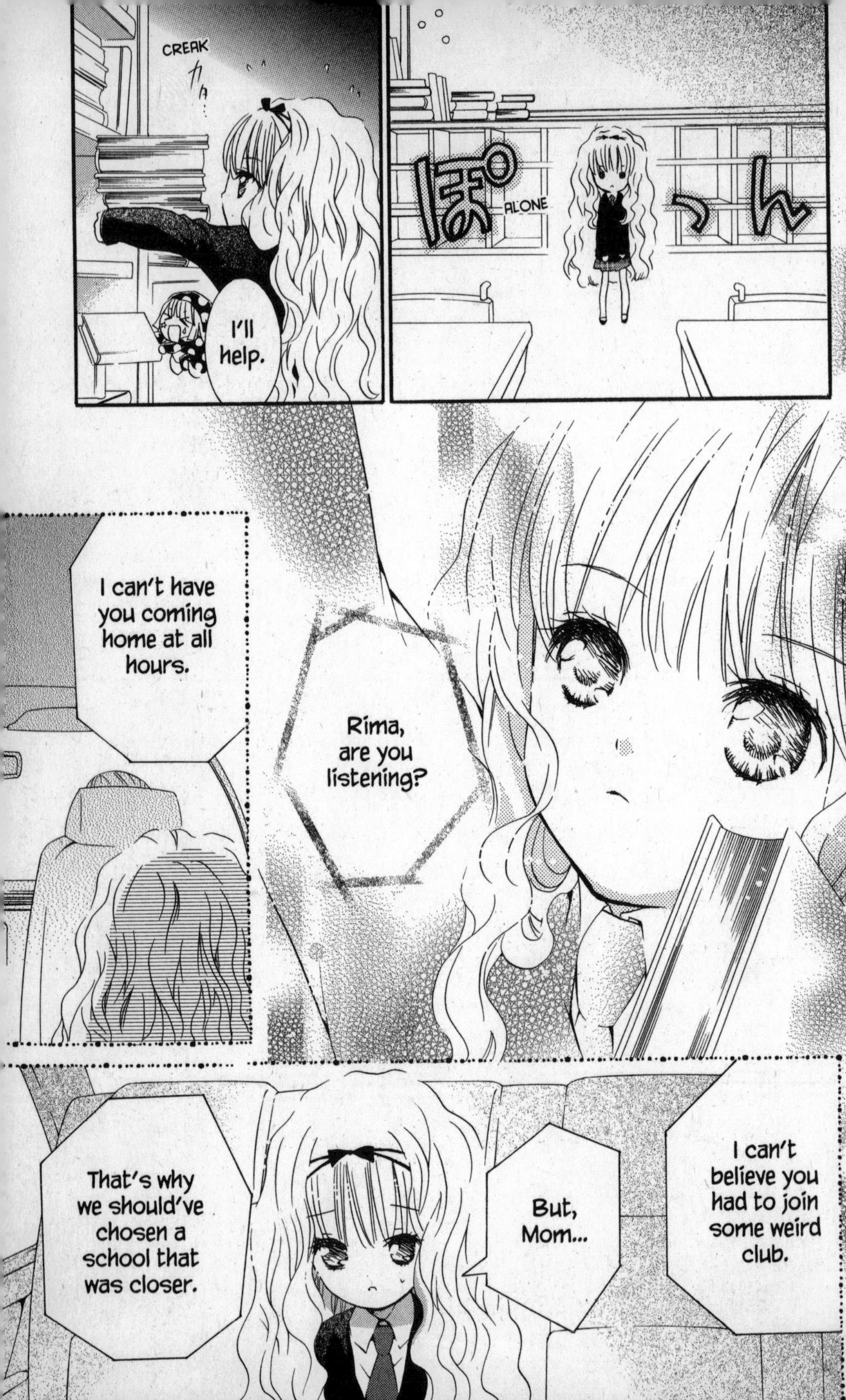
ぽ
っん
ALONE
CREAK
I'll help.
Rima, are you listening?
I can't have you coming home at all hours.
I can't believe you had to join some weird club.
But, Mom...
That's why we should've chosen a school that was closer.

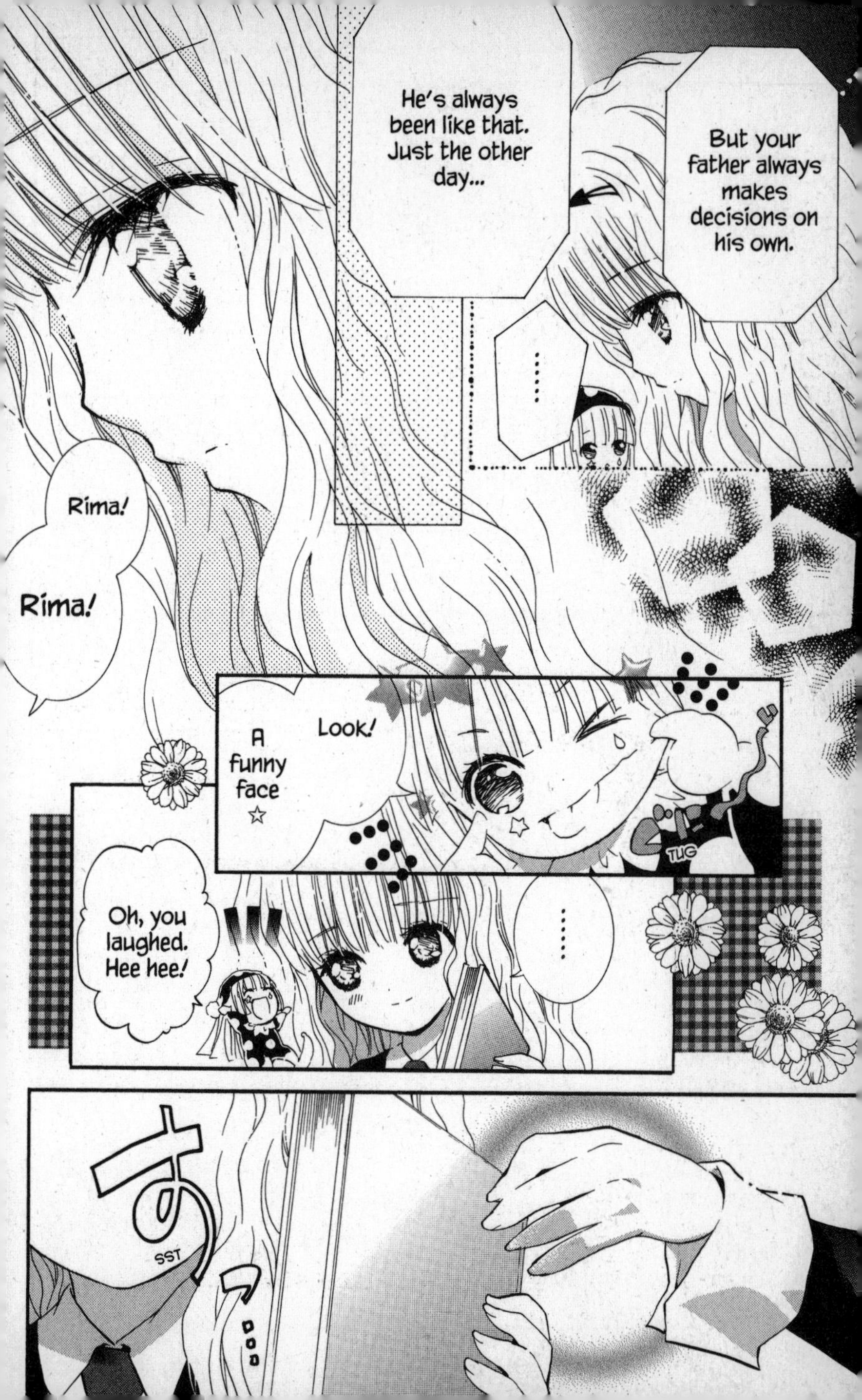
But your father always makes decisions on his own.
He's always been like that. Just the other day...
......
Rima!
Rima!
Look!
A funny face ☆
TUG
......
Oh, you laughed. Hee hee!
SST

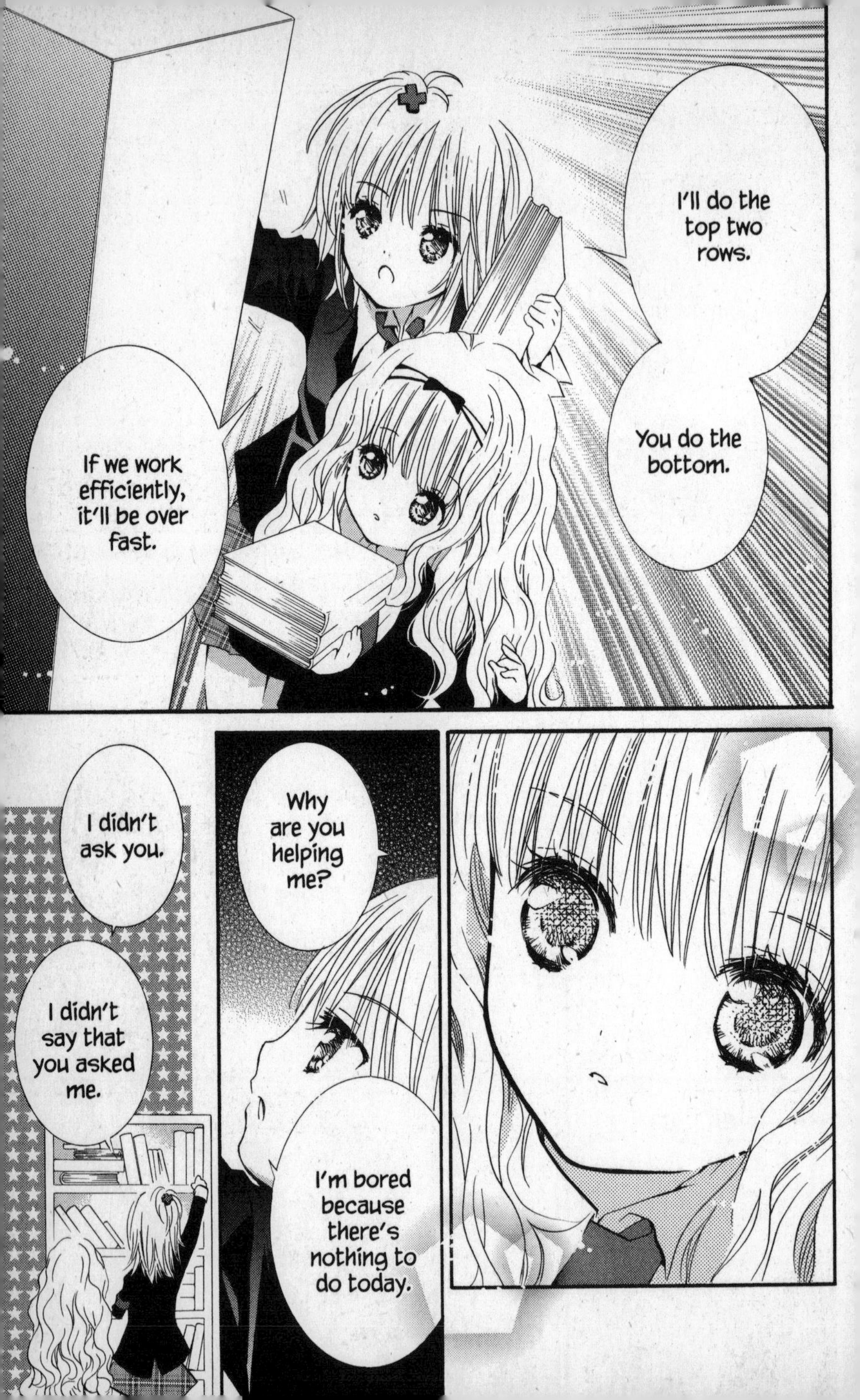
I'll do the top two rows.
You do the bottom.
If we work efficiently, it'll be over fast.
Why are you helping me?
I'm bored because there's nothing to do today.
I didn't ask you.
I didn't say that you asked me.

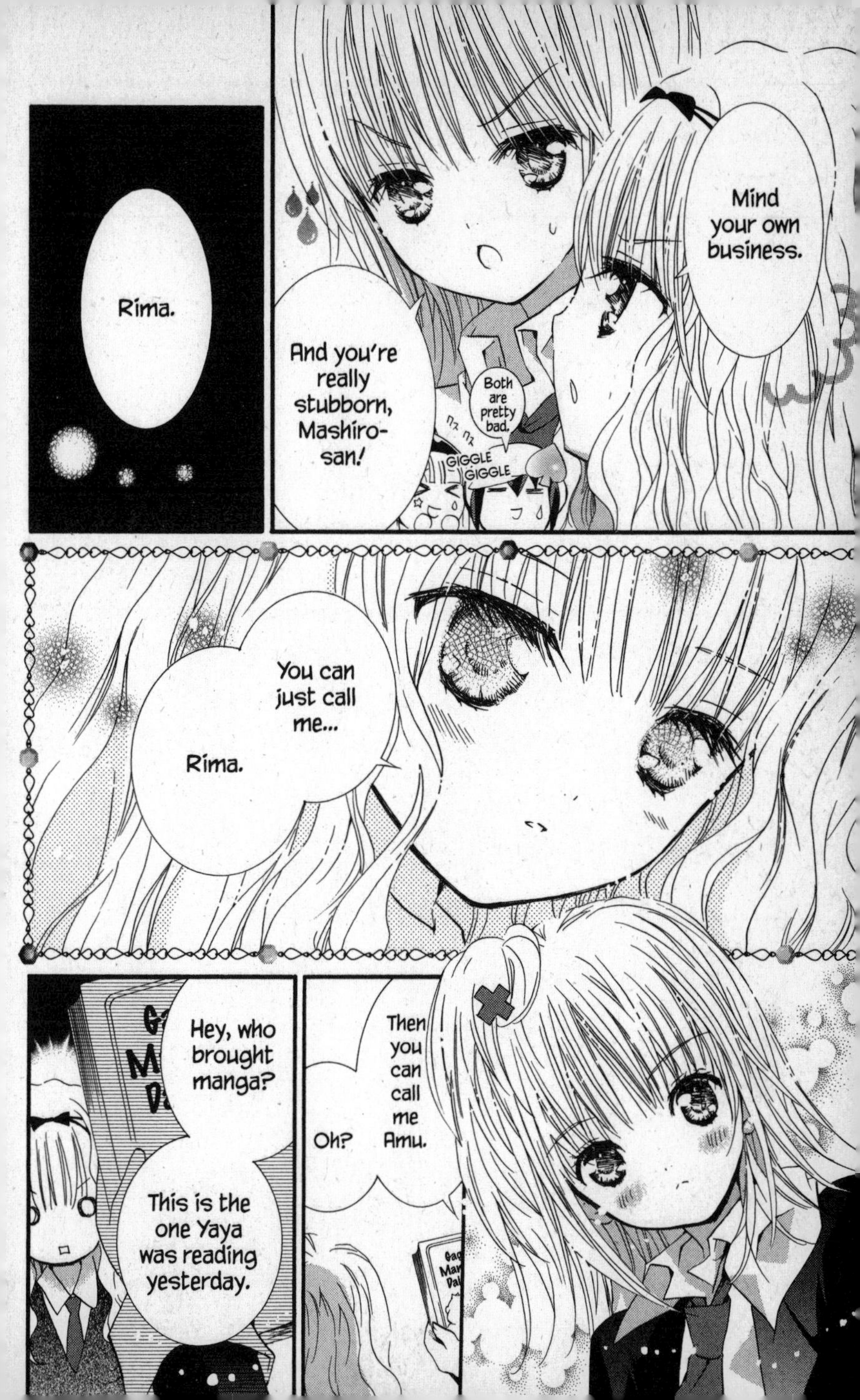

Mind your own business.
And you're really stubborn, Mashiro-san!
Both are pretty bad.
GIGGLE GIGGLE
Rima.
You can just call me...
Rima.
Then you can call me Amu.
Oh?
Hey, who brought manga?
This is the one Yaya was reading yesterday.

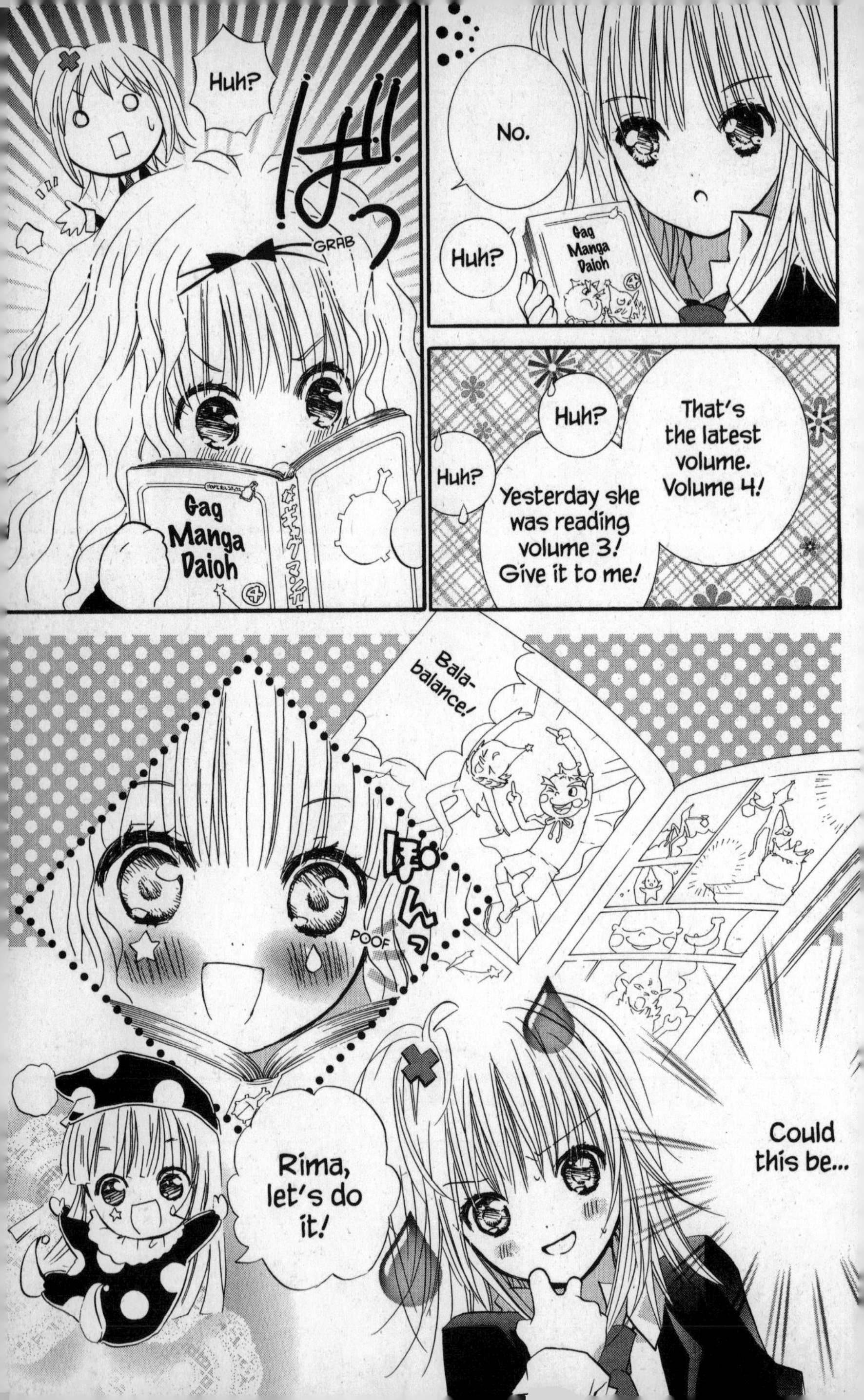
No.
Huh?
Gag Manga Daioh
That's the latest volume. Volume 4!
Huh?
Huh?
Yesterday she was reading volume 3! Give it to me!
Huh?
GRAB
Gag Manga Daioh
Bala-balance!
Could this be...
POOF
Rima, let's do it!

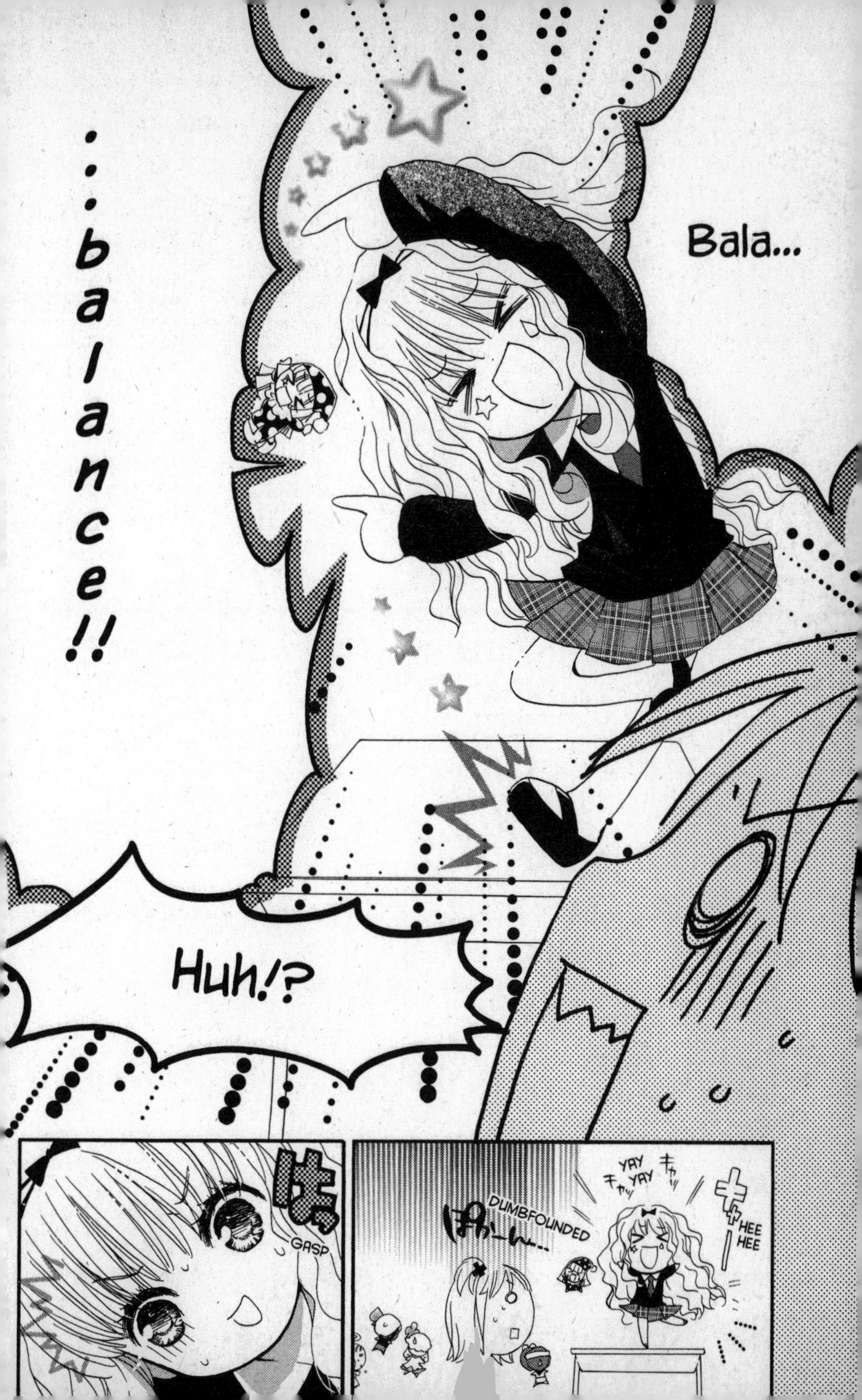

Bala...
...balance!!
Huh!?
YAY YAY
DUMBFOUNDED
HEE HEE
GASP

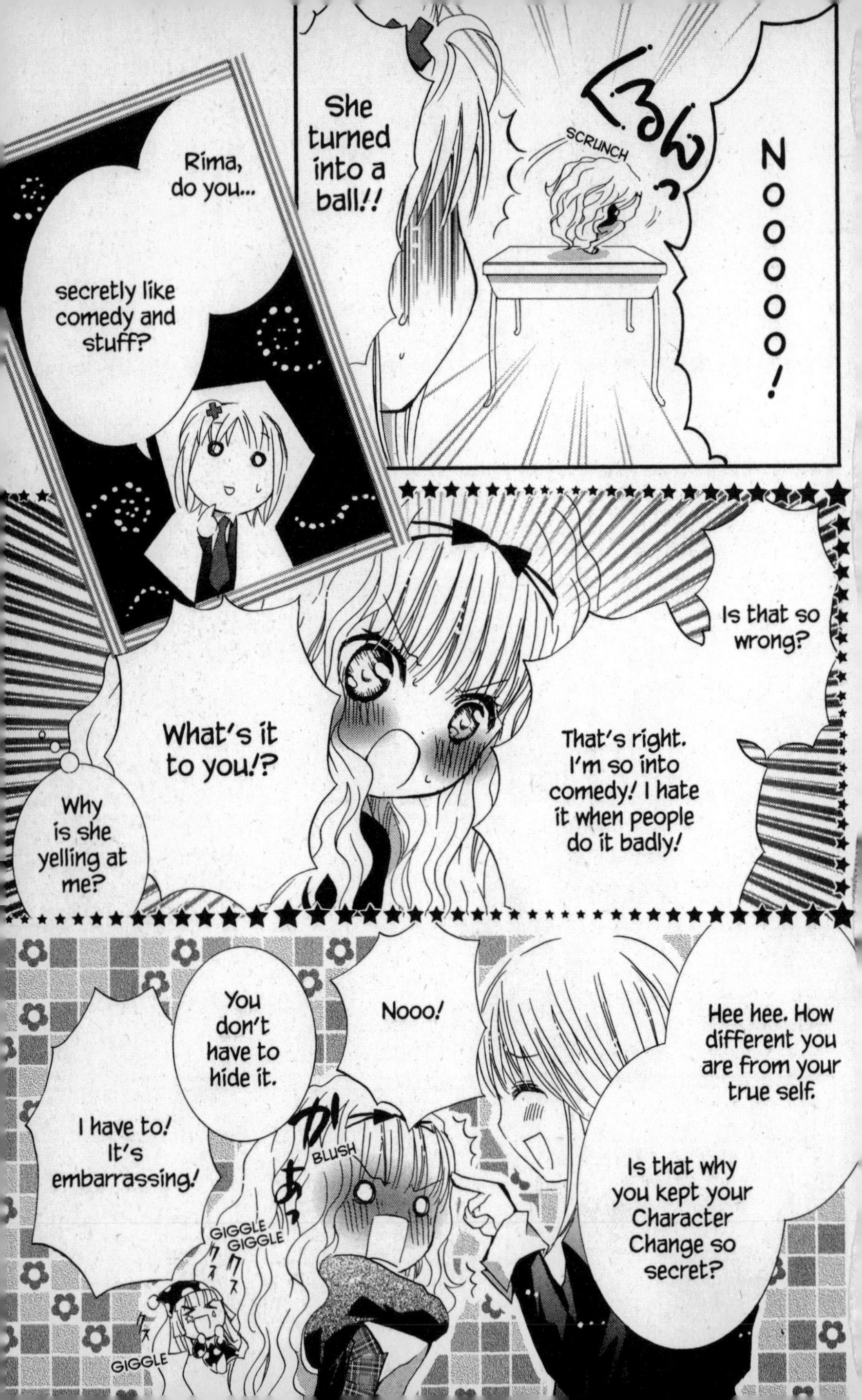
NOOOOO!
SCRUNCH
She turned into a ball!!
Rima, do you...
secretly like comedy and stuff?
Is that so wrong?
That's right. I'm so into comedy! I hate it when people do it badly!
What's it to you!?
Why is she yelling at me?
Hee hee. How different you are from your true self.
Is that why you kept your Character Change so secret?
Nooo!
BLUSH
You don't have to hide it.
I have to! It's embarrassing!
GIGGLE GIGGLE
GIGGLE

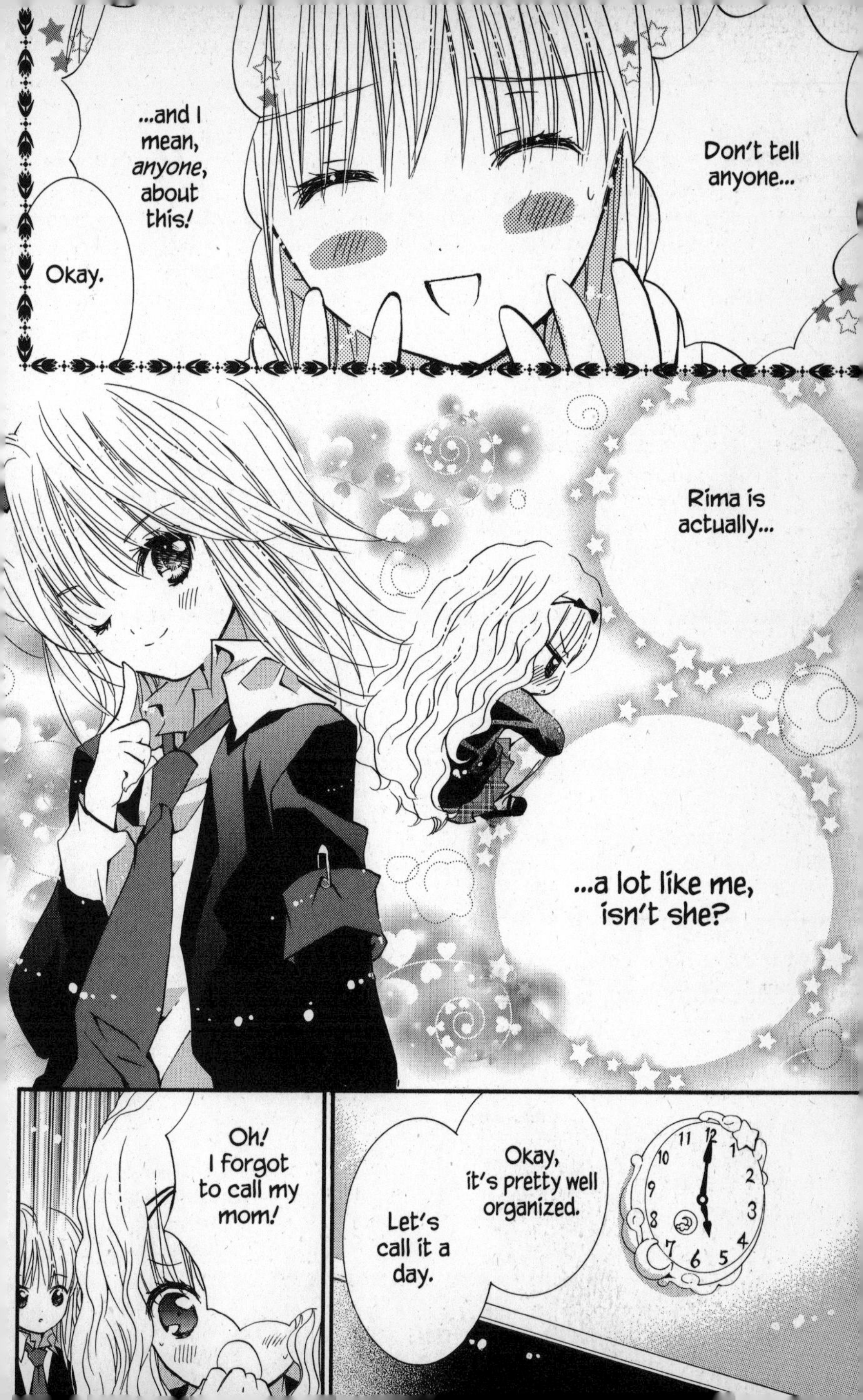
Don't tell anyone...
...and I mean, anyone, about this!
Okay.
Rima is actually...
...a lot like me, isn't she?
Okay, it's pretty well organized.
Let's call it a day.
Oh! I forgot to call my mom!

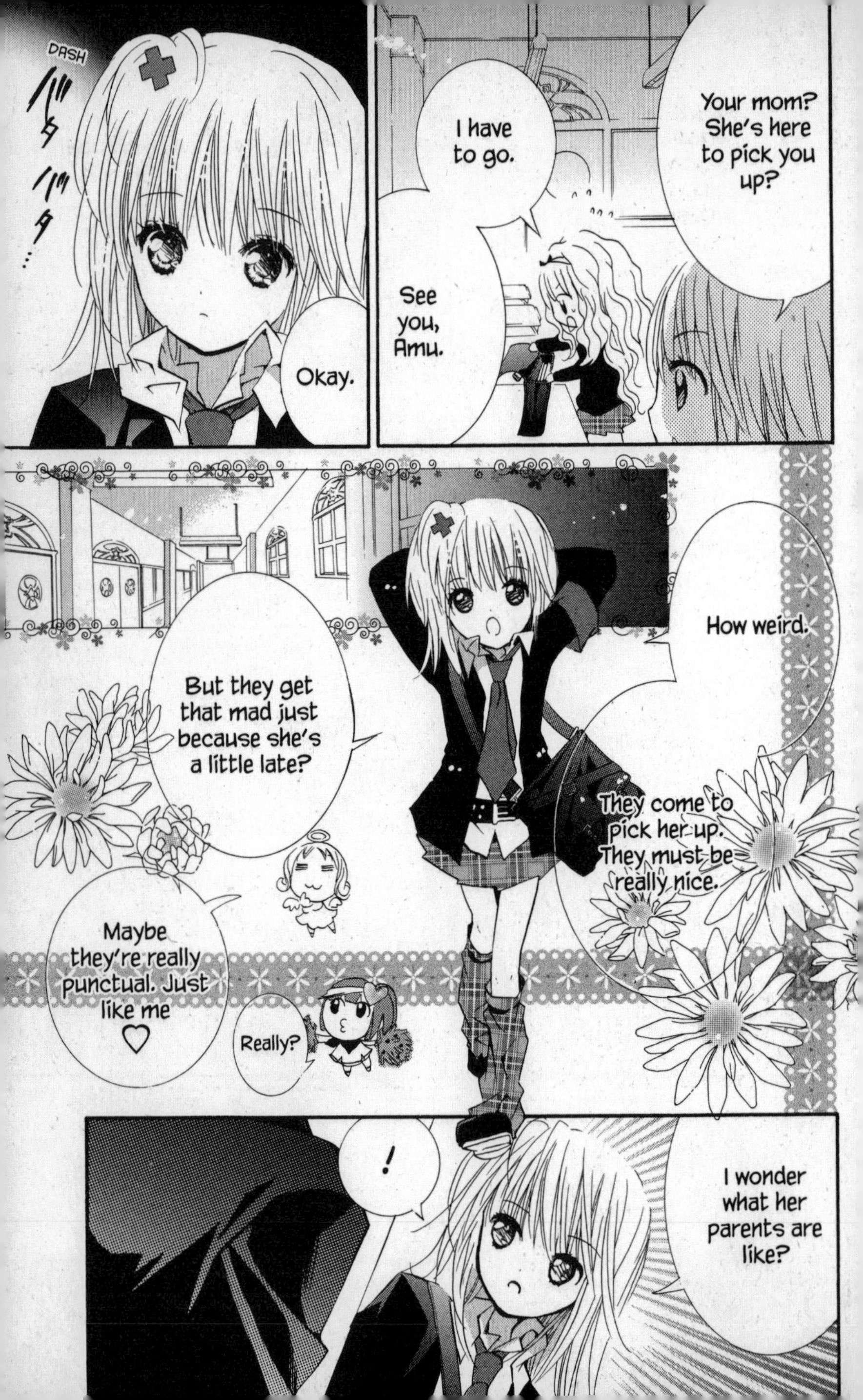
Your mom? She's here to pick you up?
I have to go.
See you, Amu.
DASH
バタバタ…
Okay.
How weird.
They come to pick her up. They must be really nice.
But they get that mad just because she's a little late?
Maybe they're really punctual. Just like me ♡
Really?
I wonder what her parents are like?
!

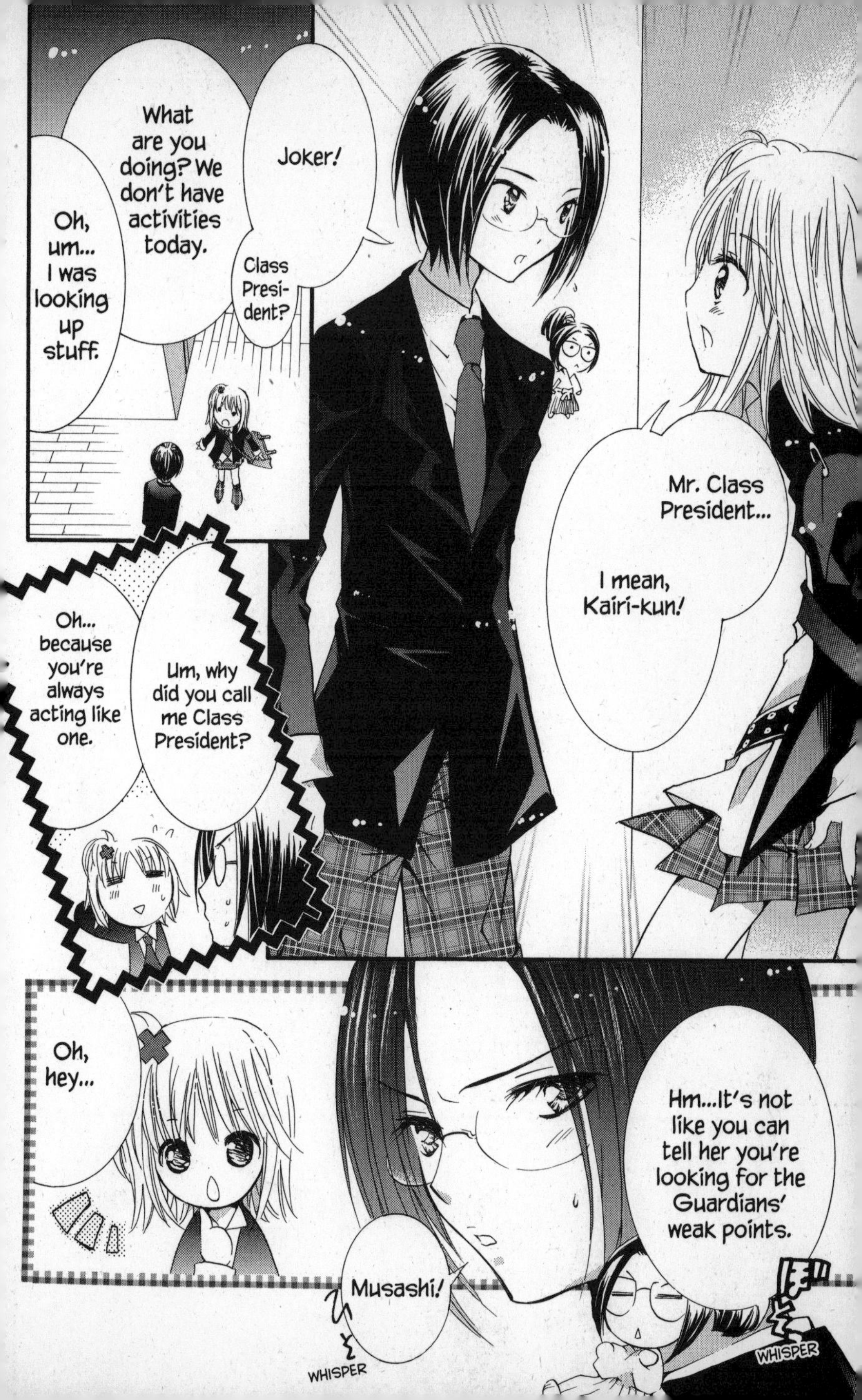
Mr. Class President...
I mean, Kairi-kun!
Joker!
Class President?
What are you doing? We don't have activities today.
Oh, um... I was looking up stuff.
Um, why did you call me Class President?
Oh... because you're always acting like one.
Hm...It's not like you can tell her you're looking for the Guardians' weak points.
WHISPER
Musashi!
WHISPER
Oh, hey...

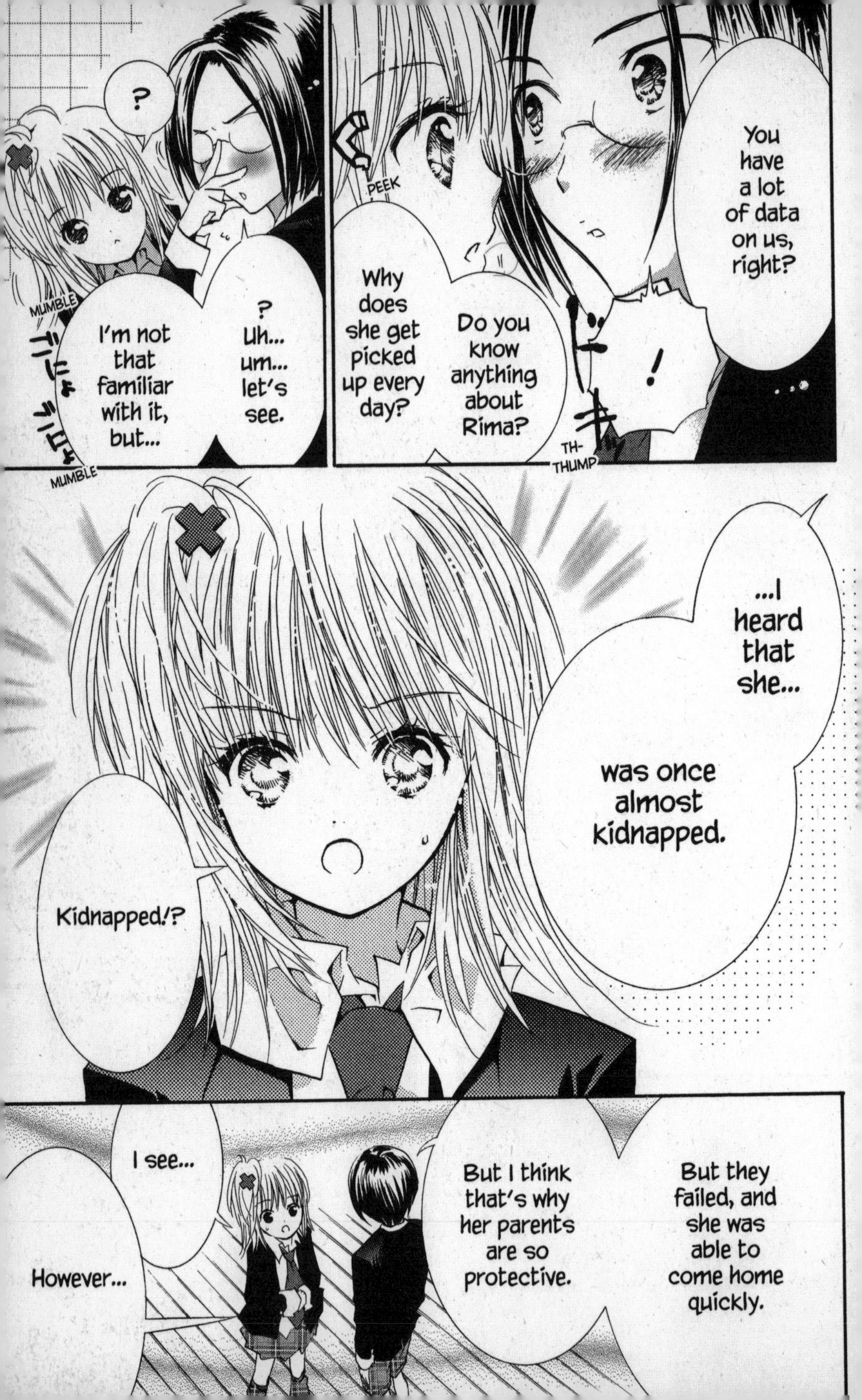

You have a lot of data on us, right?
!
TH-THUMP
Do you know anything about Rima?
Why does she get picked up every day?
PEEK
?
? uh... um... let's see.
I'm not that familiar with it, but...
MUMBLE
MUMBLE
...I heard that she...
was once almost kidnapped.
Kidnapped!?
But they failed, and she was able to come home quickly.
But I think that's why her parents are so protective.
I see...
However...

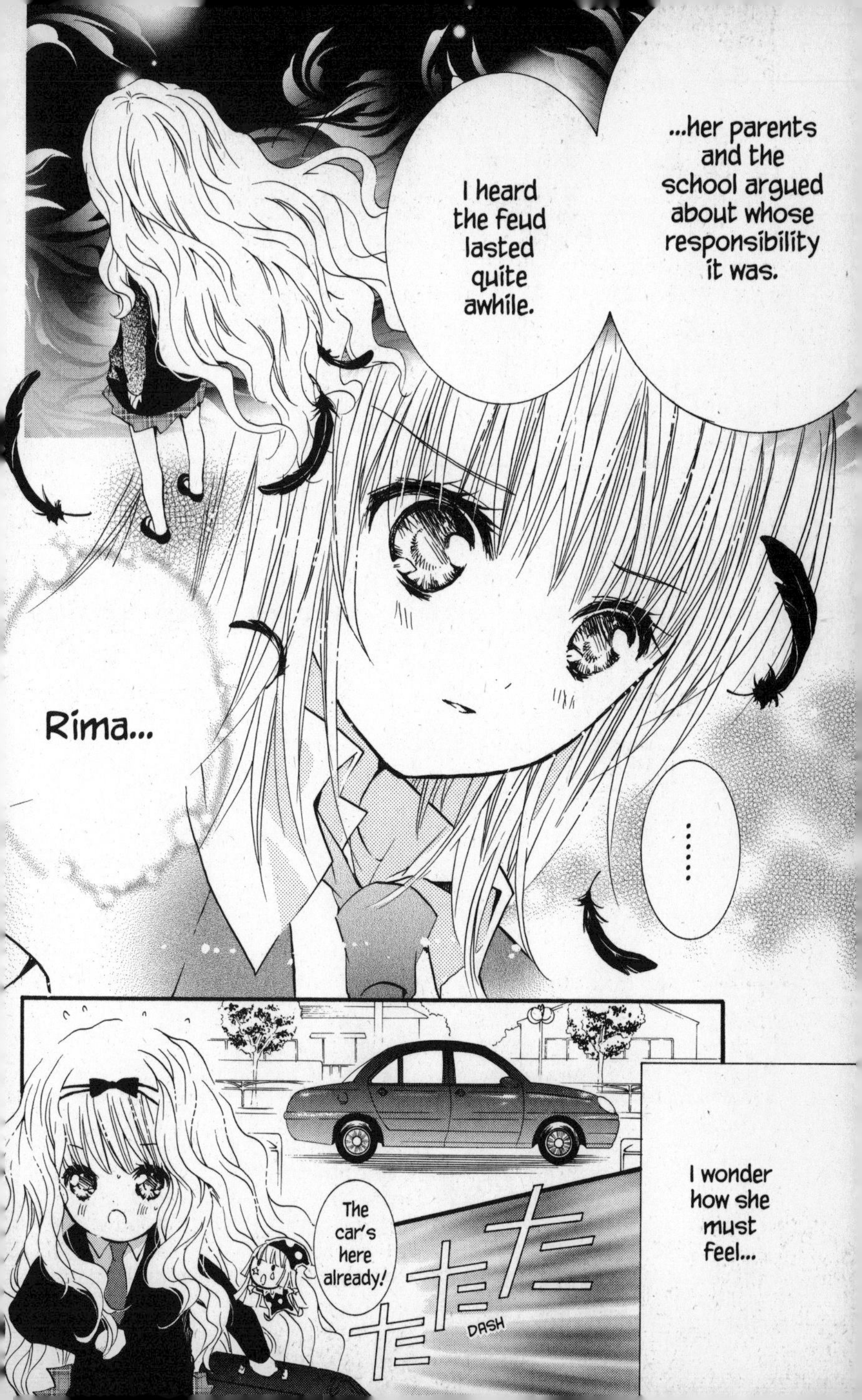
...her parents and the school argued about whose responsibility it was.
I heard the feud lasted quite awhile.
......
Rima...
I wonder how she must feel...
DASH
The car's here already!

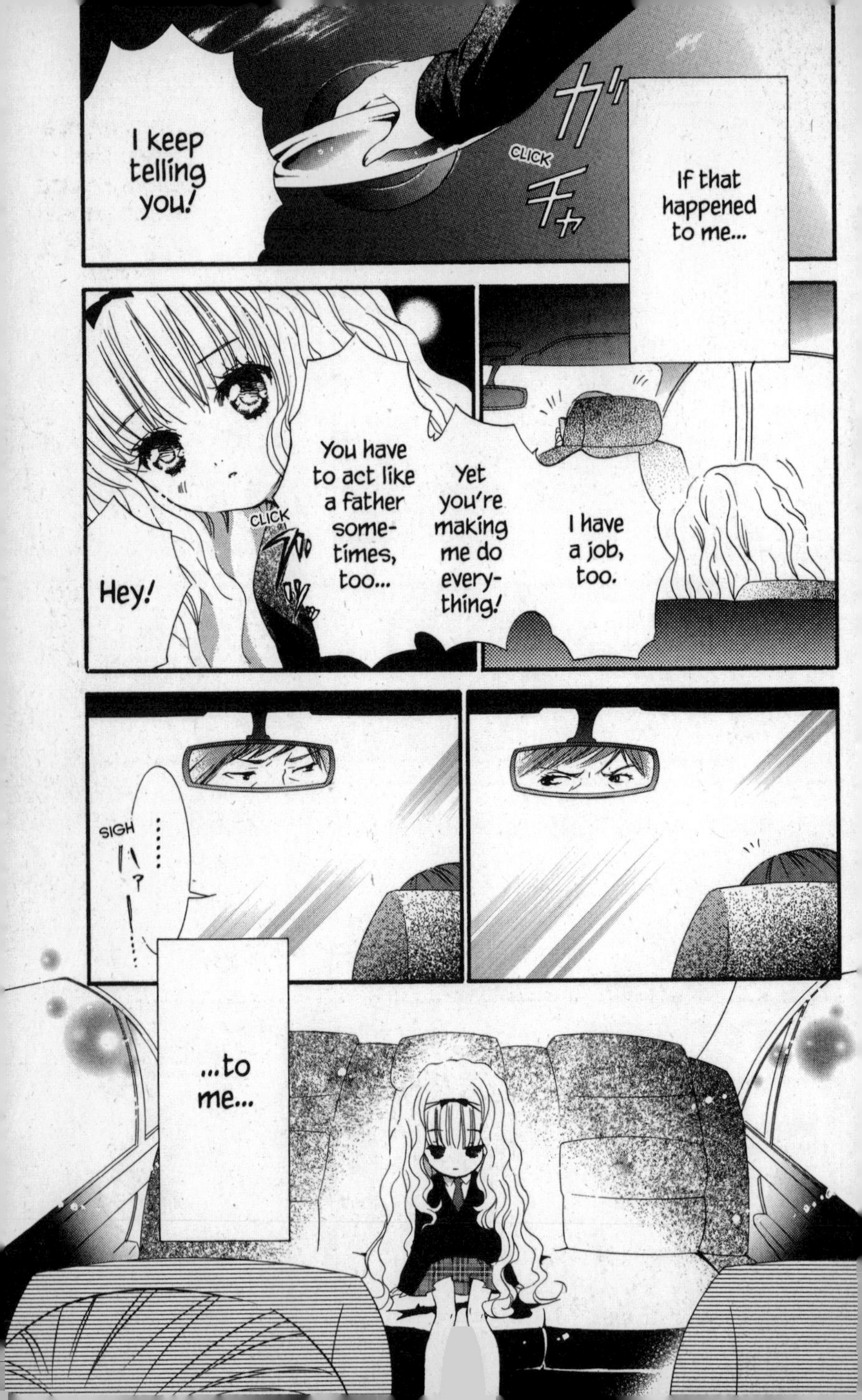
If that happened to me...
ガチャ
CLICK
I keep telling you!
I have a job, too.
Yet you're making me do everything!
You have to act like a father sometimes, too...
CLICK
Hey!
......
SIGH
...to me...

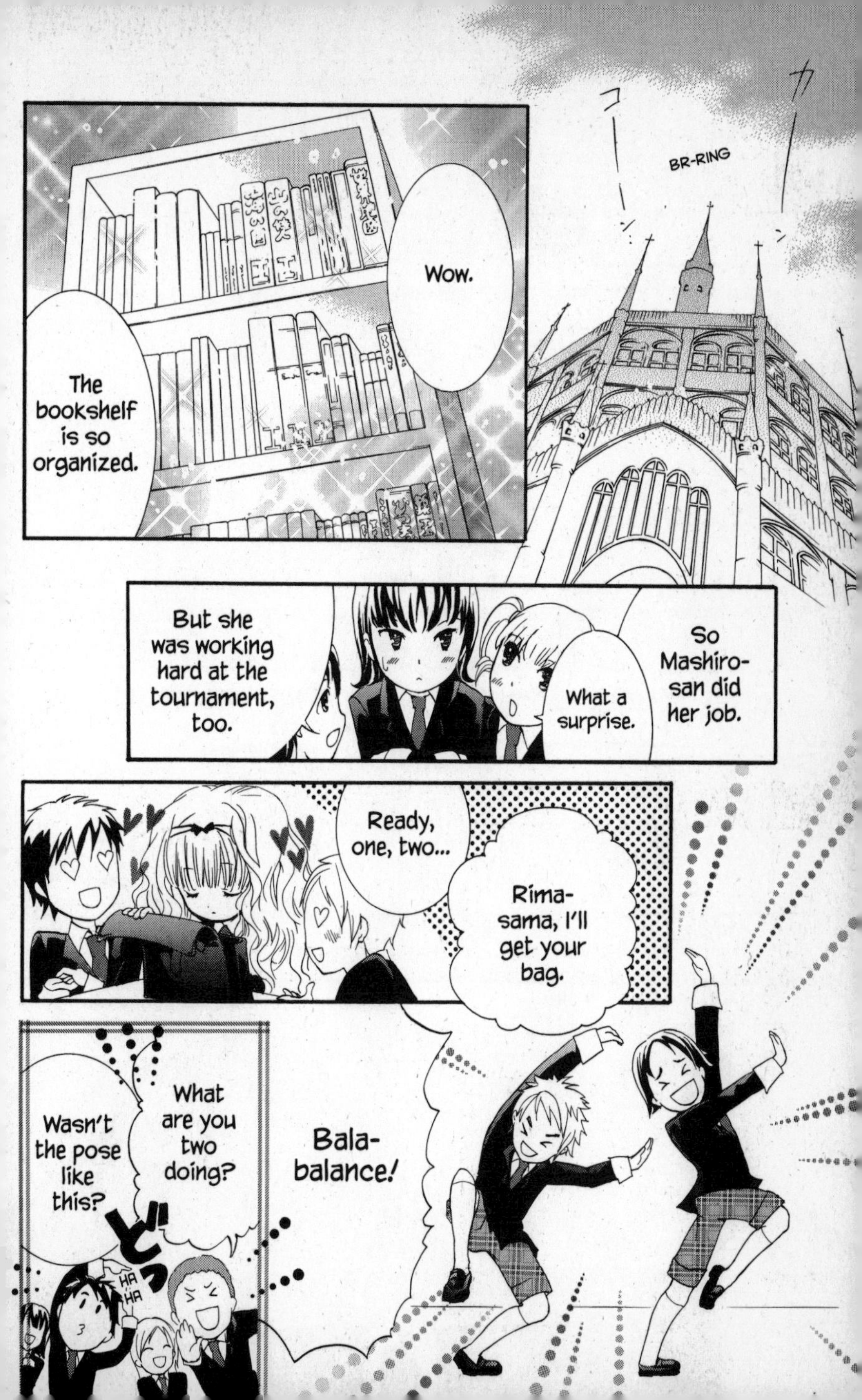
BR-RING
Wow.
The bookshelf is so organized.
So Mashiro-san did her job.
What a surprise.
But she was working hard at the tournament, too.
Rima-sama, I'll get your bag.
Ready, one, two...
Bala-balance!
What are you two doing?
Wasn't the pose like this?
HA HA

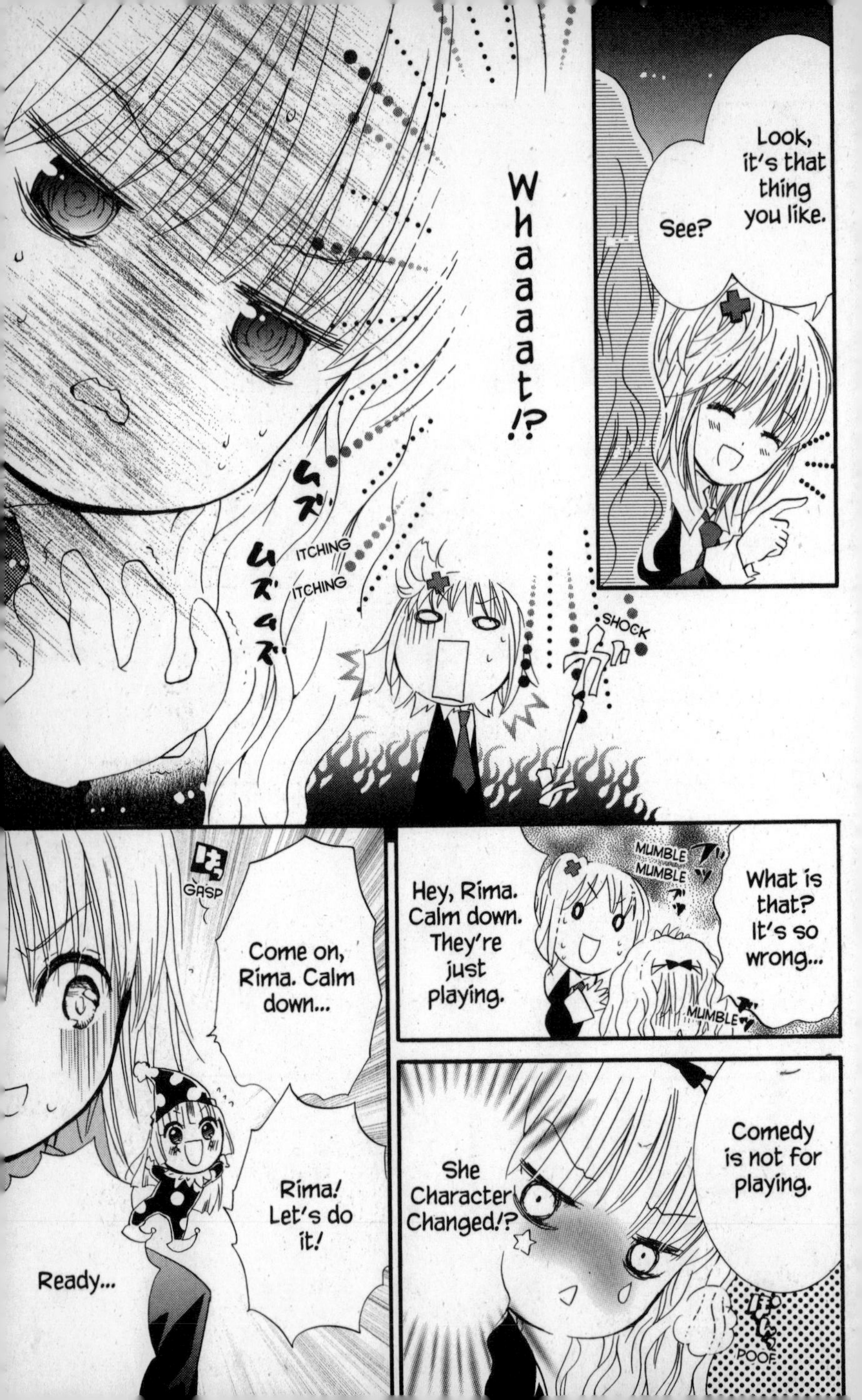

Look, it's that thing you like.
See?
Whaaaat!?
SHOCK
ITCHING
ITCHING
What is that? It's so wrong...
MUMBLE
MUMBLE
Hey, Rima. Calm down. They're just playing.
MUMBLE
Comedy is not for playing.
She Character Changed!?
POOF
GASP
Come on, Rima. Calm down...
Rima! Let's do it!
Ready...

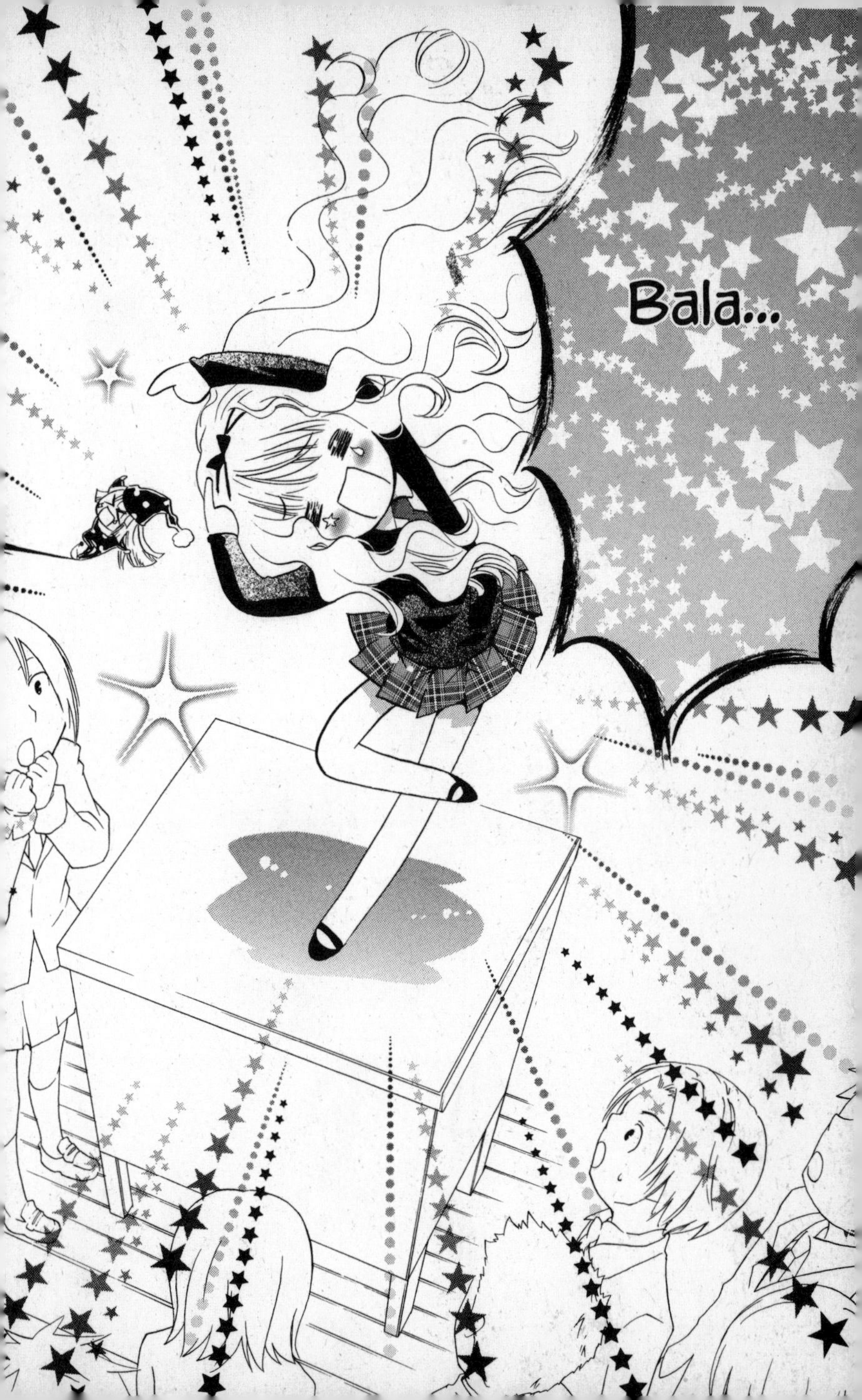
Bala...

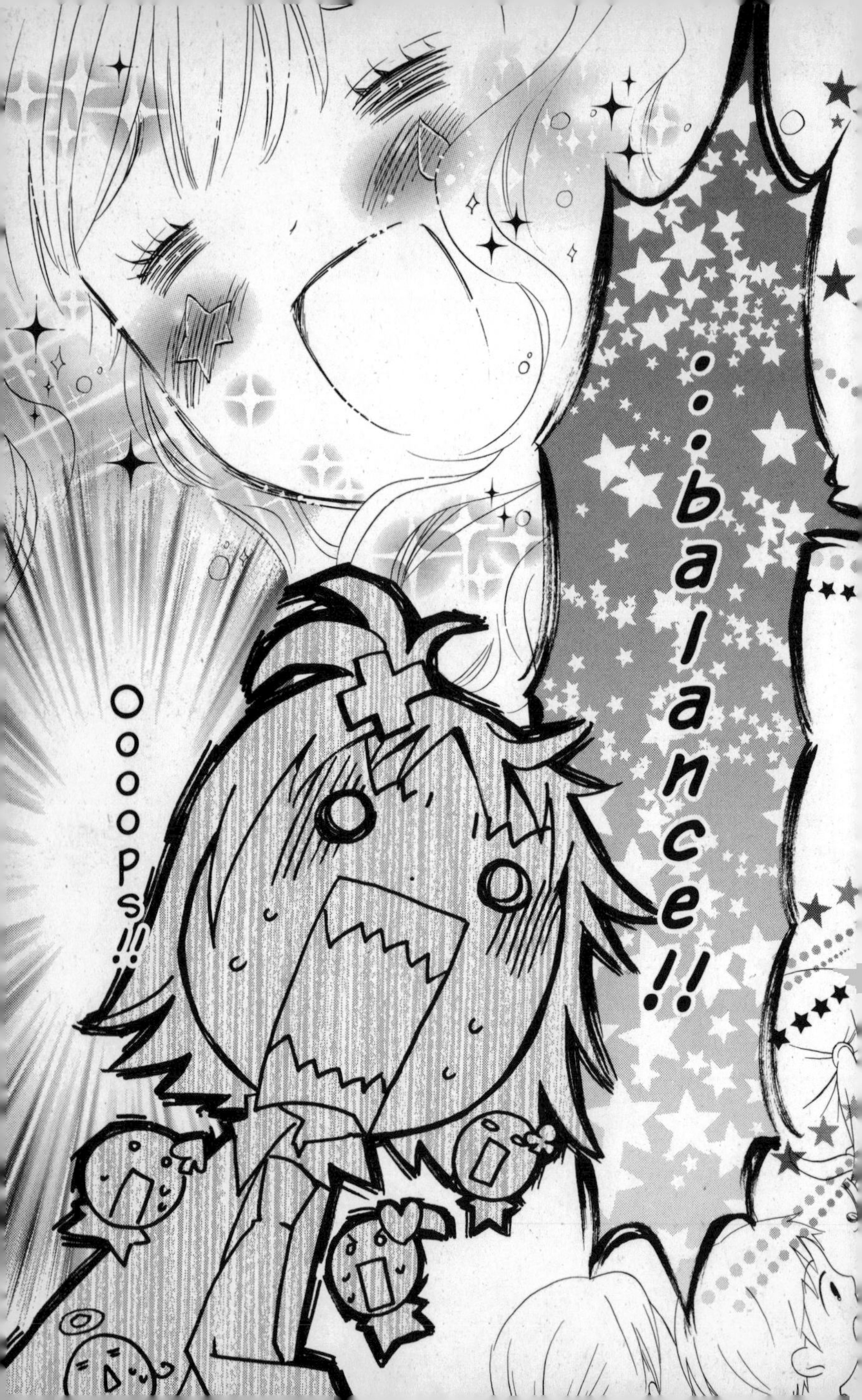
...balance!!
Oooops!!

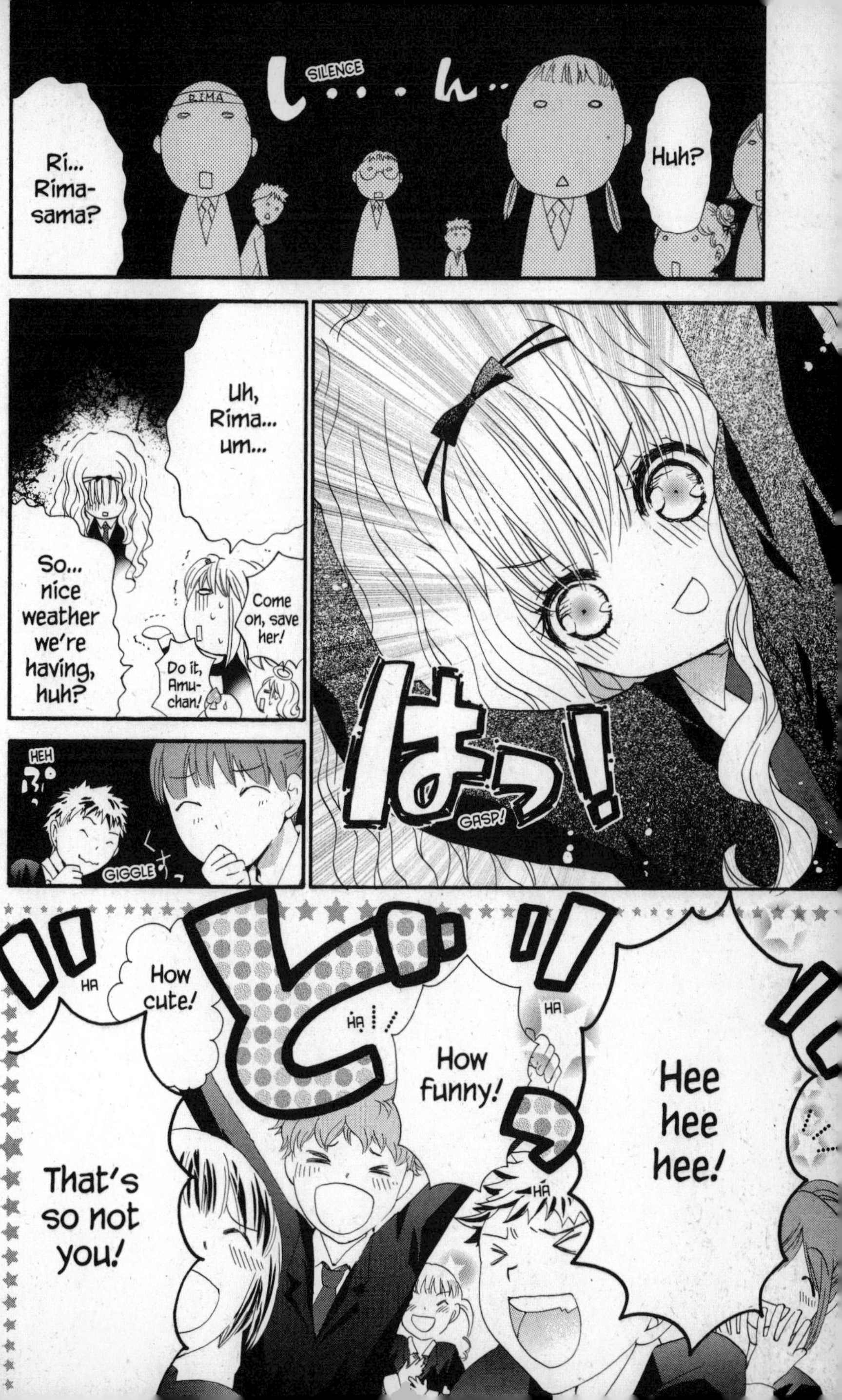
Huh?
SILENCE
RIMA
Ri... Rima-sama?
GASP!
Uh, Rima... um...
Come on, save her!
Do it, Amu-chan!
So... nice weather we're having, huh?
HEH
GIGGLE
Hee hee hee!
HA
How funny!
HA
HA
How cute!
HA
That's so not you!

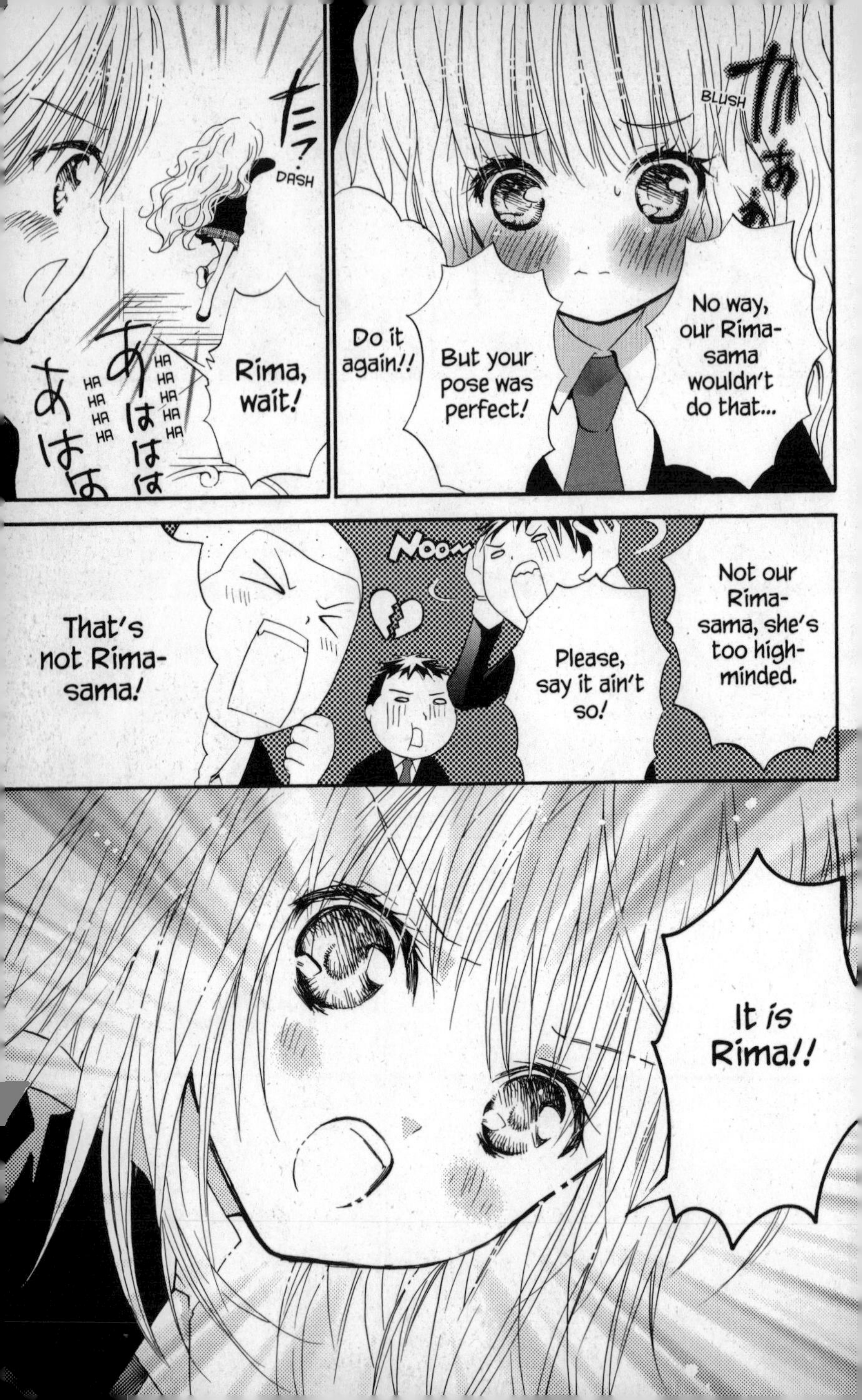
BLUSH
No way, our Rima-sama wouldn't do that...
But your pose was perfect!
Do it again!!
DASH
Rima, wait!
HA HA HA HA HA
HA HA HA HA
Not our Rima-sama, she's too high-minded.
Please, say it ain't so!
NOO~
That's not Rima-sama!
It is Rima!!

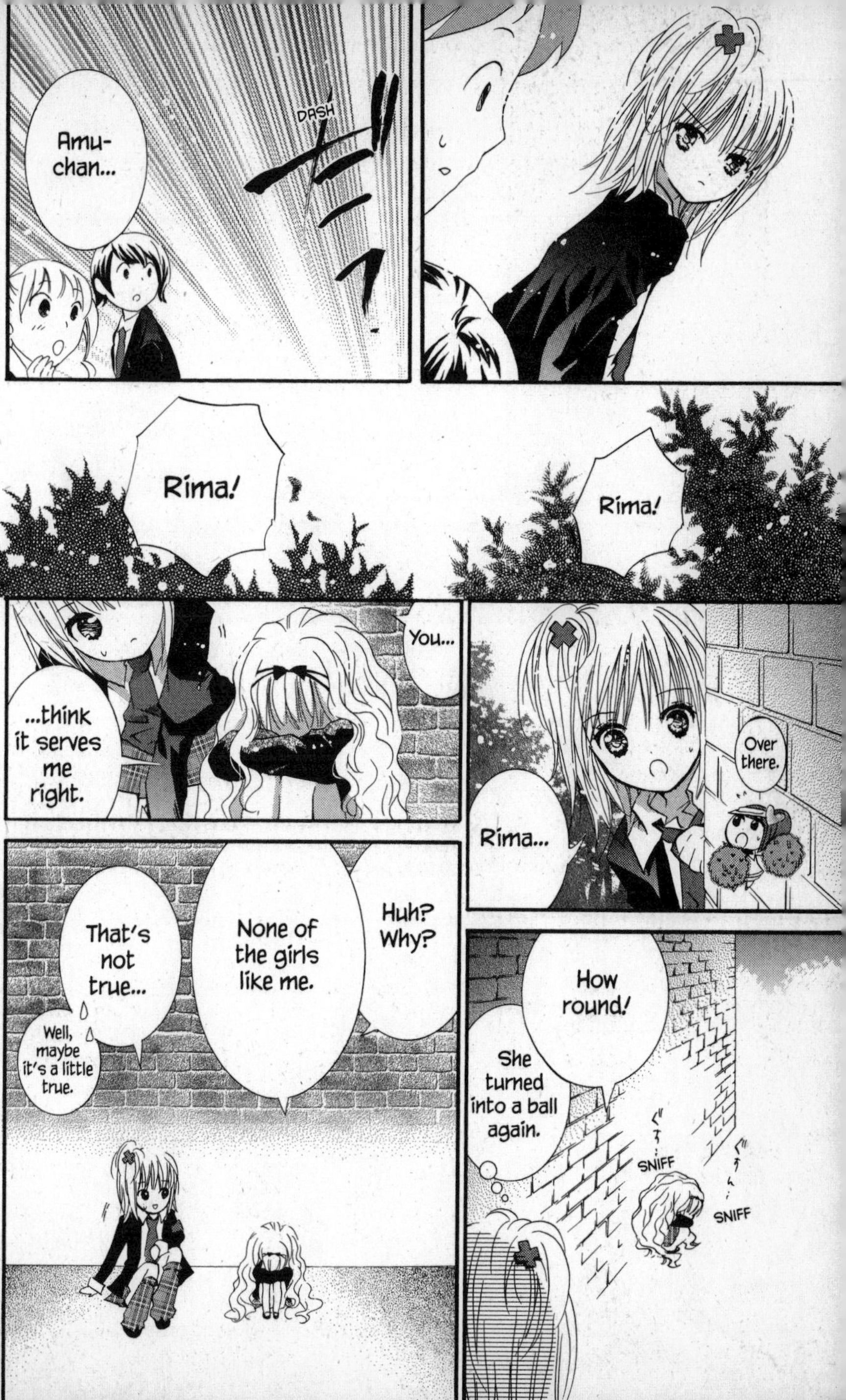
DASH
Amu-chan...
Rima!
Rima!
Over there.
Rima...
You...
...think it serves me right.
How round!
She turned into a ball again.
SNIFF
SNIFF
Huh? Why?
None of the girls like me.
That's not true...
Well, maybe it's a little true.

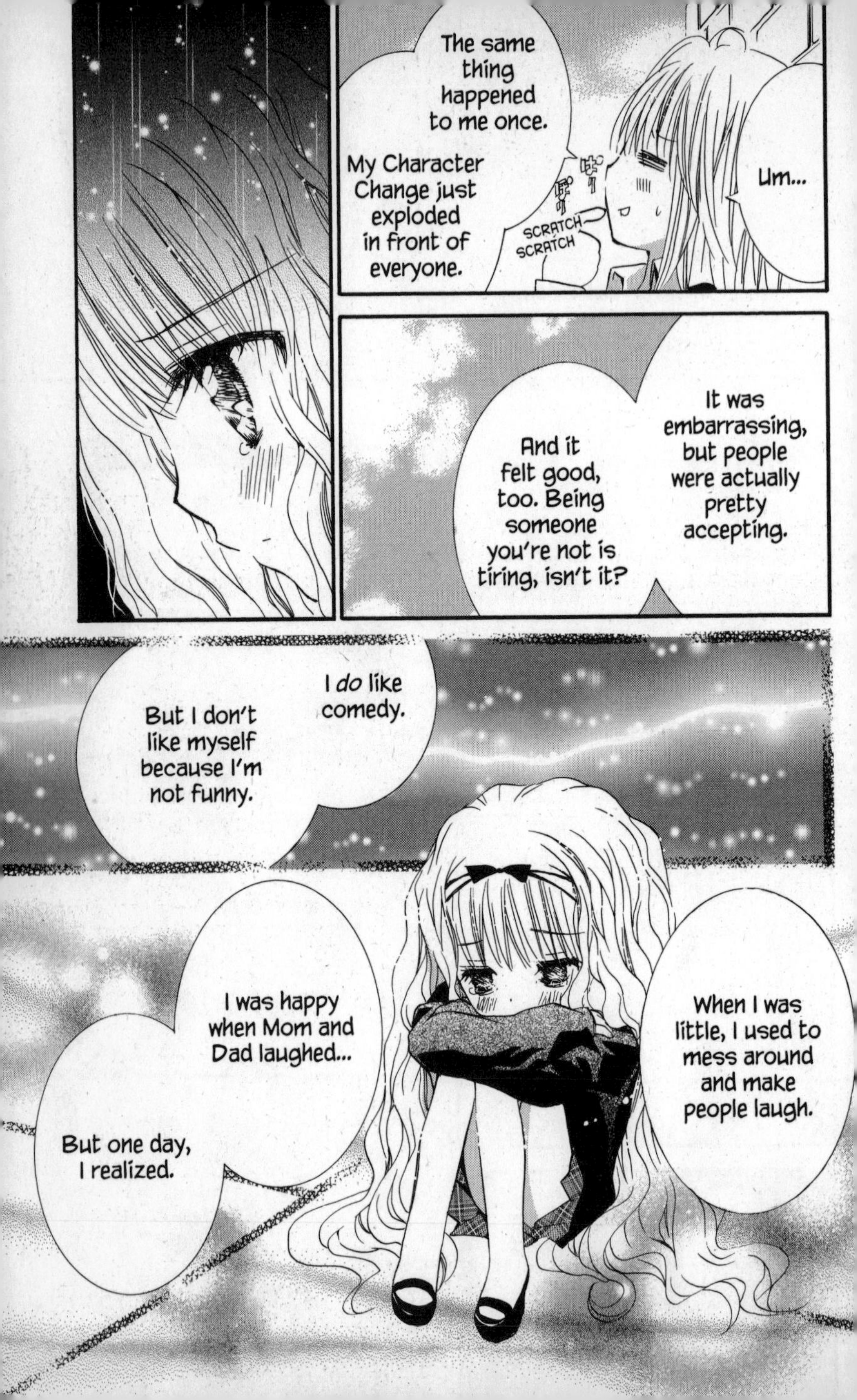
Um...
The same thing happened to me once.
My Character Change just exploded in front of everyone.
SCRATCH SCRATCH
It was embarrassing, but people were actually pretty accepting.
And it felt good, too. Being someone you're not is tiring, isn't it?
I *do* like comedy.
But I don't like myself because I'm not funny.
When I was little, I used to mess around and make people laugh.
I was happy when Mom and Dad laughed...
But one day, I realized.

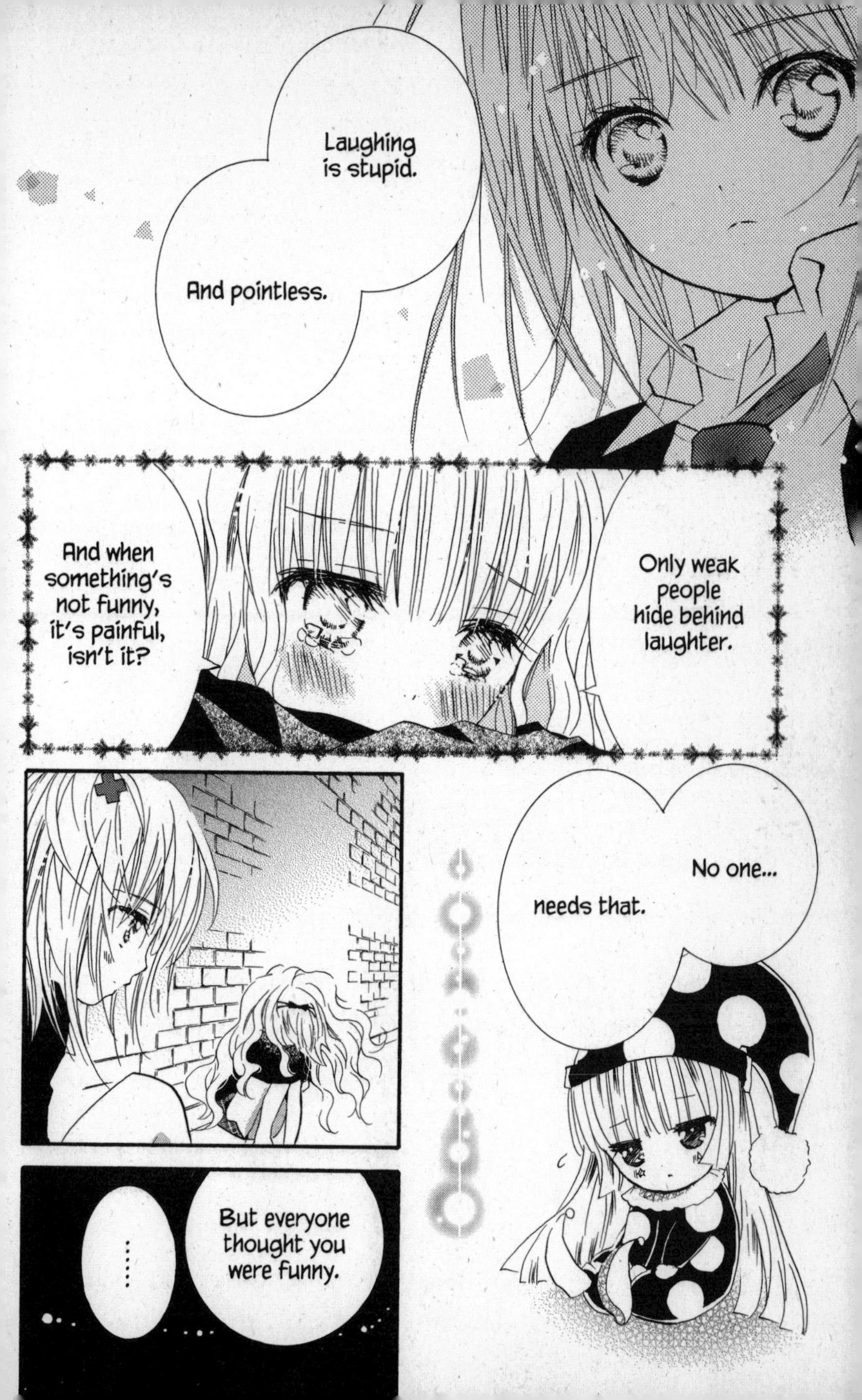
Laughing is stupid.
And pointless.
Only weak people hide behind laughter.
And when something's not funny, it's painful, isn't it?
No one...
needs that.
But everyone thought you were funny.
......

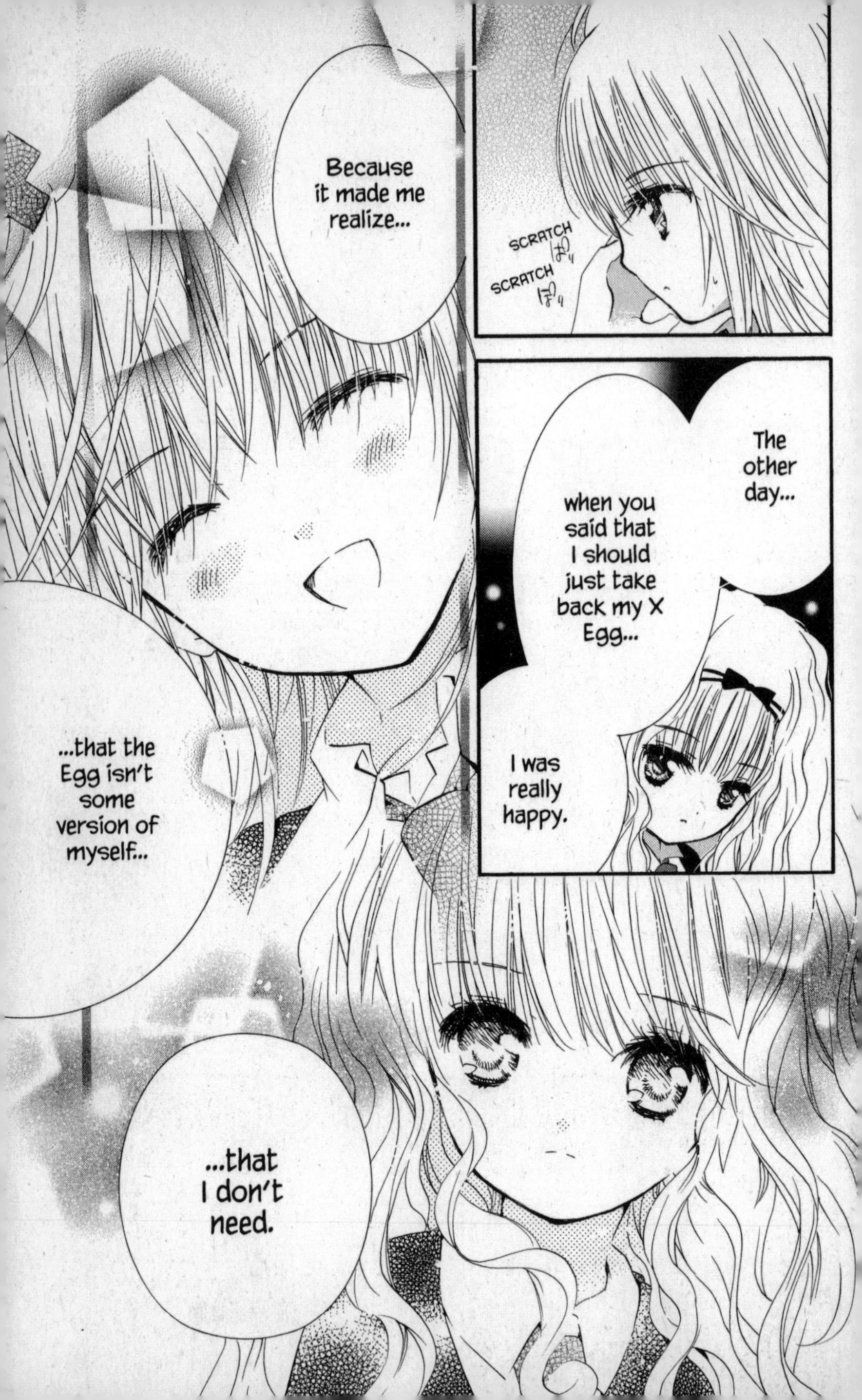
SCRATCH
SCRATCH
The other day...
when you said that I should just take back my X Egg...
I was really happy.
Because it made me realize...
...that the Egg isn't some version of myself...
...that I don't need.

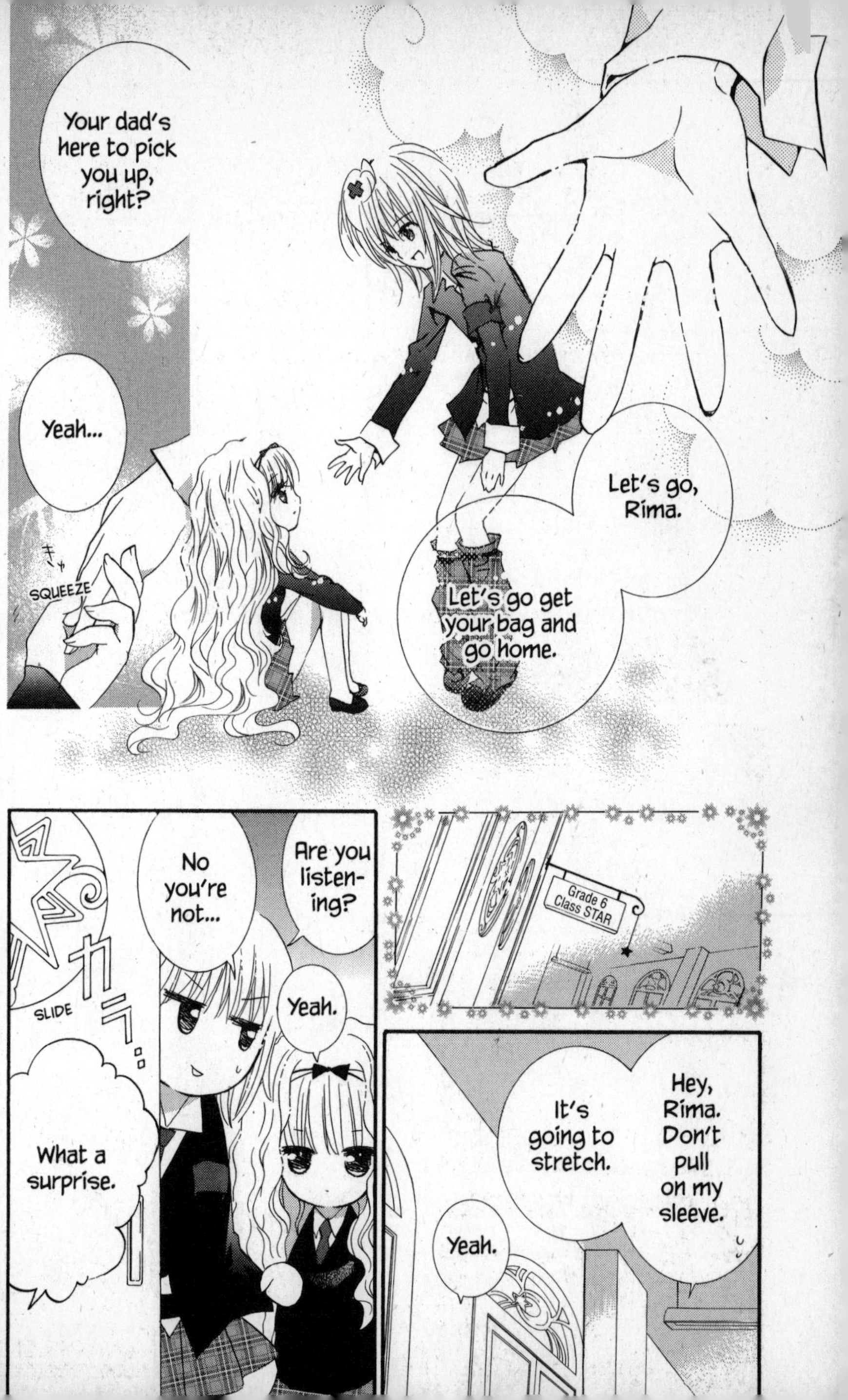
Let's go, Rima.
Let's go get your bag and go home.
Your dad's here to pick you up, right?
Yeah...
SQUEEZE
Grade 6 Class STAR
Hey, Rima. Don't pull on my sleeve.
It's going to stretch.
Yeah.
Are you listening?
No you're not...
Yeah.
SLIDE
What a surprise.

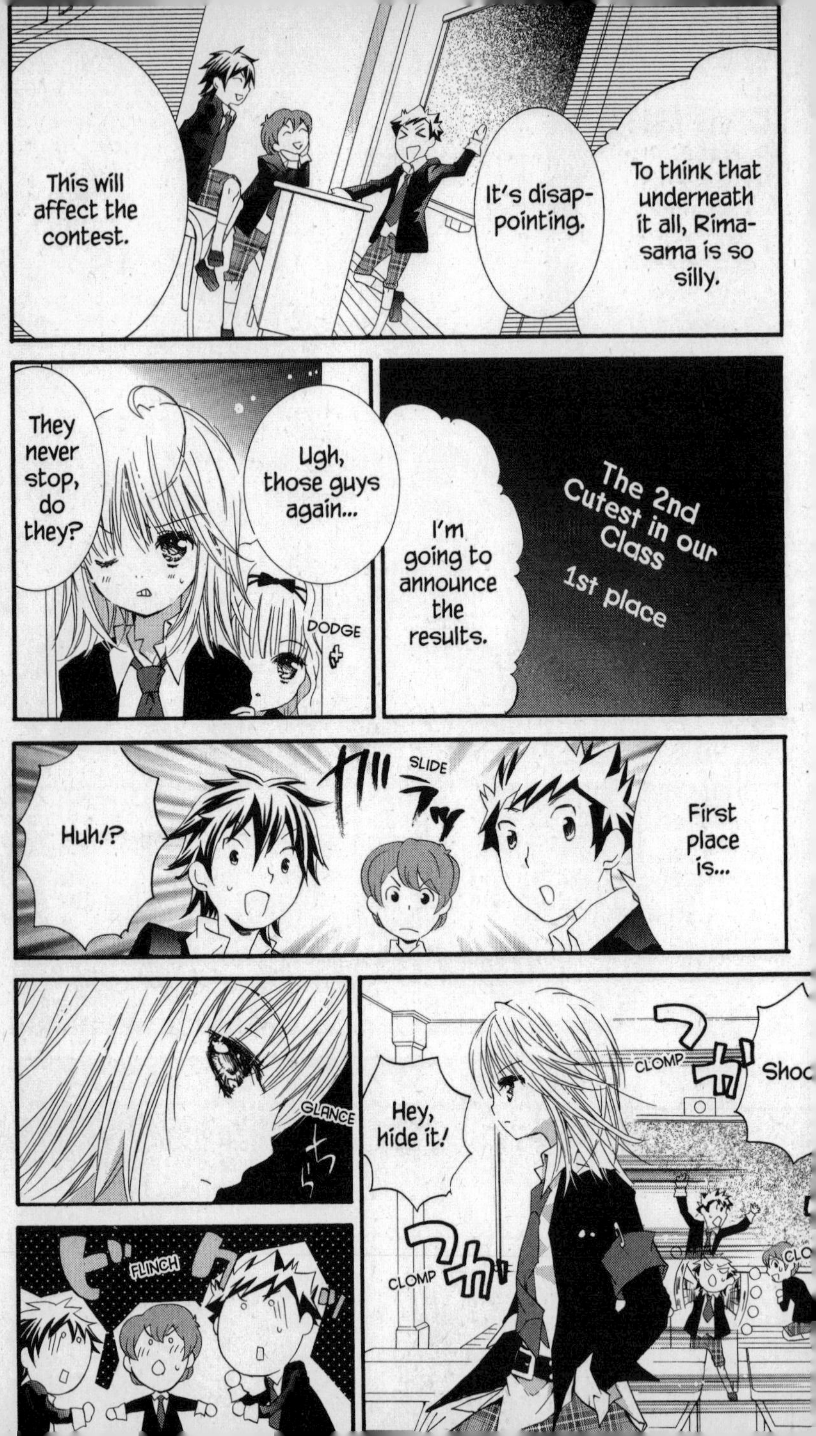
To think that underneath it all, Rima-sama is so silly.
It's disap-pointing.
This will affect the contest.
The 2nd Cutest in our Class
1st place
I'm going to announce the results.
Ugh, those guys again...
They never stop, do they?
DODGE
First place is...
SLIDE
Huh!?
Shoc
CLOMP
Hey, hide it!
CLOMP
GLANCE
FLINCH

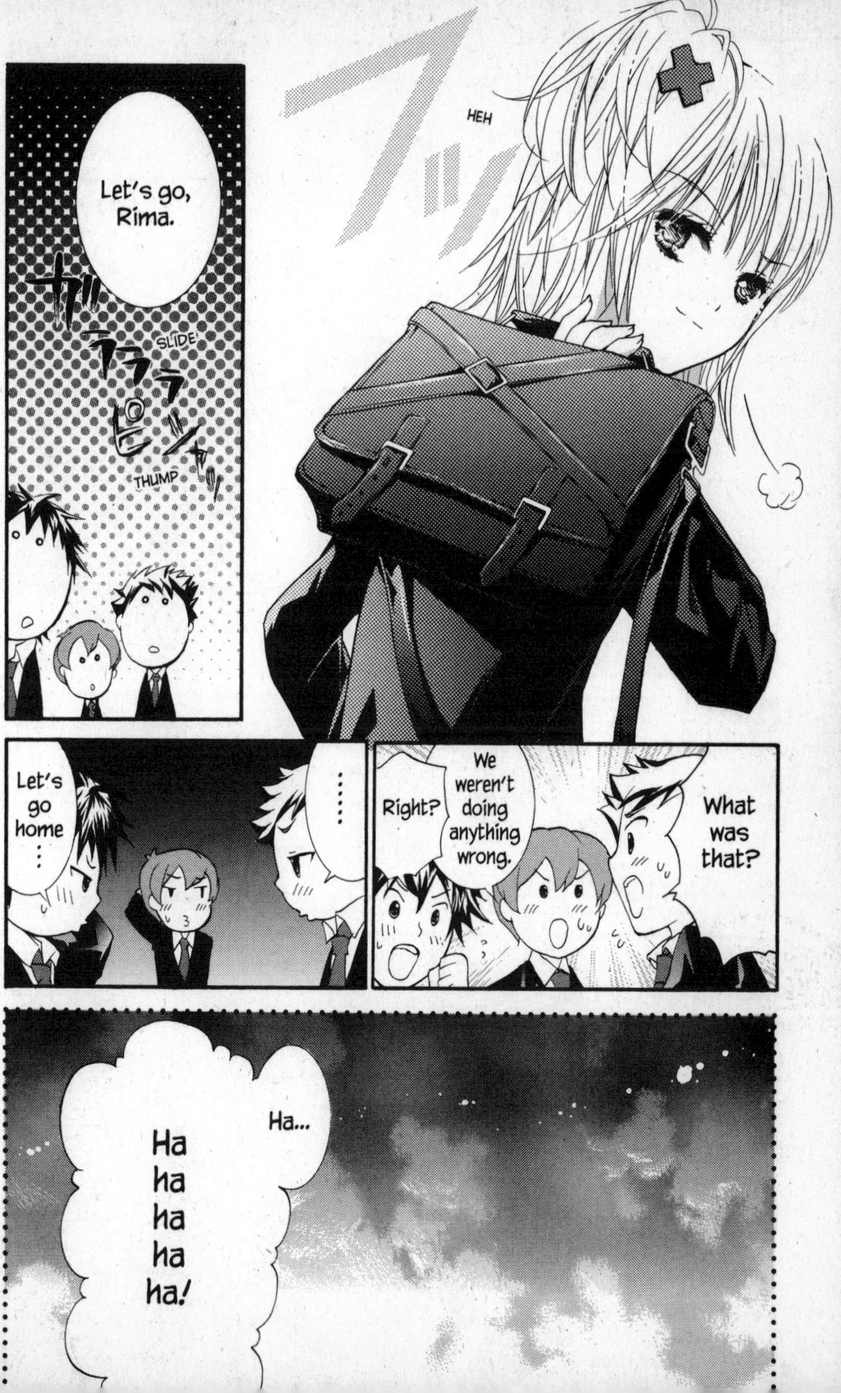
HEH
Let's go, Rima.
SLIDE
THUMP
What was that?
We weren't doing anything wrong.
Right?
......
Let's go home...
Ha...
Ha ha ha ha ha!

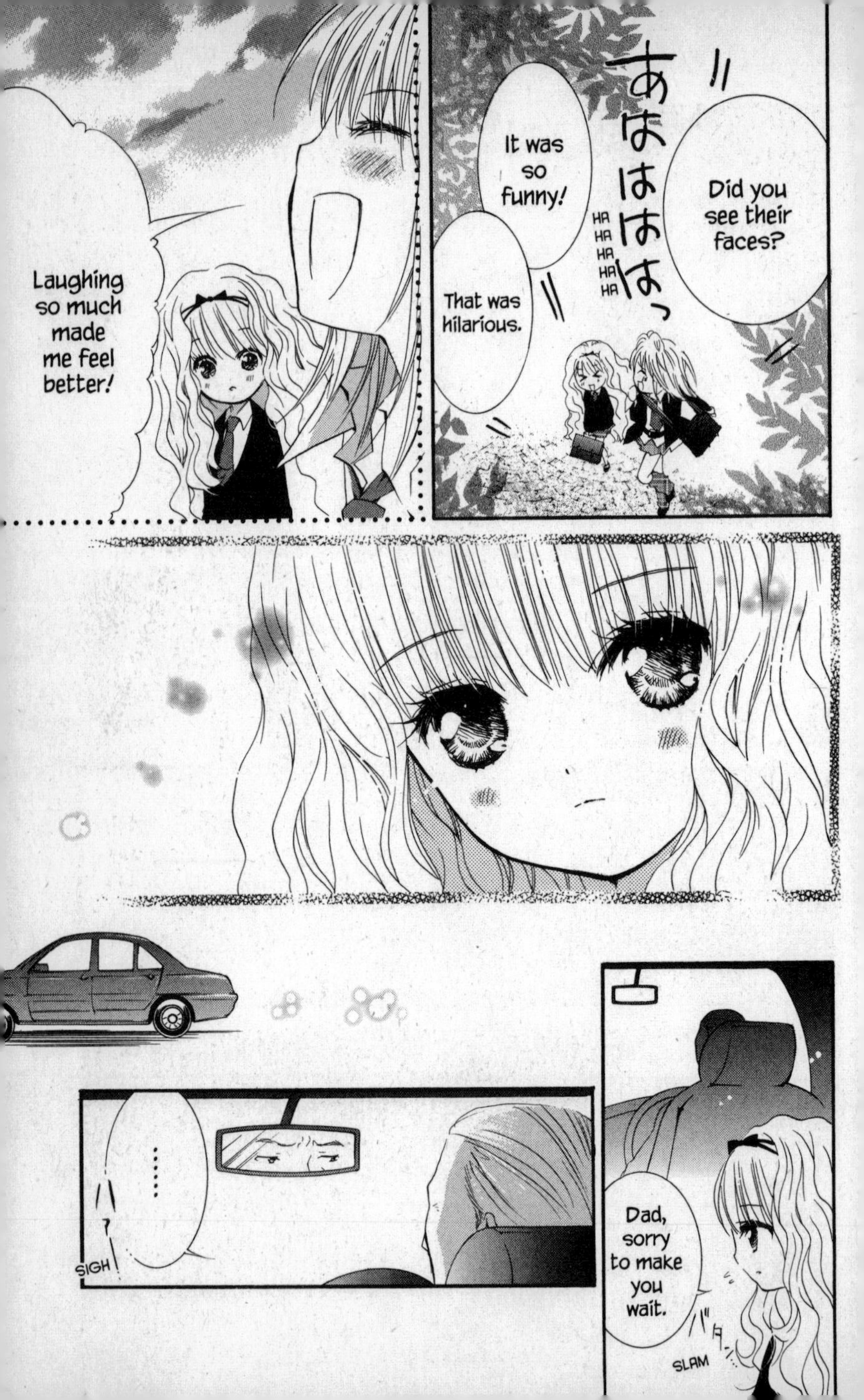
Did you see their faces?
あははは、
HA HA HA HA HA
It was so funny!
That was hilarious.
Laughing so much made me feel better!
Dad, sorry to make you wait.
バタン
SLAM
......
SIGH

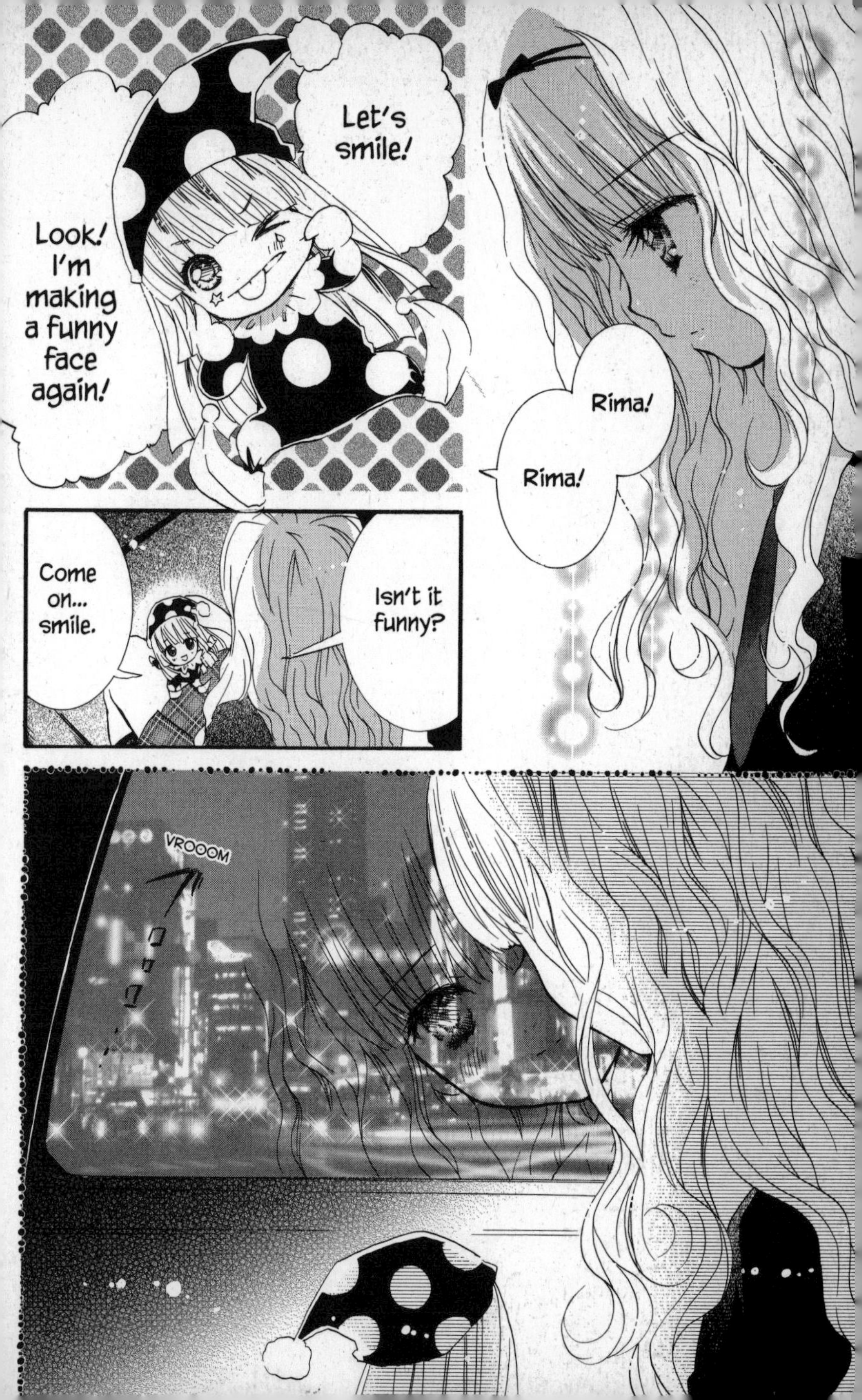
Rima!
Rima!
Let's smile!
Look! I'm making a funny face again!
Isn't it funny?
Come on... smile.
VROOOM

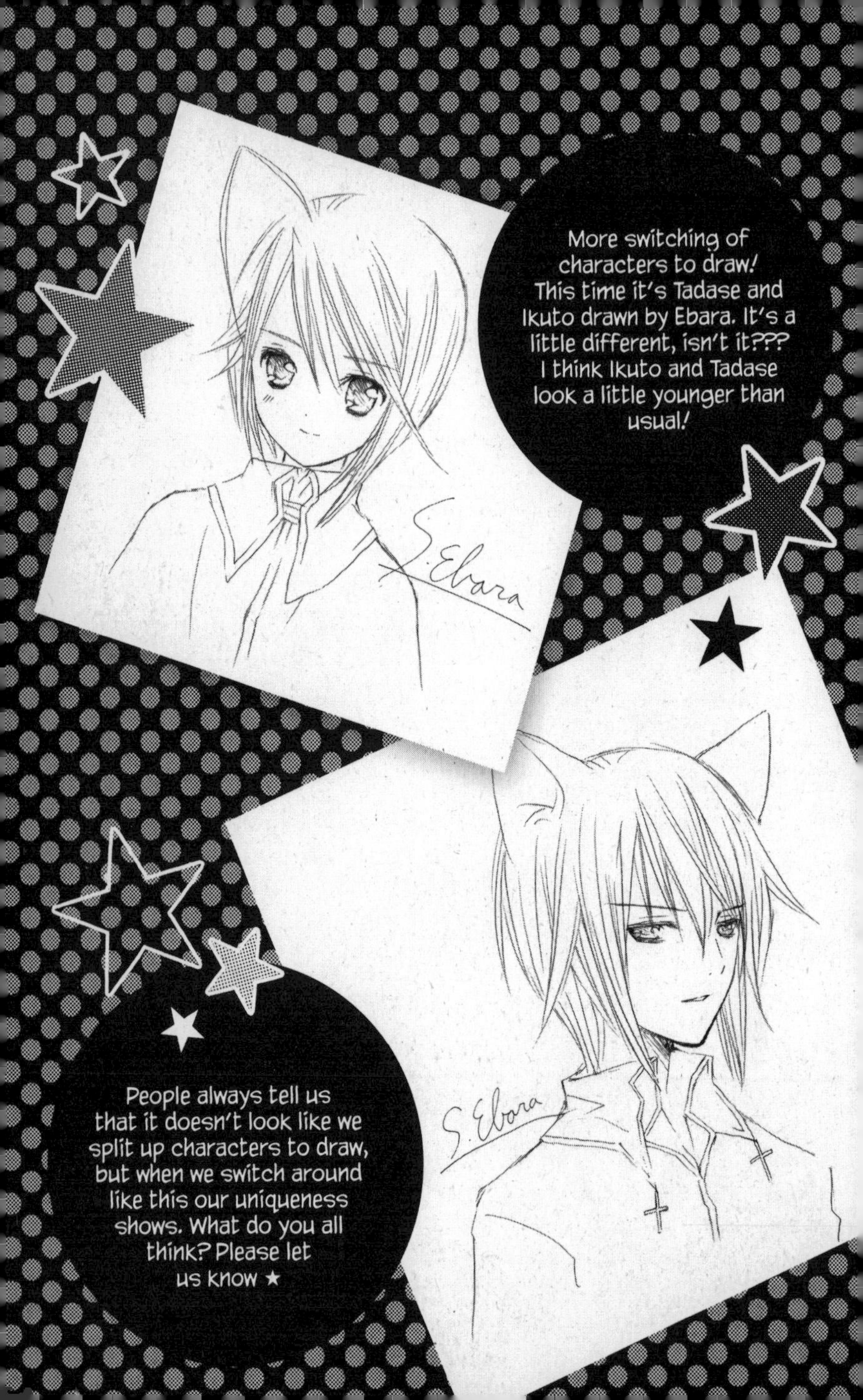
More switching of characters to draw! This time it's Tadase and Ikuto drawn by Ebara. It's a little different, isn't it??? I think Ikuto and Tadase look a little younger than usual!
S.Ebara
S.Ebara
People always tell us that it doesn't look like we split up characters to draw, but when we switch around like this our uniqueness shows. What do you all think? Please let us know ★

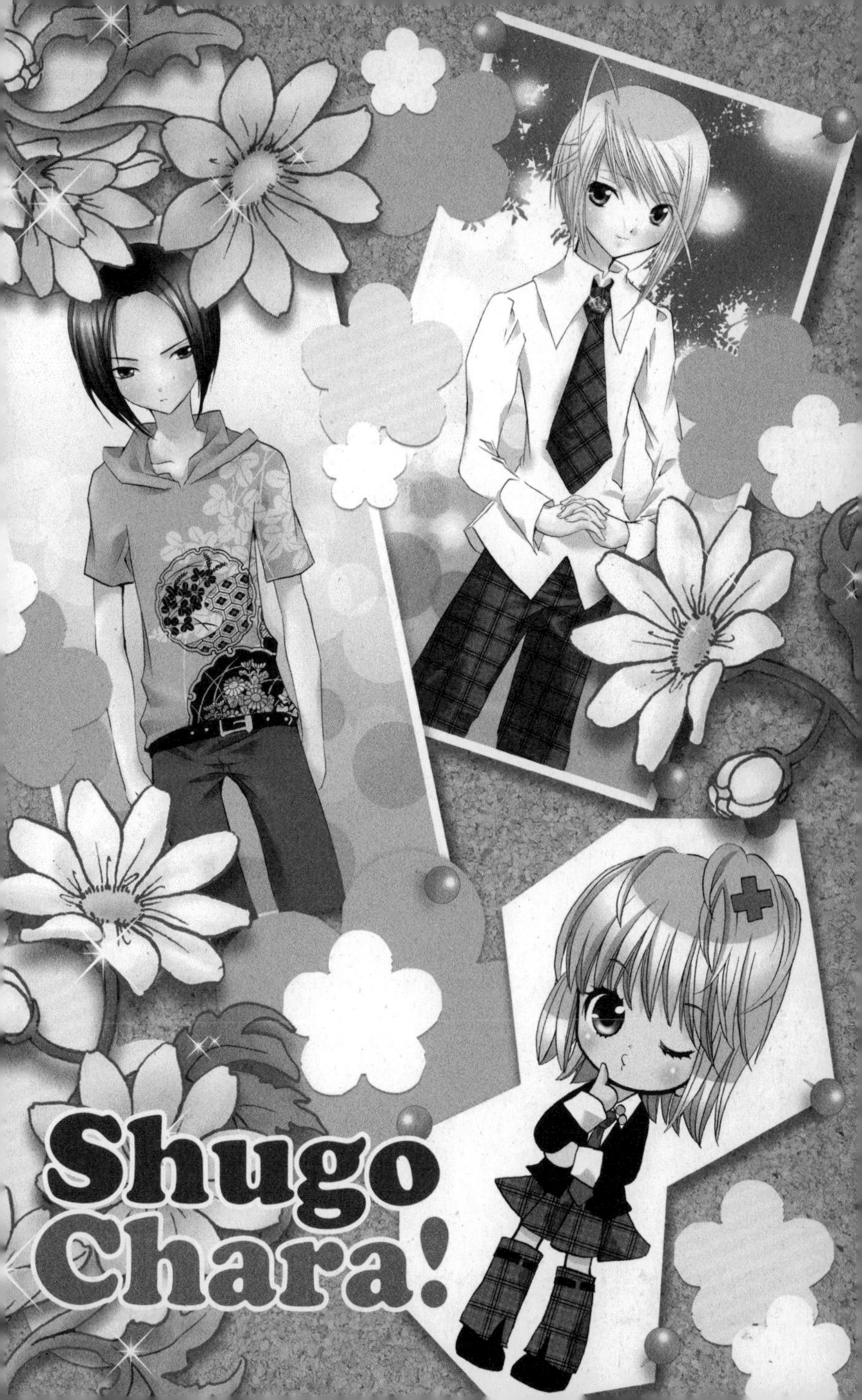
Shugo
Chara!

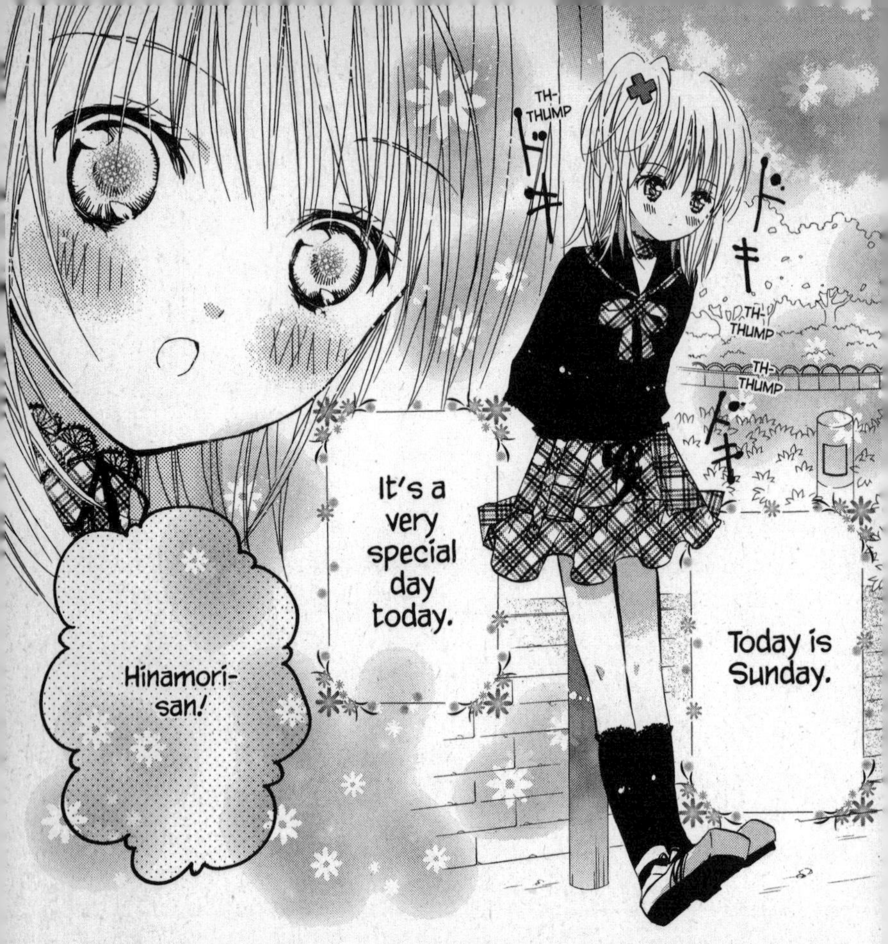
TH-THUMP
TH-THUMP
TH-THUMP
Today is Sunday.
It's a very special day today.
Hinamori-san!

Q4: Isn't Rima going to change her hair? Like tie it up?

A4: She has such long hair, it must be hot in the summer. If you would send us hairstyle ideas, we'd be really happy! For those of you whose ideas we choose, you can become Rima's slave (laugh). Okay, our Q&A for this volume is coming to an end. Please send us more! We'll work hard to answer them!

Many kids draw this, and it makes us smile ♡

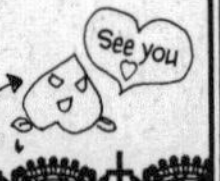
See you ♡

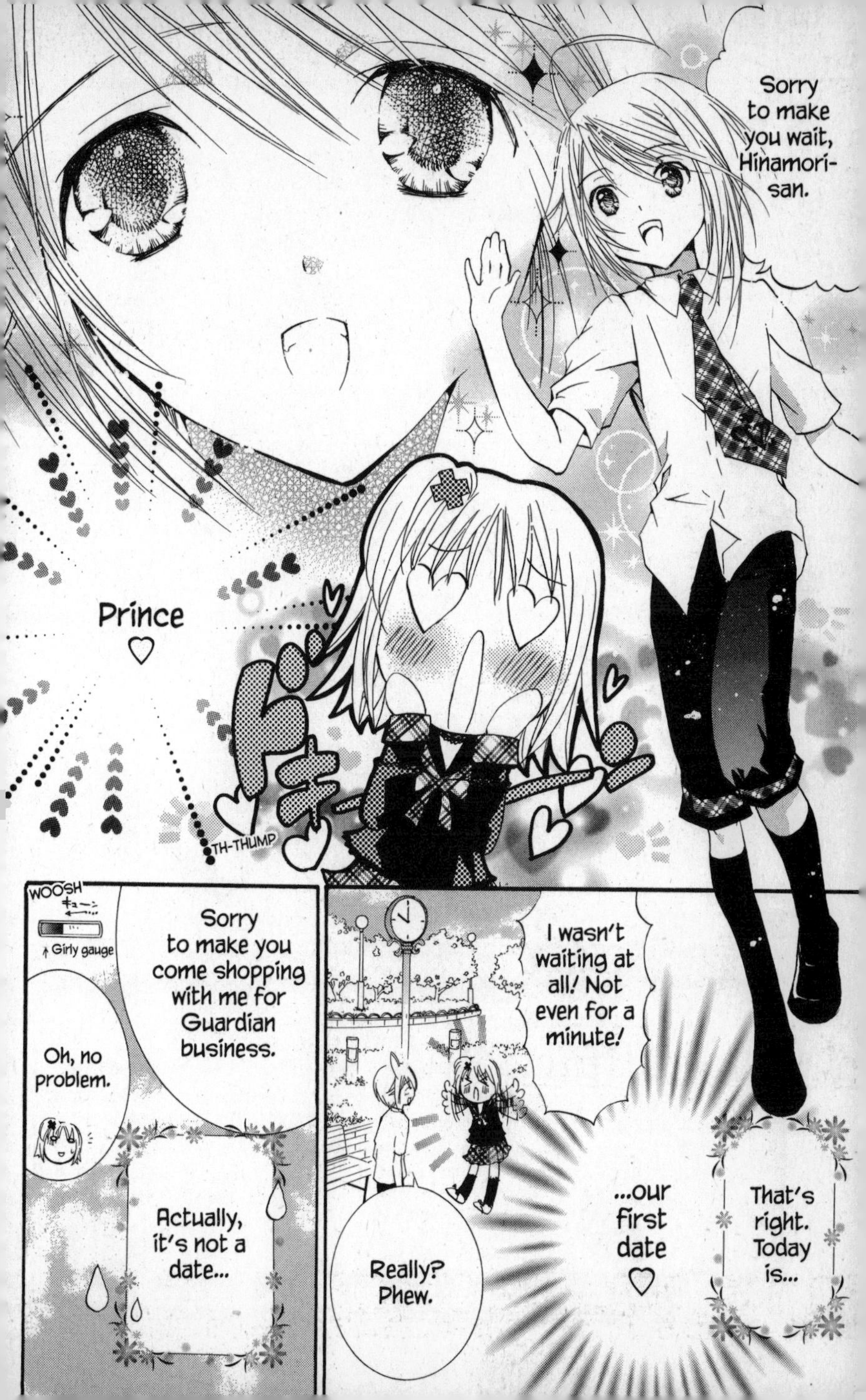
Sorry to make you wait, Hinamori-san.
Prince ♡
TH-THUMP
I wasn't waiting at all! Not even for a minute!
Really? Phew.
That's right. Today is...
...our first date ♡
WOOSH
↑ Girly gauge
Sorry to make you come shopping with me for Guardian business.
Oh, no problem.
Actually, it's not a date...

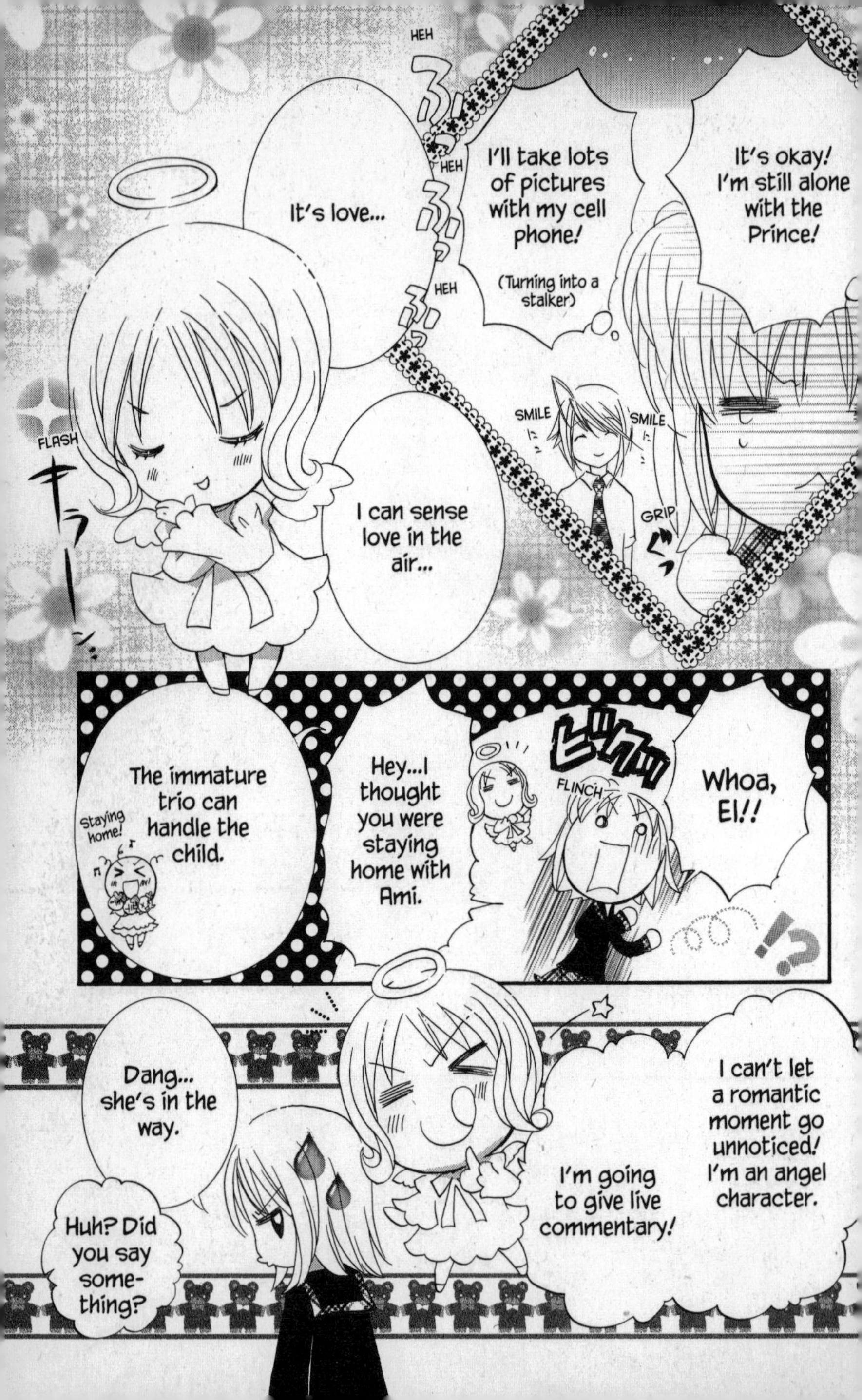

It's okay! I'm still alone with the Prince!
I'll take lots of pictures with my cell phone!
(Turning into a stalker)
HEH
HEH
HEH
It's love...
SMILE
SMILE
GRIP
I can sense love in the air...
FLASH
Whoa, El!!
FLINCH
Hey...I thought you were staying home with Ami.
The immature trio can handle the child.
Staying home!
I can't let a romantic moment go unnoticed! I'm an angel character.
I'm going to give live commentary!
Dang... she's in the way.
Huh? Did you say something?

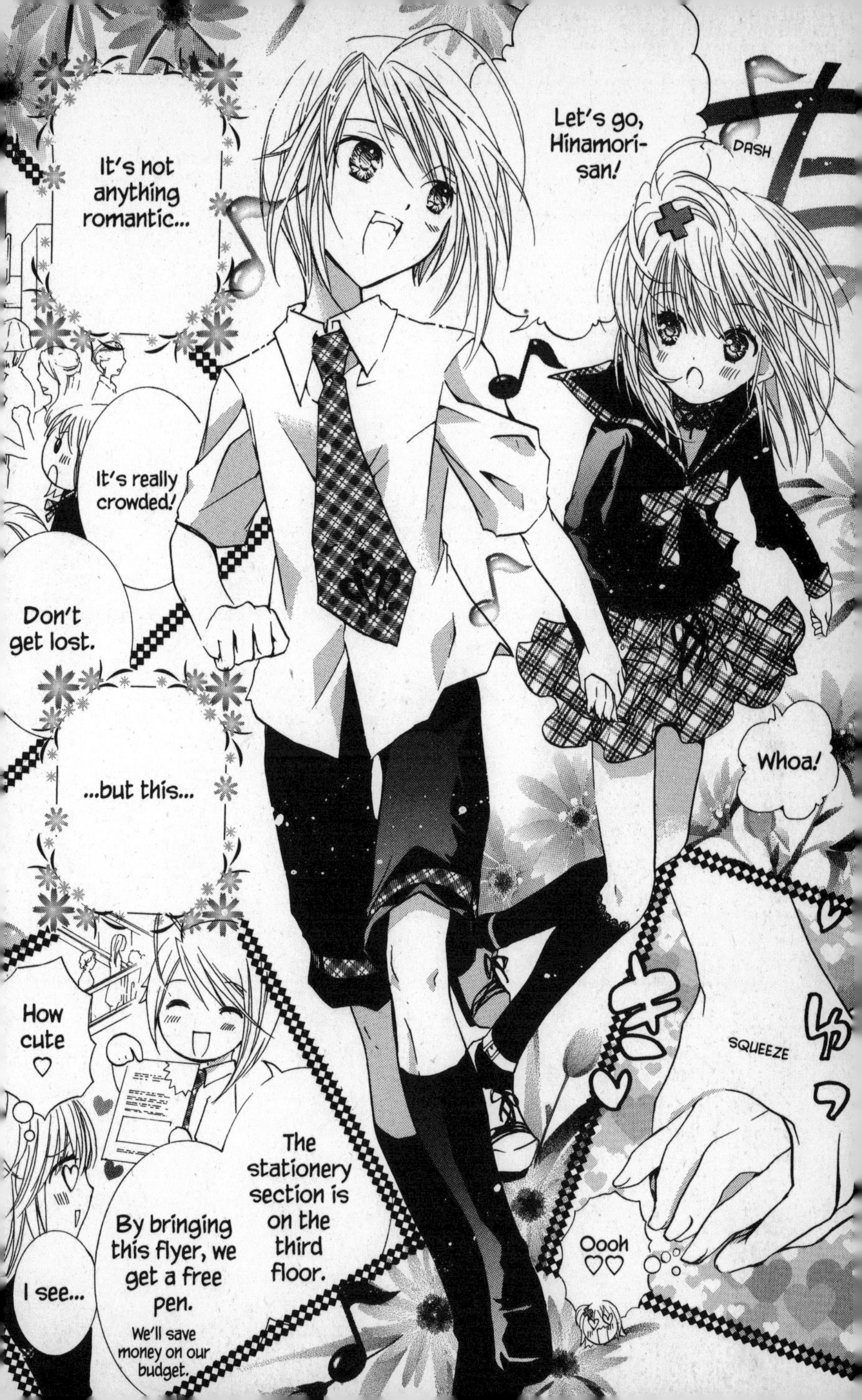
Let's go, Hinamori-san!
DASH
It's not anything romantic...
It's really crowded!
Don't get lost.
Whoa!
...but this...
SQUEEZE
Oooh ♡♡
The stationery section is on the third floor.
How cute ♡
By bringing this flyer, we get a free pen.
We'll save money on our budget.
I see...

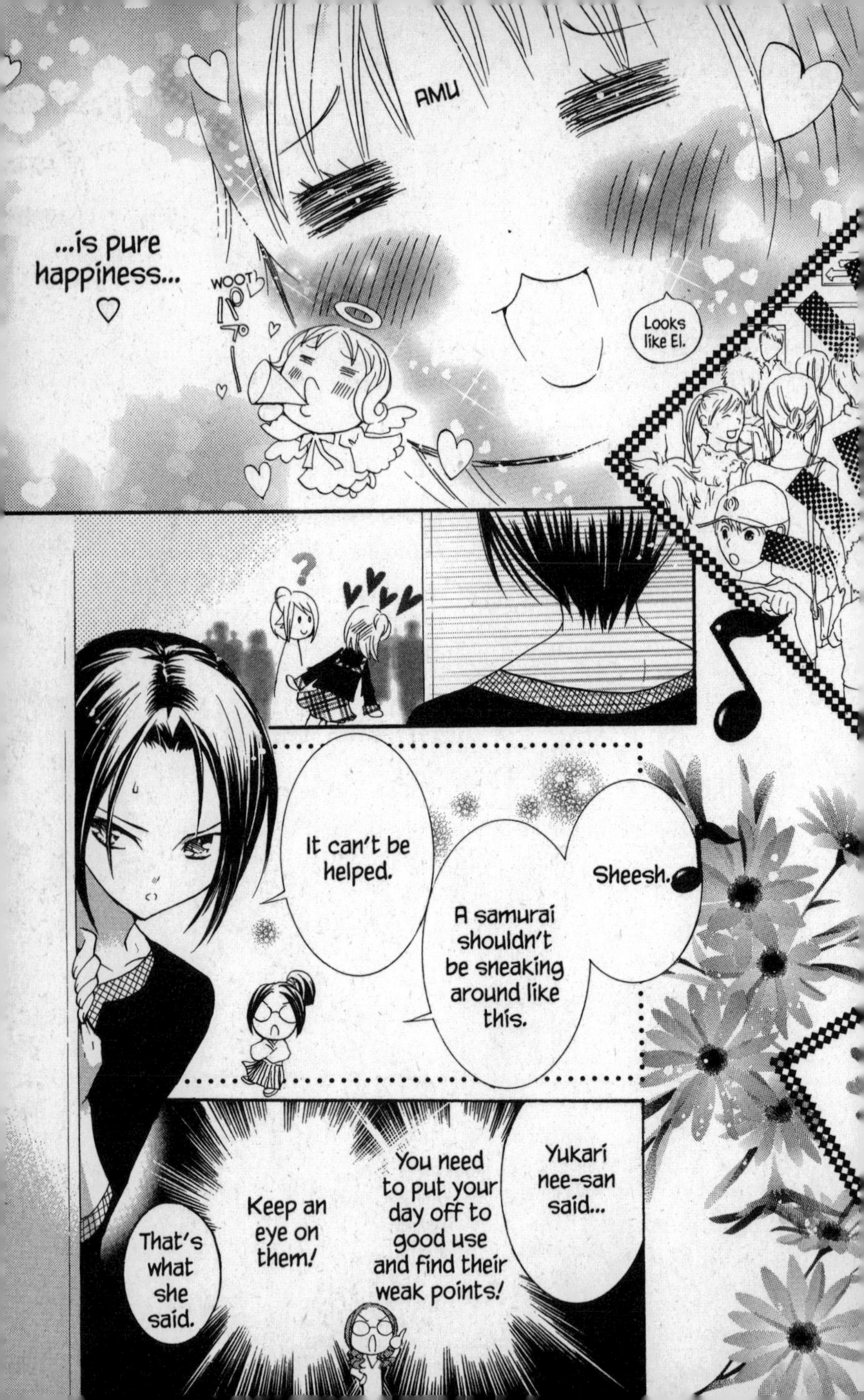
AMU
...is pure happiness... ♡
WOOT
Looks like El.
Sheesh.
A samurai shouldn't be sneaking around like this.
It can't be helped.
Yukari nee-san said...
You need to put your day off to good use and find their weak points!
Keep an eye on them!
That's what she said.

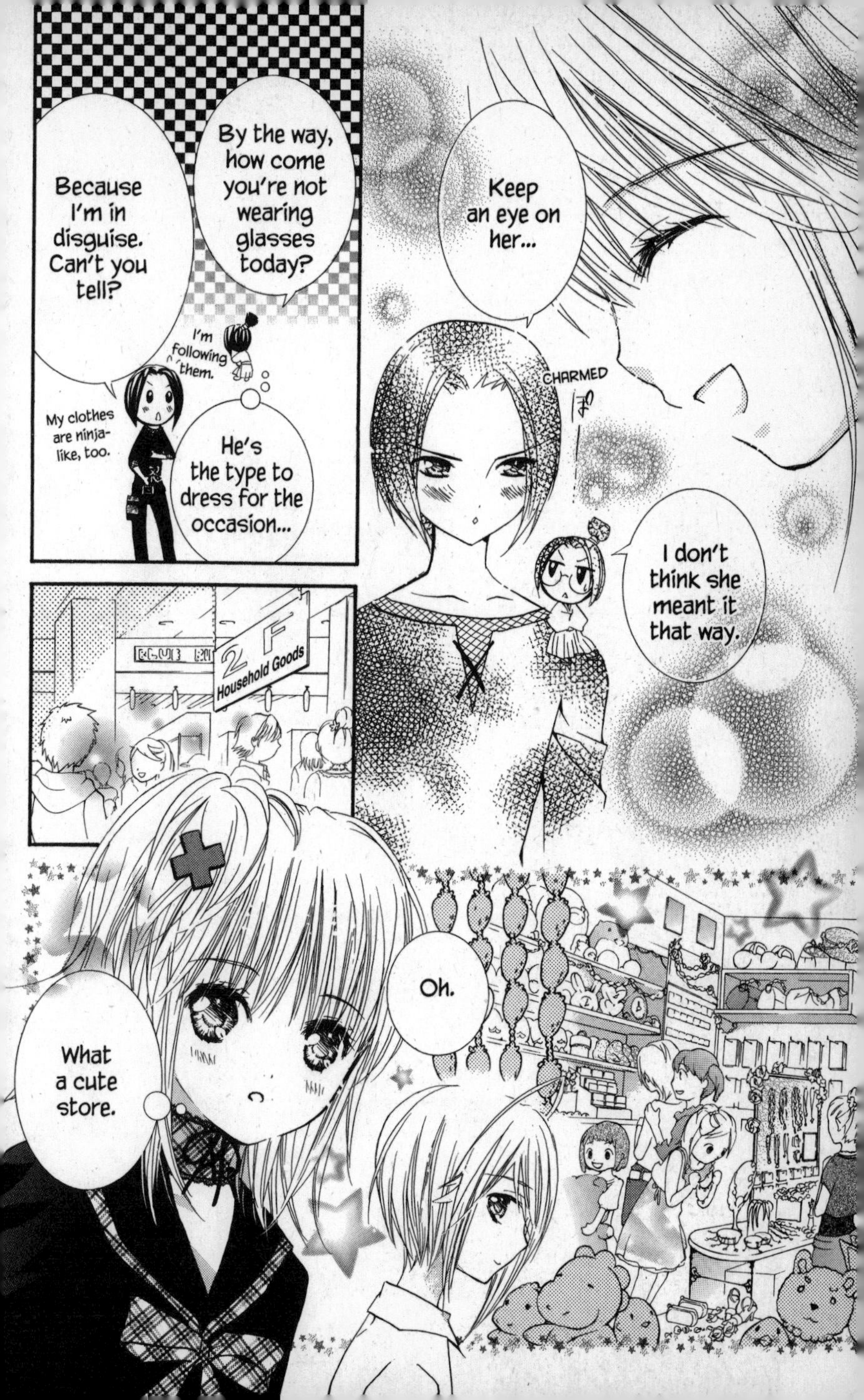

Keep an eye on her...
CHARMED
I don't think she meant it that way.
By the way, how come you're not wearing glasses today?
Because I'm in disguise. Can't you tell?
I'm following them.
He's the type to dress for the occasion...
My clothes are ninja-like, too.
2F
Household Goods
Oh.
What a cute store.

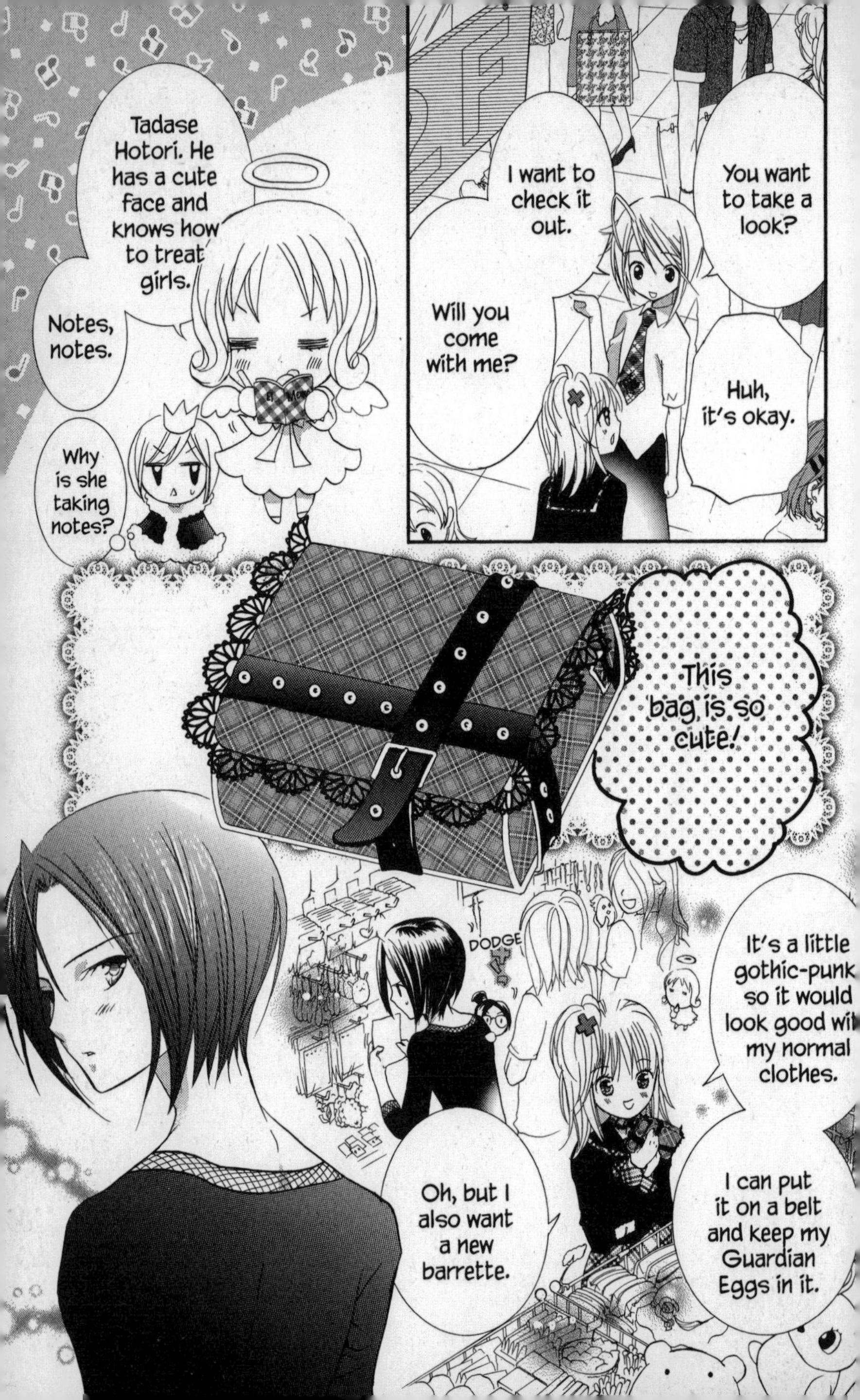
You want to take a look?
I want to check it out.
Huh, it's okay.
Will you come with me?
Tadase Hotori. He has a cute face and knows how to treat girls.
Notes, notes.
Why is she taking notes?
This bag is so cute!
It's a little gothic-punk so it would look good wit my normal clothes.
DODGE
I can put it on a belt and keep my Guardian Eggs in it.
Oh, but I also want a new barrette.

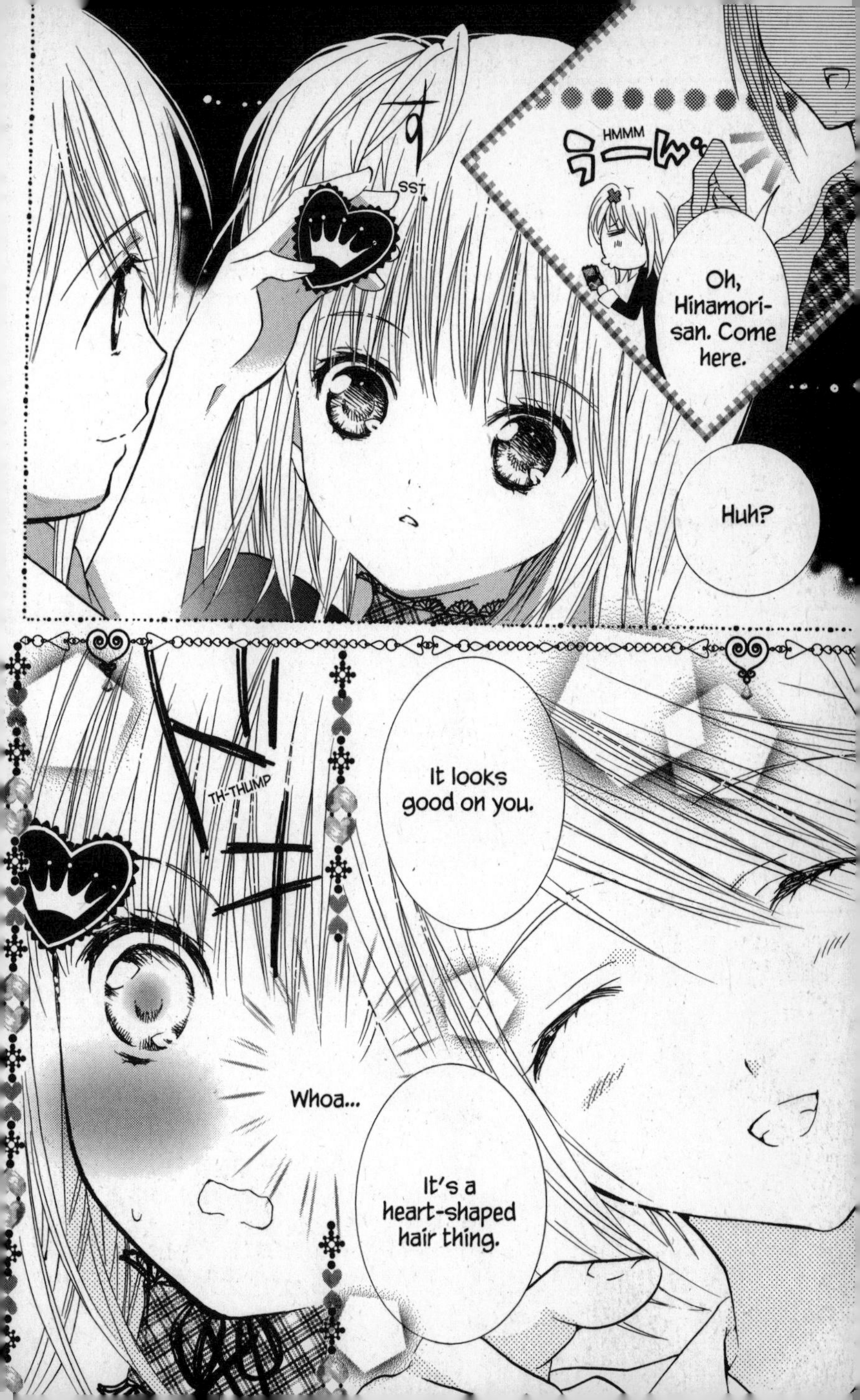
HMMM
Oh, Hinamori-san. Come here.
Huh?
SST
It looks good on you.
Whoa...
It's a heart-shaped hair thing.
TH-THUMP

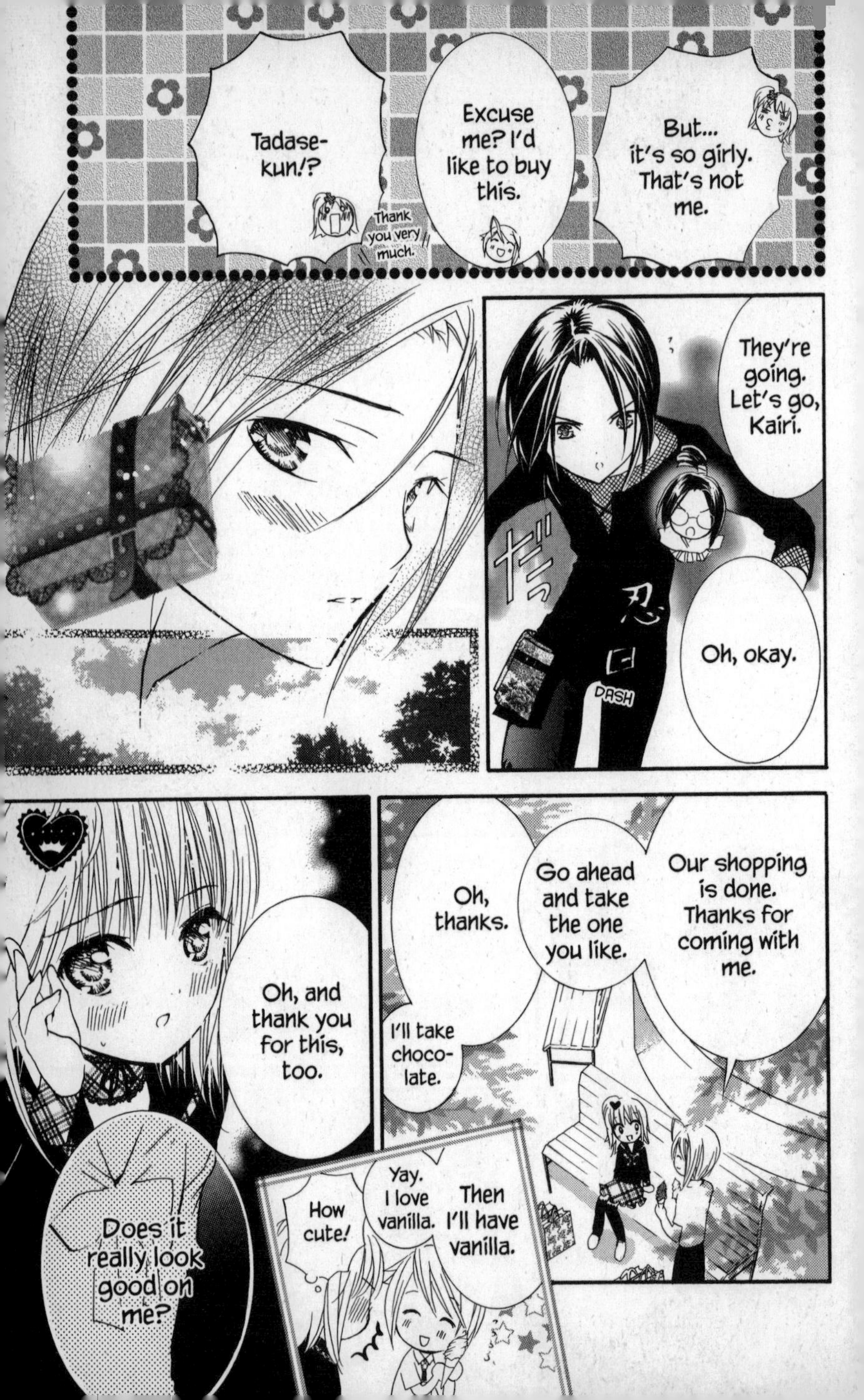
But... it's so girly. That's not me.
Excuse me? I'd like to buy this.
Thank you very much.
Tadase-kun!?
They're going. Let's go, Kairi.
Oh, okay.
DASH
Our shopping is done. Thanks for coming with me.
Go ahead and take the one you like.
Oh, thanks.
I'll take chocolate.
Then I'll have vanilla.
Yay. I love vanilla.
How cute!
Oh, and thank you for this, too.
Does it really look good on me?

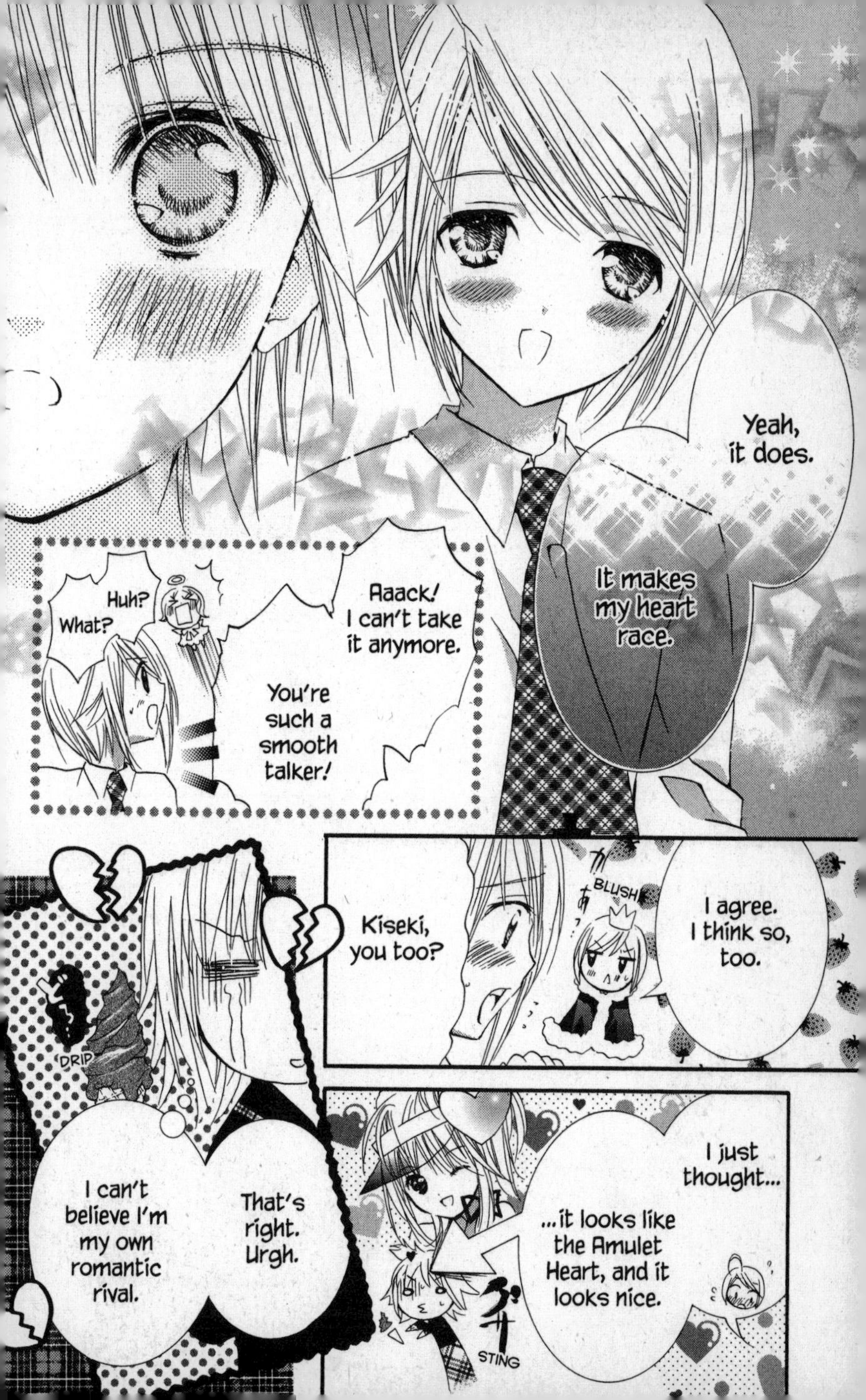

Yeah, it does.
It makes my heart race.
Aaack! I can't take it anymore.
You're such a smooth talker!
Huh? What?
I agree. I think so, too.
BLUSH
Kiseki, you too?
I just thought...
...it looks like the Amulet Heart, and it looks nice.
STING
DRIP
That's right. Urgh.
I can't believe I'm my own romantic rival.

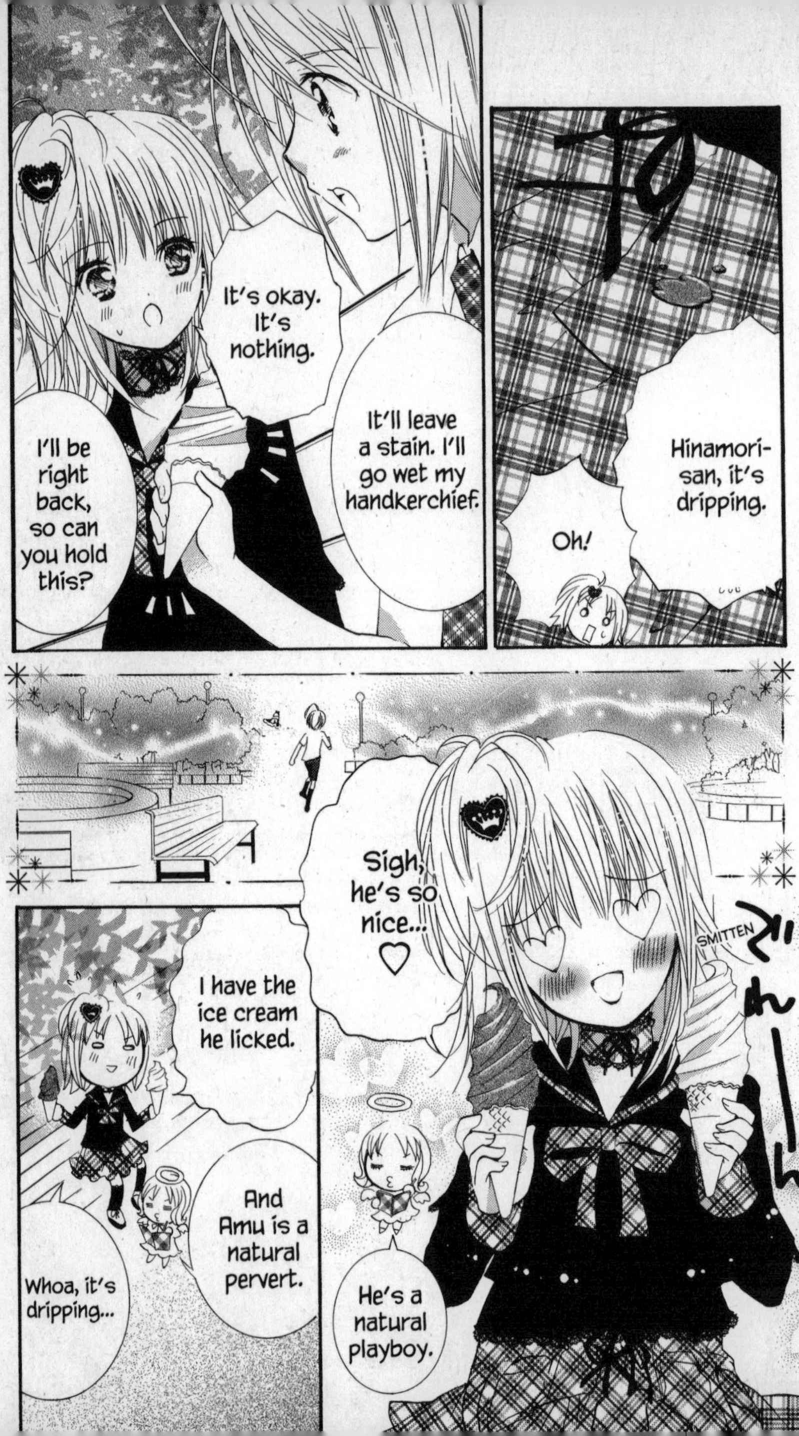

Hinamori-san, it's dripping.
Oh!
It's okay. It's nothing.
It'll leave a stain. I'll go wet my handkerchief.
I'll be right back, so can you hold this?
Sigh, he's so nice... ♡
SMITTEN
He's a natural playboy.
I have the ice cream he licked.
And Amu is a natural pervert.
Whoa, it's dripping...

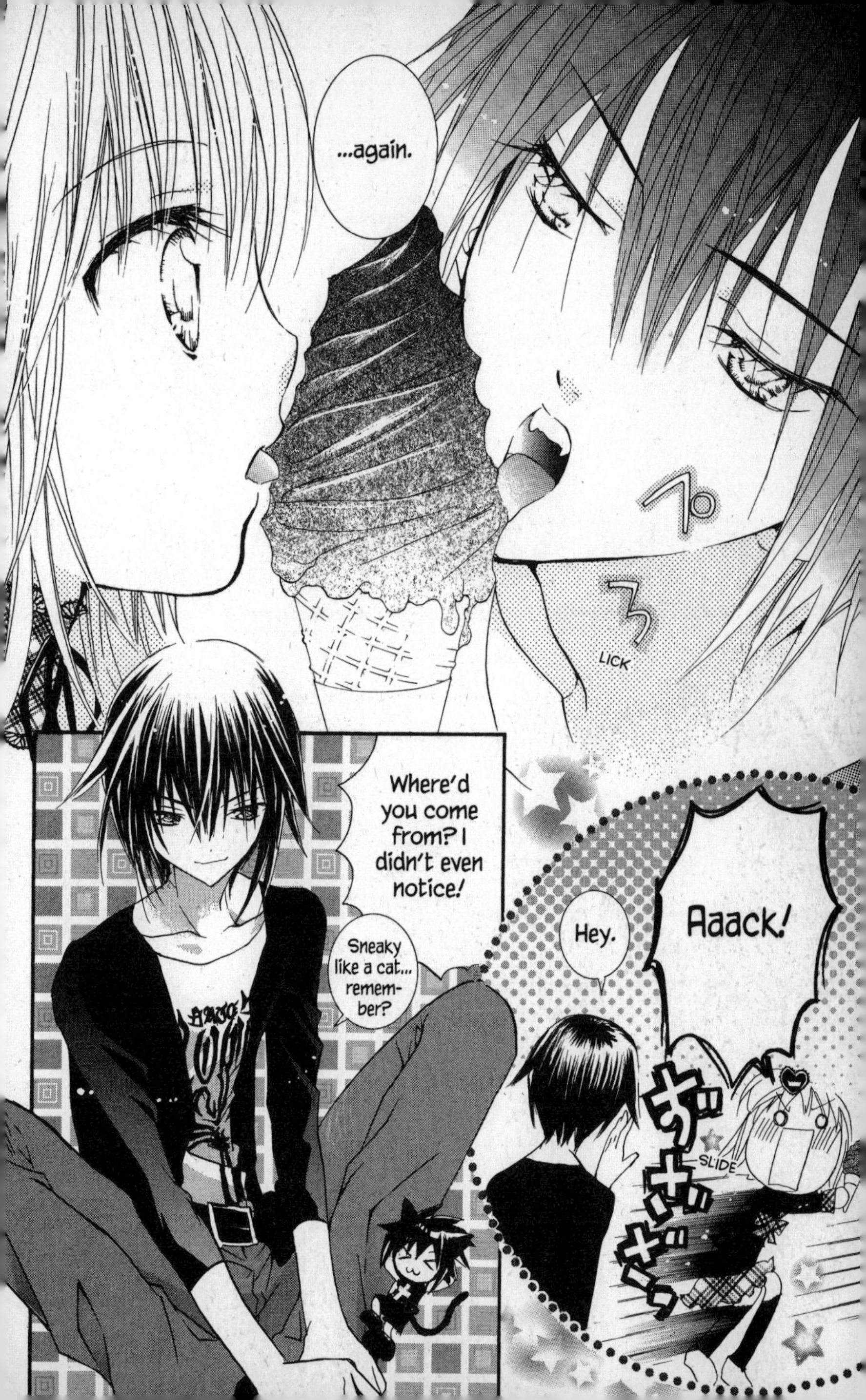
...again.
LICK
Aaack!
Hey.
SLIDE
Where'd you come from? I didn't even notice!
Sneaky like a cat... remember?

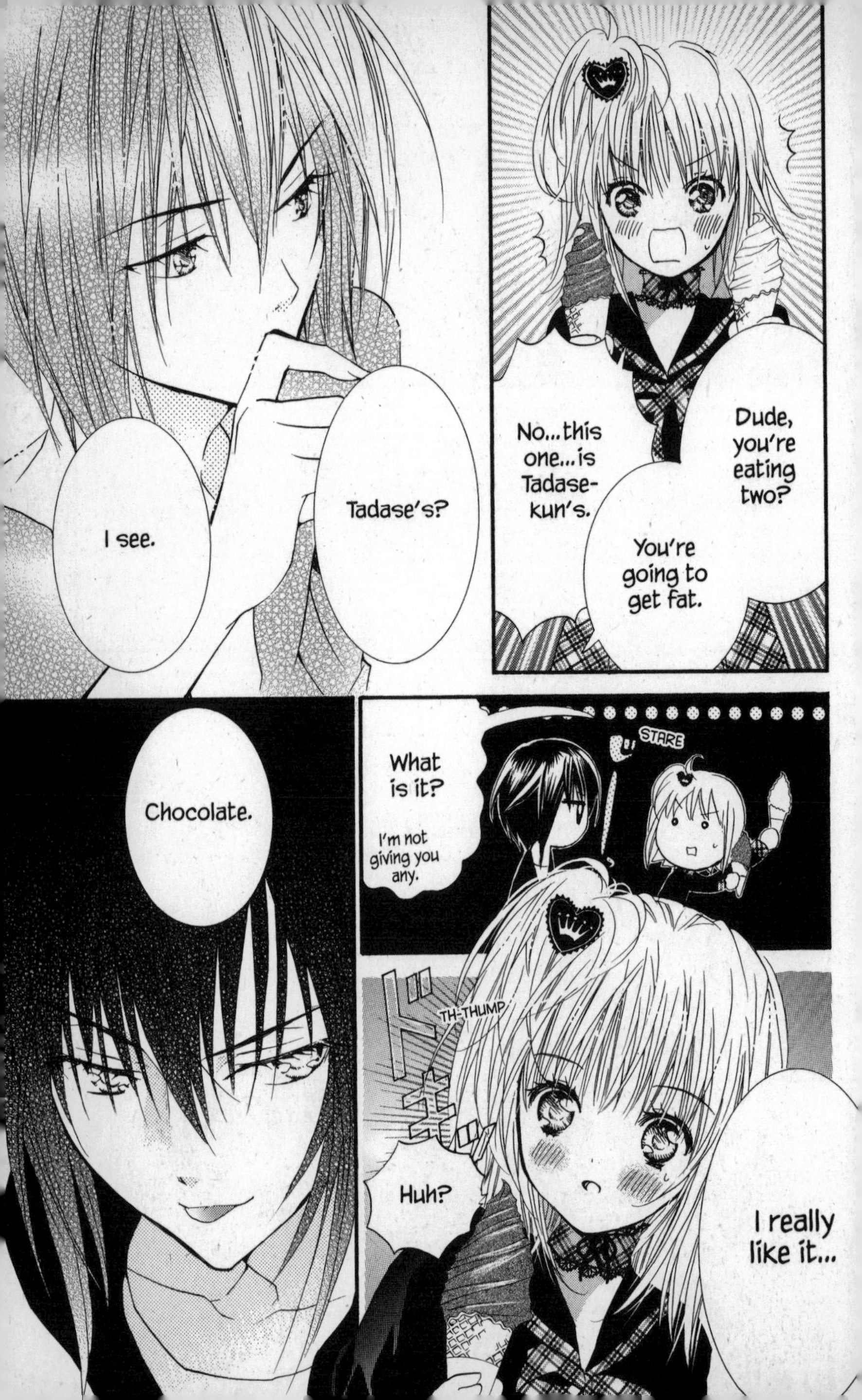
Dude, you're eating two?
You're going to get fat.
No...this one...is Tadase-kun's.
Tadase's?
I see.
STARE
What is it?
I'm not giving you any.
I really like it...
TH-THUMP
Huh?
Chocolate.

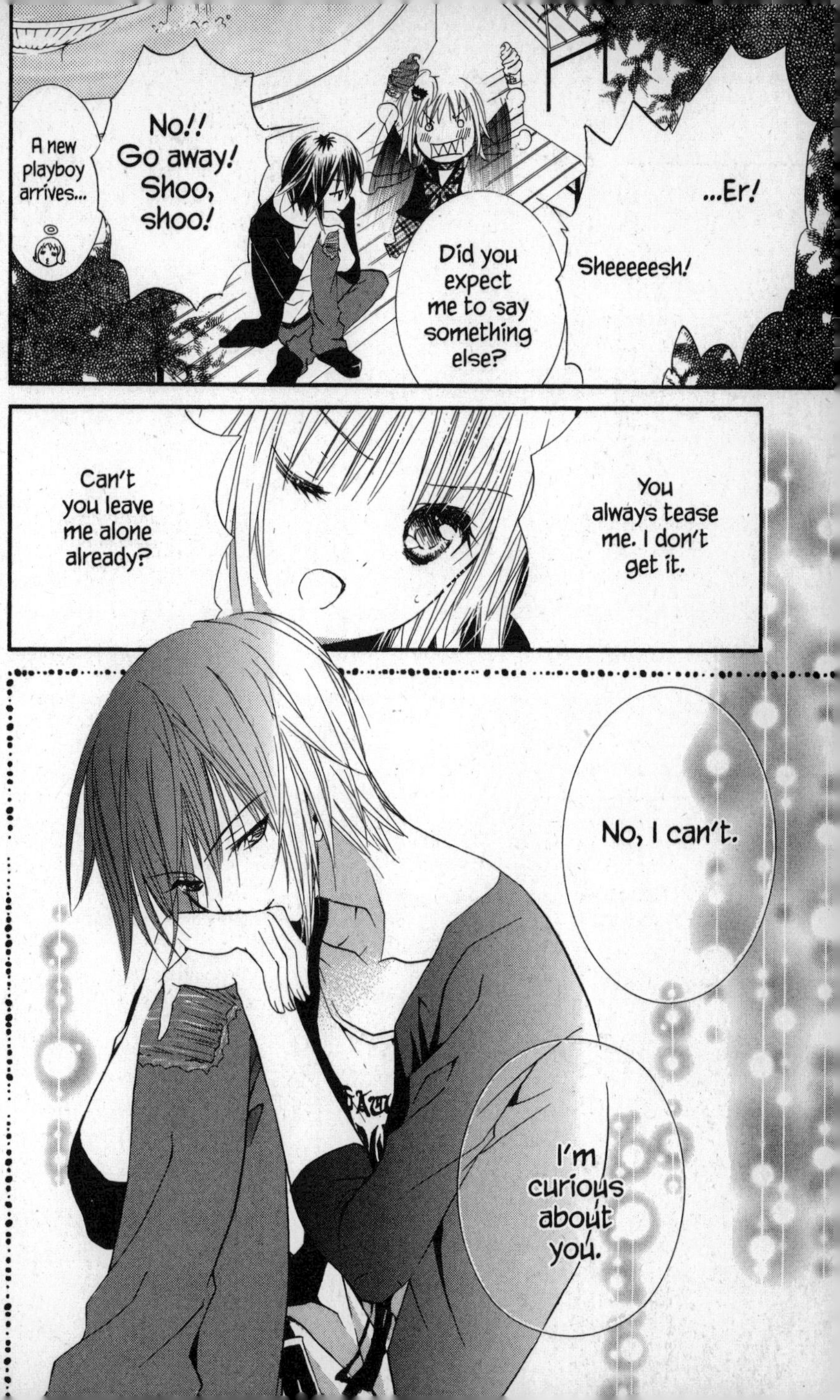
...Er!
Sheeeeesh!
Did you expect me to say something else?
No!! Go away! Shoo, shoo!
A new playboy arrives...
You always tease me. I don't get it.
Can't you leave me alone already?
No, I can't.
I'm curious about you.

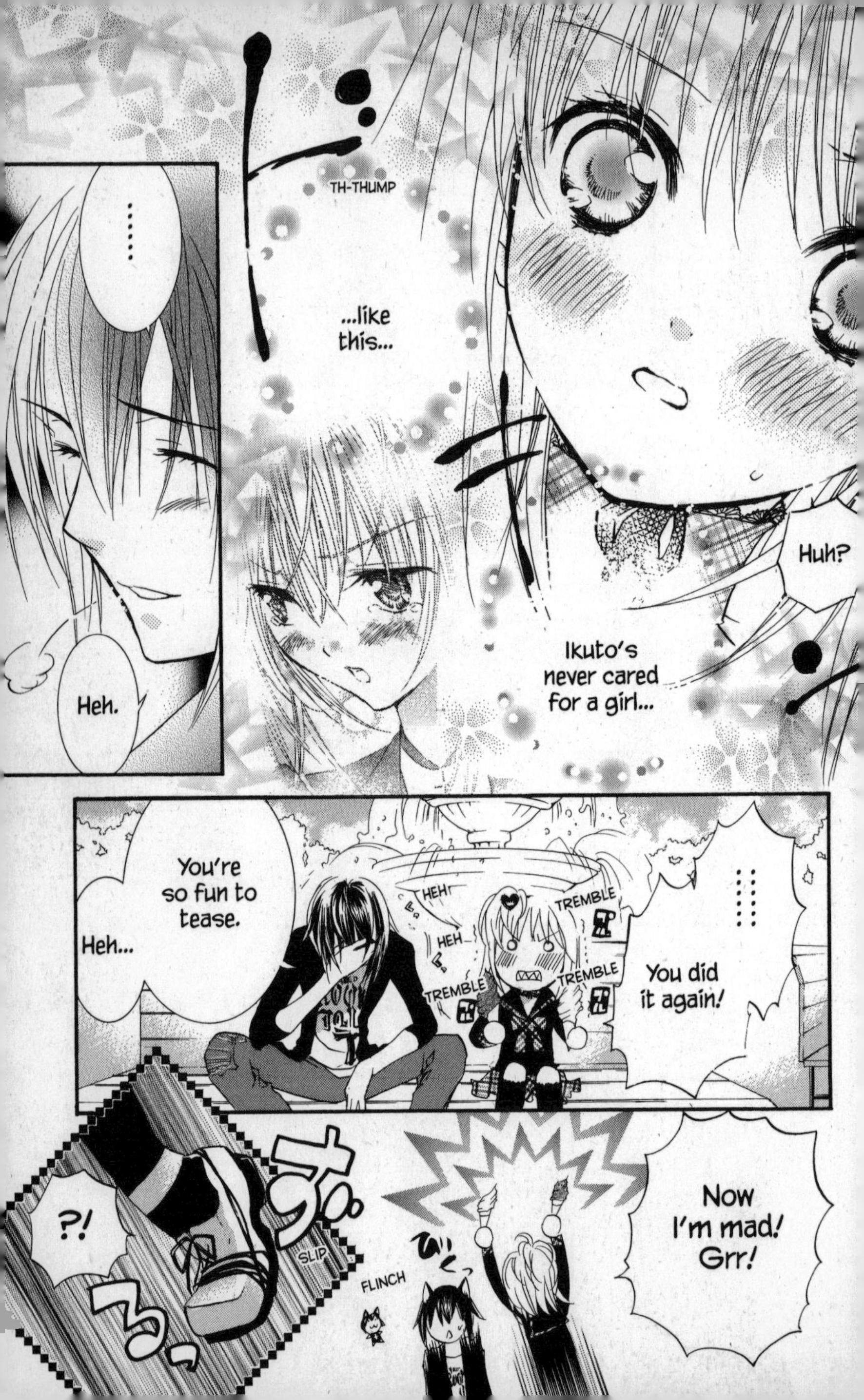
TH-THUMP
...like this...
Huh?
Ikuto's never cared for a girl...
......
Heh.
......
You did it again!
TREMBLE
TREMBLE
TREMBLE
HEH
HEH
You're so fun to tease.
Heh...
Now I'm mad! Grr!
FLINCH
SLIP
?!

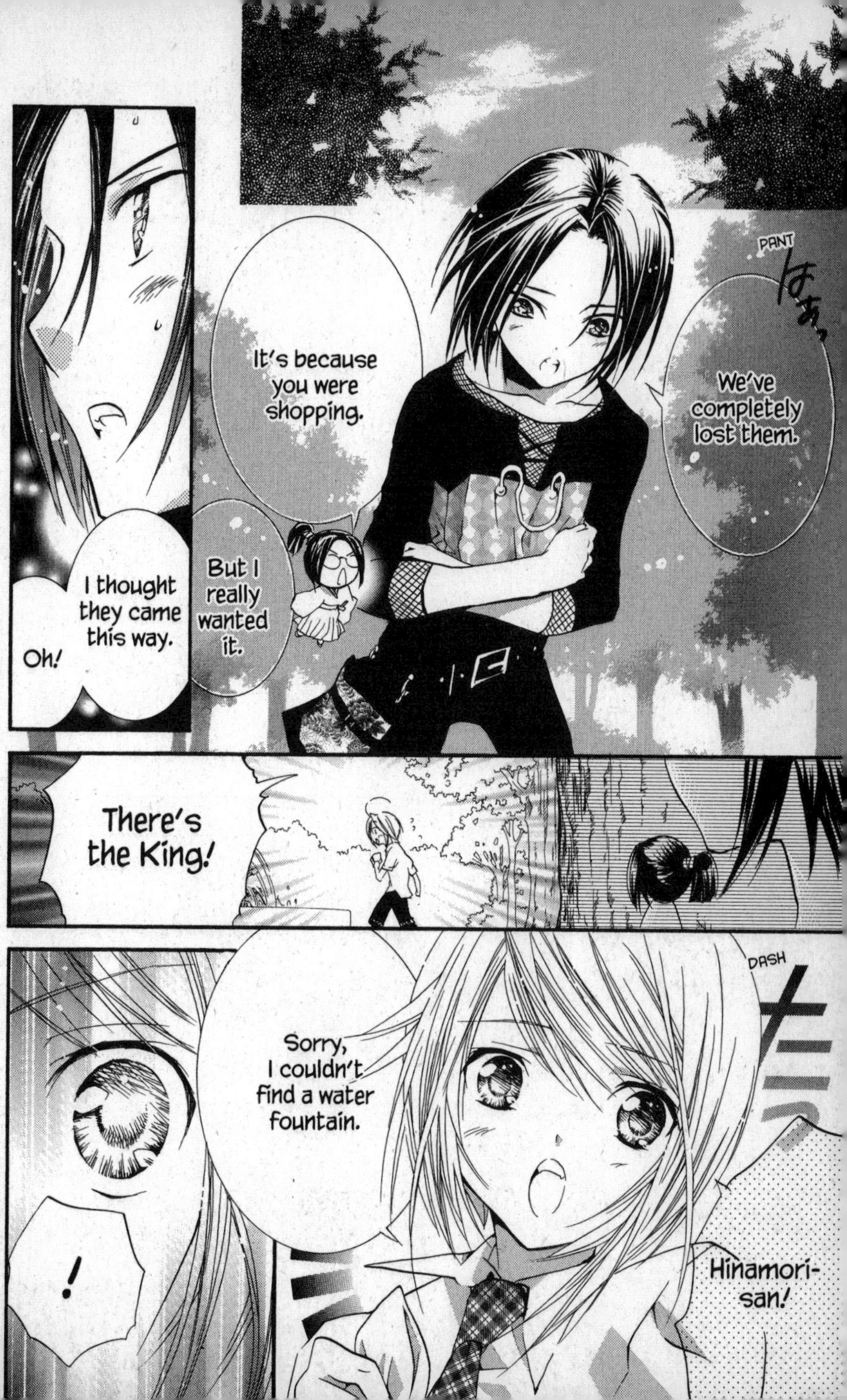
PANT
We've completely lost them.
It's because you were shopping.
But I really wanted it.
I thought they came this way.
Oh!
There's the King!
DASH
Hinamori-san!
Sorry, I couldn't find a water fountain.
!

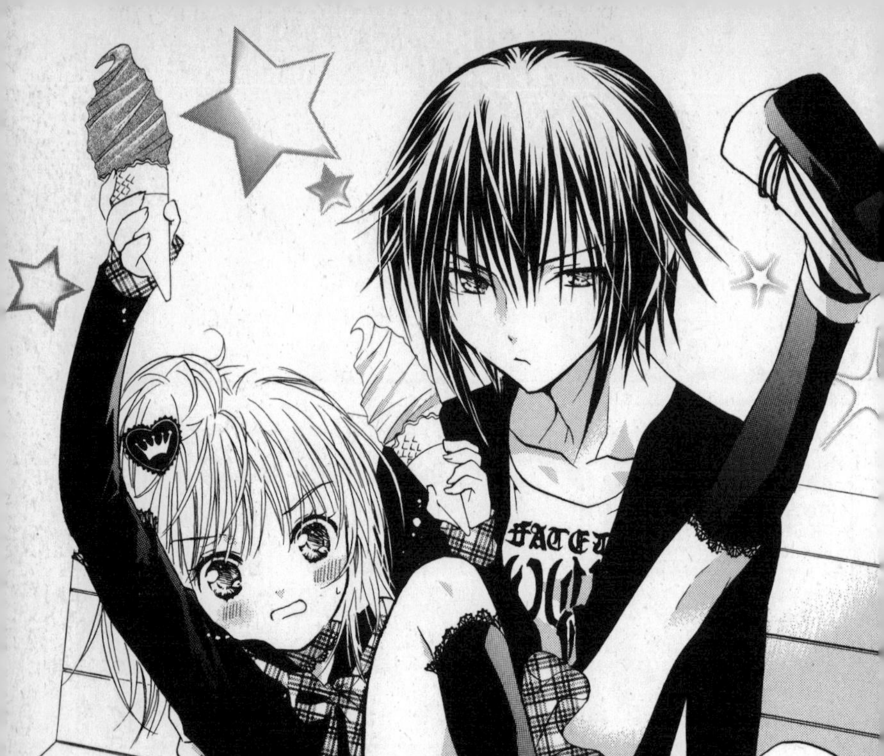
Ta..dase-
kun...

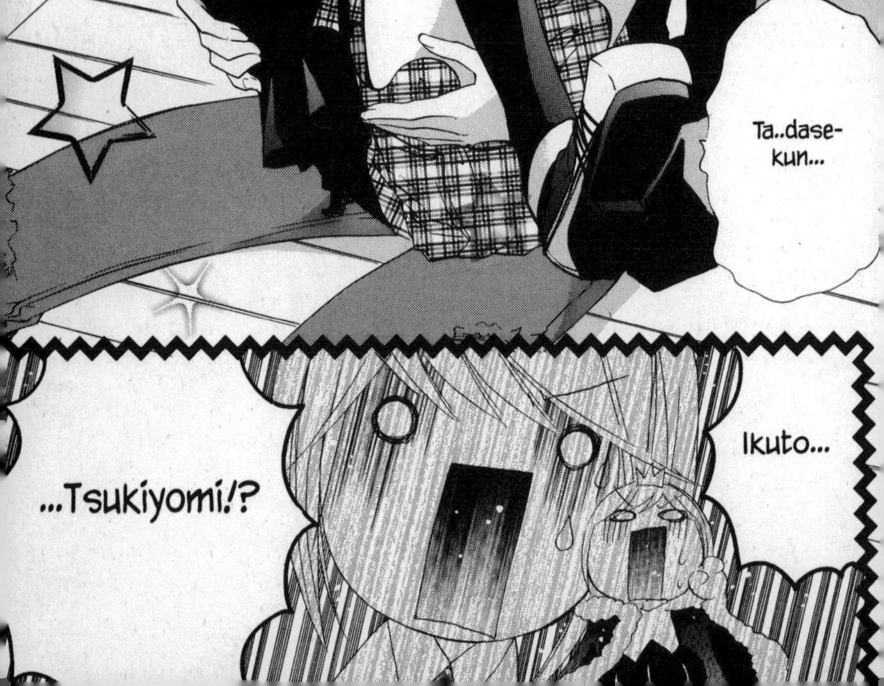
Ikuto...
...Tsukiyomi!?

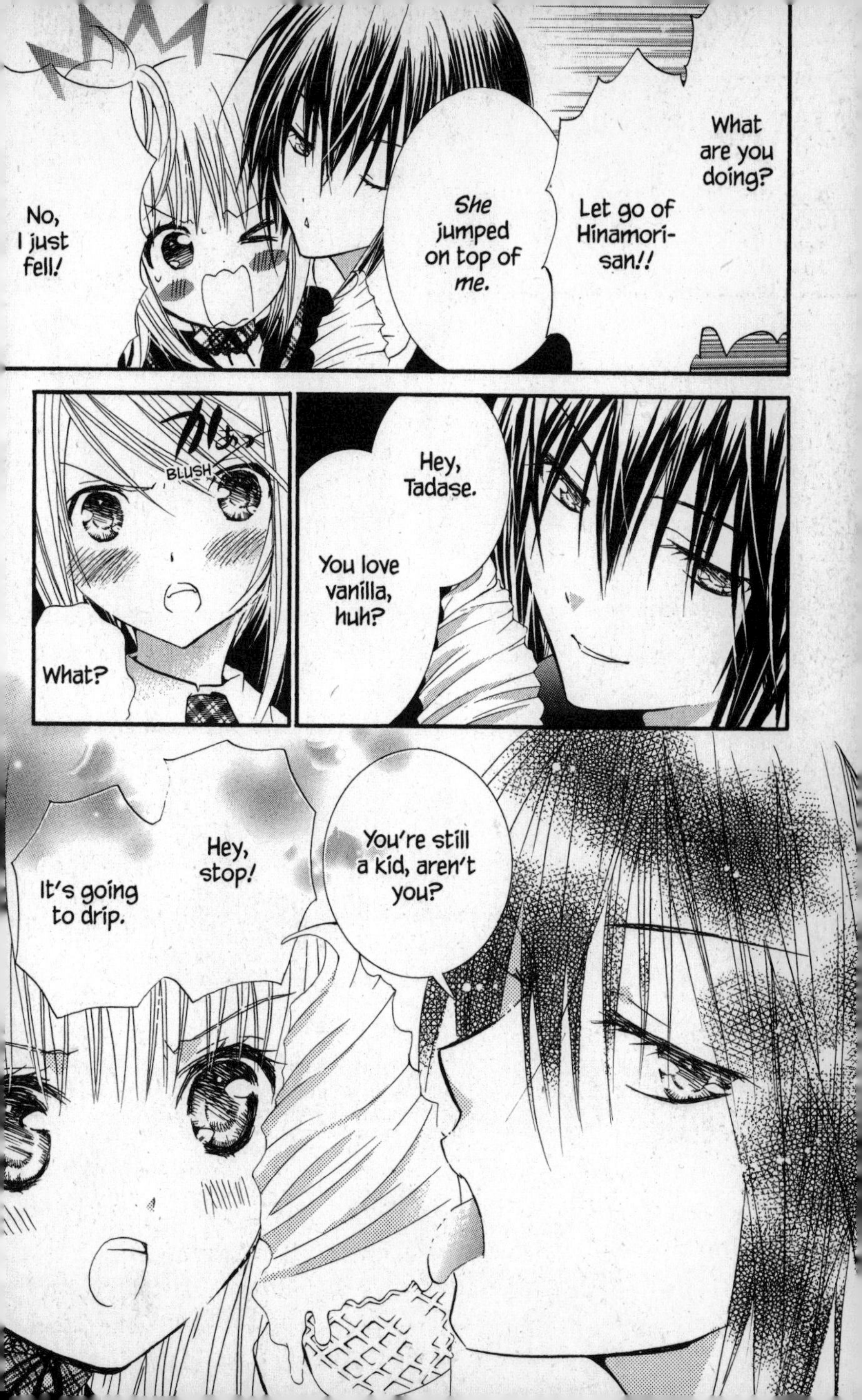
What are you doing?
Let go of Hinamori-san!!
She jumped on top of me.
No, I just fell!
Hey, Tadase.
You love vanilla, huh?
BLUSH
What?
You're still a kid, aren't you?
Hey, stop!
It's going to drip.

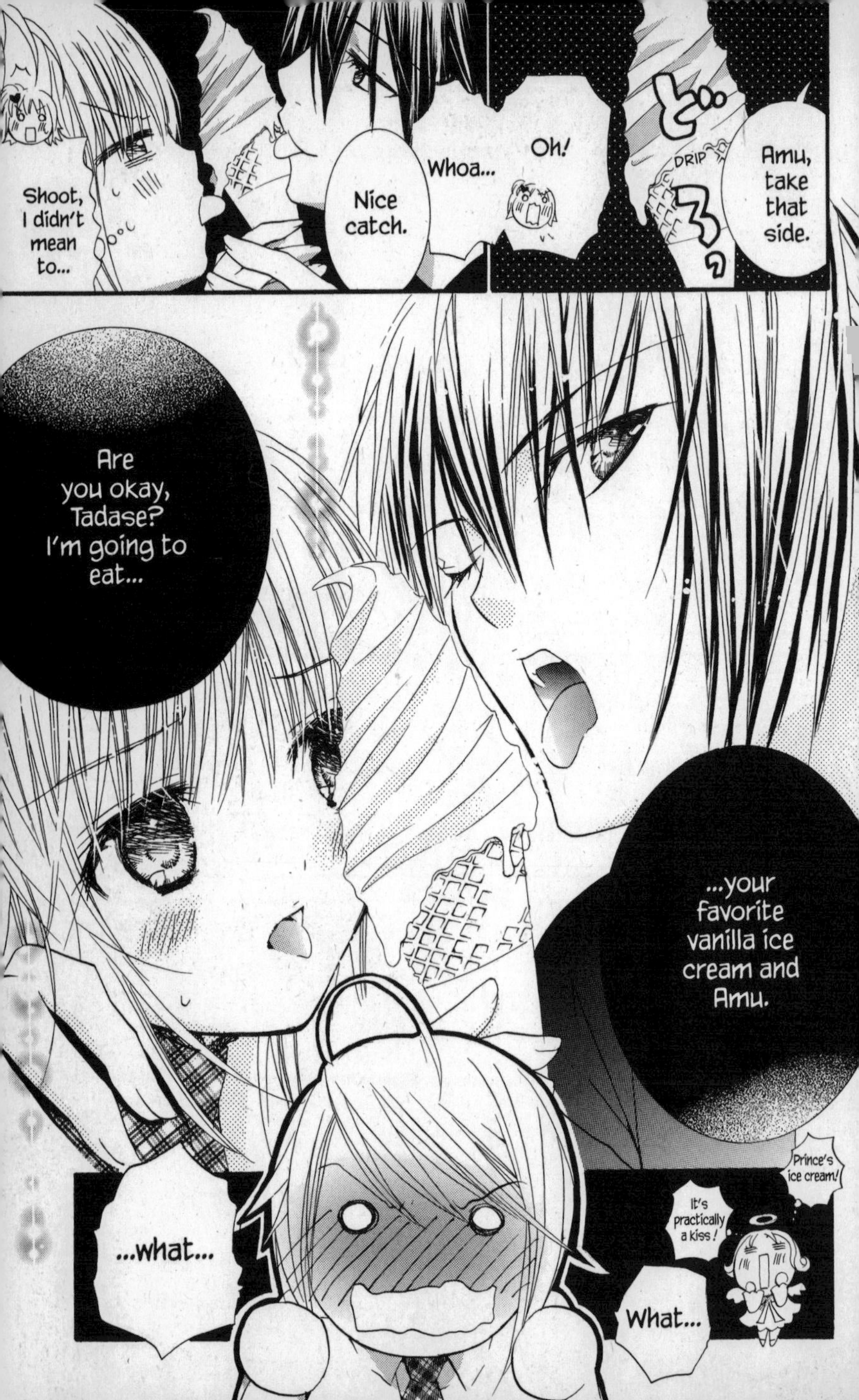
Amu, take that side.
DRIP
Oh!
Whoa...
Nice catch.
Shoot, I didn't mean to...
Are you okay, Tadase? I'm going to eat...
...your favorite vanilla ice cream and Amu.
Prince's ice cream!
It's practically a kiss!
What...
...what...

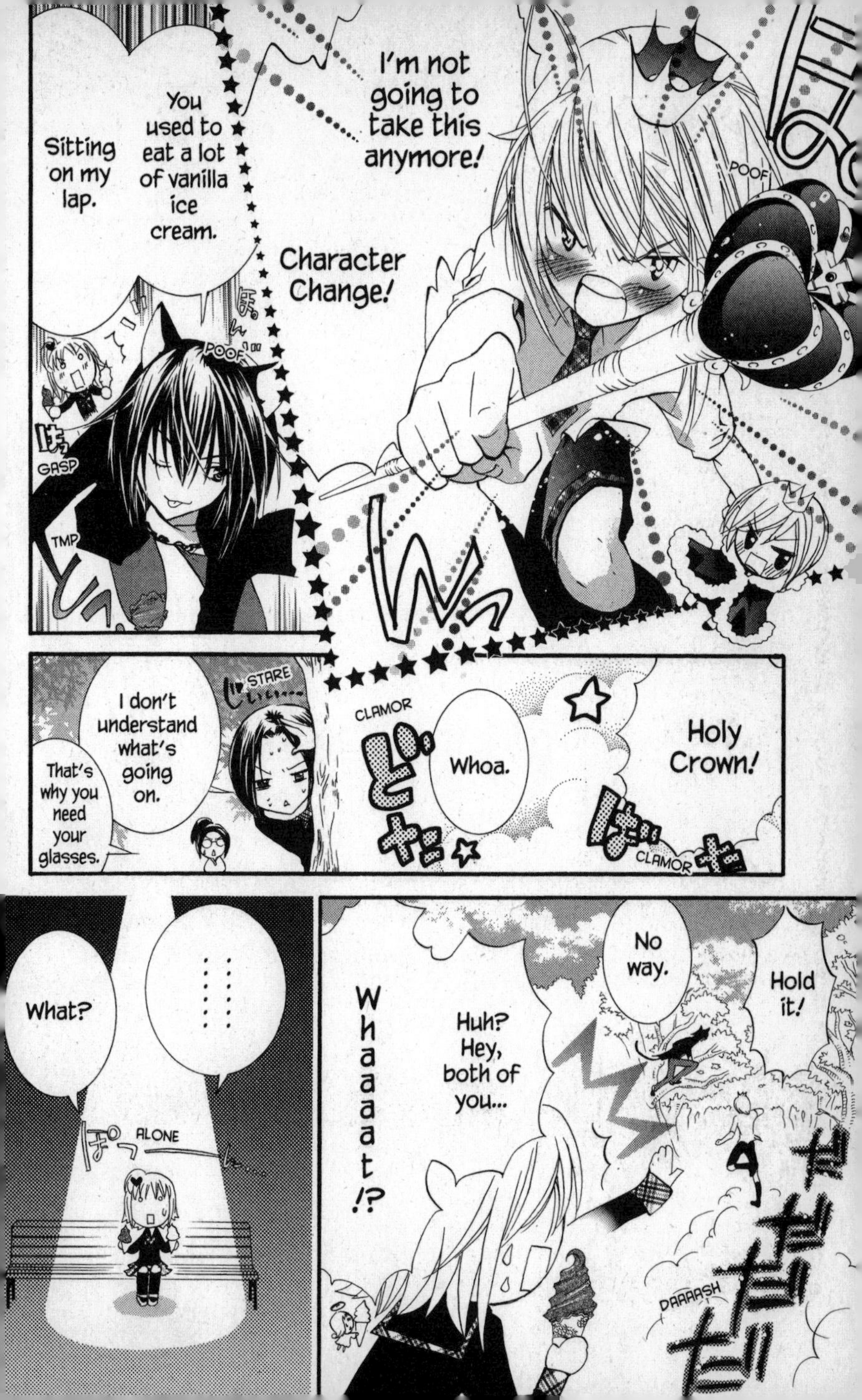

I'm not going to take this anymore!
POOF
Character Change!
You used to eat a lot of vanilla ice cream.
Sitting on my lap.
POOF
GASP
TMP
Holy Crown!
Whoa.
CLAMOR
CLAMOR
STARE
I don't understand what's going on.
That's why you need your glasses.
Hold it!
No way.
Huh? Hey, both of you...
Whaaaat!?
DAAAASH
......
What?
ALONE

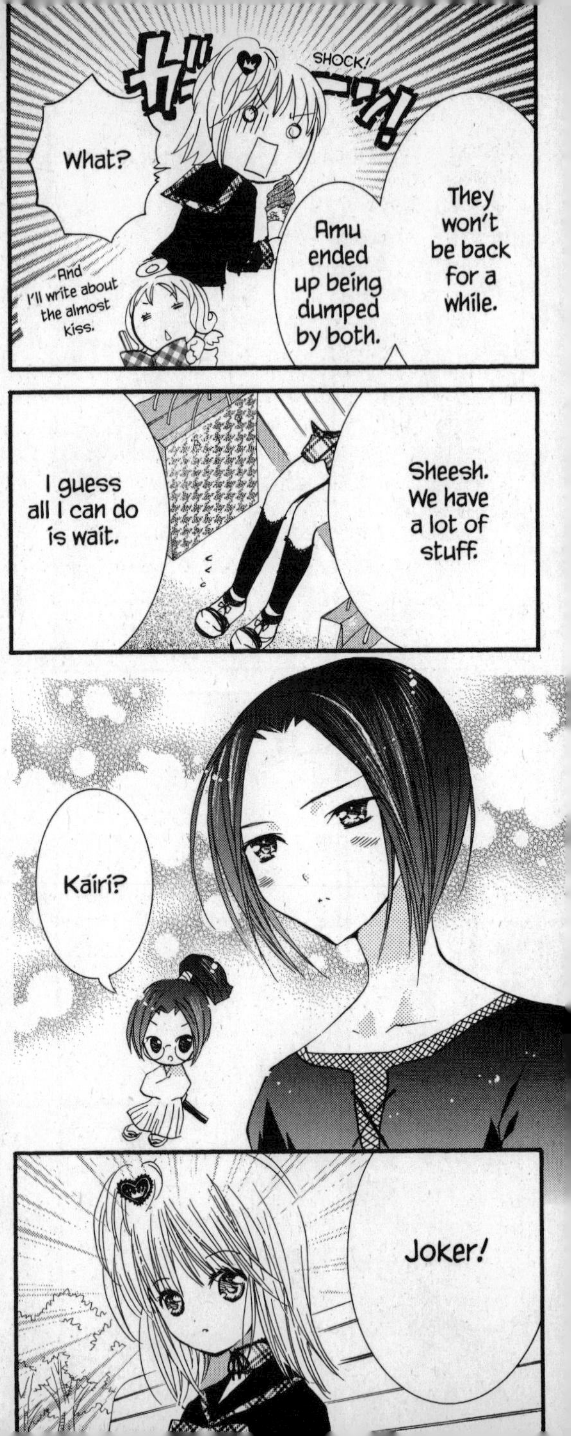
They won't be back for a while.
Amu ended up being dumped by both.
SHOCK!
What?
And I'll write about the almost kiss.
Sheesh. We have a lot of stuff.
I guess all I can do is wait.
Kairi?
Joker!

character profile

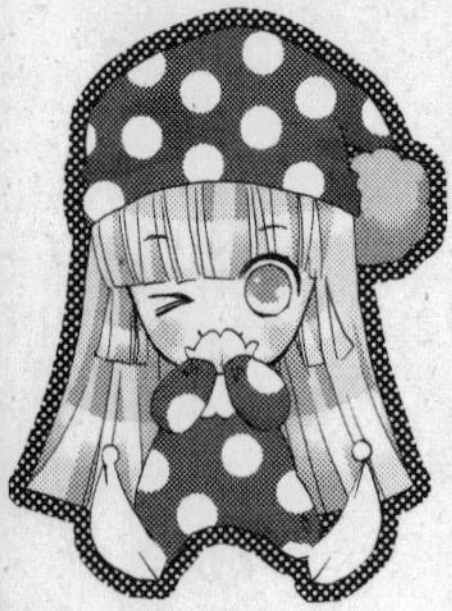

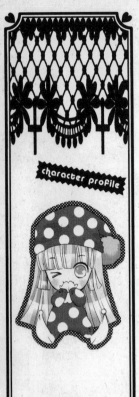

KUSUKUSU

Guardian Character of: Rima
Special Skill: Comedy
Hates: Staring

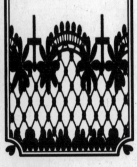

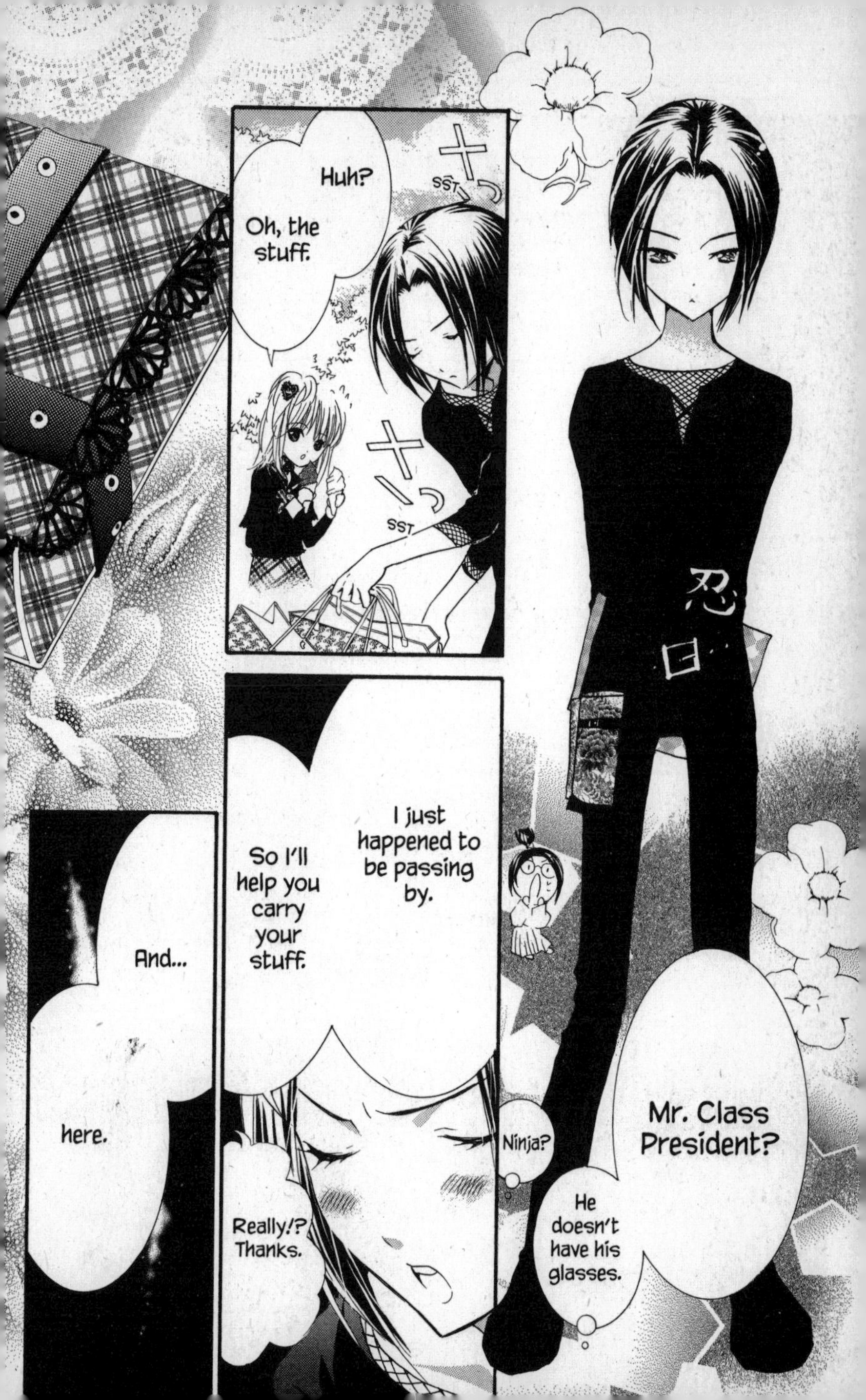
Mr. Class President?
Ninja?
He doesn't have his glasses.
SST
Huh?
Oh, the stuff.
SST
I just happened to be passing by.
So I'll help you carry your stuff.
Really!? Thanks.
And...
here.

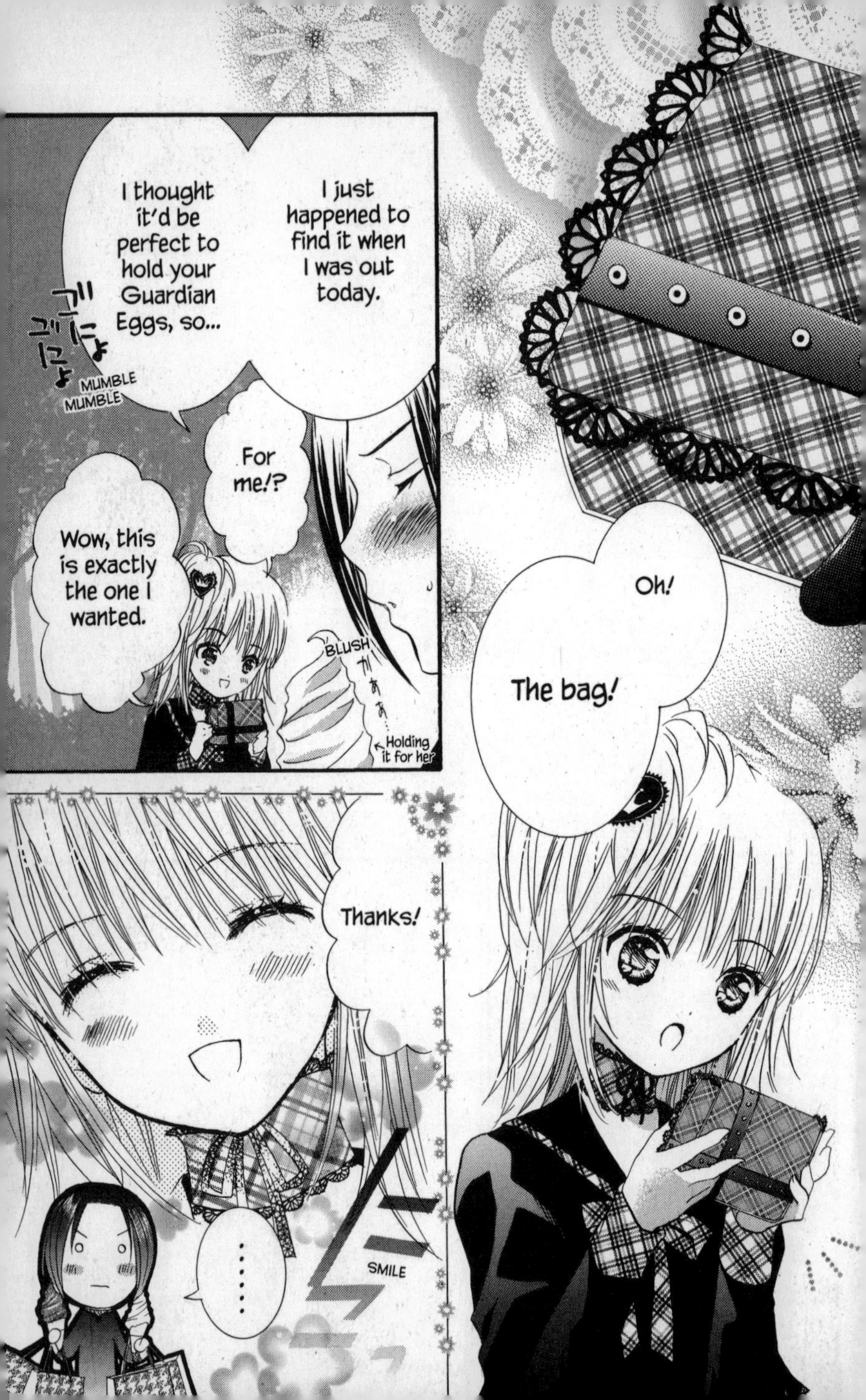
Oh!
The bag!
I just happened to find it when I was out today.
I thought it'd be perfect to hold your Guardian Eggs, so...
ごにょごにょ
MUMBLE MUMBLE
For me!?
Wow, this is exactly the one I wanted.
BLUSH
かああ…
← Holding it for her
Thanks!
SMILE
......

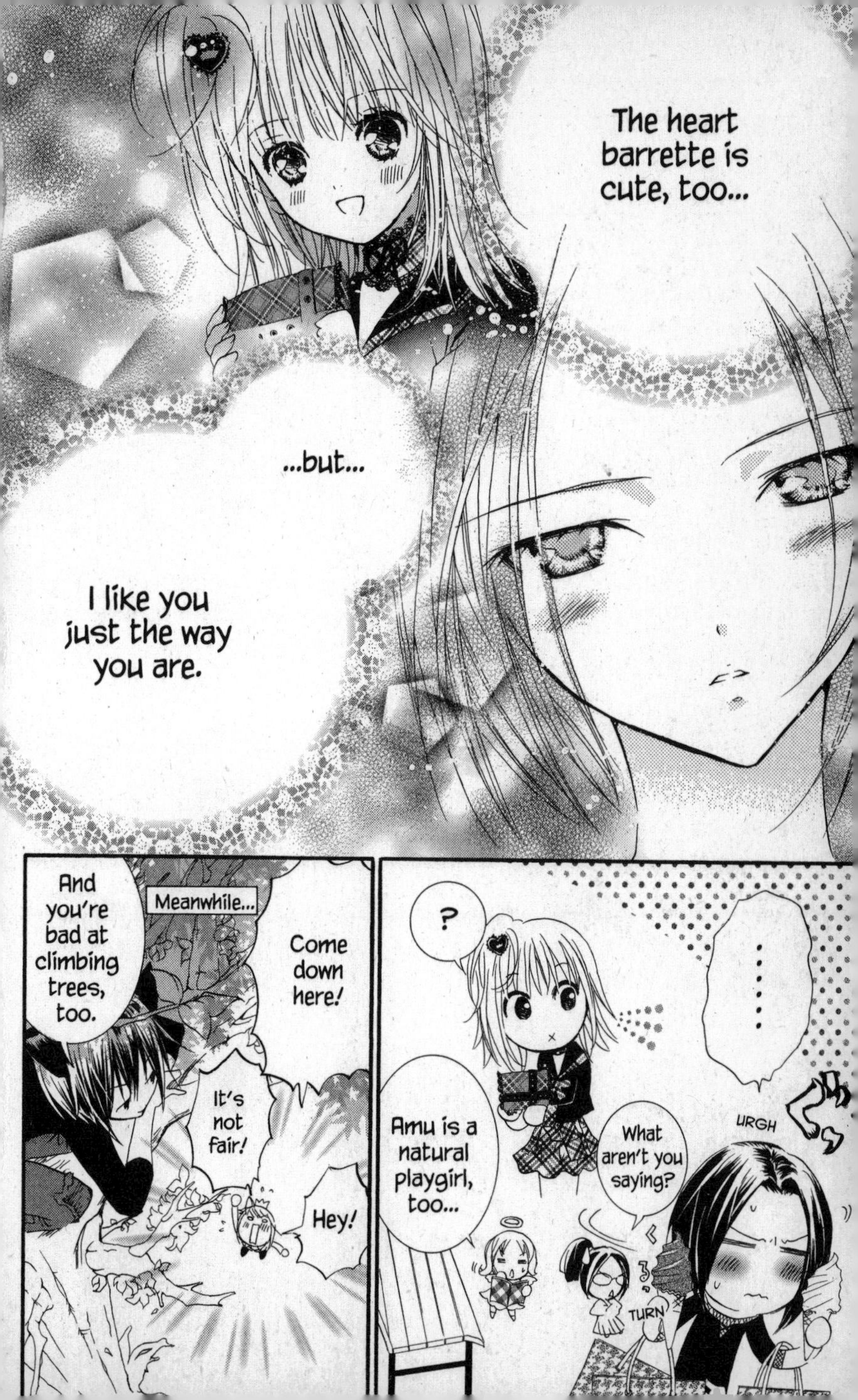

The heart barrette is cute, too...
...but...
I like you just the way you are.
?
......
URGH
What aren't you saying?
TURN
Amu is a natural playgirl, too...
Meanwhile...
Come down here!
And you're bad at climbing trees, too.
It's not fair!
Hey!

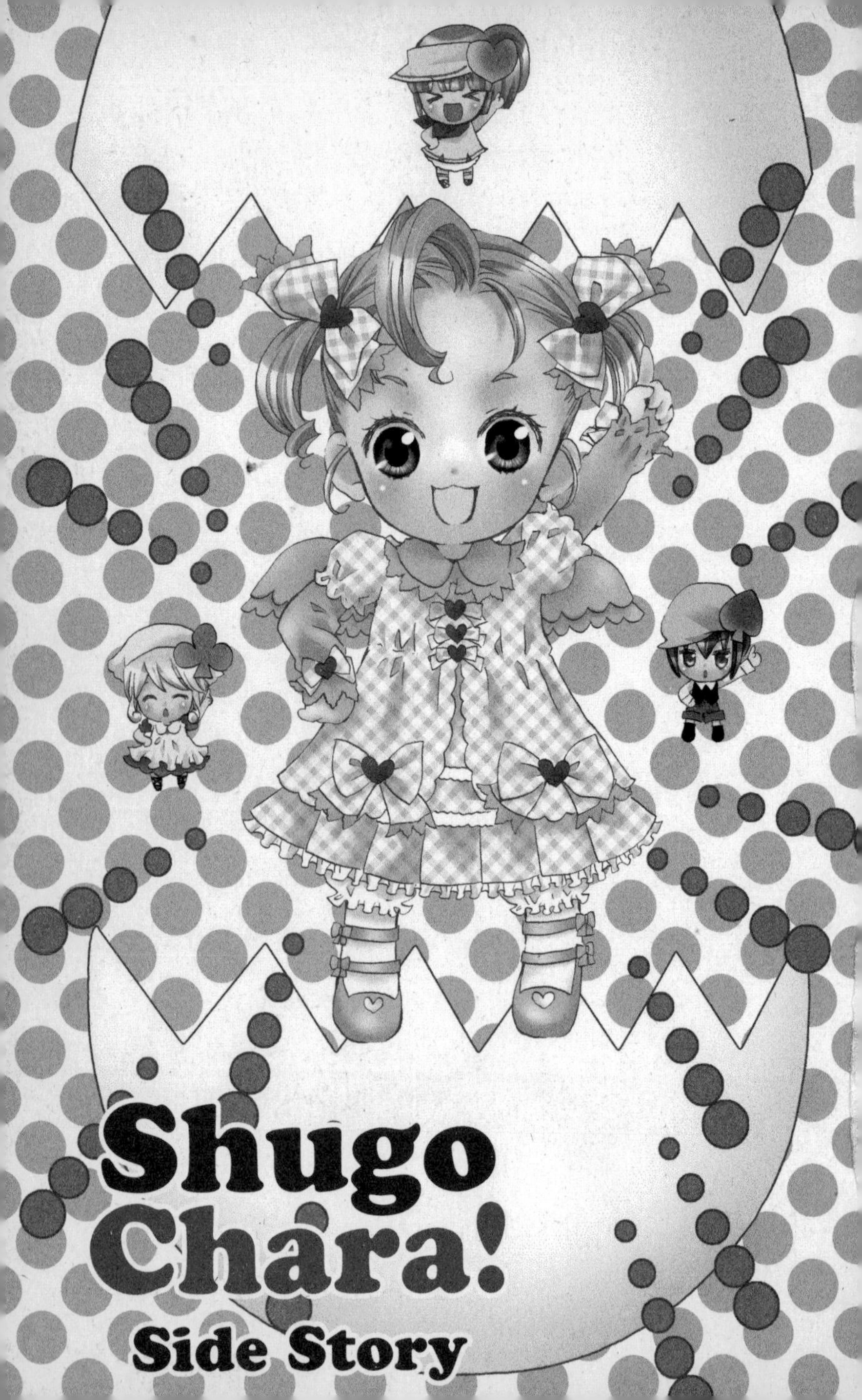
Shugo Chara!
Side Story

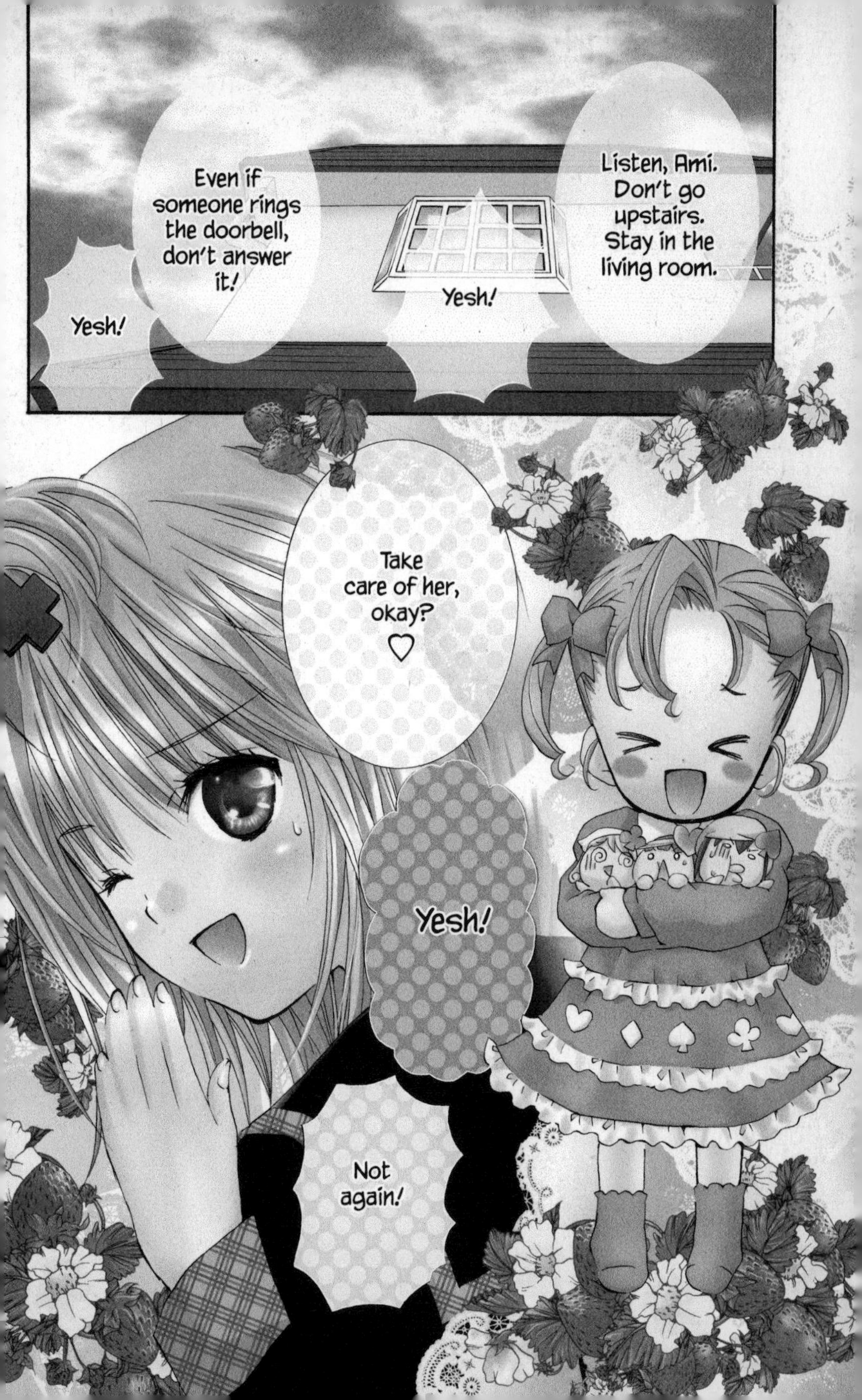
Listen, Ami. Don't go upstairs. Stay in the living room.
Yesh!
Even if someone rings the doorbell, don't answer it!
Yesh!
Take care of her, okay? ♡
Yesh!
Not again!

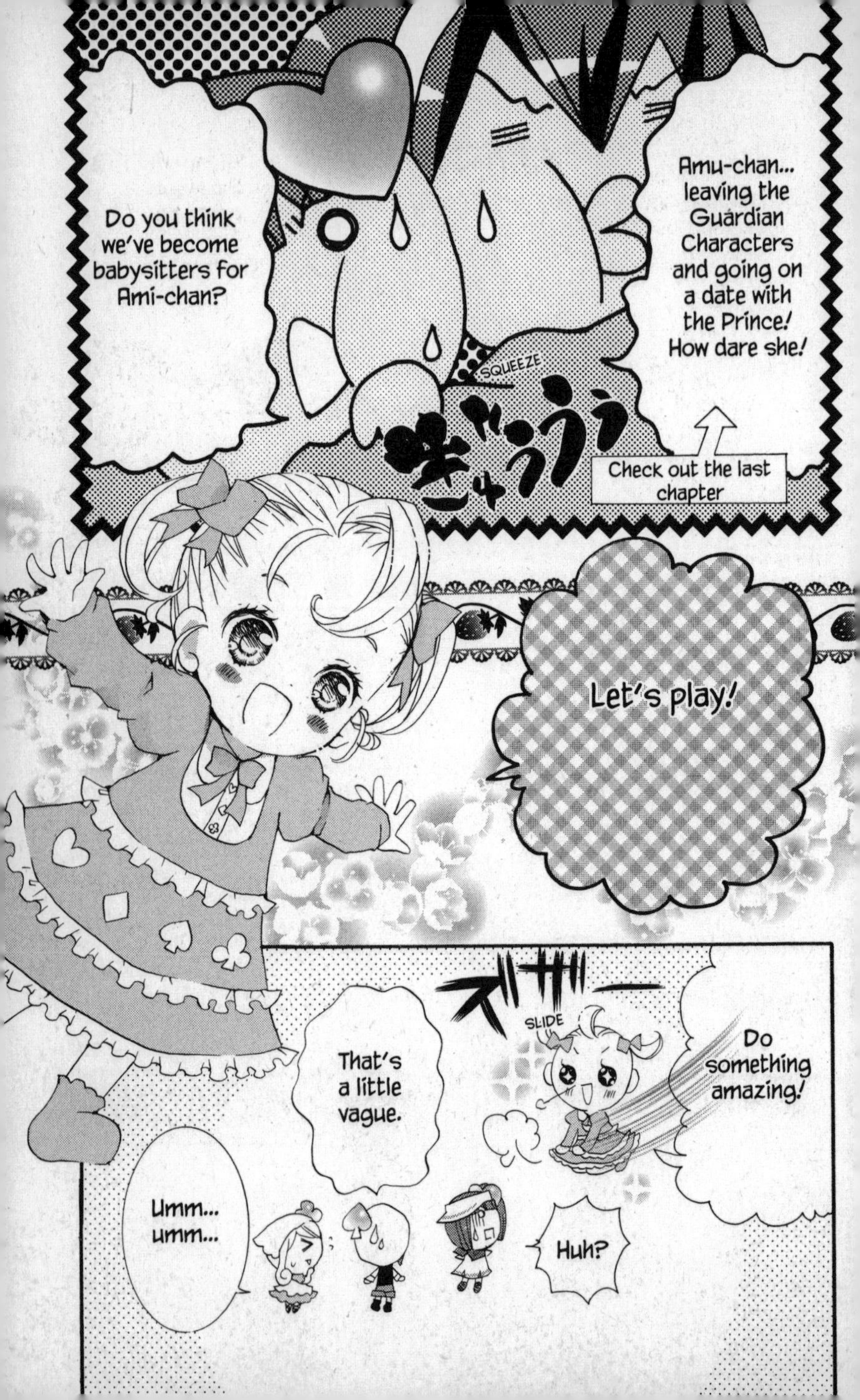
Amu-chan... leaving the Guardian Characters and going on a date with the Prince! How dare she!
Do you think we've become babysitters for Ami-chan?
SQUEEZE
Check out the last chapter
Let's play!
SLIDE
Do something amazing!
That's a little vague.
Huh?
Umm... umm...

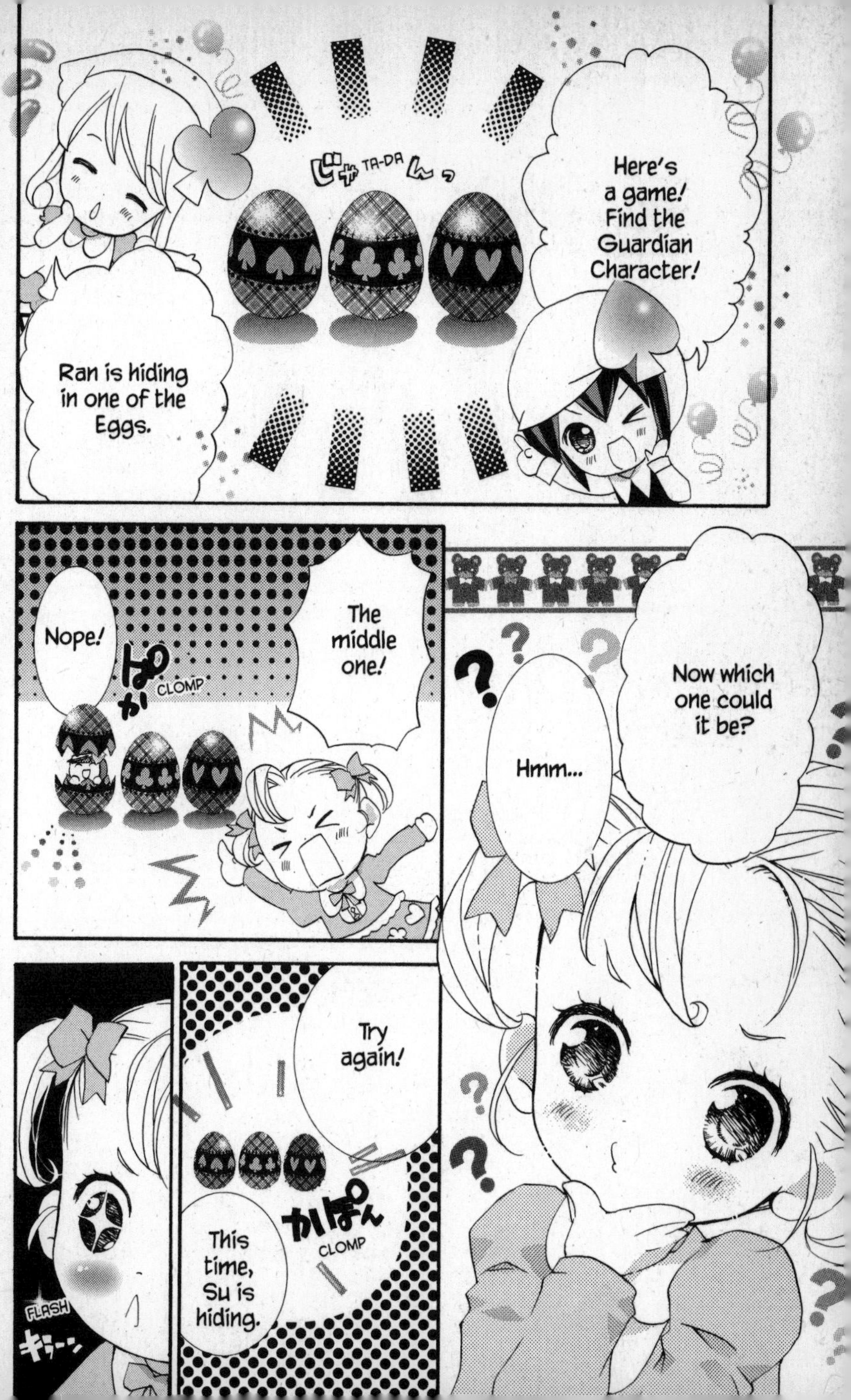

Here's a game! Find the Guardian Character!
TA-DA
Ran is hiding in one of the Eggs.
Now which one could it be?
Hmm...
The middle one!
Nope!
CLOMP
Try again!
CLOMP
This time, Su is hiding.
FLASH

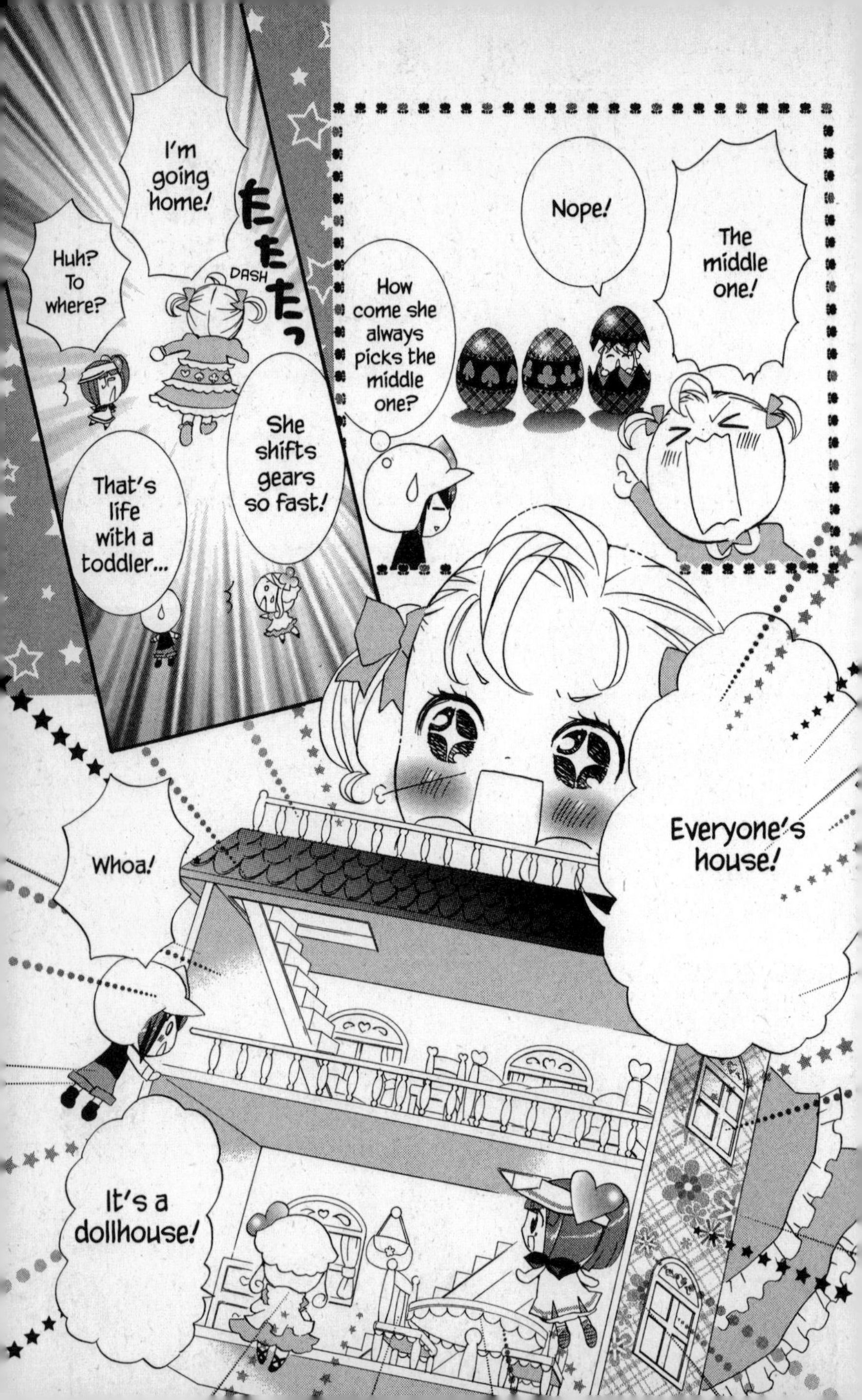
The middle one!
Nope!
How come she always picks the middle one?
I'm going home!
たたたっ
DASH
Huh? To where?
She shifts gears so fast!
That's life with a toddler...
Everyone's house!
Whoa!
It's a dollhouse!

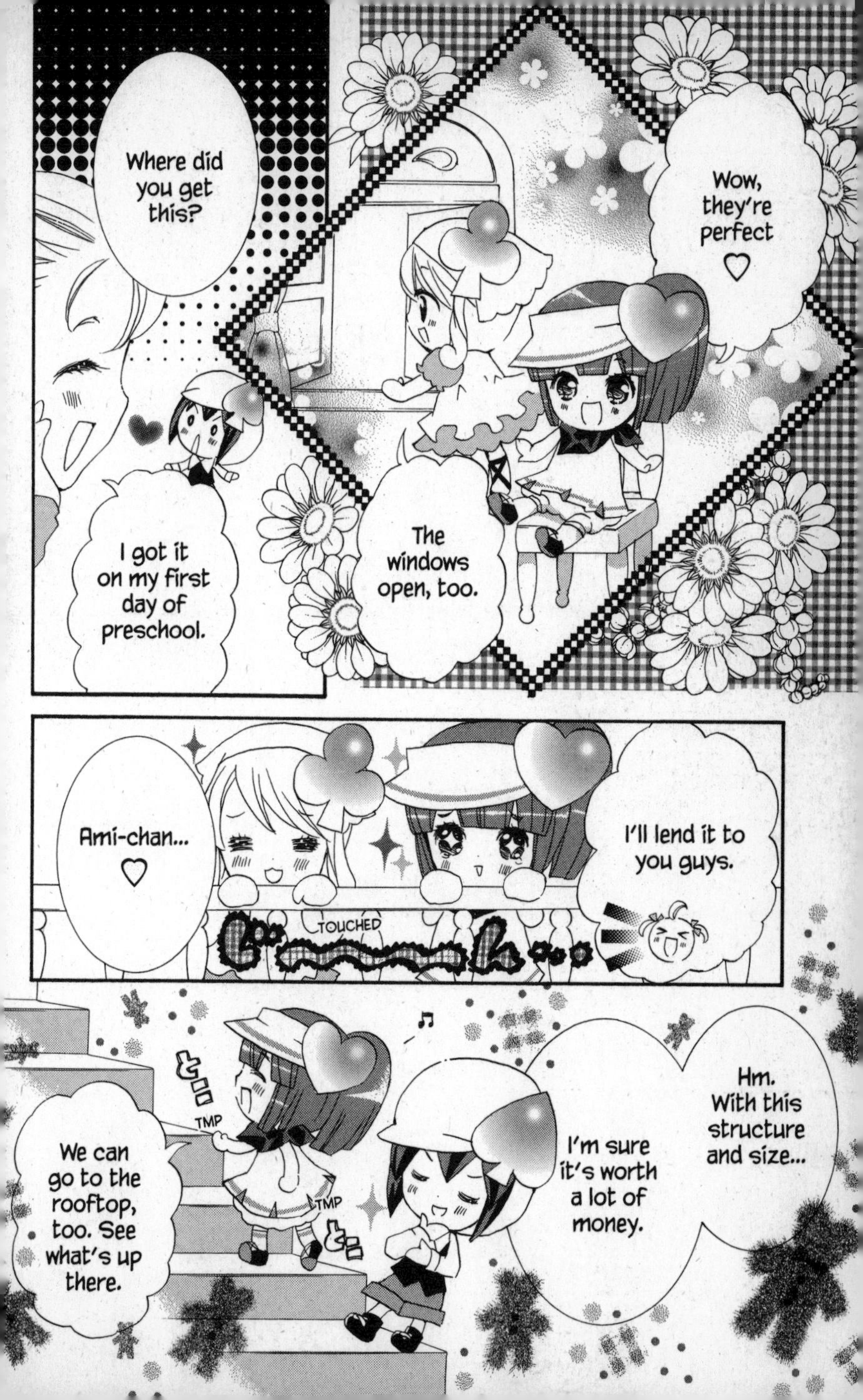
Wow, they're perfect ♡
The windows open, too.
Where did you get this?
I got it on my first day of preschool.
I'll lend it to you guys.
TOUCHED
Ami-chan... ♡
Hm. With this structure and size...
I'm sure it's worth a lot of money.
TMP
TMP
We can go to the rooftop, too. See what's up there.

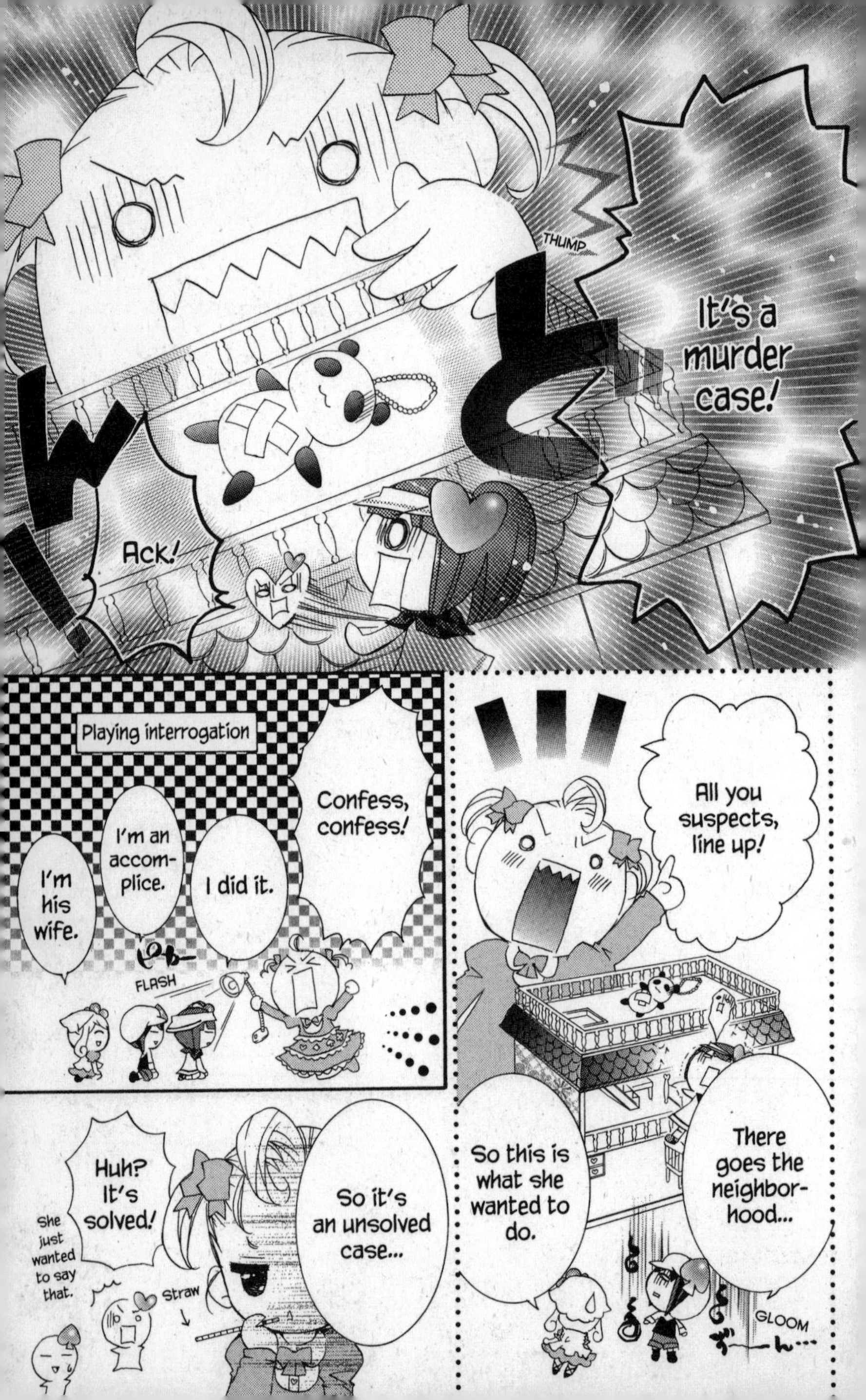
It's a murder case!
THUMP
Ack!
All you suspects, line up!
There goes the neighborhood...
So this is what she wanted to do.
GLOOM
Playing interrogation
Confess, confess!
I did it.
I'm an accomplice.
I'm his wife.
FLASH
So it's an unsolved case...
Huh? It's solved!
Straw
She just wanted to say that.

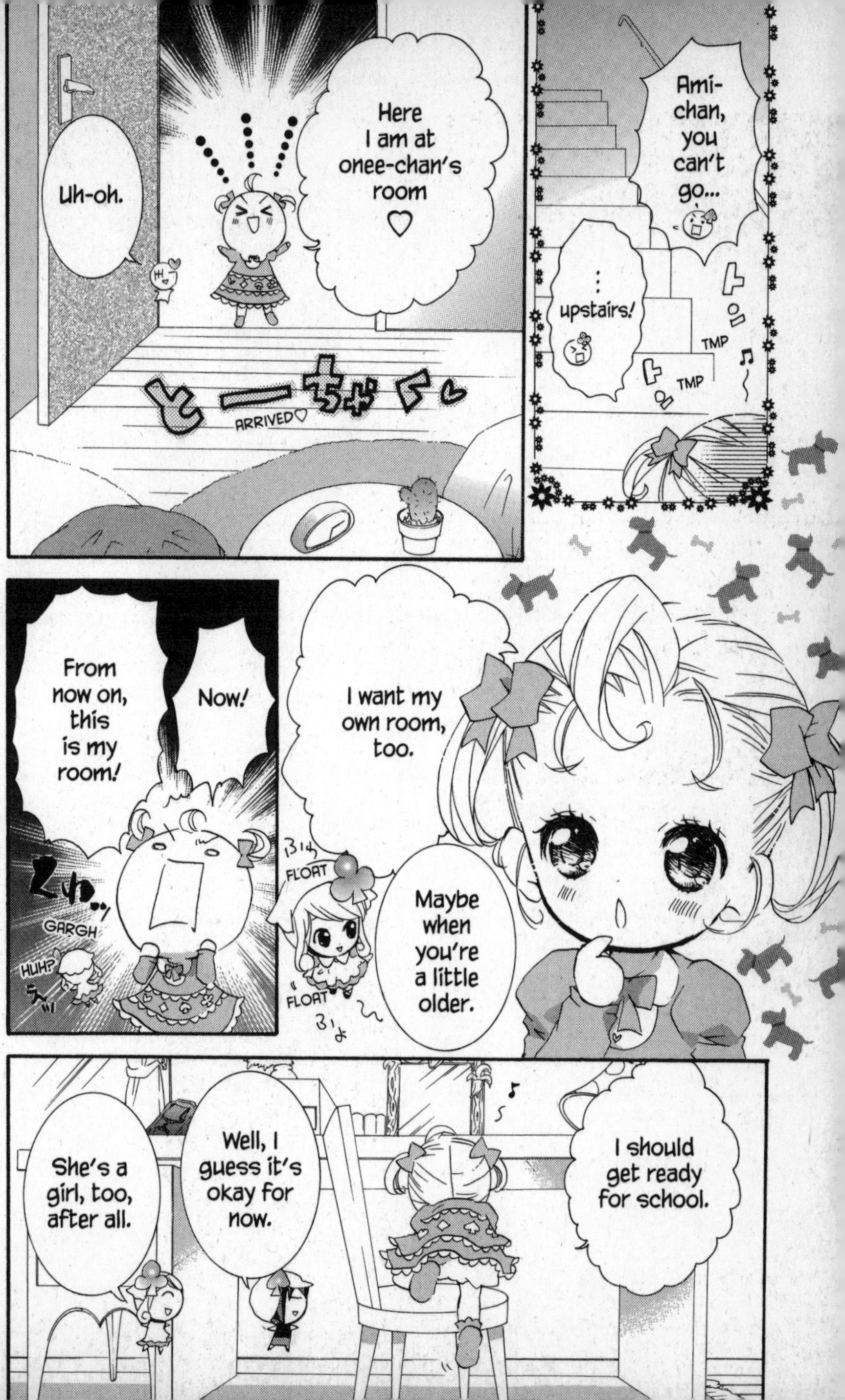
Ami-chan, you can't go...
... upstairs!
TMP
TMP
Here I am at onee-chan's room ♡
Uh-oh.
ARRIVED♡
I want my own room, too.
FLOAT
Maybe when you're a little older.
FLOAT
Now!
From now on, this is my room!
GARGH
HUH?
I should get ready for school.
Well, I guess it's okay for now.
She's a girl, too, after all.

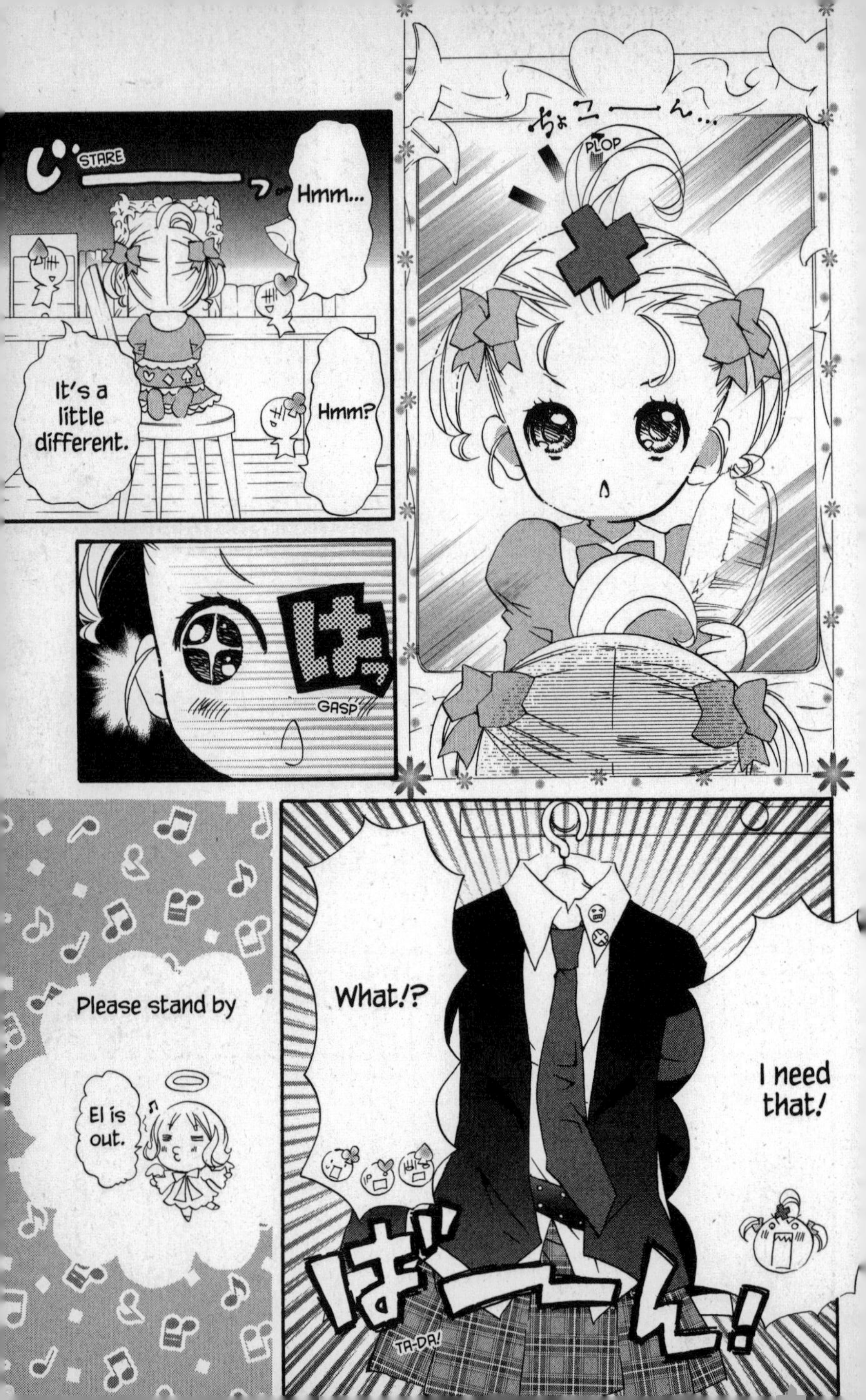
ちょこーーん...
PLOP
Hmm...
じーーー
STARE
Hmm?
It's a little different.
は
GASP
What!?
I need that!
ぱーーん!
TA-DA!
Please stand by
El is out.

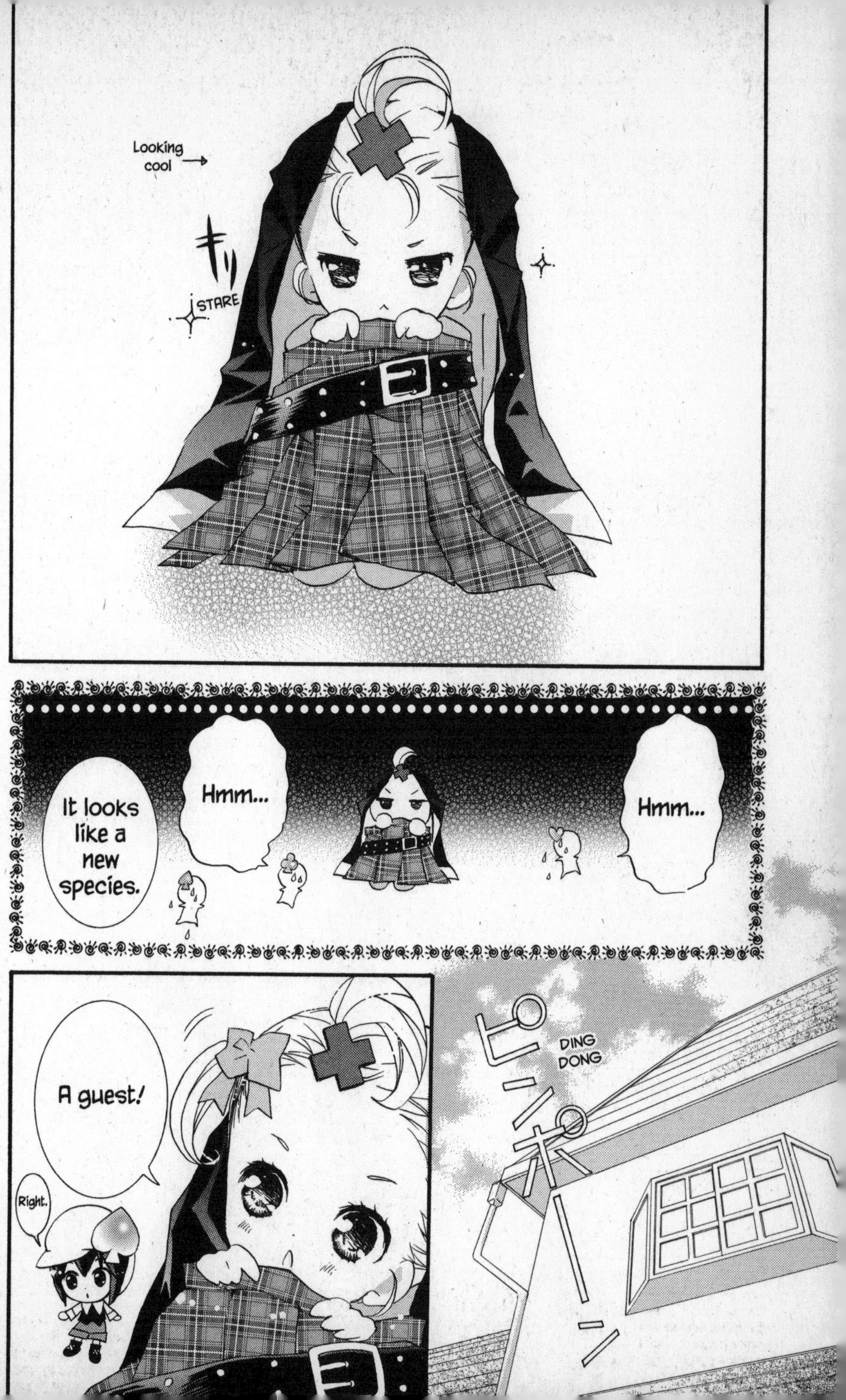
Looking cool
キリ
STARE
Hmm...
Hmm...
It looks like a new species.
ピンポーン
DING DONG
A guest!
Right.

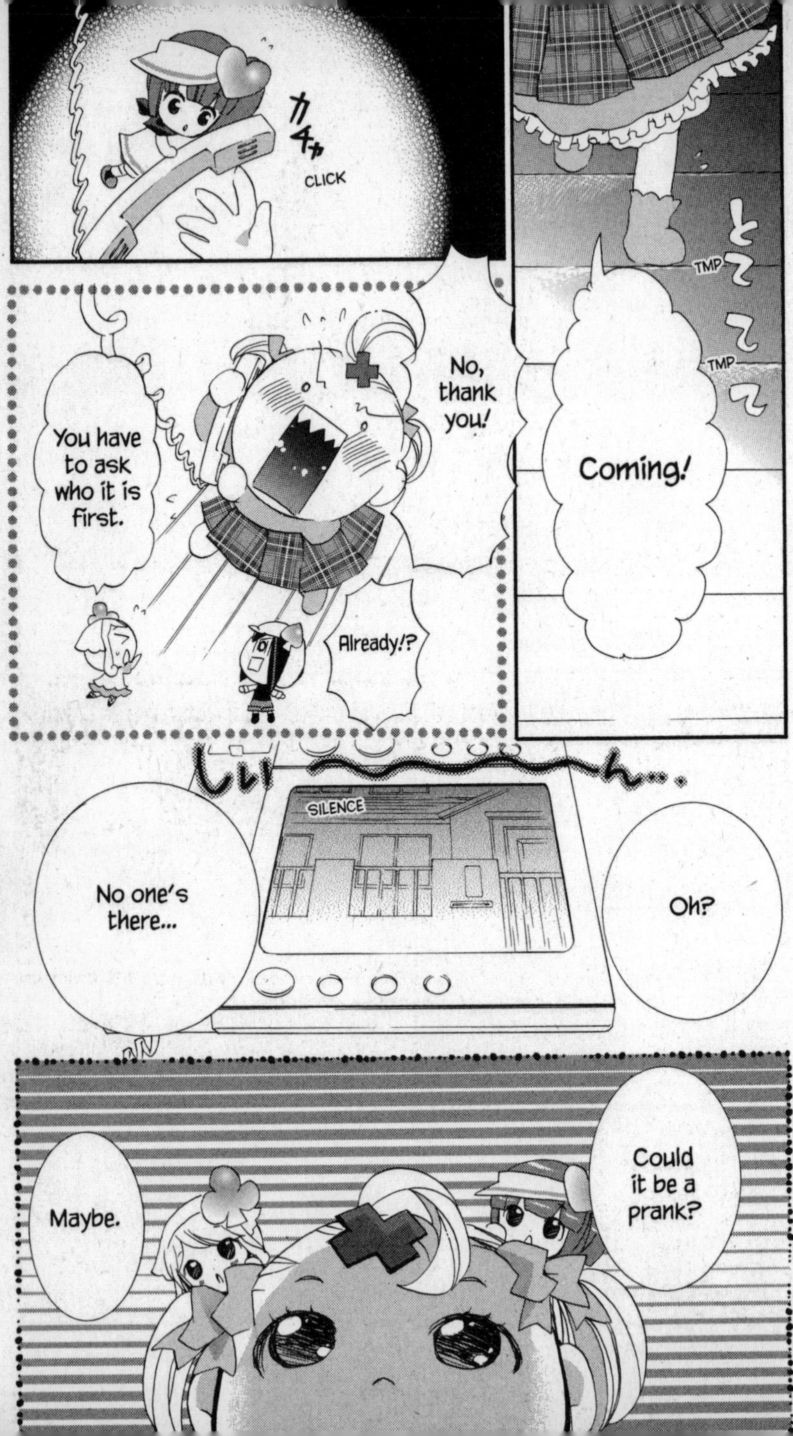
TMP
TMP
Coming!
カチャ
CLICK
No, thank you!
You have to ask who it is first.
Already!?
Oh?
SILENCE
No one's there...
Could it be a prank?
Maybe.

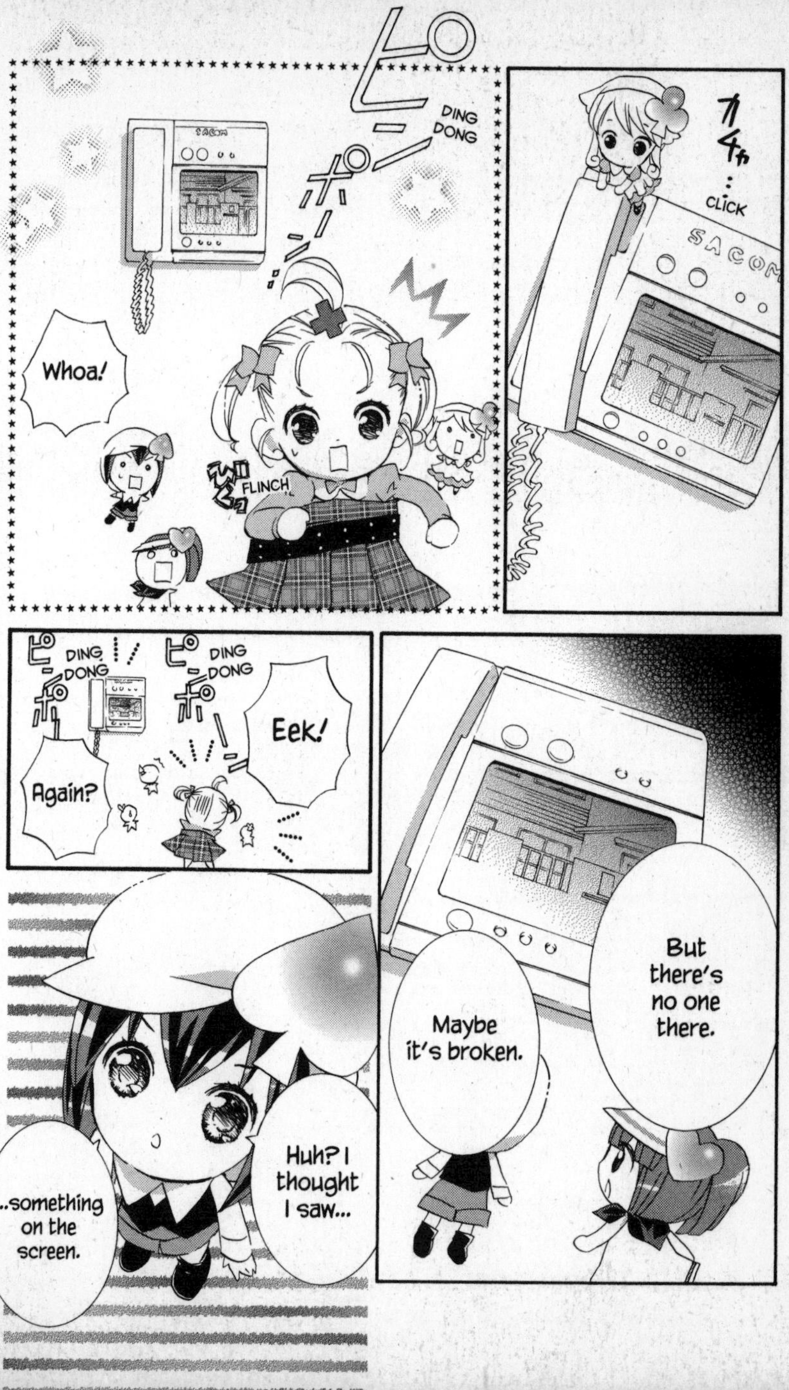

CLICK
DING DONG
Whoa!
FLINCH
But there's no one there.
Maybe it's broken.
DING DONG
Eek!
DING DONG
Again?
Huh? I thought I saw...
...something on the screen.

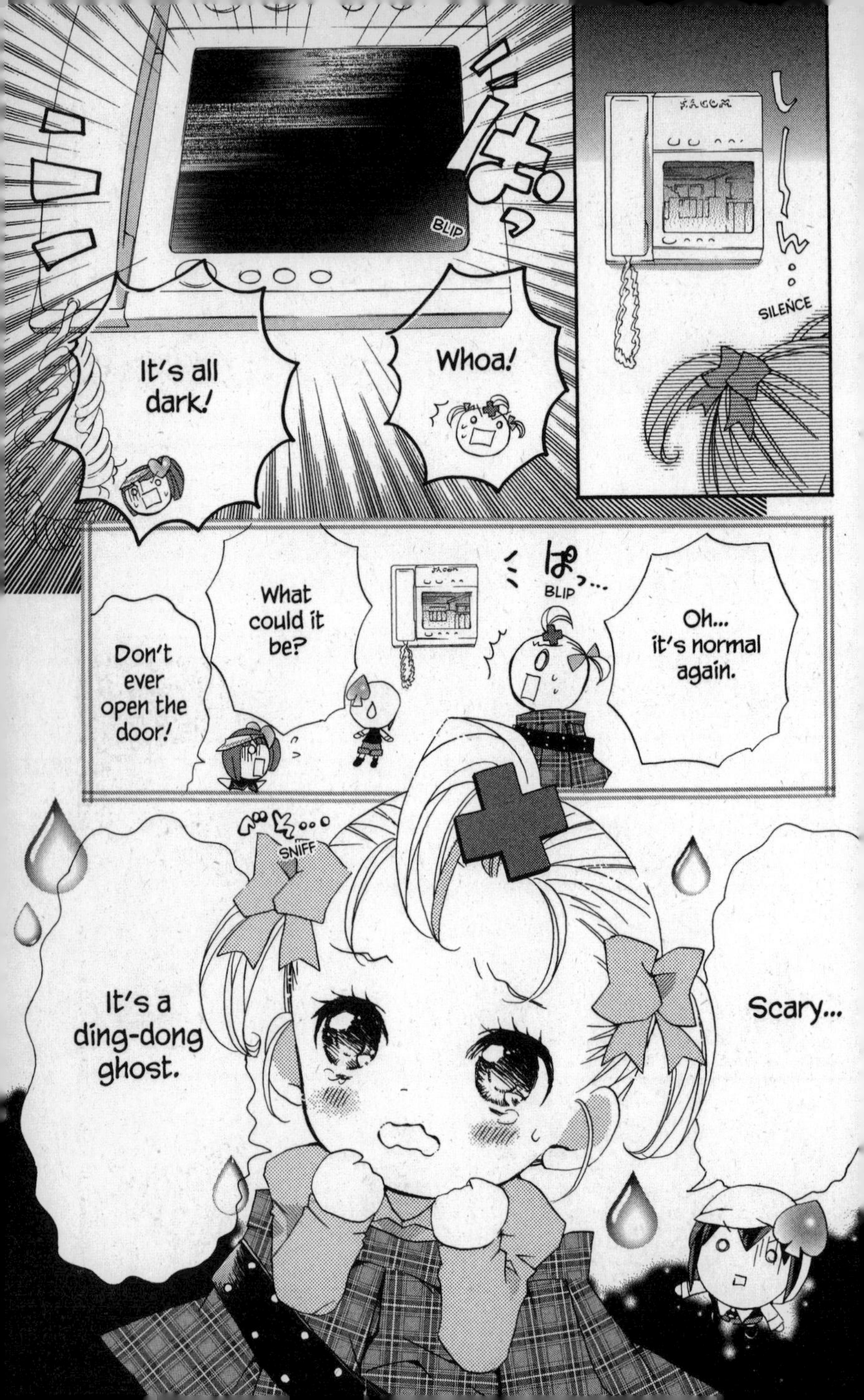
しーん。
SILENCE
BLIP
Whoa!
It's all dark!
ぱっ…
BLIP
Oh... it's normal again.
What could it be?
Don't ever open the door!
SNIFF
Scary...
It's a ding-dong ghost.

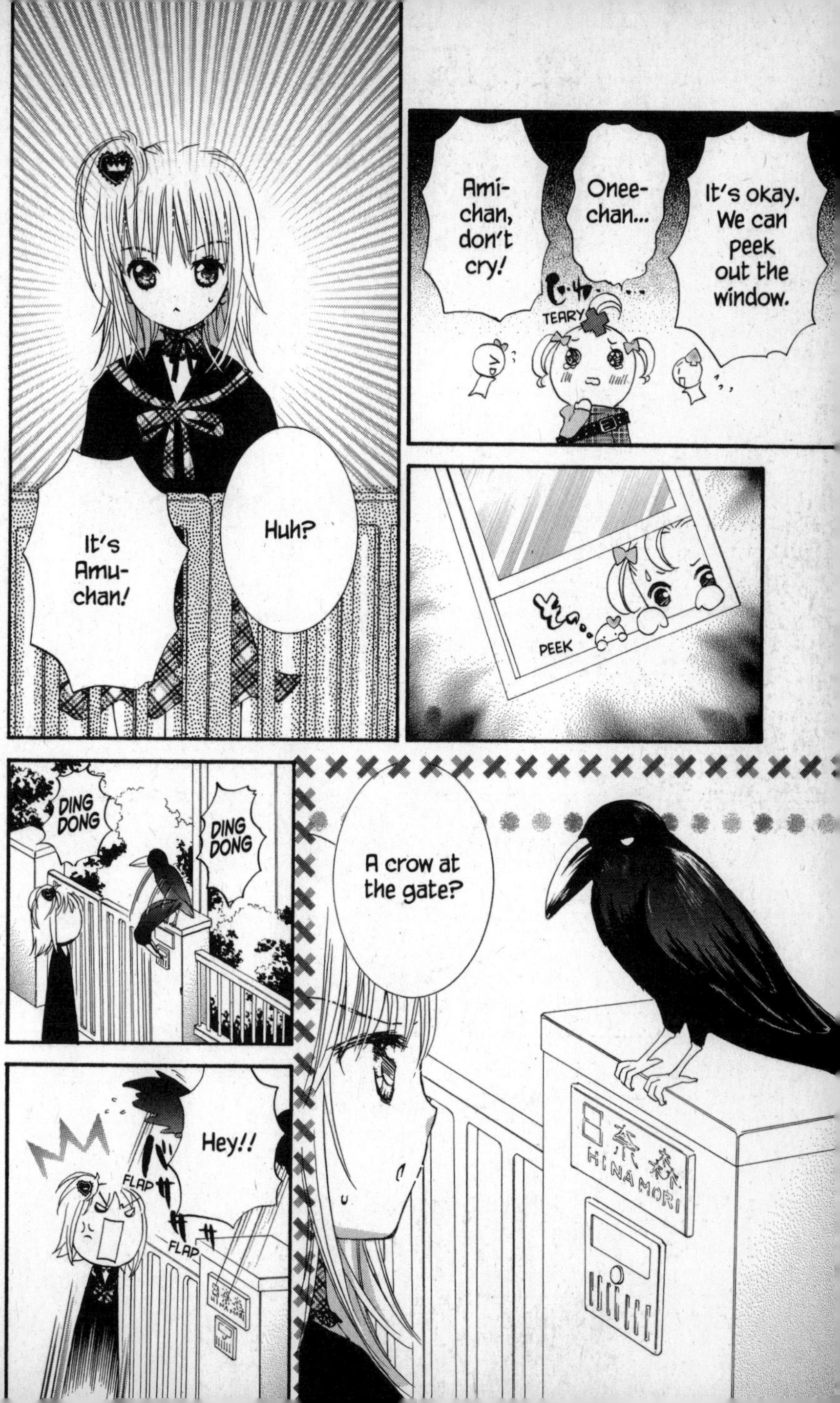
It's okay. We can peek out the window.
Onee-chan...
Ami-chan, don't cry!
TEARY
PEEK
Huh?
It's Amu-chan!
A crow at the gate?
HINAMORI
DING DONG
DING DONG
Hey!!
FLAP
FLAP

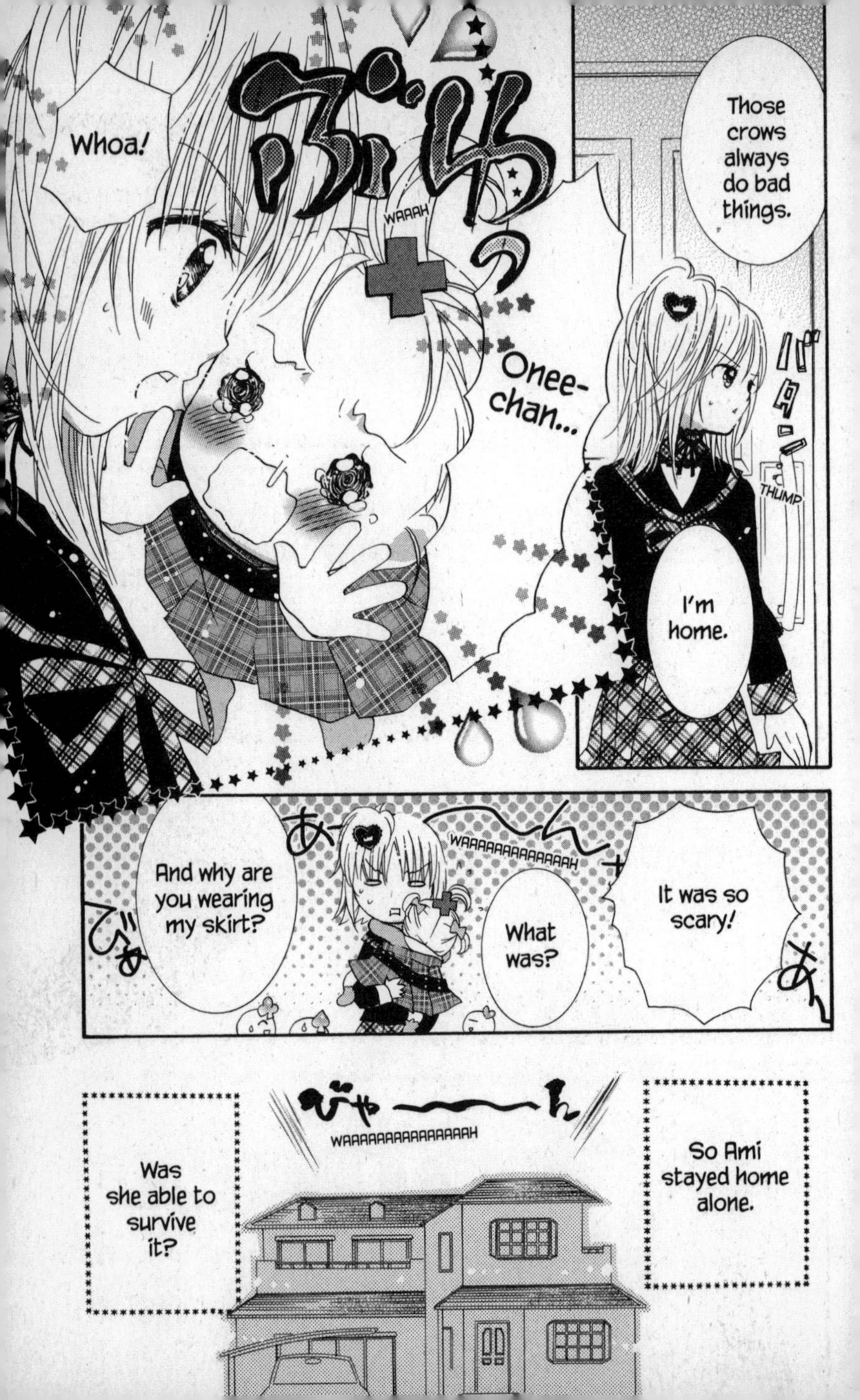

Those crows always do bad things.
THUMP
I'm home.
WAAAH
Onee-chan...
Whoa!
It was so scary!
What was?
WAAAAAAAAAAAAAAAH
And why are you wearing my skirt?
So Ami stayed home alone.
WAAAAAAAAAAAAAAAAH
Was she able to survive it?

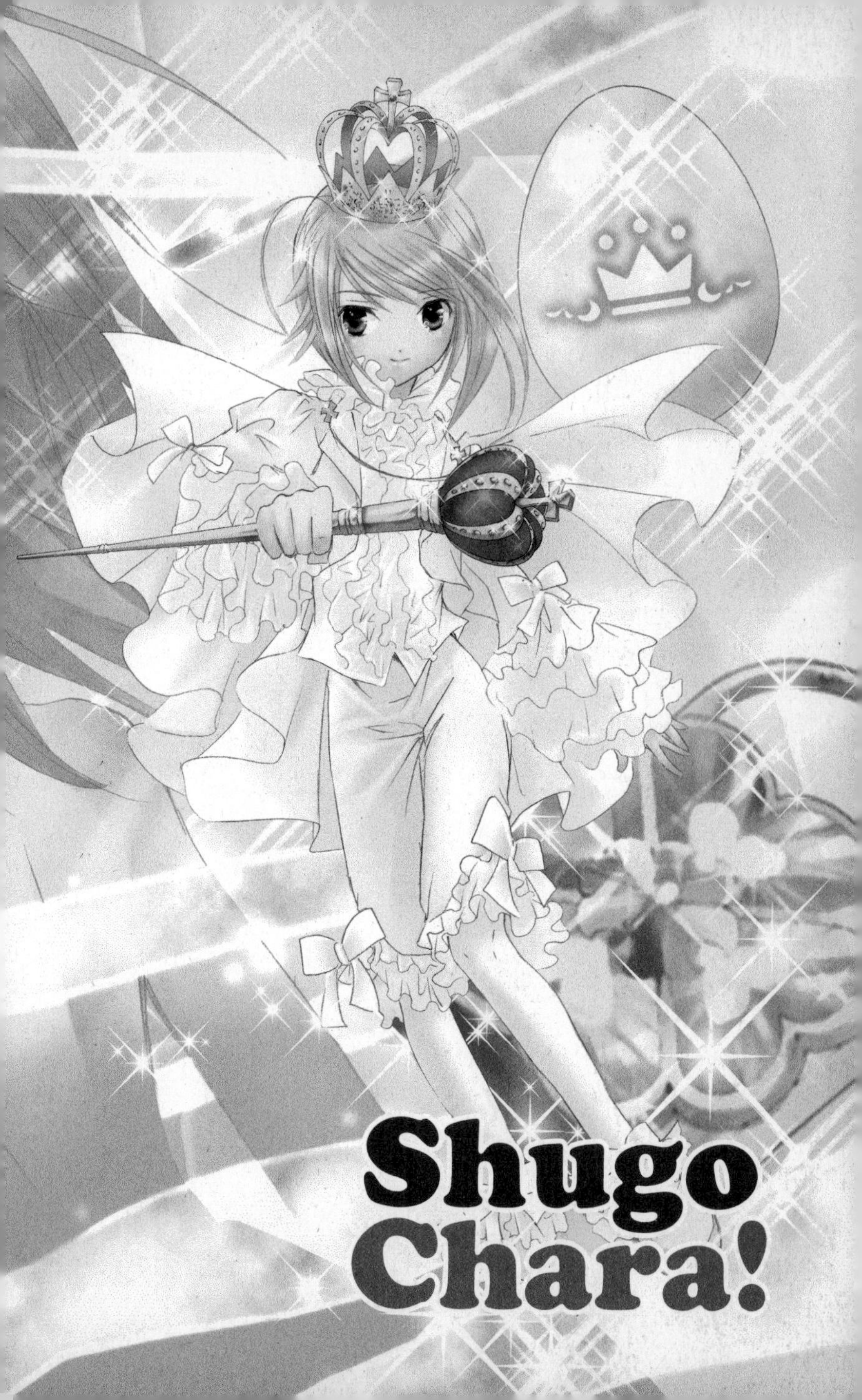
Shugo Chara!

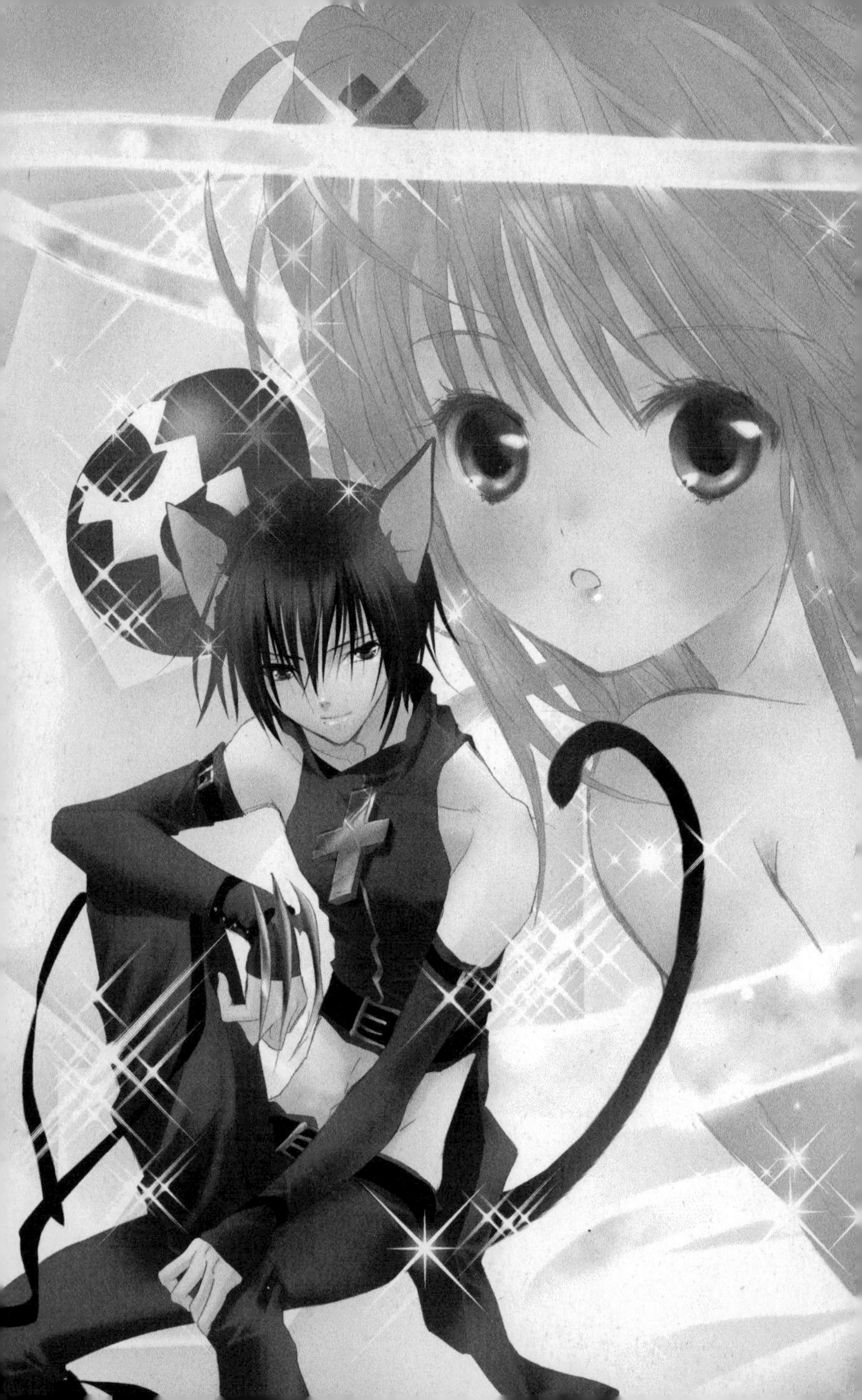

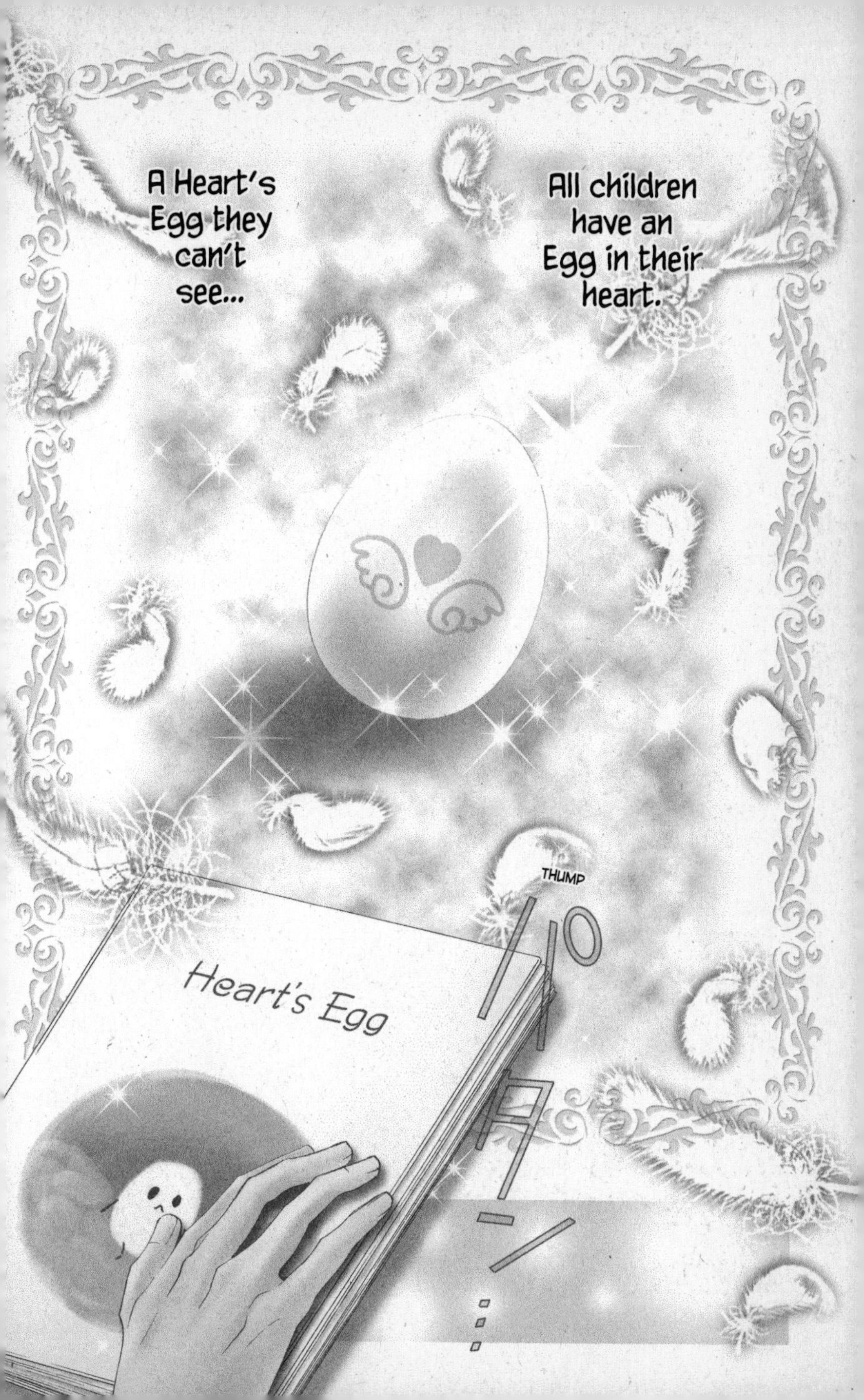
All children have an Egg in their heart.
A Heart's Egg they can't see...
Heart's Egg
THUMP

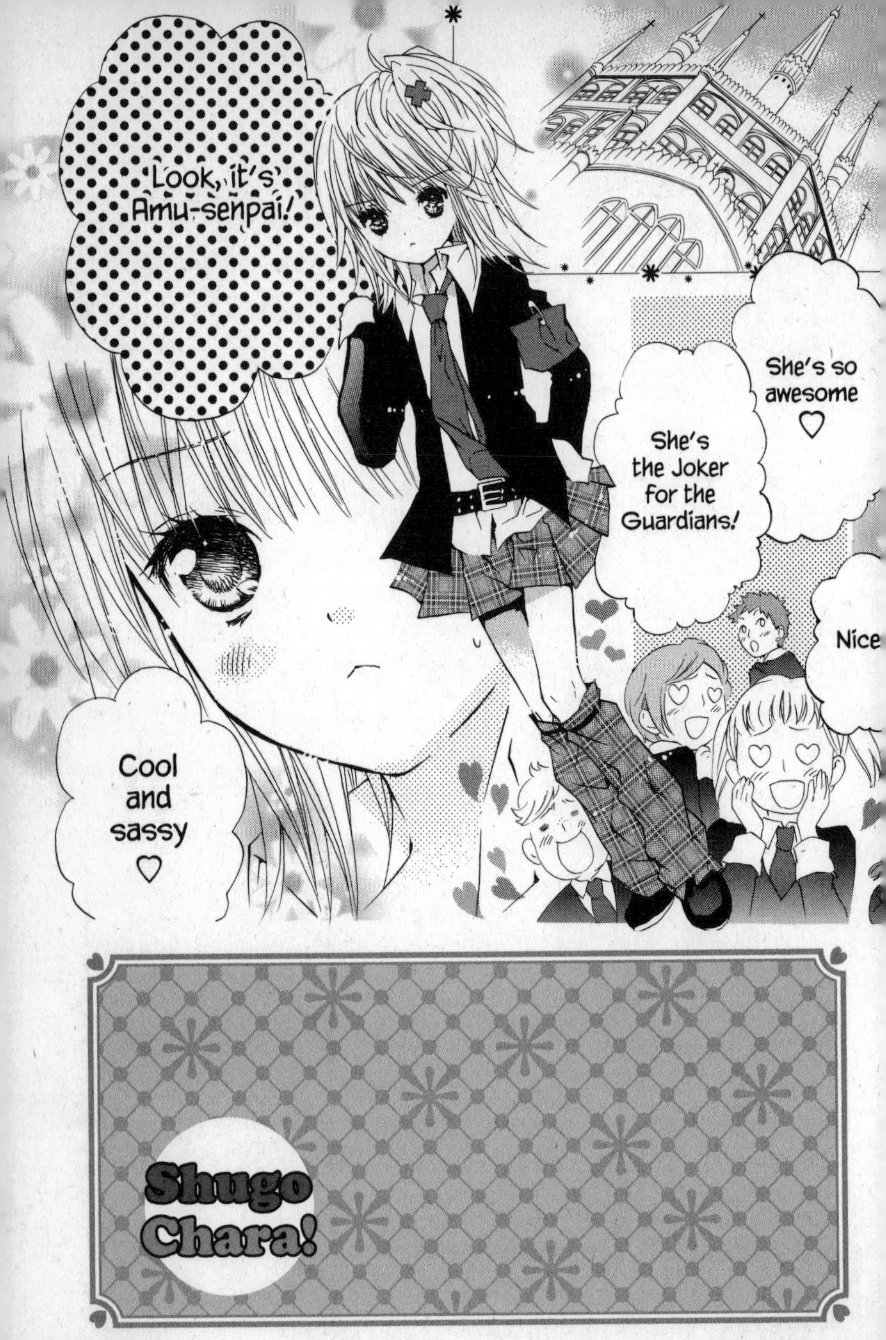
Look, it's Amu-senpai!
She's so awesome ♡
She's the Joker for the Guardians!
Nice
Cool and sassy ♡

Shugo Chara!

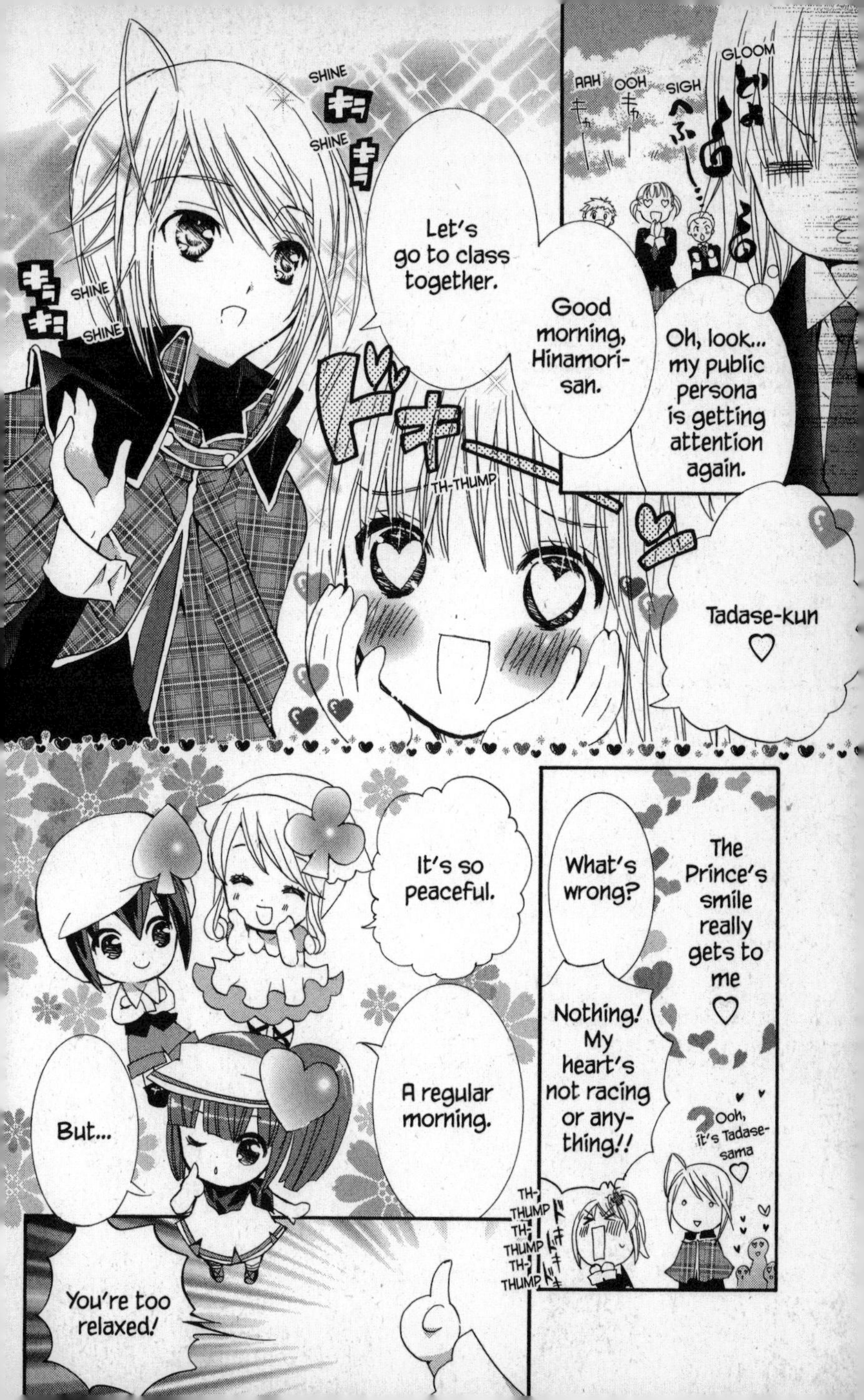
GLOOM
SIGH
OOH
AAH
Oh, look... my public persona is getting attention again.
SHINE SHINE
SHINE SHINE
Good morning, Hinamori-san.
Let's go to class together.
TH-THUMP
Tadase-kun ♡
The Prince's smile really gets to me ♡
What's wrong?
Nothing! My heart's not racing or anything!!
Ooh, it's Tadase-sama ♡
TH-THUMP TH-THUMP TH-THUMP
It's so peaceful.
A regular morning.
But...
You're too relaxed!

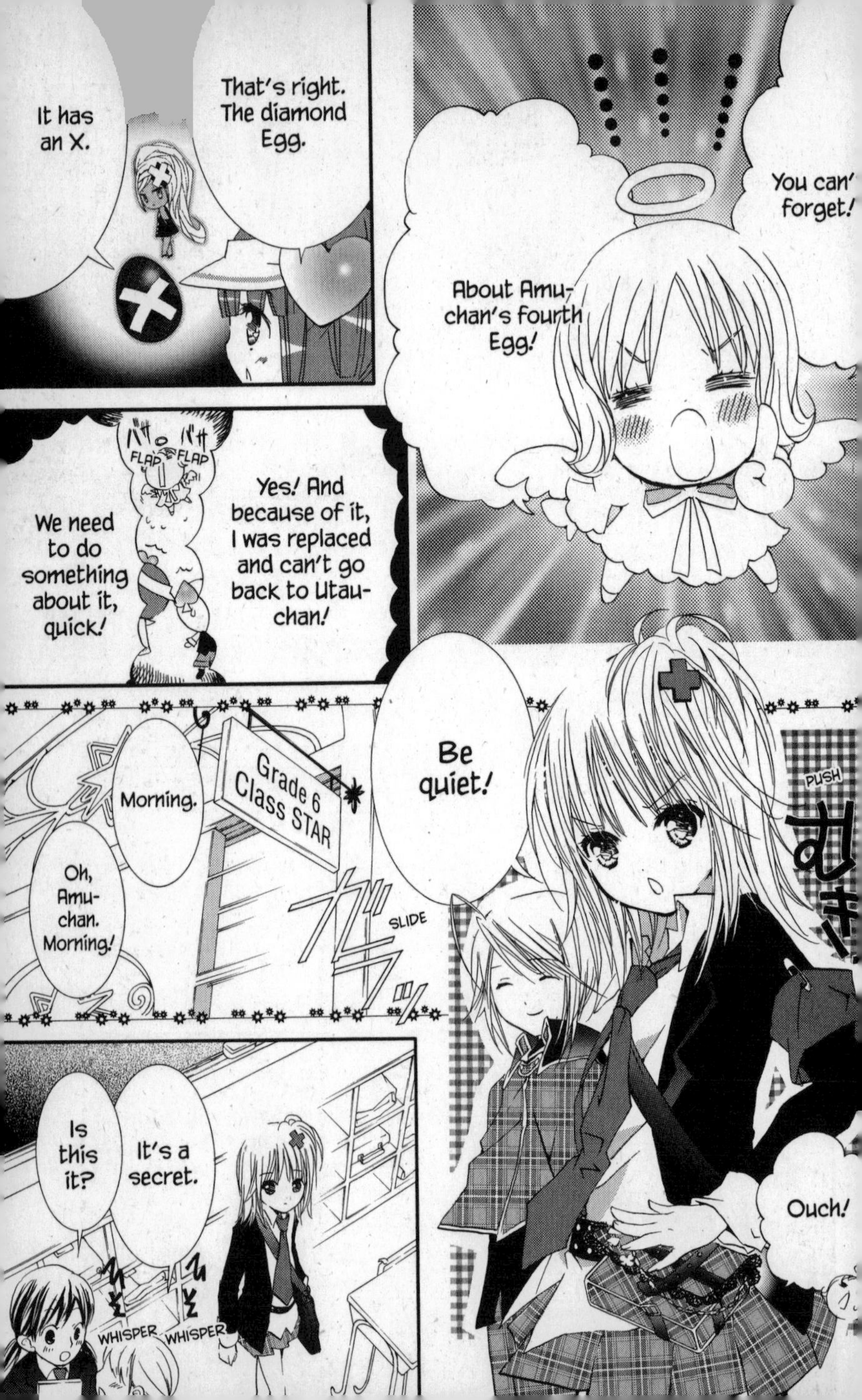

You can' forget!
About Amu-chan's fourth Egg!
That's right. The diamond Egg.
It has an X.
FLAP FLAP
Yes! And because of it, I was replaced and can't go back to Utau-chan!
We need to do something about it, quick!
Be quiet!
PUSH
Ouch!
SLIDE
Grade 6 Class STAR
Morning.
Oh, Amu-chan. Morning!
It's a secret.
Is this it?
WHISPER WHISPER

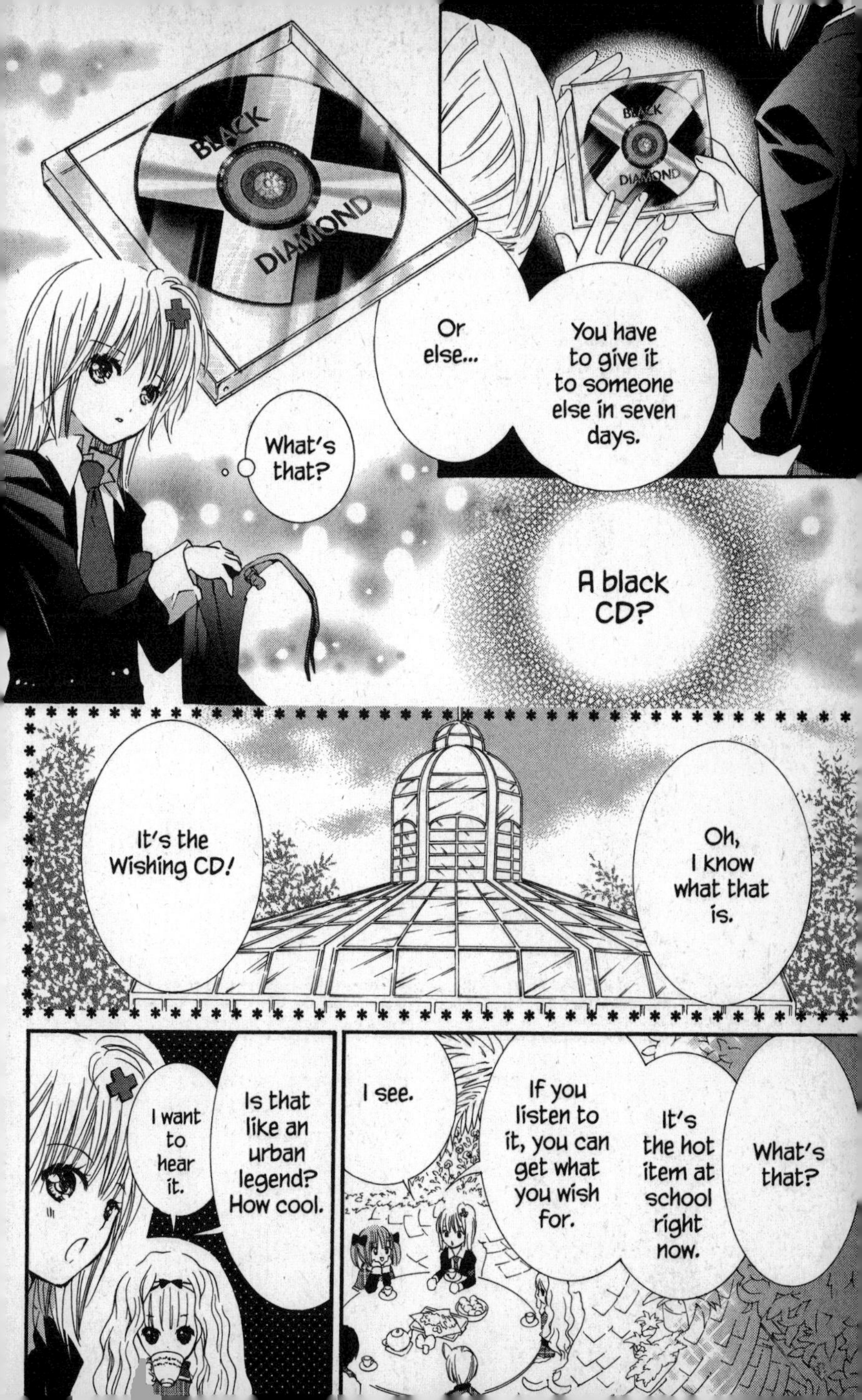

BLACK DIAMOND
You have to give it to someone else in seven days.
Or else...
A black CD?
BLACK DIAMOND
What's that?
Oh, I know what that is.
It's the Wishing CD!
What's that?
It's the hot item at school right now.
If you listen to it, you can get what you wish for.
I see.
Is that like an urban legend? How cool.
I want to hear it.

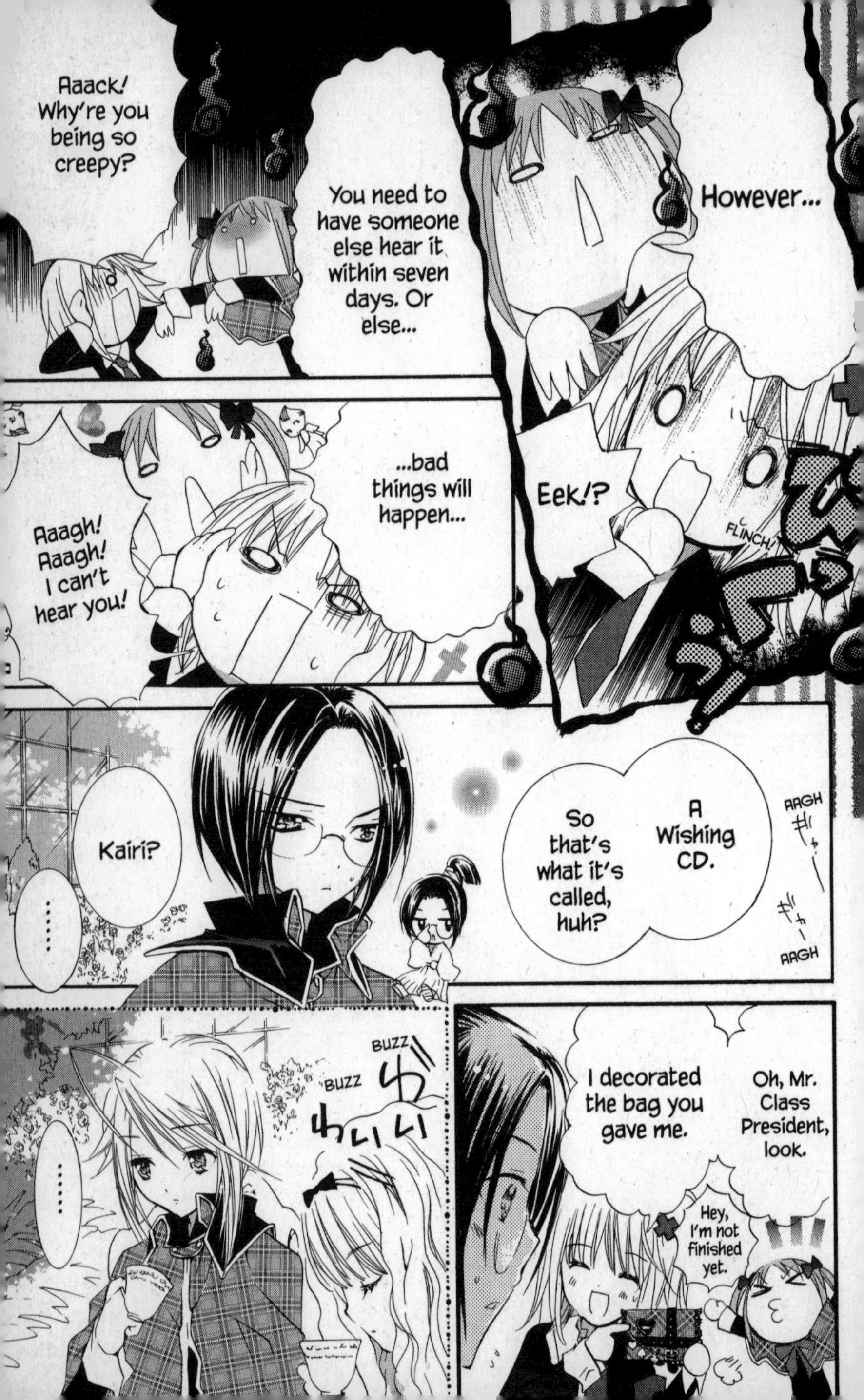
However...
Eek!?
FLINCH!
You need to have someone else hear it within seven days. Or else...
Aaack! Why're you being so creepy?
...bad things will happen...
Aaagh! Aaagh! I can't hear you!
AARGH
AARGH
A Wishing CD.
So that's what it's called, huh?
Kairi?
......
Oh, Mr. Class President, look.
I decorated the bag you gave me.
Hey, I'm not finished yet.
BUZZ
BUZZ
......

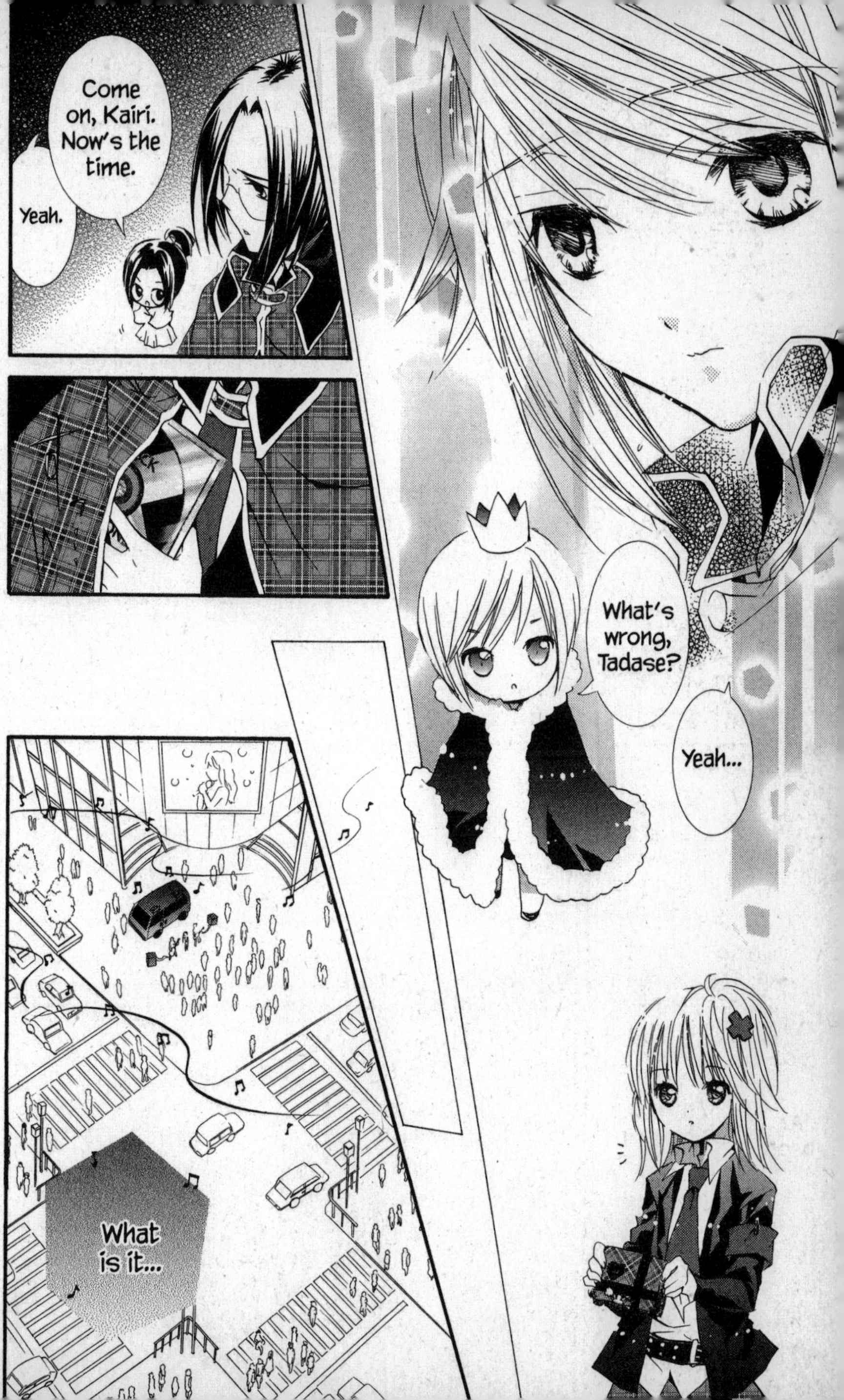

What's wrong, Tadase?
Yeah...
Come on, Kairi. Now's the time.
Yeah.
What is it...

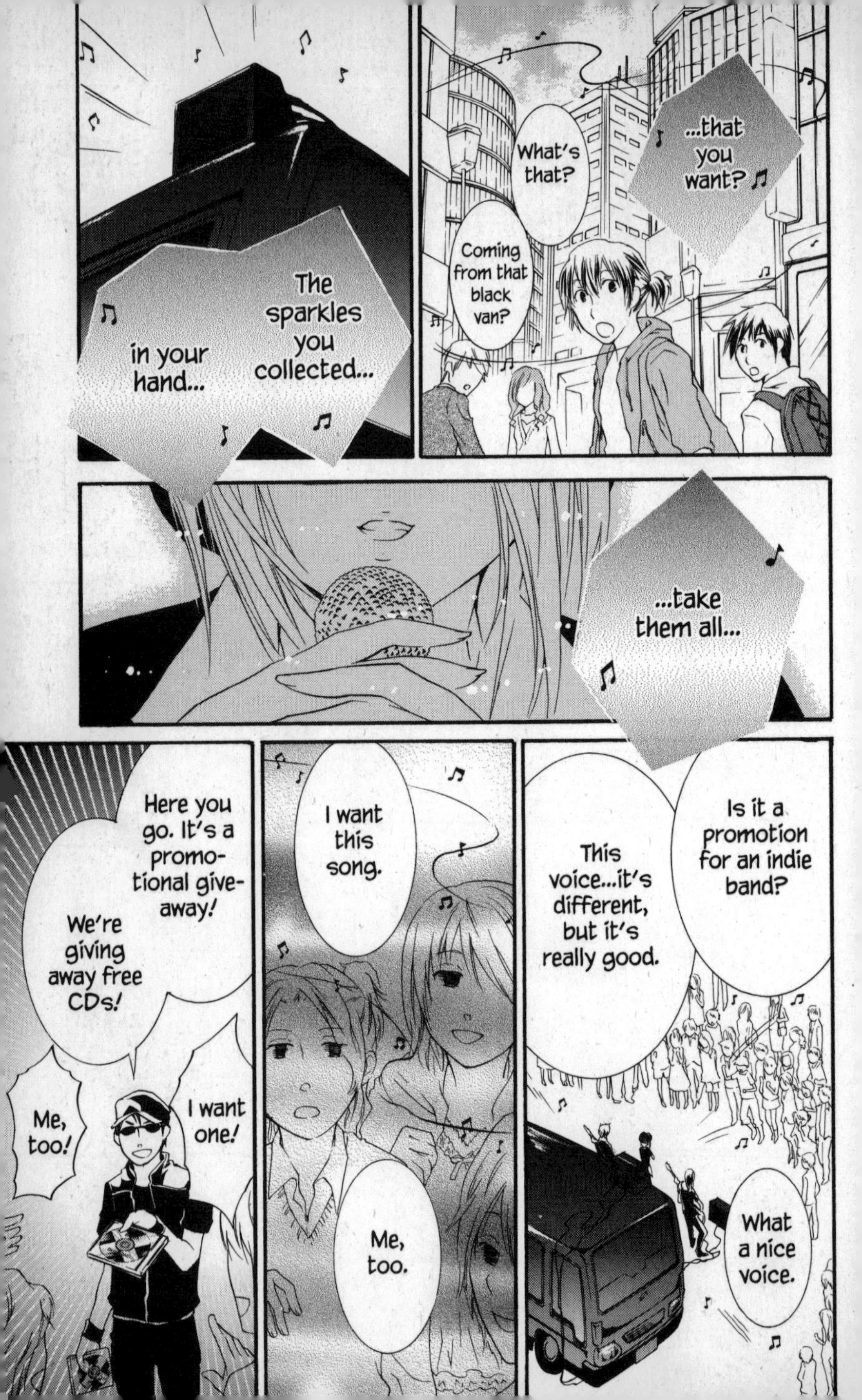
...that you want?
What's that?
Coming from that black van?
The sparkles you collected...
in your hand...
...take them all...
Is it a promotion for an indie band?
This voice...it's different, but it's really good.
What a nice voice.
I want this song.
Me, too.
Here you go. It's a promotional give-away!
We're giving away free CDs!
I want one!
Me, too!

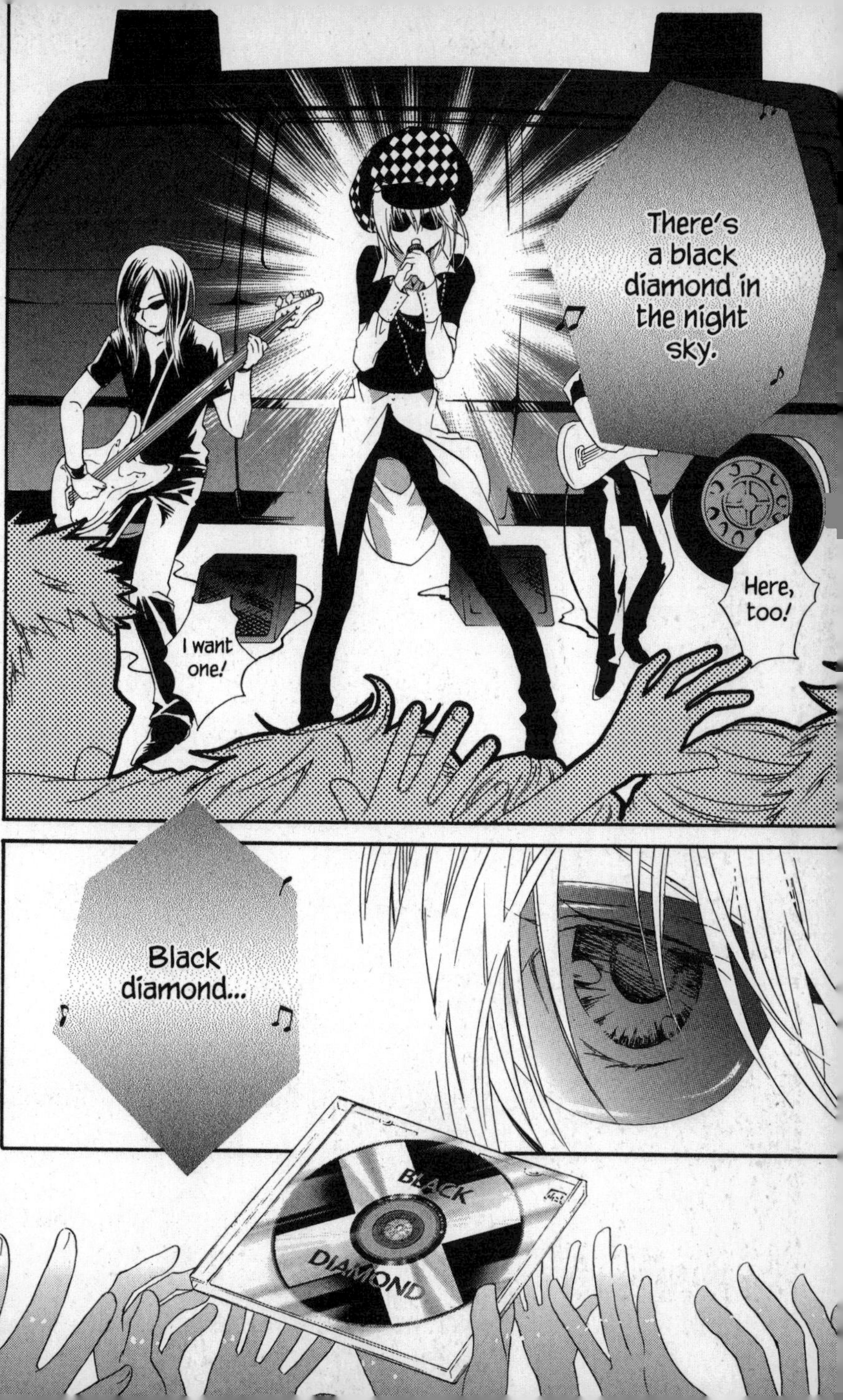
There's a black diamond in the night sky.
Here, too!
I want one!
Black diamond...
BLACK DIAMOND

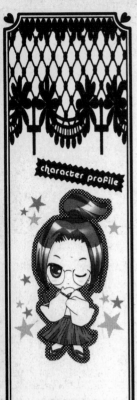

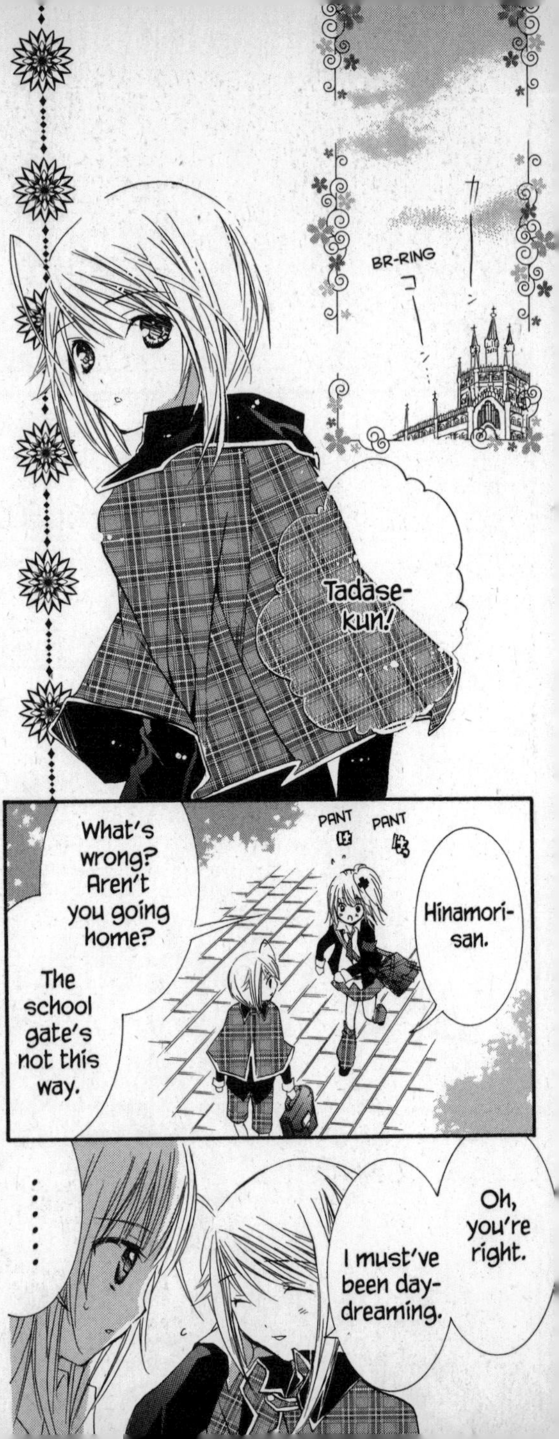
BR-RING
Tadase-kun!
PANT PANT
Hinamori-san.
What's wrong? Aren't you going home?
The school gate's not this way.
Oh, you're right.
I must've been day-dreaming.
......

character profile

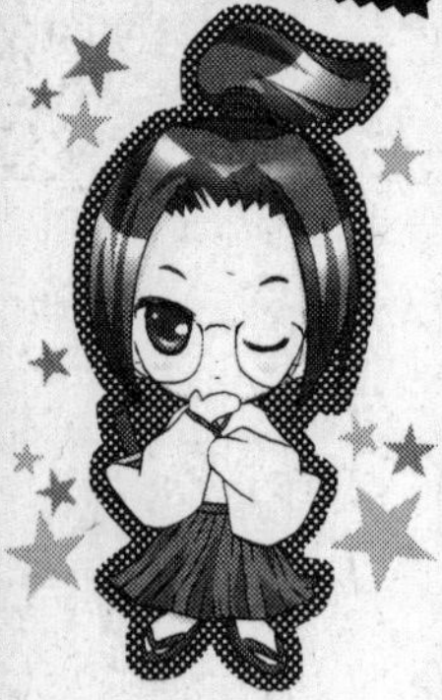

MUSASHI

Guardian Character of: Kairi
Special Skill: Swords
Hates: Girls

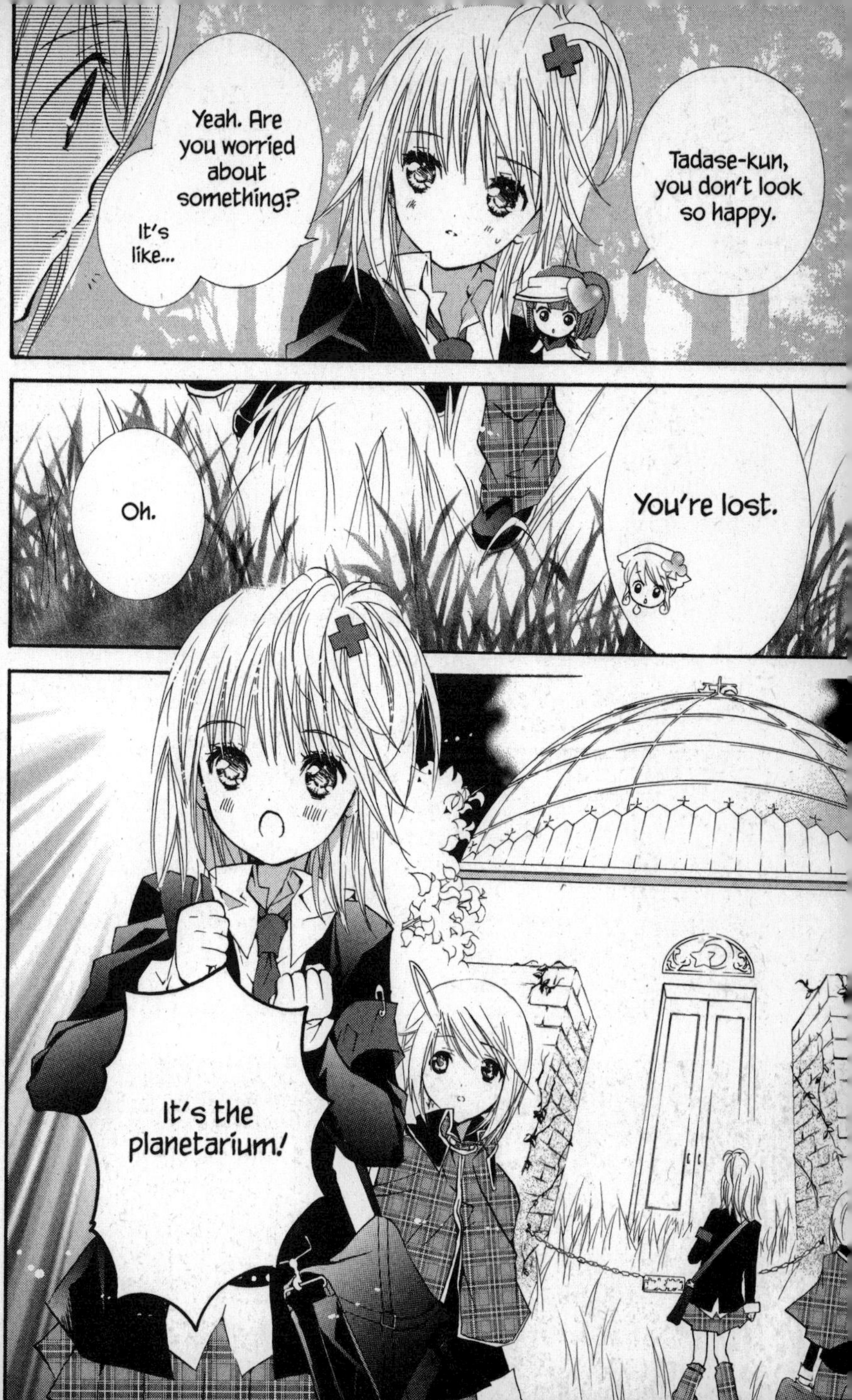
Tadase-kun, you don't look so happy.
Yeah. Are you worried about something?
It's like...
You're lost.
Oh.
It's the planetarium!

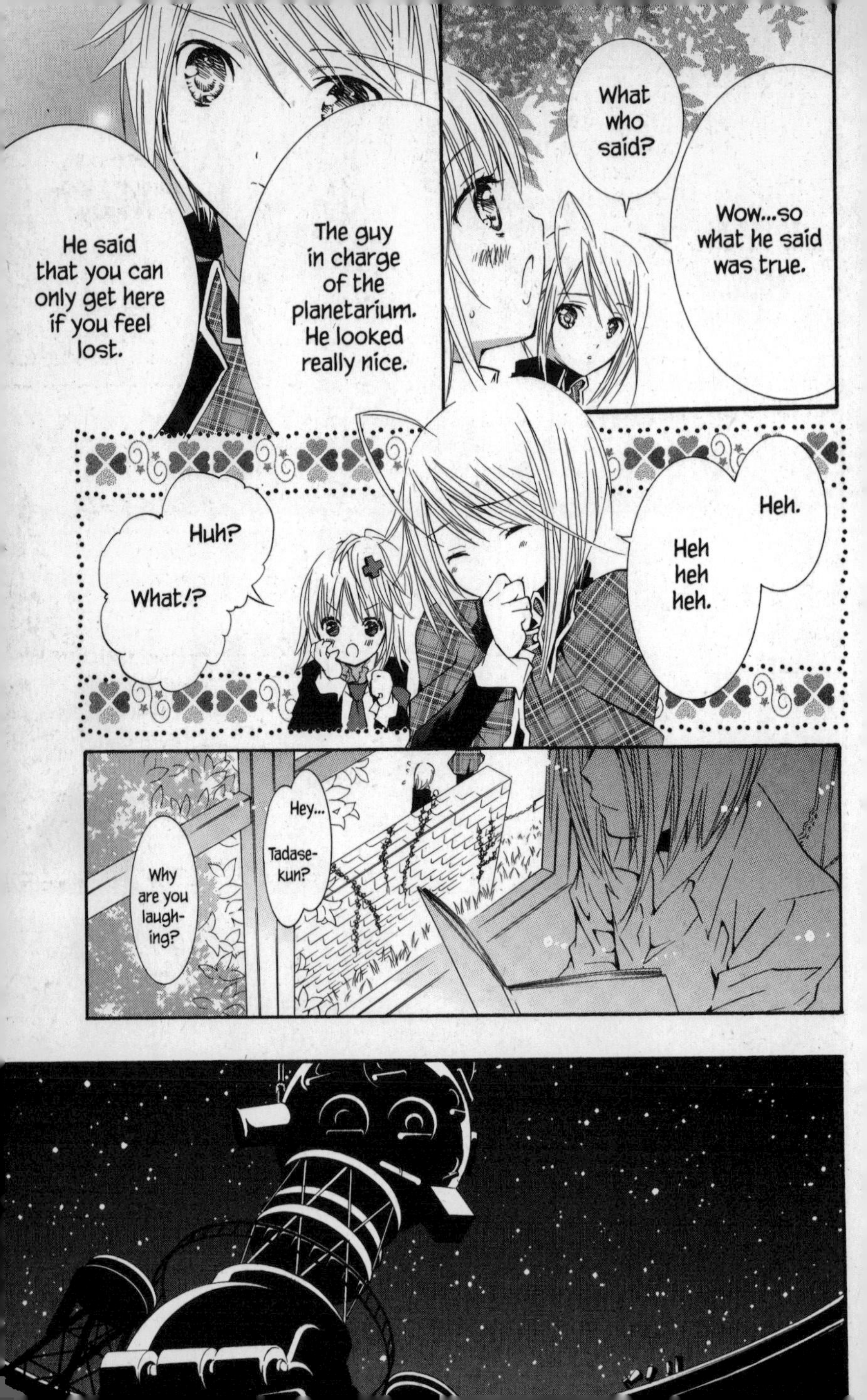
Wow...so what he said was true.
What who said?
The guy in charge of the planetarium. He looked really nice.
He said that you can only get here if you feel lost.
Heh.
Heh heh heh.
Huh?
What!?
Hey...
Tadase-kun?
Why are you laughing?

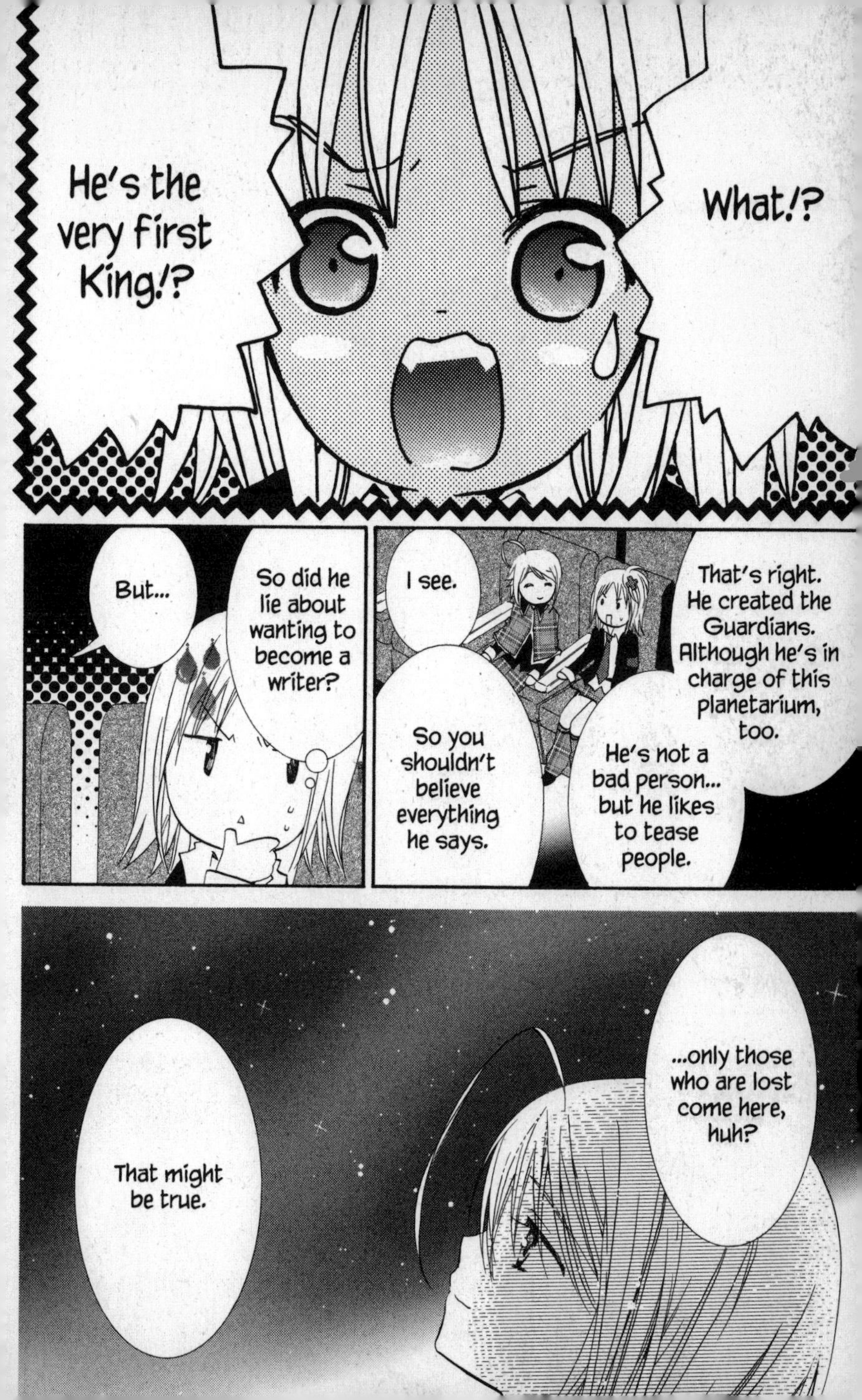
What!?
He's the very first King!?
That's right. He created the Guardians. Although he's in charge of this planetarium, too.
I see.
He's not a bad person... but he likes to tease people.
So you shouldn't believe everything he says.
So did he lie about wanting to become a writer?
But...
...only those who are lost come here, huh?
That might be true.

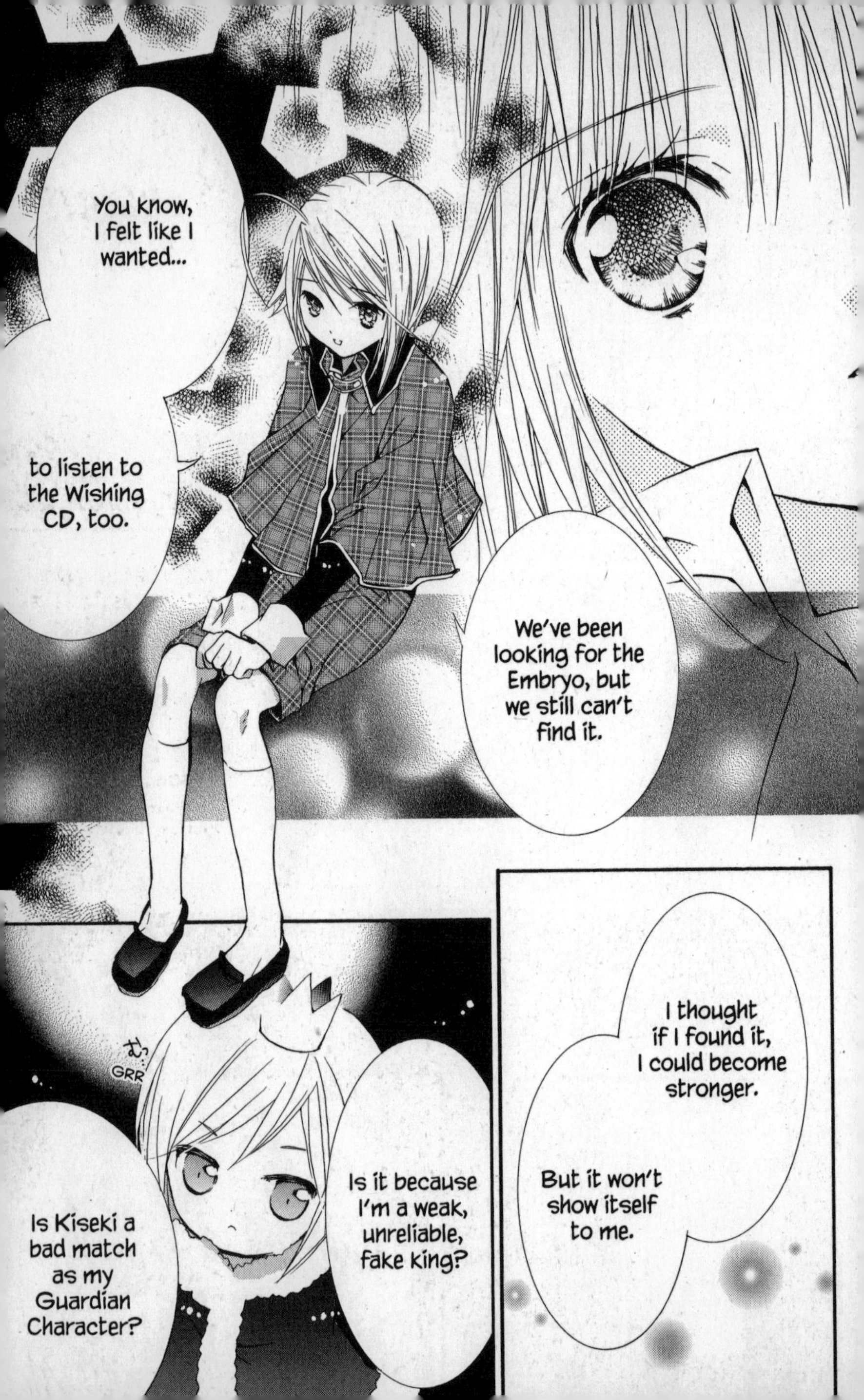
You know, I felt like I wanted...
to listen to the Wishing CD, too.
We've been looking for the Embryo, but we still can't find it.
I thought if I found it, I could become stronger.
But it won't show itself to me.
GRR
Is it because I'm a weak, unreliable, fake king?
Is Kiseki a bad match as my Guardian Character?

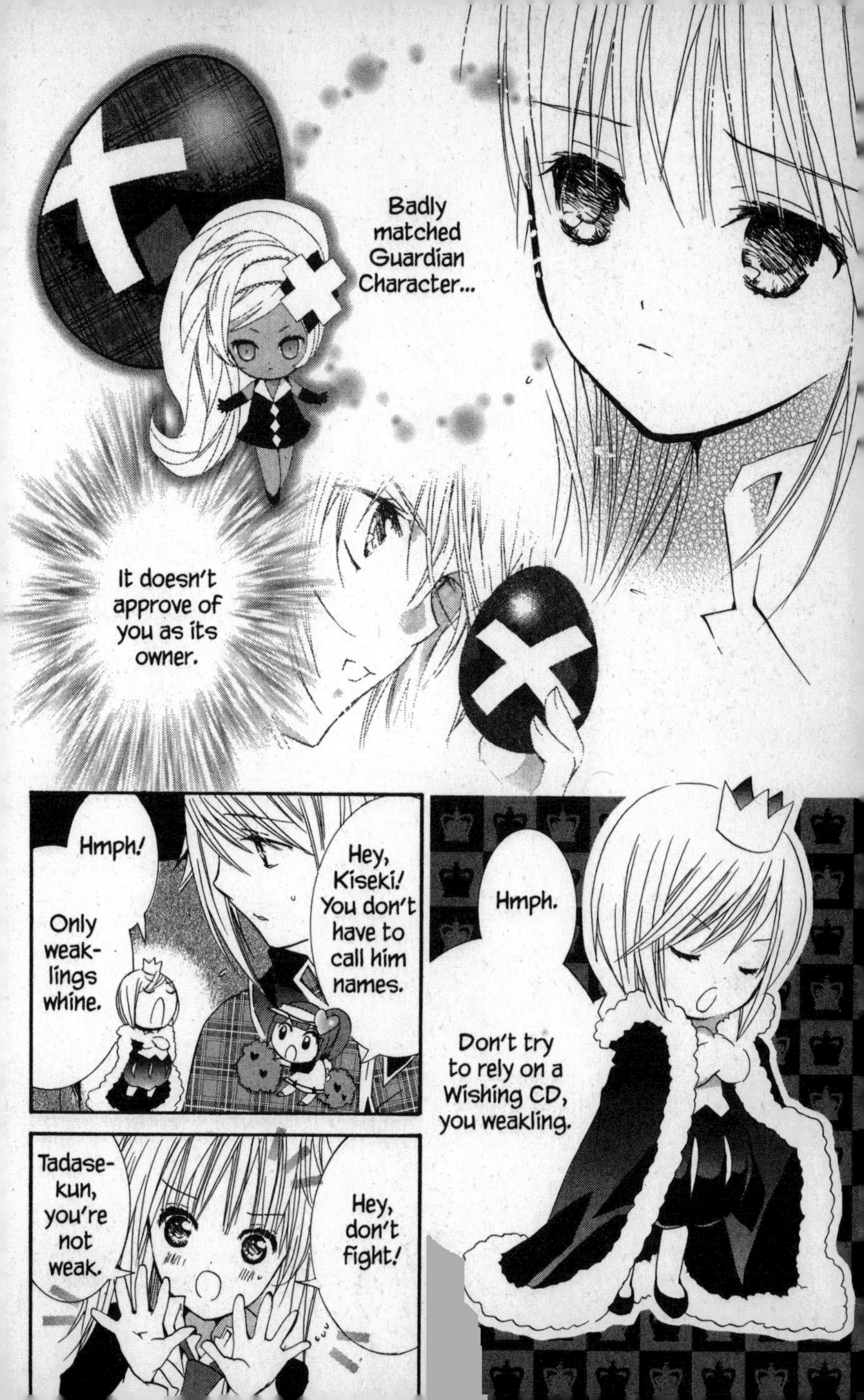
Badly matched Guardian Character...
It doesn't approve of you as its owner.
Hmph.
Don't try to rely on a Wishing CD, you weakling.
Hey, Kiseki! You don't have to call him names.
Hmph!
Only weak-lings whine.
Hey, don't fight!
Tadase-kun, you're not weak.

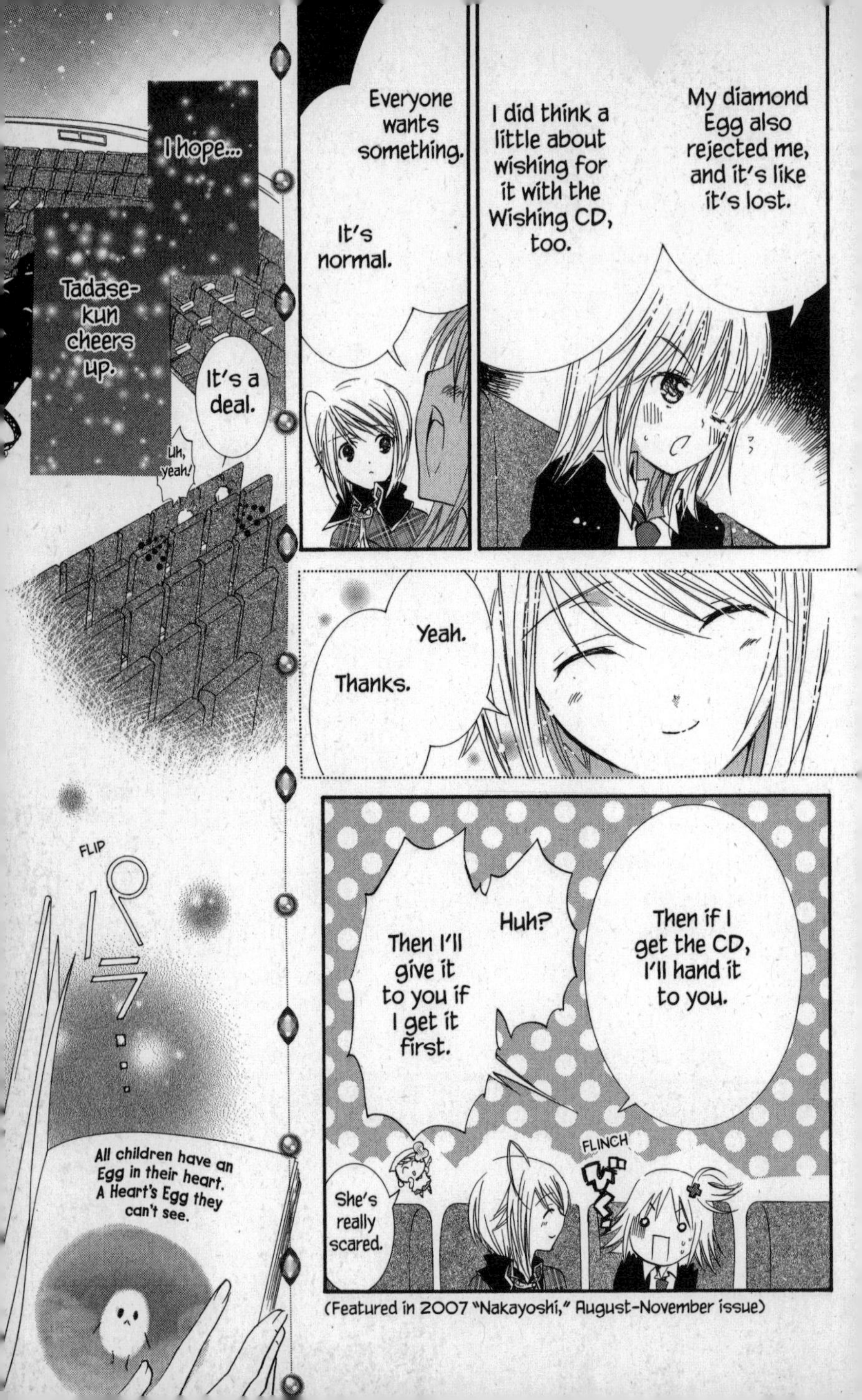
My diamond Egg also rejected me, and it's like it's lost.
I did think a little about wishing for it with the Wishing CD, too.
Everyone wants something.
It's normal.
Yeah.
Thanks.
Then if I get the CD, I'll hand it to you.
Huh?
Then I'll give it to you if I get it first.
FLINCH
She's really scared.
I hope...
Tadase-kun cheers up.
It's a deal.
Uh, yeah!
FLIP
All children have an Egg in their heart. A Heart's Egg they can't see.

(Featured in 2007 "Nakayoshi," August-November issue)

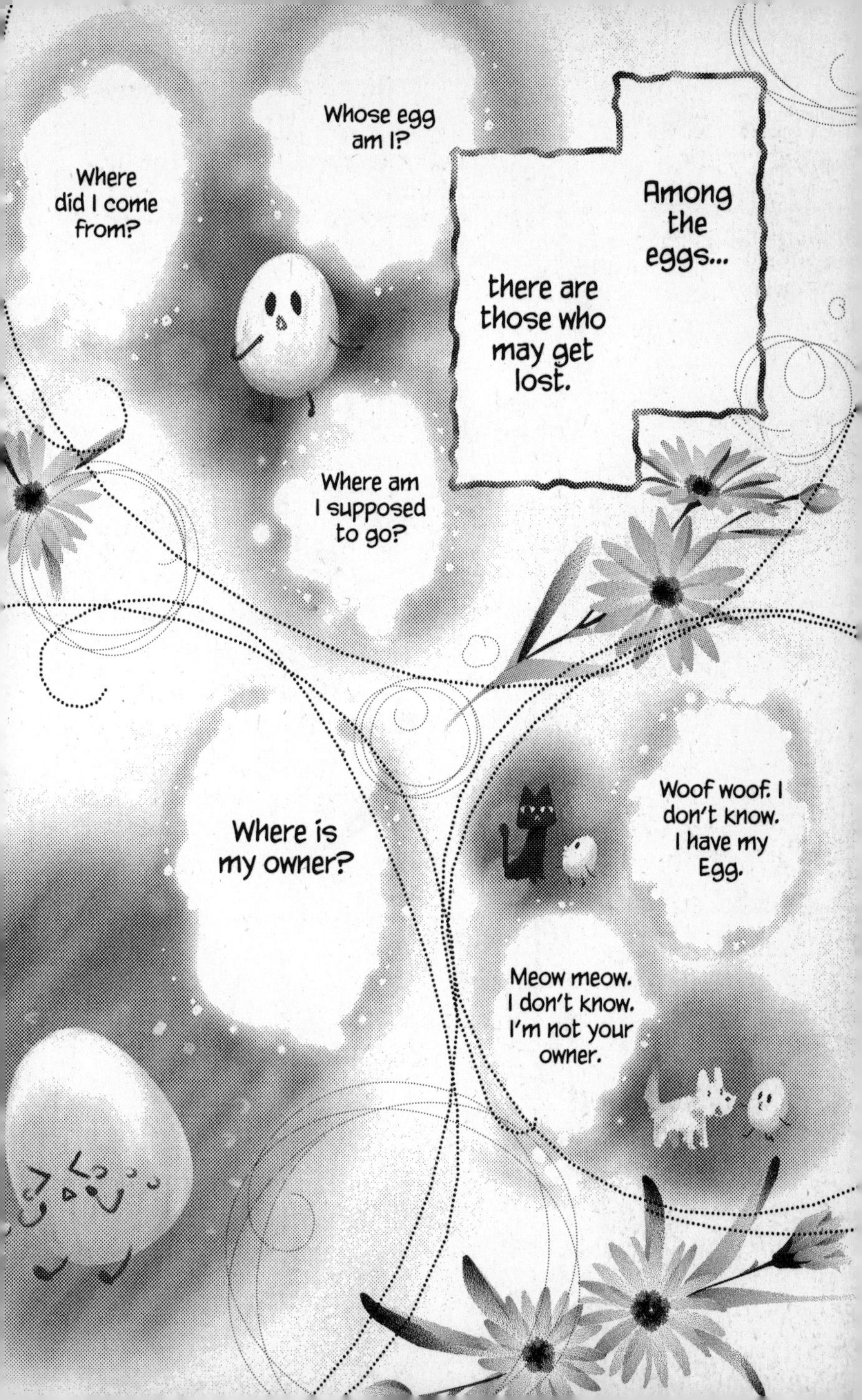
Among the eggs...
there are those who may get lost.
Whose egg am I?
Where did I come from?
Where am I supposed to go?
Woof woof. I don't know. I have my Egg.
Where is my owner?
Meow meow. I don't know. I'm not your owner.

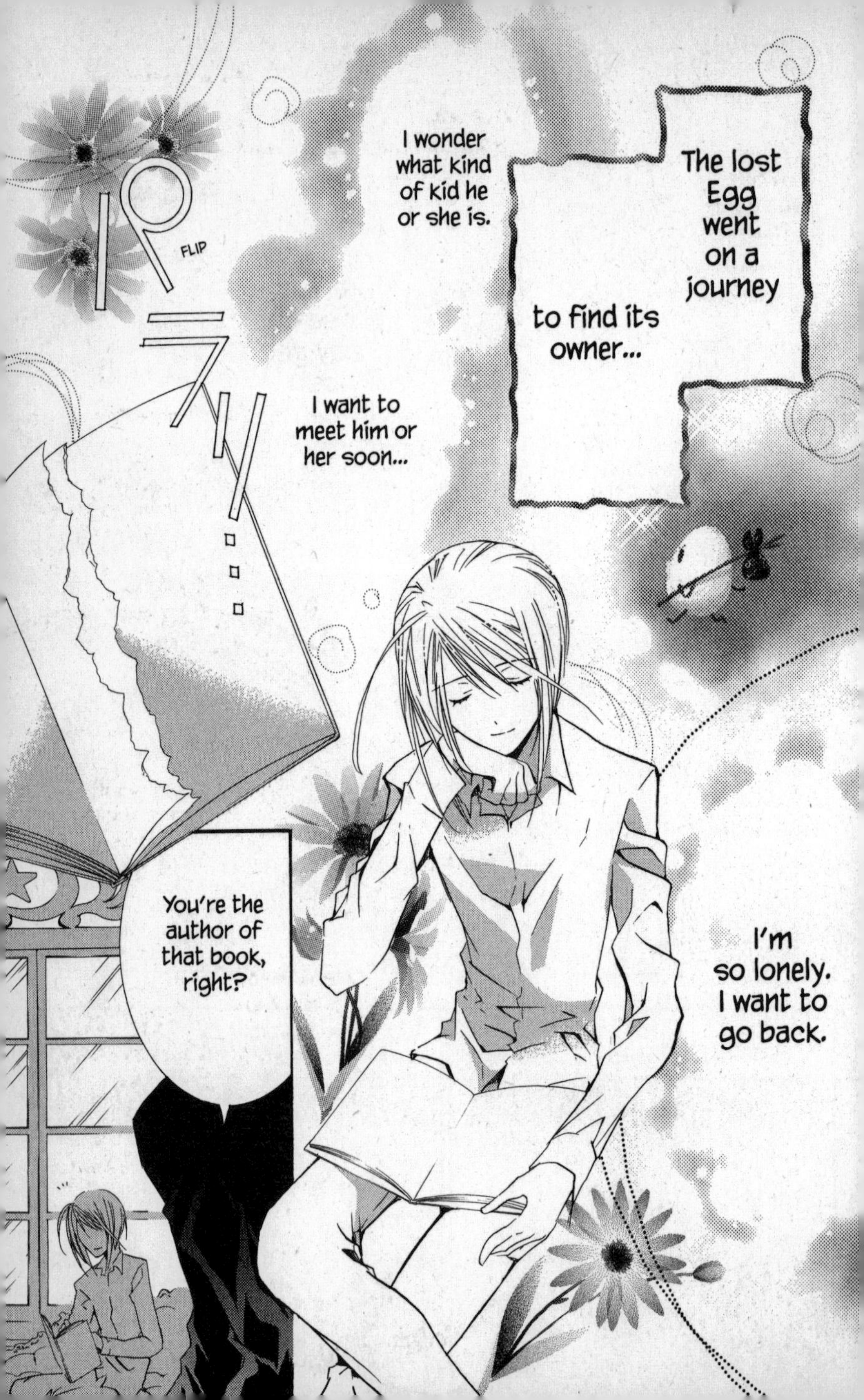
The lost Egg went on a journey
to find its owner...
I wonder what kind of kid he or she is.
I want to meet him or her soon...
パラリ…
FLIP
I'm so lonely. I want to go back.
You're the author of that book, right?

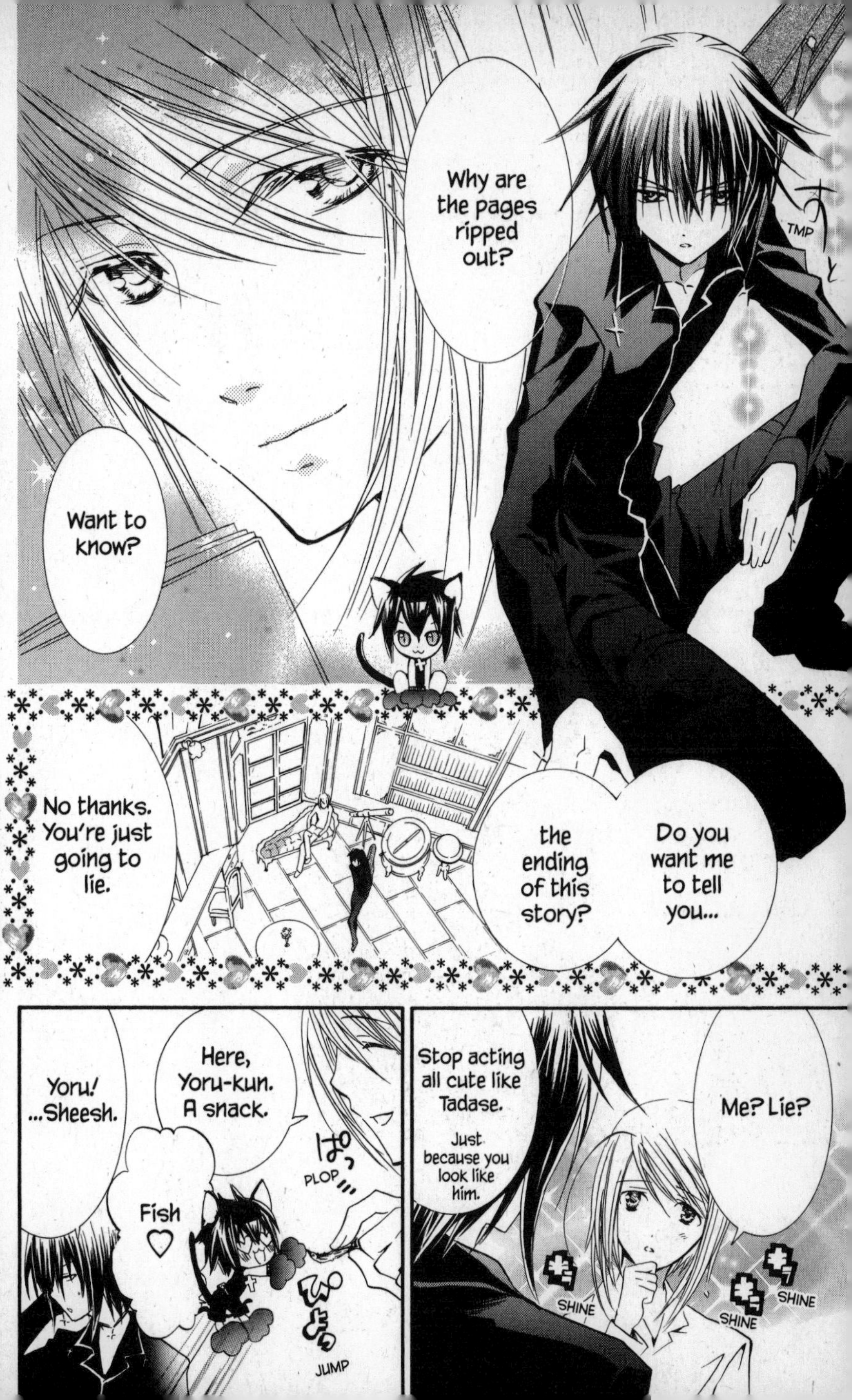
Why are the pages ripped out?
TMP
Want to know?
Do you want me to tell you...
the ending of this story?
No thanks. You're just going to lie.
Me? Lie?
Stop acting all cute like Tadase.
Just because you look like him.
SHINE
SHINE
SHINE
Here, Yoru-kun. A snack.
PLOP
Yoru! ...Sheesh.
Fish ♡
JUMP

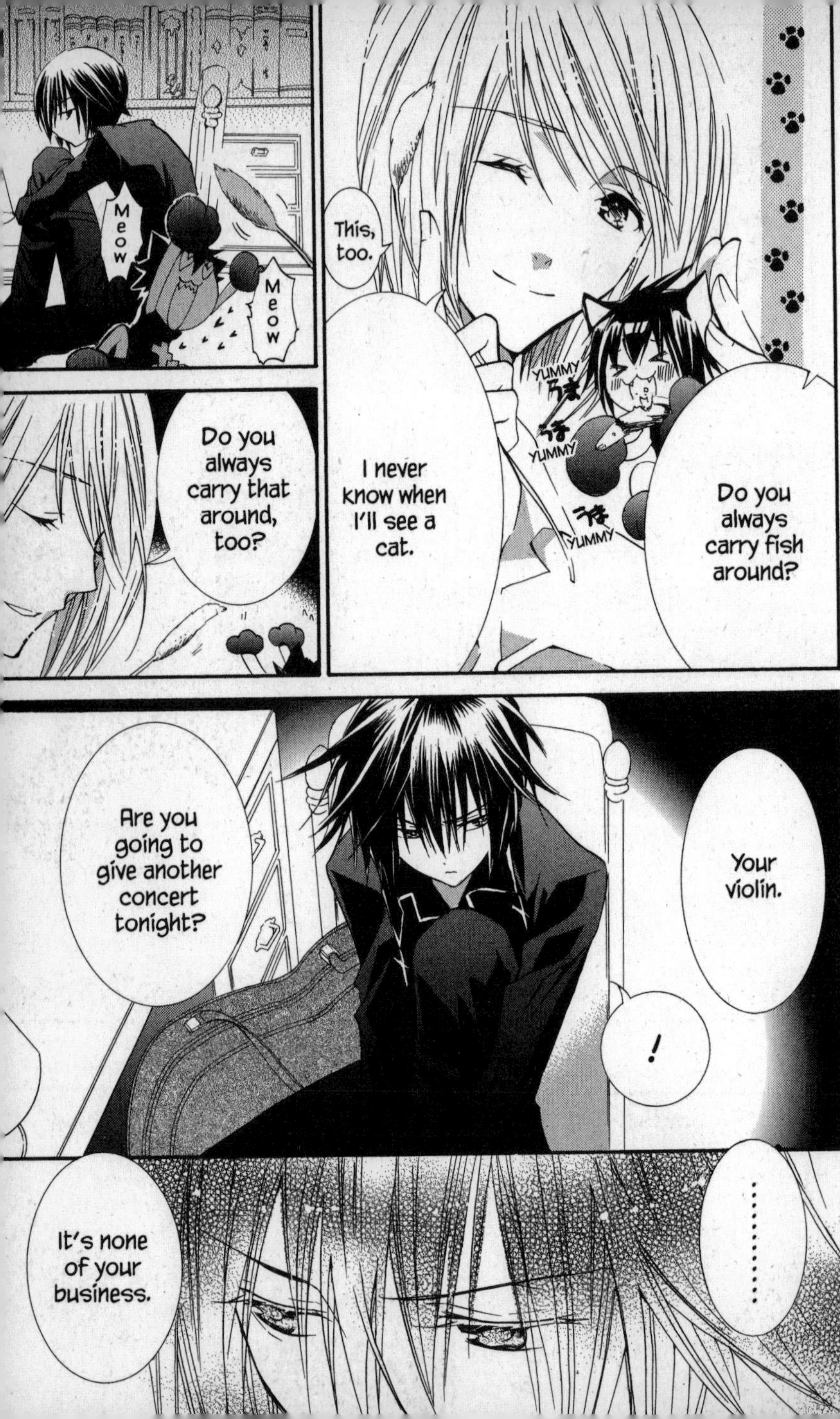

YUMMY
YUMMY
YUMMY
Do you always carry fish around?
I never know when I'll see a cat.
This, too.
Meow
Meow
Do you always carry that around, too?
Your violin.
!
Are you going to give another concert tonight?
......
It's none of your business.

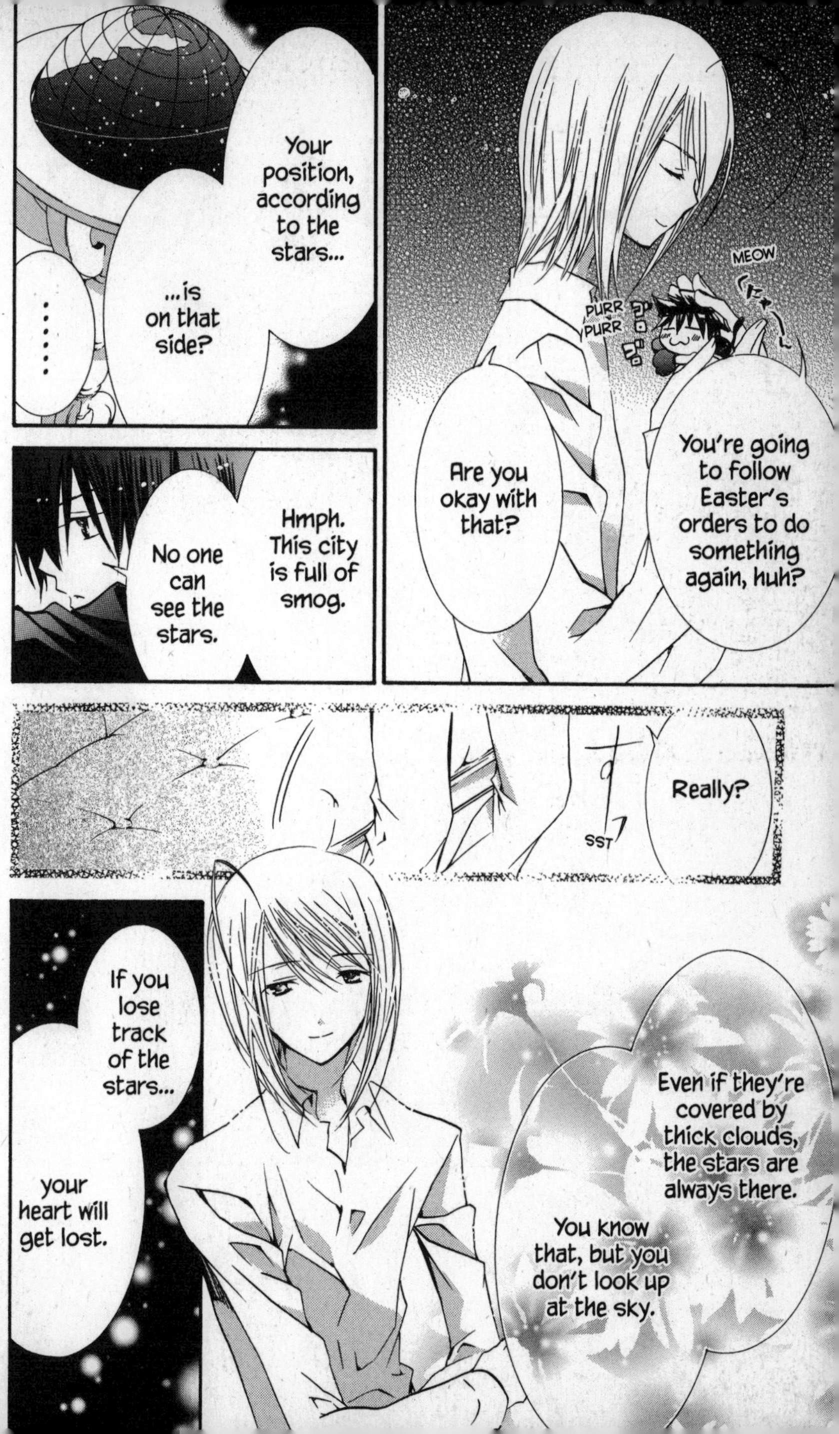
MEOW
PURR PURR
You're going to follow Easter's orders to do something again, huh?
Are you okay with that?
Your position, according to the stars...
...is on that side?
......
Hmph. This city is full of smog.
No one can see the stars.
Really?
SST
Even if they're covered by thick clouds, the stars are always there.
You know that, but you don't look up at the sky.
If you lose track of the stars...
your heart will get lost.

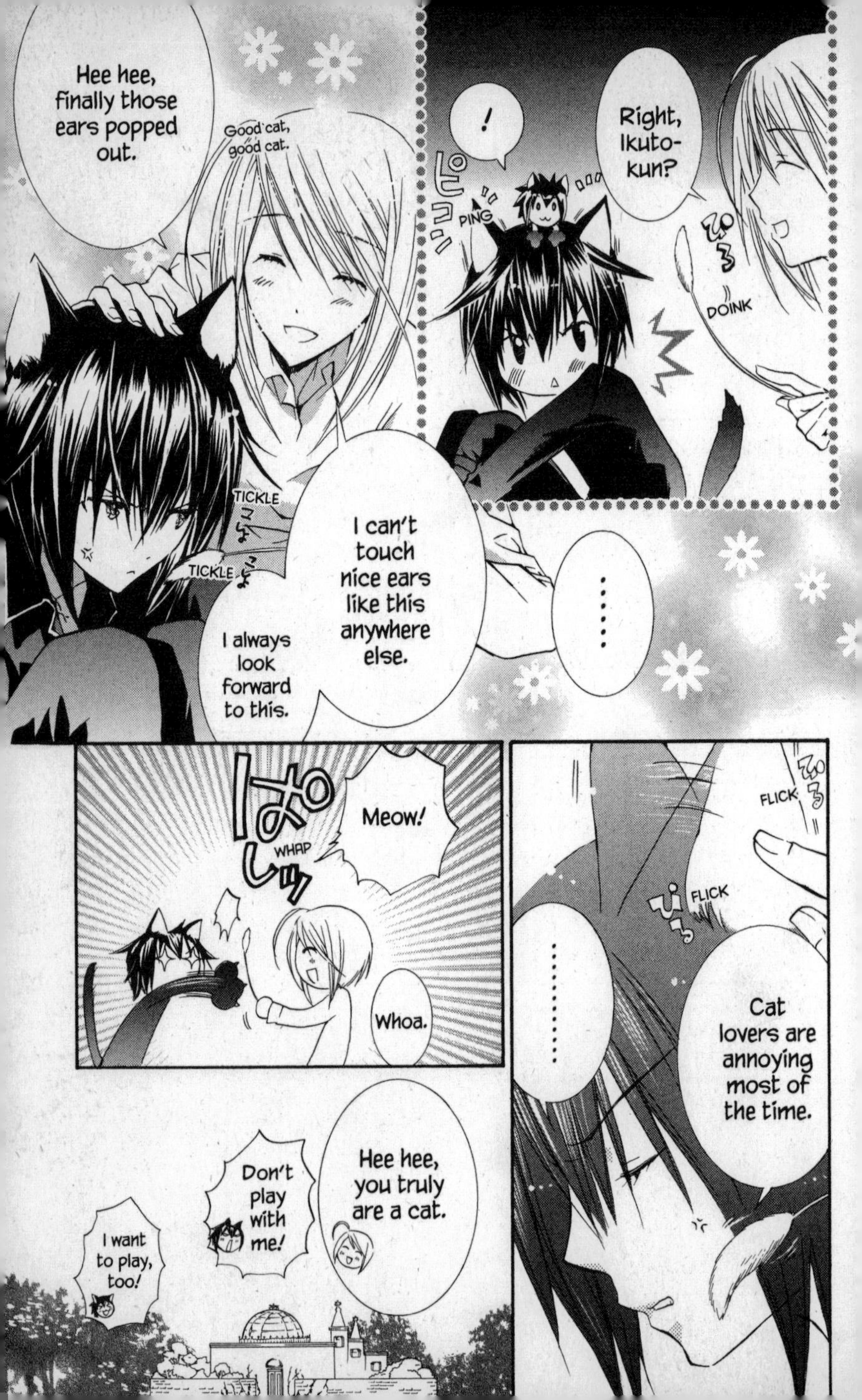
Right, Ikuto-kun?
!
PING
DOINK
Hee hee, finally those ears popped out.
Good cat, good cat.
TICKLE
TICKLE
I can't touch nice ears like this anywhere else.
I always look forward to this.
......
FLICK
FLICK
......
Cat lovers are annoying most of the time.
Meow!
WHAP
Whoa.
Hee hee, you truly are a cat.
Don't play with me!
I want to play, too!

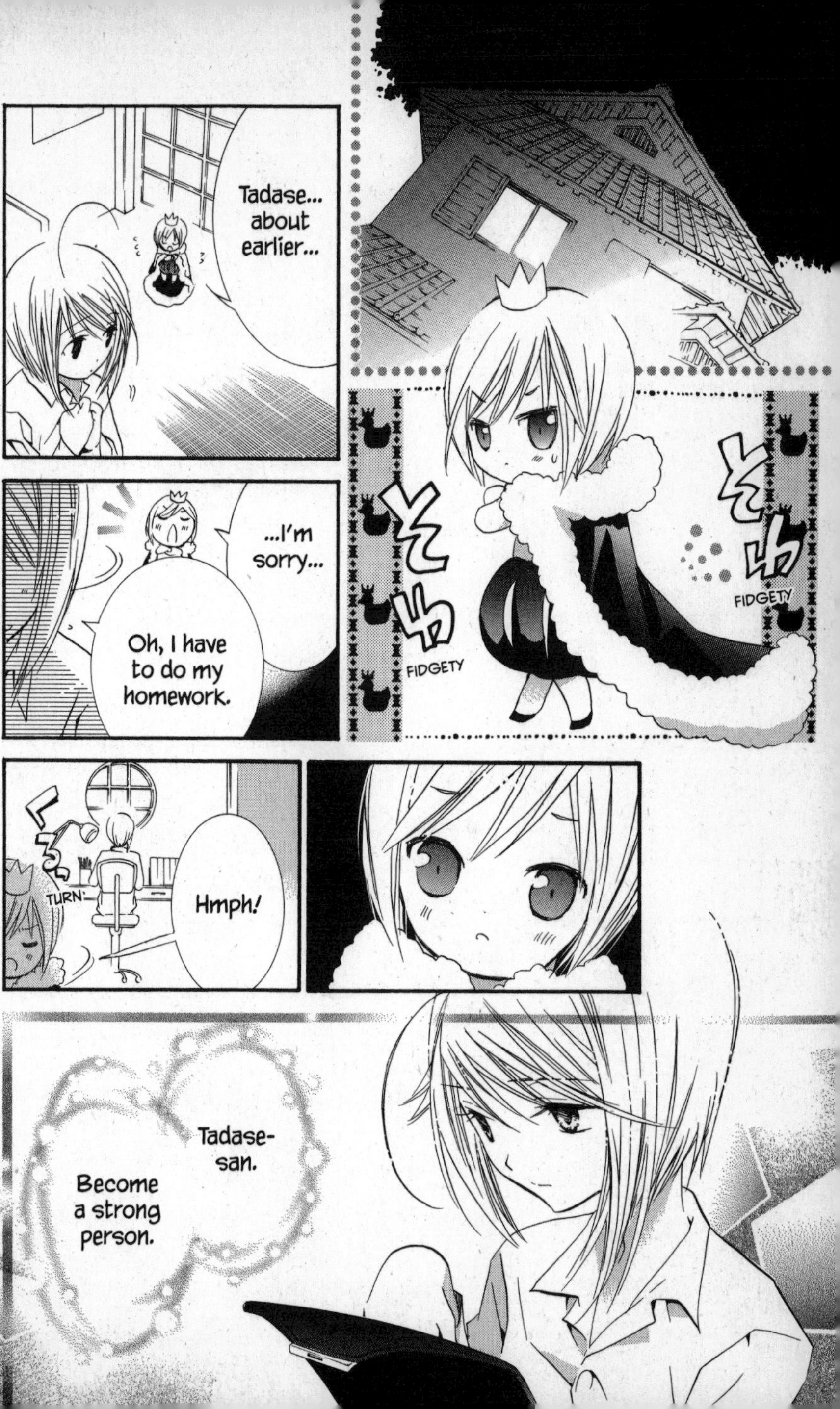

そわ
FIDGETY
そわ
FIDGETY
Tadase... about earlier...
...I'm sorry...
Oh, I have to do my homework.
Hmph!
TURN
Tadase-san.
Become a strong person.

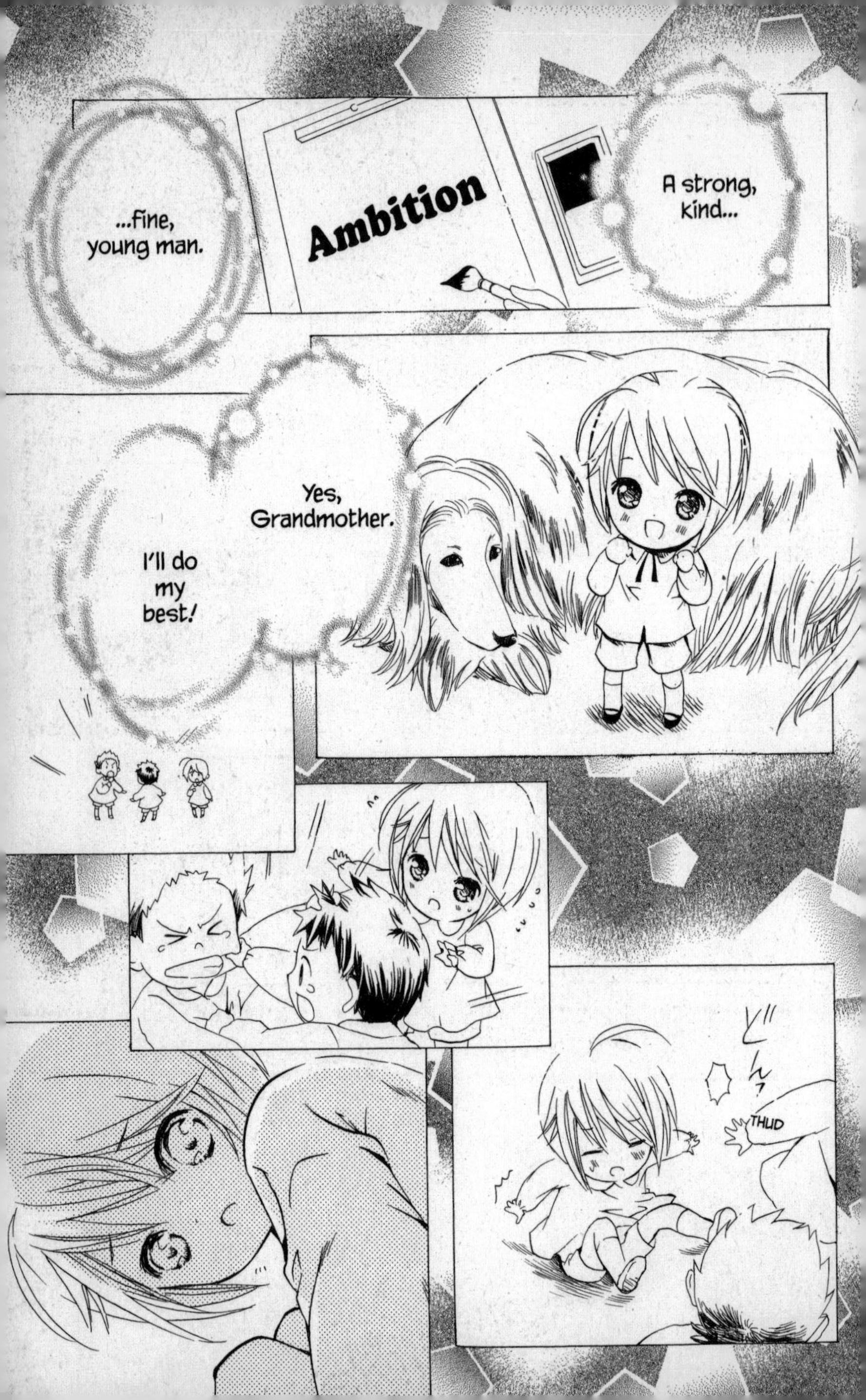
A strong, kind...
Ambition
...fine, young man.
Yes, Grandmother.
I'll do my best!
THUD

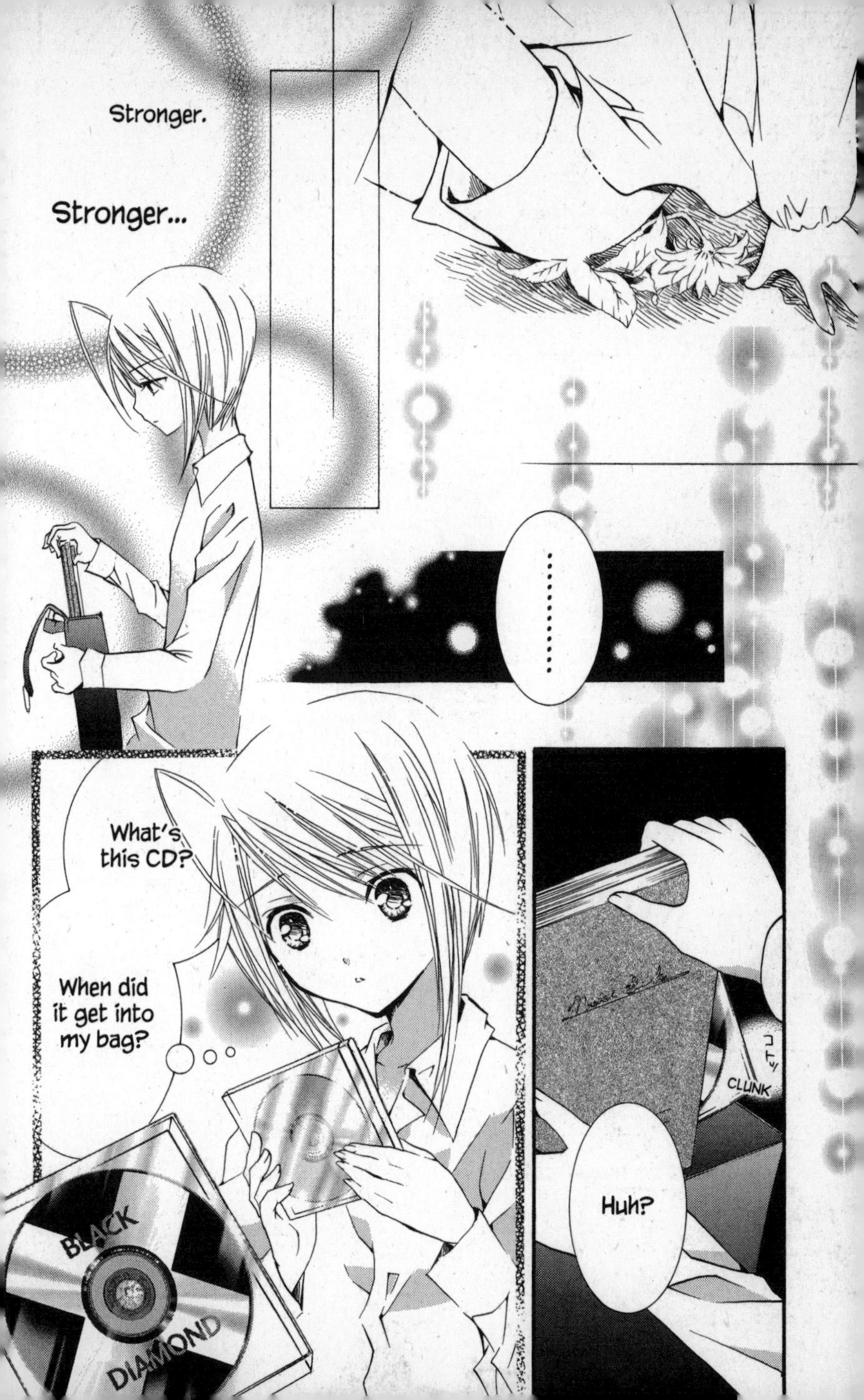
Stronger.
Stronger...
......
Huh?
CLUNK
What's this CD?
When did it get into my bag?
BLACK DIAMOND

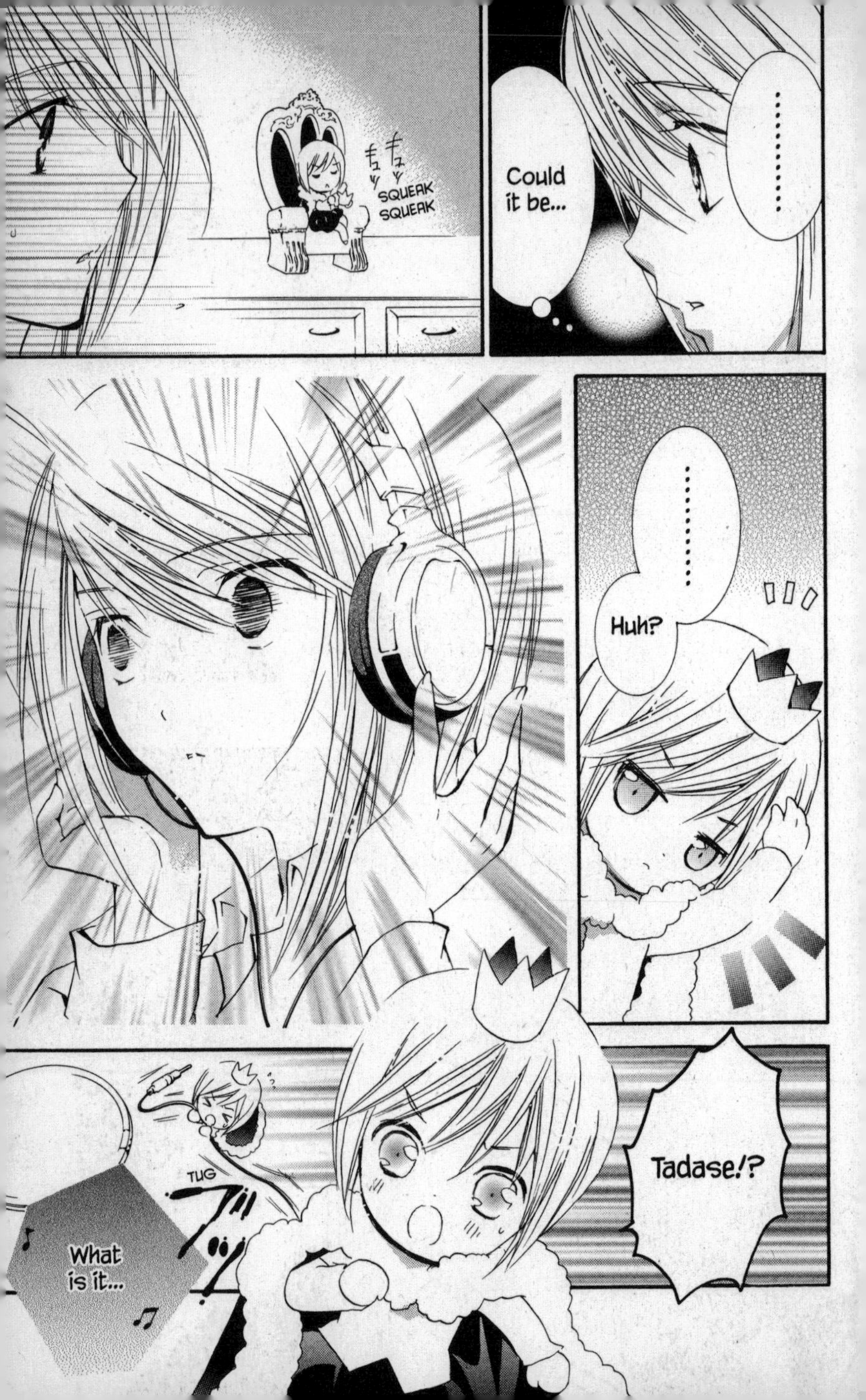
……
Could it be...
SQUEAK SQUEAK
……
Huh?
Tadase!?
TUG
What is it...

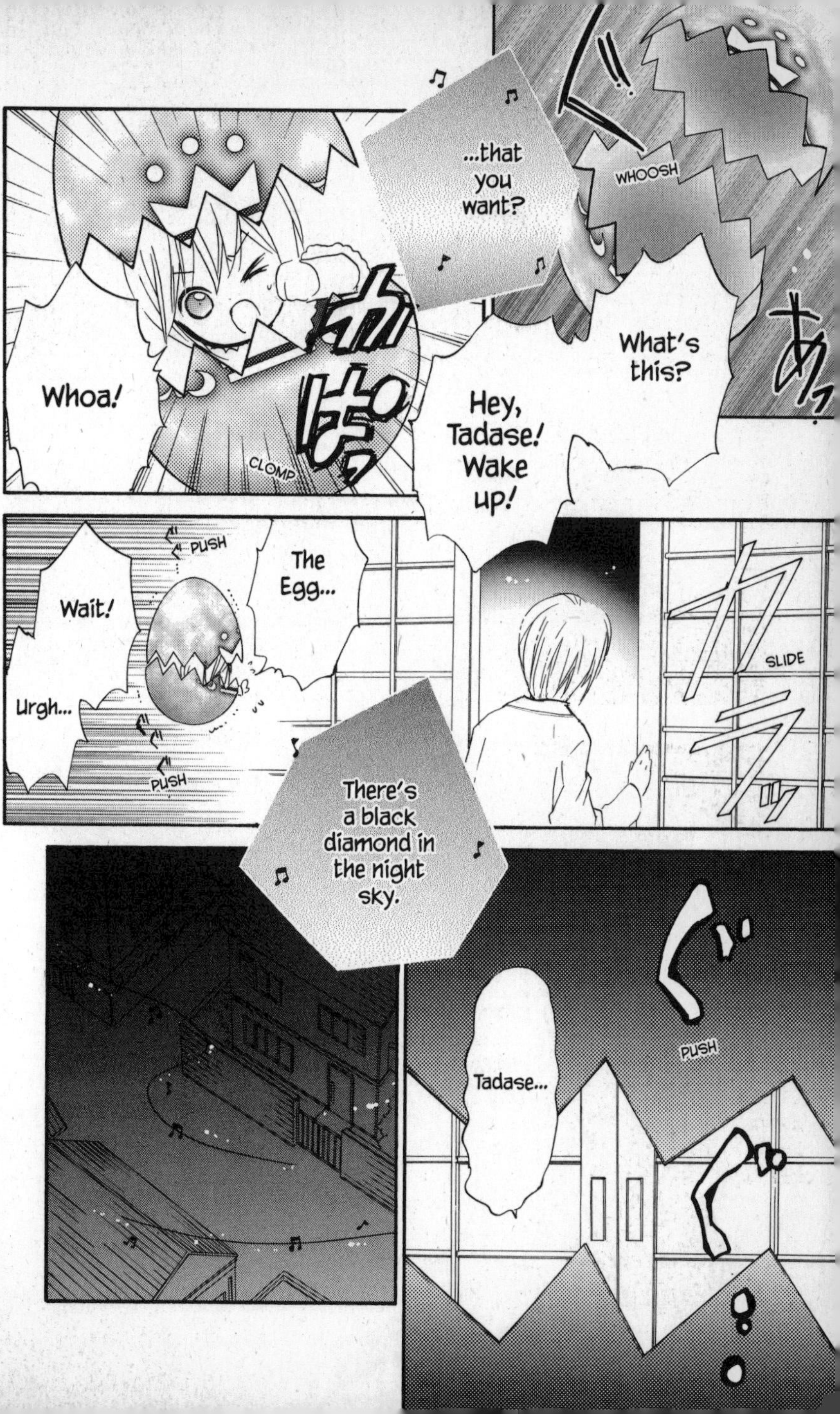
...that you want?
WHOOSH
What's this?
Whoa!
CLOMP
Hey, Tadase! Wake up!
SLIDE
The Egg...
PUSH
Wait!
Urgh...
PUSH
There's a black diamond in the night sky.
PUSH
Tadase...

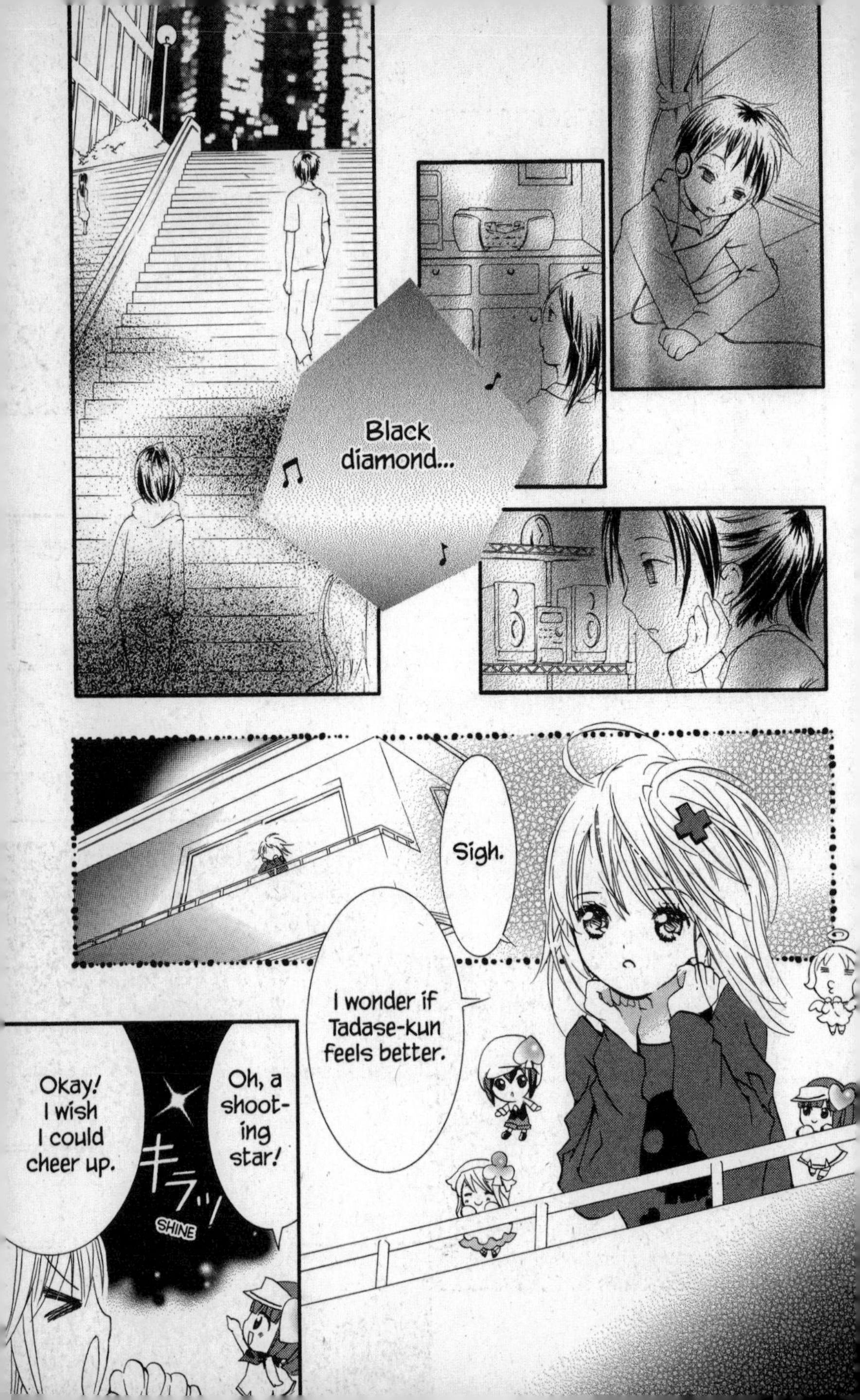
Black diamond...
Sigh.
I wonder if Tadase-kun feels better.
Oh, a shooting star!
キラッ
SHINE
Okay! I wish I could cheer up.

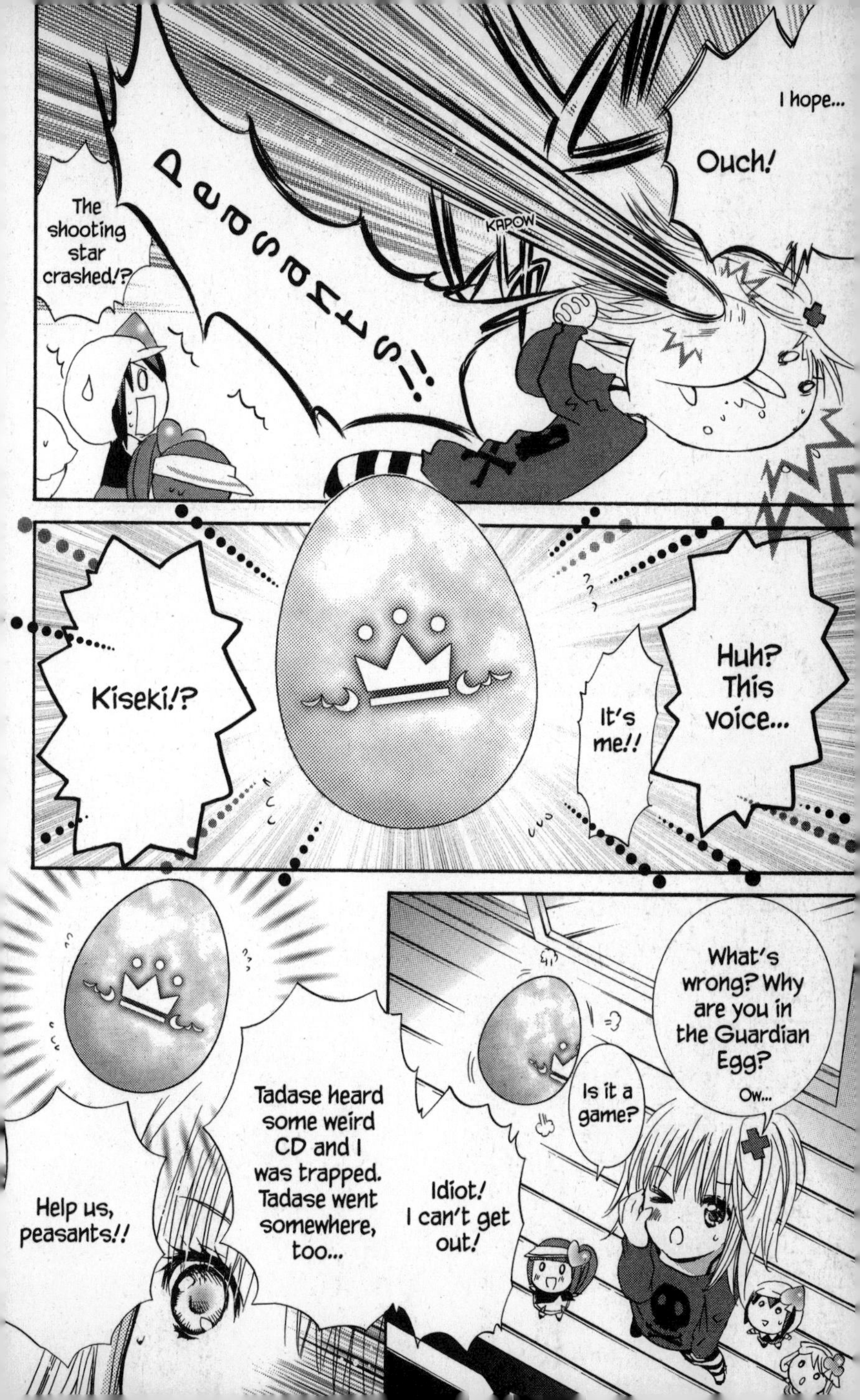
I hope...
Ouch!
KAPOW
Peasants!!
The shooting star crashed!?
Huh? This voice...
It's me!!
Kiseki!?
What's wrong? Why are you in the Guardian Egg?
Ow...
Is it a game?
Idiot! I can't get out!
Tadase heard some weird CD and I was trapped. Tadase went somewhere, too...
Help us, peasants!!

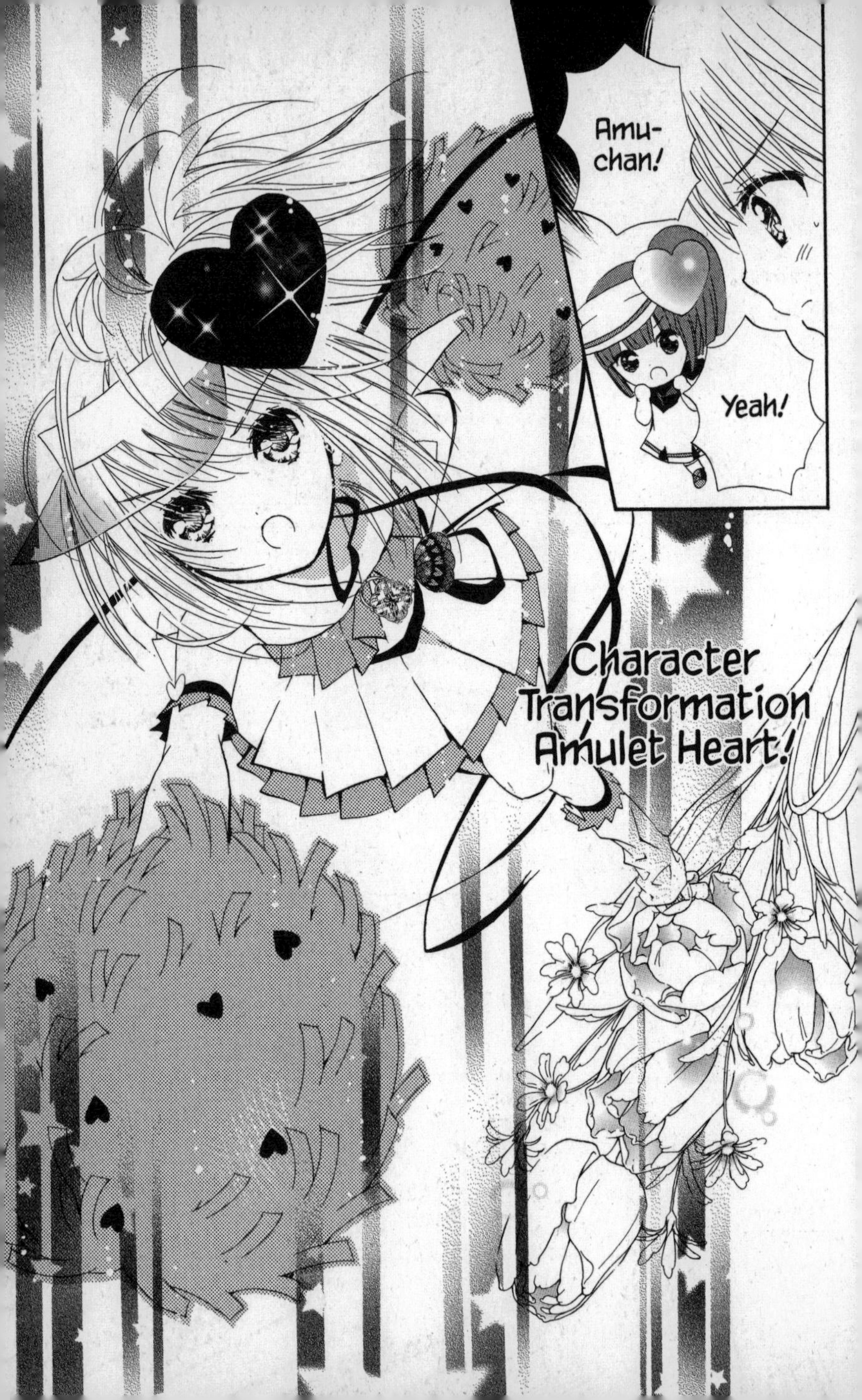
Amu-chan!
Yeah!
Character Transformation Amulet Heart!

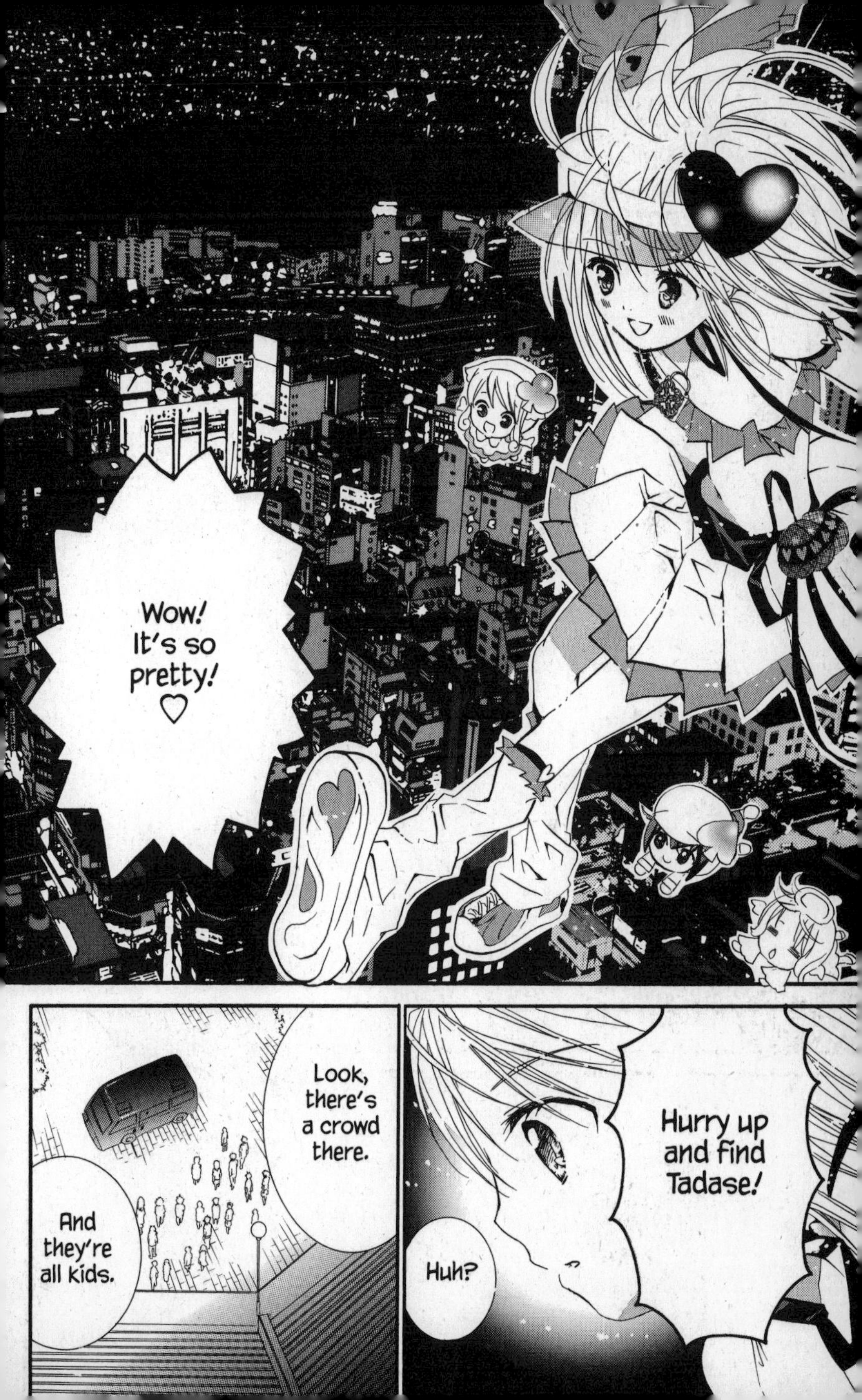
Wow! It's so pretty! ♡
Hurry up and find Tadase!
Huh?
Look, there's a crowd there.
And they're all kids.

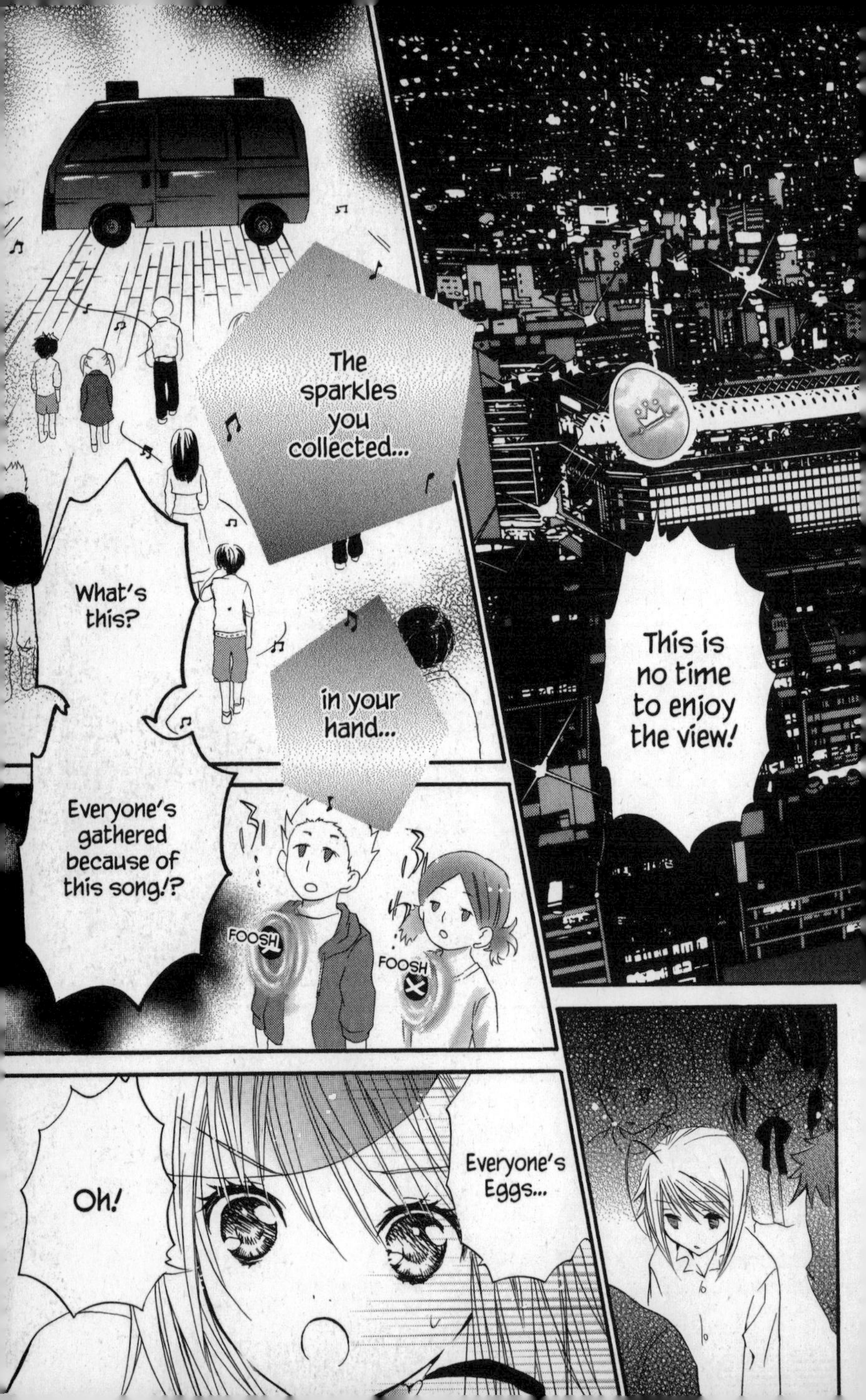
This is no time to enjoy the view!
The sparkles you collected...
in your hand...
What's this?
Everyone's gathered because of this song!?
FOOSH
FOOSH
Everyone's Eggs...
Oh!

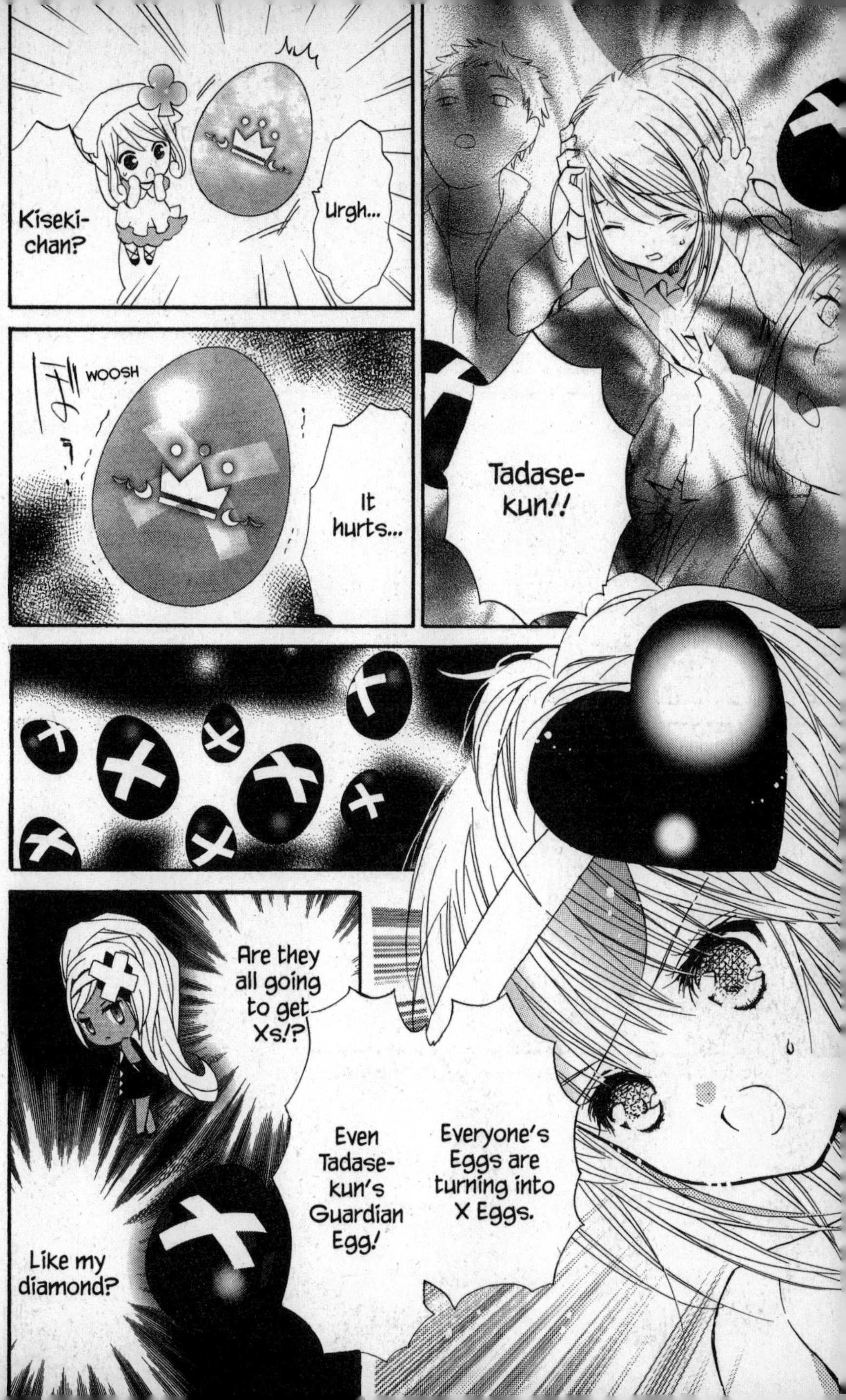
Tadase-kun!!
Urgh...
Kiseki-chan?
WOOSH
It hurts...
Everyone's Eggs are turning into X Eggs.
Even Tadase-kun's Guardian Egg!
Are they all going to get Xs!?
Like my diamond?

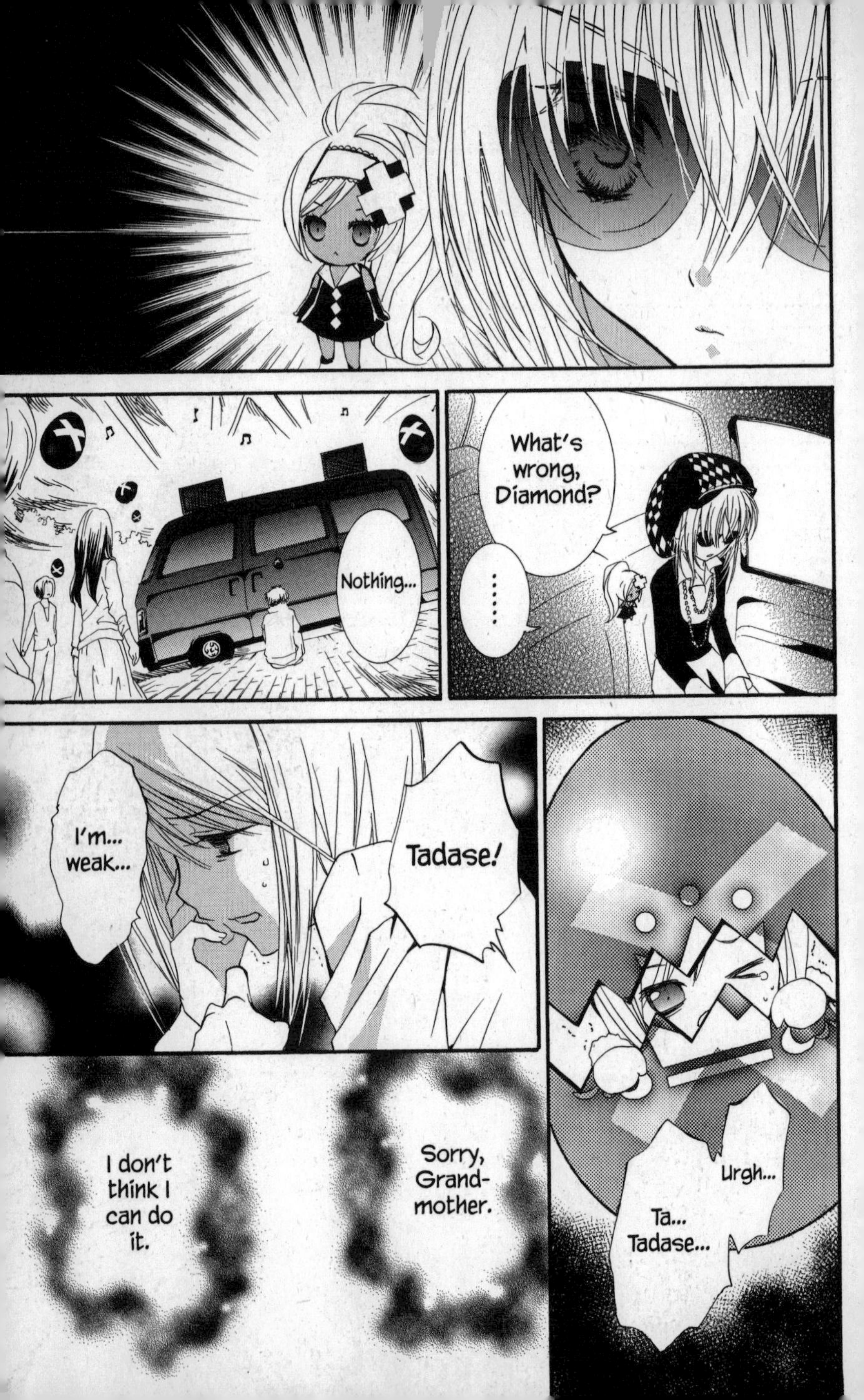
What's wrong, Diamond?
......
Nothing...
Urgh...
Ta... Tadase...
Tadase!
I'm... weak...
Sorry, Grand-mother.
I don't think I can do it.

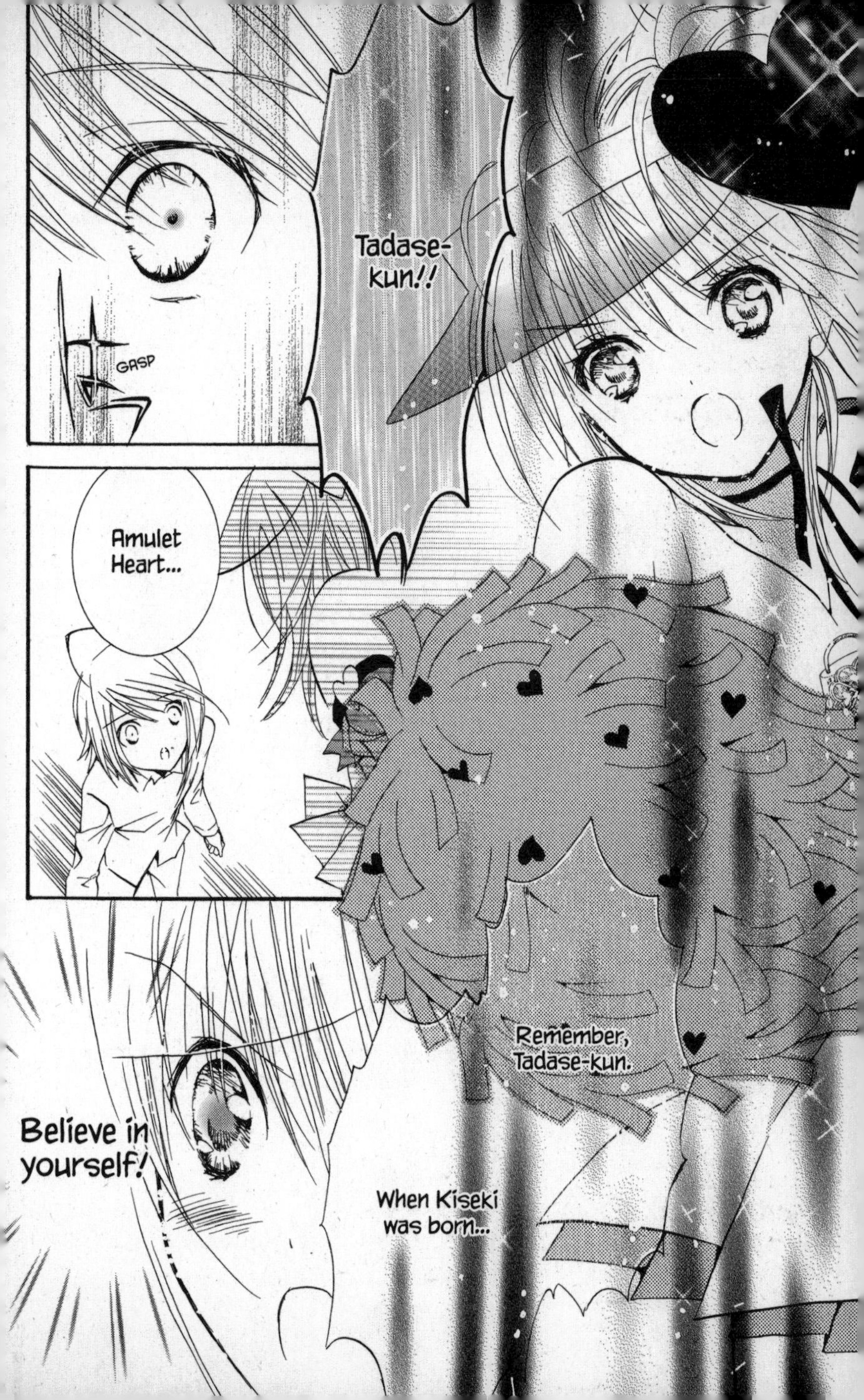

Tadase-kun!!
Remember, Tadase-kun.
When Kiseki was born...
GASP
Amulet Heart...
Believe in yourself!

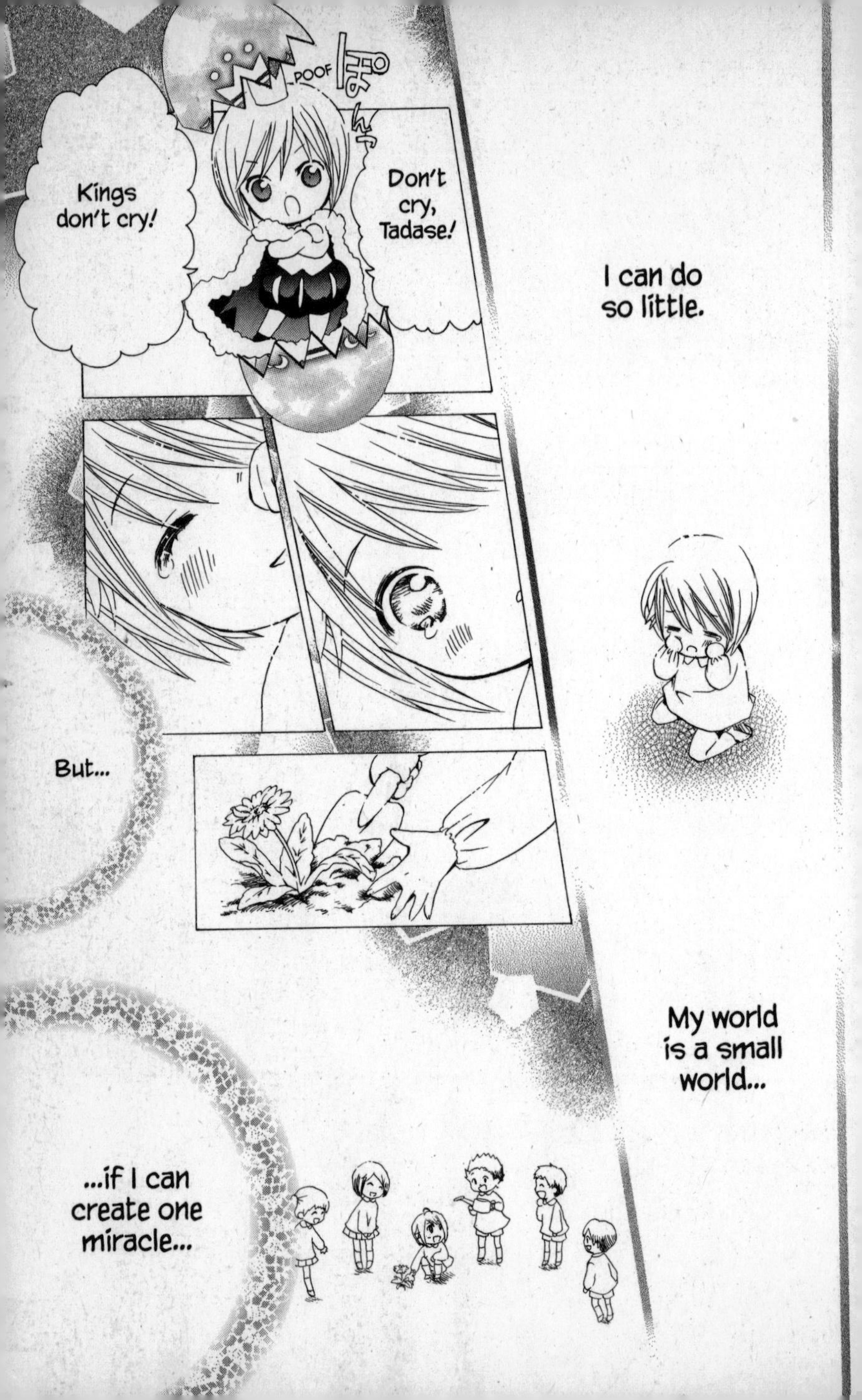
I can do so little.
My world is a small world...
POOF ぽん
Don't cry, Tadase!
Kings don't cry!
But...
...if I can create one miracle...

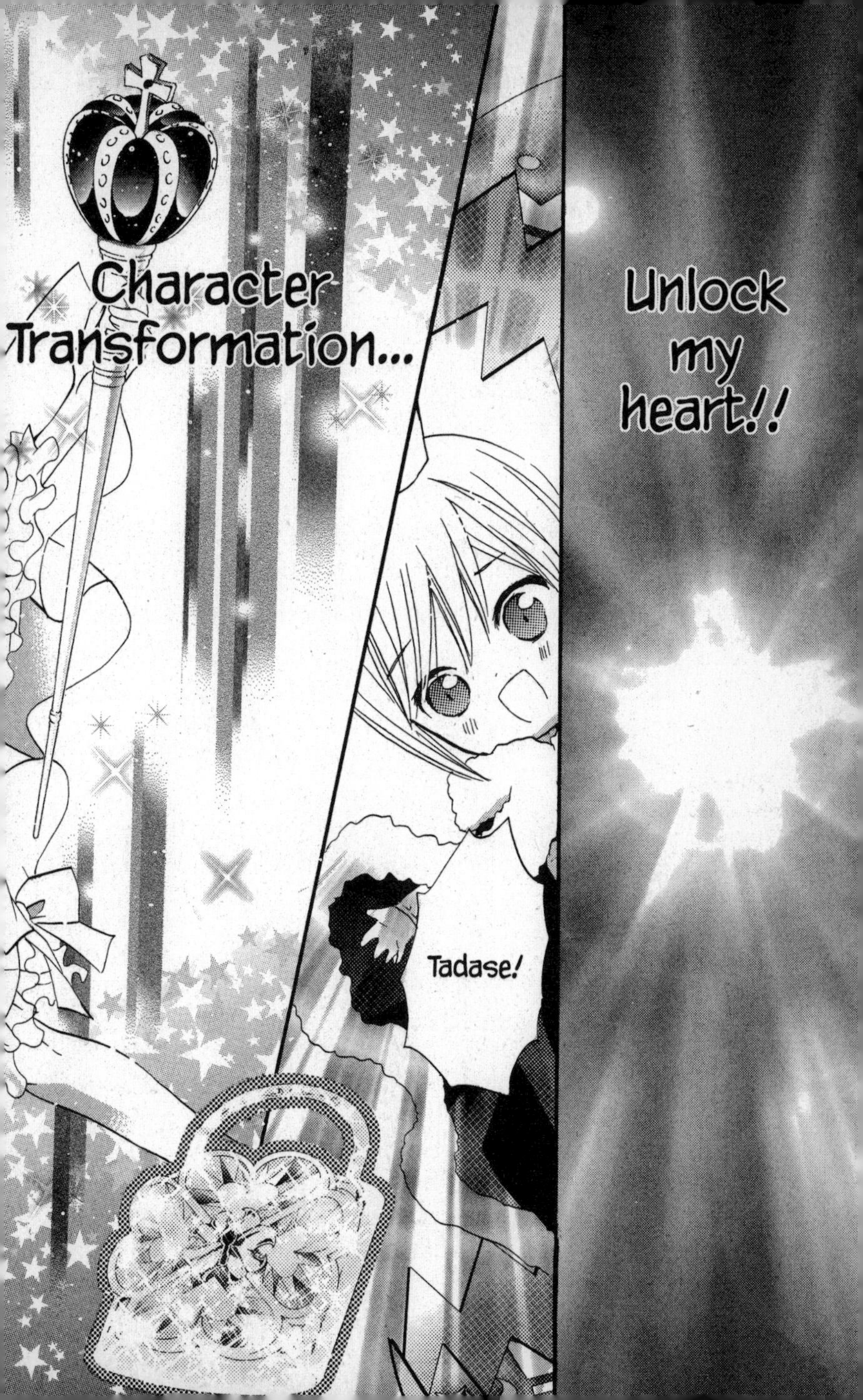
Unlock my heart!!
Tadase!
Character Transformation...

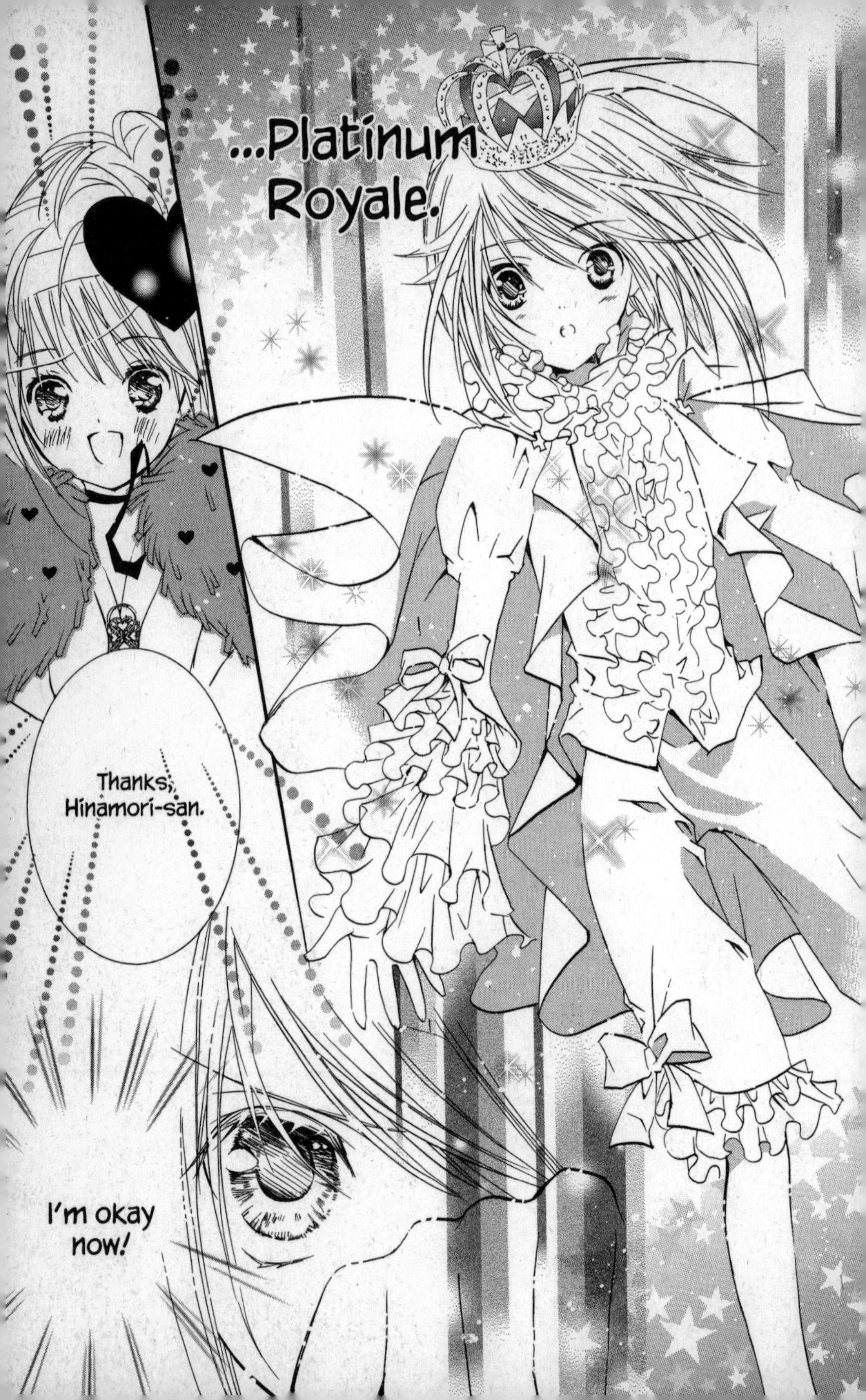
...Platinum Royale.
Thanks, Hinamori-san.
I'm okay now!

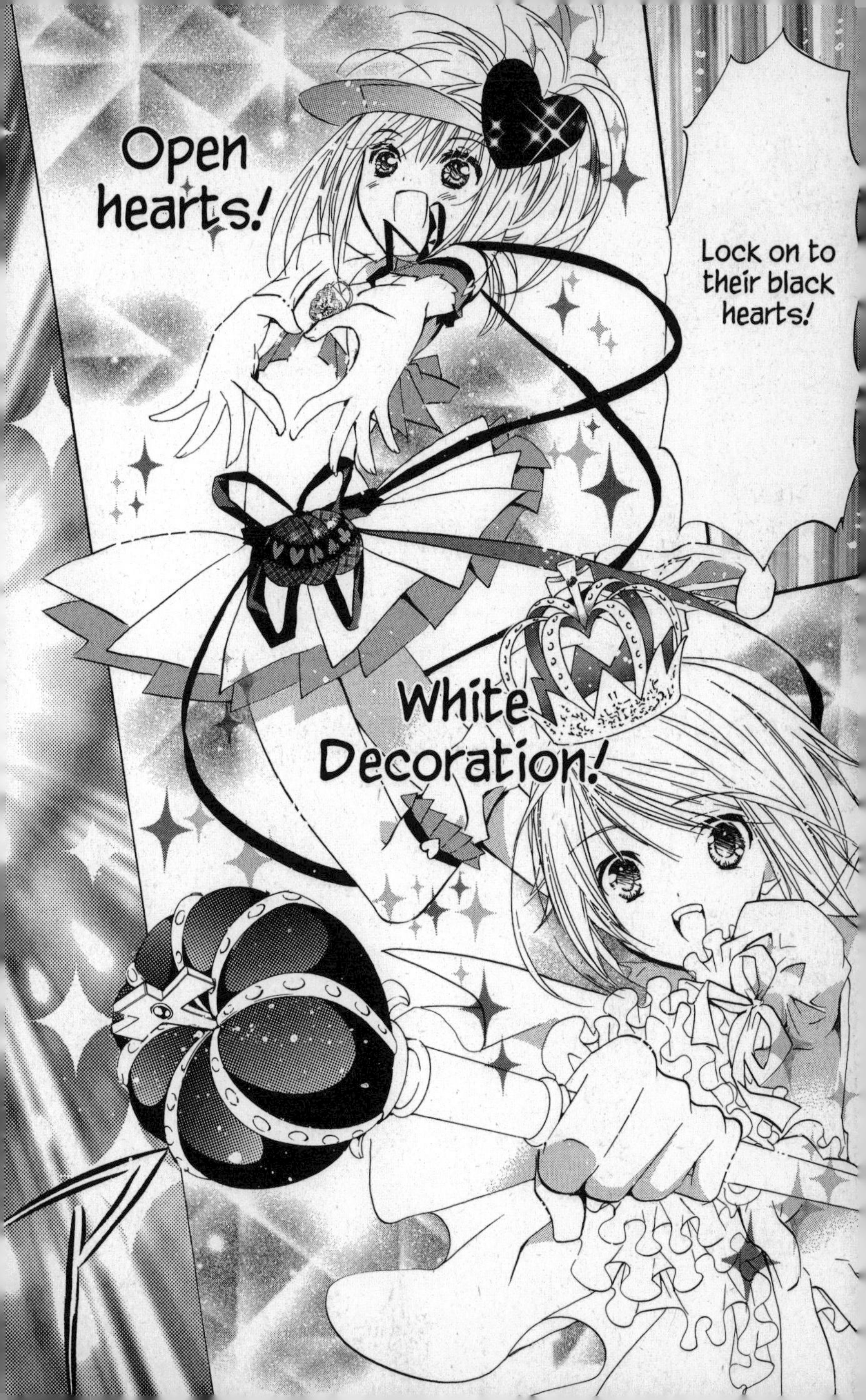
Lock on to their black hearts!
Open hearts!
White Decoration!

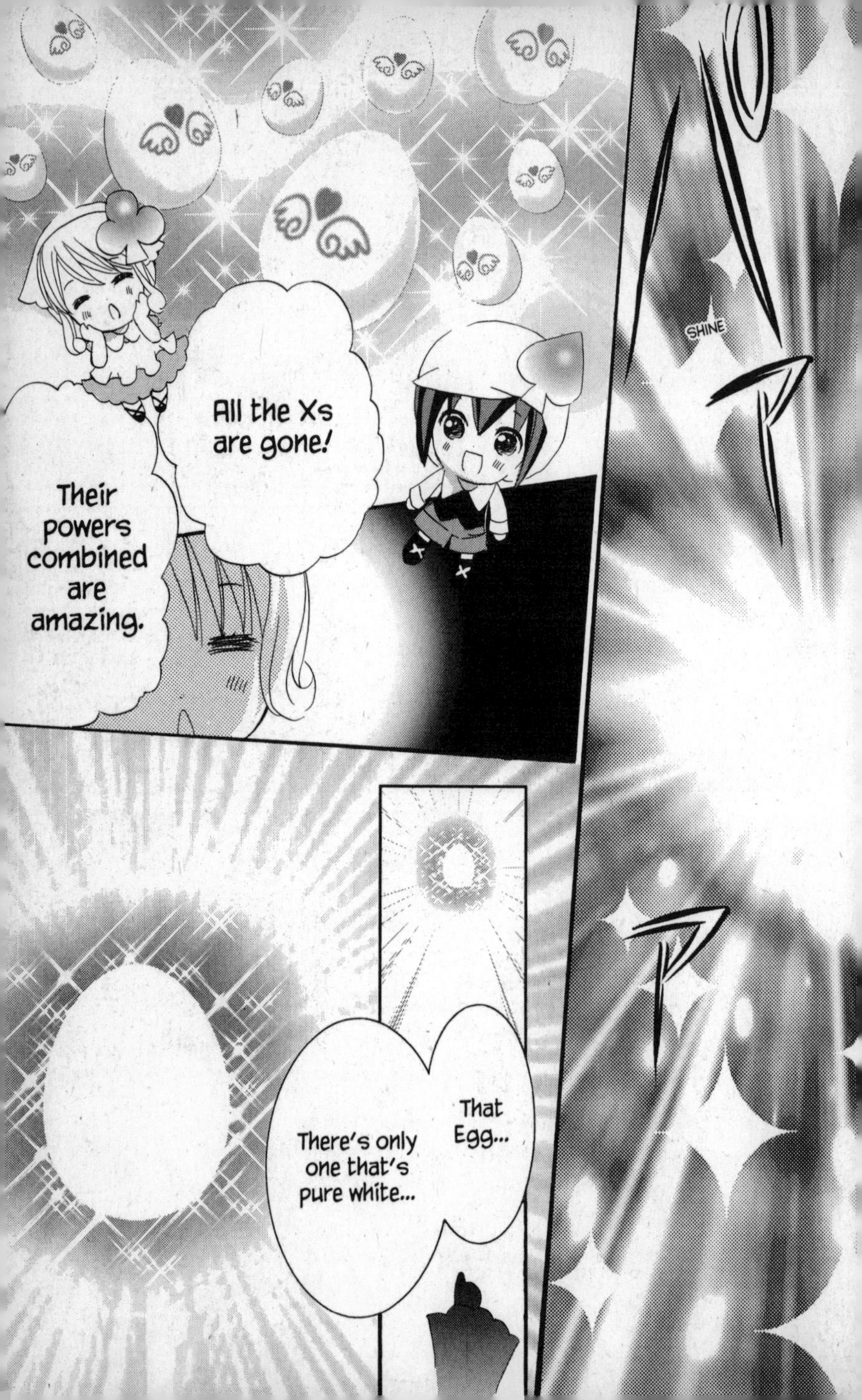
SHINE
All the Xs are gone!
Their powers combined are amazing.
That Egg...
There's only one that's pure white...

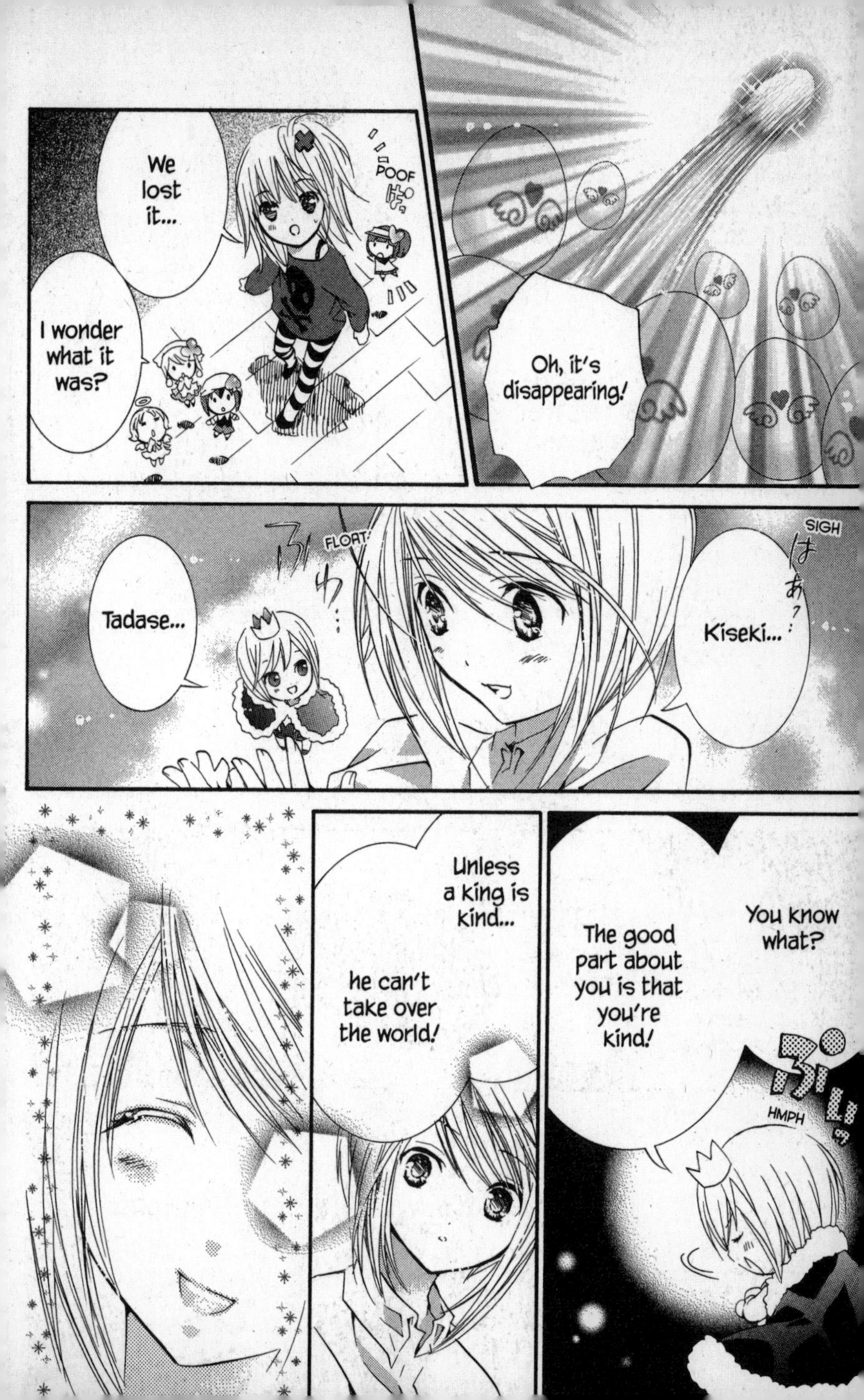
Oh, it's disappearing!
POOF
We lost it...
I wonder what it was?
SIGH
Kiseki...
FLOAT
Tadase...
You know what?
The good part about you is that you're kind!
HMPH
Unless a king is kind...
he can't take over the world!

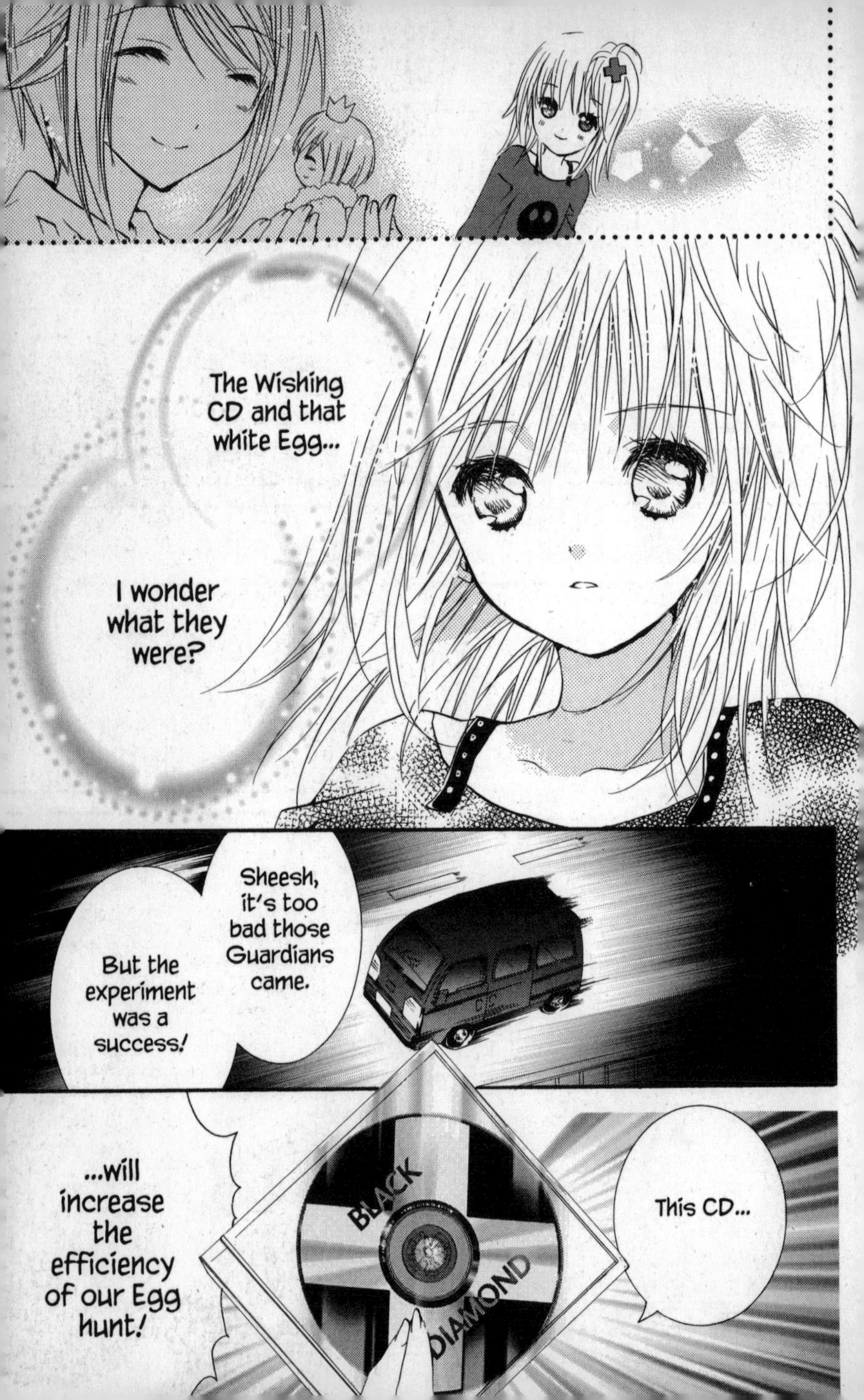
The Wishing CD and that white Egg...
I wonder what they were?
Sheesh, it's too bad those Guardians came.
But the experiment was a success!
This CD...
BLACK DIAMOND
...will increase the efficiency of our Egg hunt!

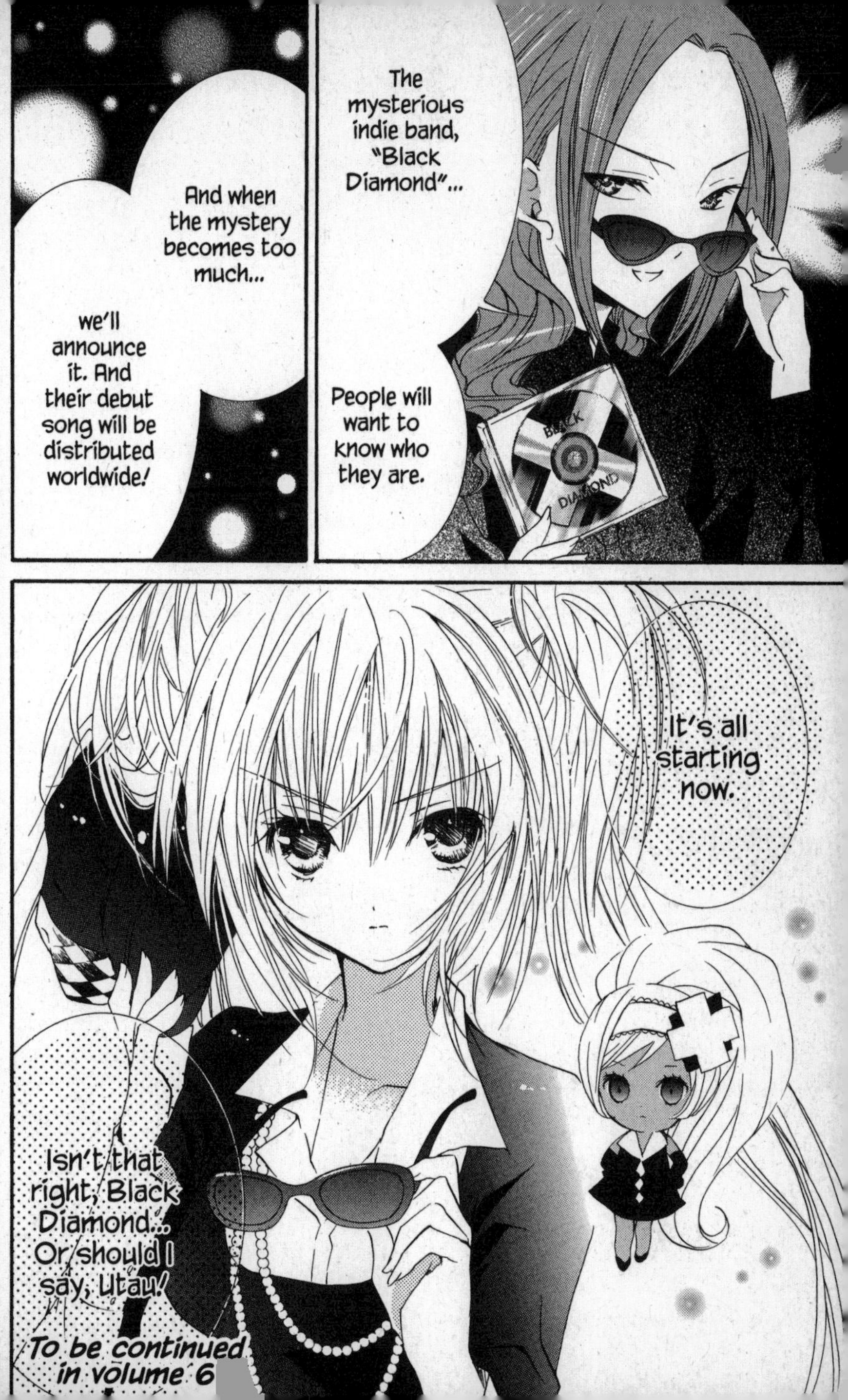
The mysterious indie band, "Black Diamond"...
People will want to know who they are.
BLACK DIAMOND
And when the mystery becomes too much...
we'll announce it. And their debut song will be distributed worldwide!
It's all starting now.
Isn't that right, Black Diamond... Or should I say, Utau!
To be continued in volume 6

Shugo
Chara!

About the Creators

PEACH-PIT:
Banri Sendo was born on June 7. Shibuko Ebara was born on June 21. They are a pair of Gemini manga artists who work together. Sendo likes to eat sweets, and Ebara likes to eat spicy stuff. Here's something that happened recently: We almost flushed our cell phones down the toilet...twice.

Translation Notes

Japanese is a tricky language for most Westerners, and translation is often more art than science. For your edification and reading pleasure, here are notes on some of the places where we could have gone in a different direction in our translation of the work, or where a Japanese cultural reference is used.

Mr. Class President, page 6

Yaya, and eventually everyone else, calls Kairi "Class President." This is not because he is the class president, but because he acts like one. Kairi will always respond, "Class President?"

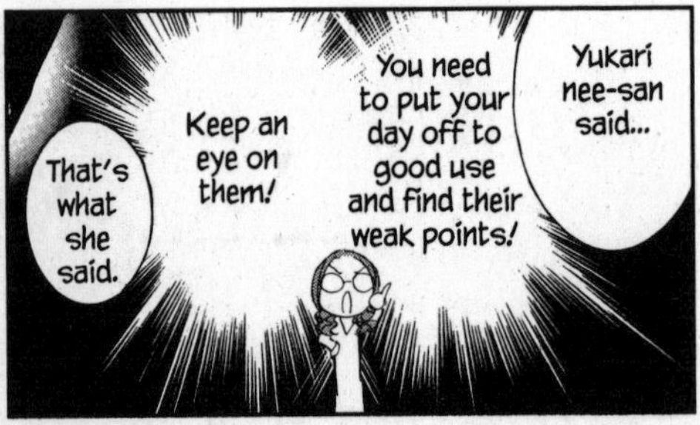
Yukari nee-san said...
You need to put your day off to good use and find their weak points!
Keep an eye on them!
That's what she said.

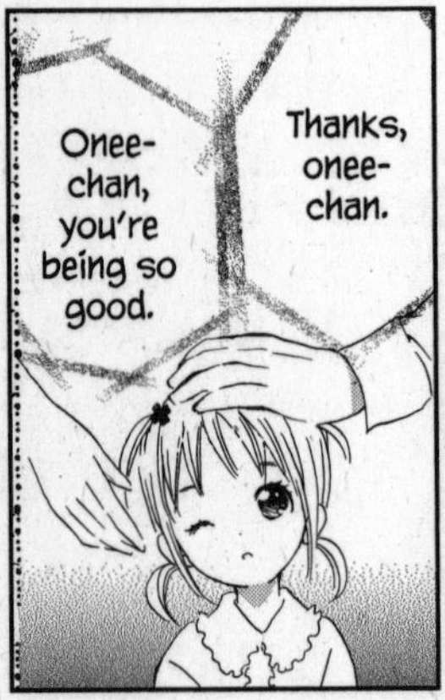
Thanks, onee-chan.
Onee-chan, you're being so good.

Onee-chan/nee-san, page 26 and page 87

Onee-chan and *nee-san* are two Japanese honorifics for a big sister.

Candies, page 43

Candies is a pop idol group that was popular in the 1970s in Japan. The three girls in the group were Ran Ito, Yoshiko Tanaka (known as Su), and Miki Fujimura. The group formed in 1973 and disbanded in 1977. They said that they wanted to "return to being normal girls," which is a phrase that is popular even today.

TOMARE!

[STOP!]

You're going the wrong way!

Manga is a completely
different type of reading
experience.

To start at the *beginning,*
go to the *end!*

That's right! Authentic manga is read the traditional Japanese way—from right to left. Exactly the *opposite* of how American books are read. It's easy to follow: Just go to the other end of the book, and read each page—and each panel—from right side to left side, starting at the top right. Now you're experiencing manga as it was meant to be!